DESTINOS

A Telecourse Designed by
Bill VanPatten
University of Illinois at Urbana-Champaign

Martha Alford Marks

Richard V. Teschner
University of Texas, El Paso

Thalia Dorwick
Coordinator of Print Material for McGraw-Hill, Inc.

McGraw-Hill, Inc.
New York St. Louis San Francisco Auckland Bogotá
Caracas Lisbon London Madrid Mexico City Milan
Montreal New Delhi San Juan Singapore
Sydney Tokyo Toronto

DESTINOS

·····•·•·•·•·•·•·•·•

An Introduction to Spanish

Workbook/Study Guide I
LECCIONES 1–26

Workbook/Study Guide I to accompany
Destinos An Introduction to Spanish

20 21 22 CUS/CUS 0 5 4 3 2 1 0

ISBN 0–07–002072–8

The senior editing supervisor was Richard Mason.
The copyeditor was Charlotte Jackson.
The editing assistant was Eileen Burke.
The art director was Francis Owens.
The text and cover designer was Juan Vargas, Vargas/Williams Design.
The production supervisor was Diane Baccianini.
Production assistance was provided by Edie Williams, Lorna Lo, and Anne Eldredge.
The illustrators were Lori Heckelman and Alan Eitzen.
The compositor was Fog Press.

Grateful acknowledgment is made for use of the following:

Realia: *Page 145* © Quino/Quipos.

Photographs: *Page 94* (*bottom*) © Steve Goldberg/Monkmeyer Press; *97* Museo del Prado. All other photographs courtesy of Olivia Tappan and Creative Television Associates (Boston).

HIGHLIGHTS OF THE VOCABULARY AND GRAMMAR TOPICS IN THE TEXTBOOK AND WORKBOOK

Note: Grammar topics are grouped by unit, not by the order of their introduction. Not all topics are included here.

	Vocabulario	*Gramática*
Lecciones 1–2 Textbook pages 2–25	cognates; family members	**ser**; articles and gender; possession

Un viaje a Sevilla (España) — Textbook page 27

Lecciones 3–6 Textbook pages 28–68	numbers (0–21); academic subjects; animals; days of the week; telling time	**hay; estar; ir**; present tense (regular verbs); subject pronouns; personal **a**; interrogatives; adjective agreement

Un viaje a Madrid (España) — Textbook page 69

Lecciones 7–11 Textbook pages 70–118	clothing; numbers (21–99); interrogatives; months; seasons; colors; descriptive adjectives	**saber; conocer**; present tense (irregular verbs, stem-changing verbs); reflexive pronouns; more on possession and adjectives; demonstratives; **ser** and **estar**

Un viaje a la Argentina — Textbook page 119

Lecciones 12–18 Textbook pages 120–188	numbers (100–1000); food groups; writing and written materials \	preterite tense; object pronouns; more on using adjectives; verbs used reflexively and nonreflexively; **gustar** and verbs like it

Un viaje a Puerto Rico — Textbook page 189

Lecciones 19–26 Textbook pages 190–260	directions; more family members; weather; changes in states and conditions; parts of a house; domestic appliances; more descriptive adjectives	present and past progressive; imperfect; using imperfect and preterite together; **por** and **para**; affirmative and negative words; **tener** idioms; comparisons; **estar** + adjectives

Vocabulario   *Gramática*

Un viaje a México: El pueblo, la capital   Textbook page 263

Lecciones 27–36
Textbook
pages 264–365

parts of the body; medical
situations; places in a city;
stores; geographical features;
professions; social life; giving
advice

future; superlatives; present subjunctive
and uses (noun and adjective clauses;
adverbial conjunctions of time);
commands; present perfect (indicative
and subjunctive)

Un viaje a México: La capital   Textbook page 367

Lecciones 37–52
Textbook
pages 368–491

money; business; renting and
buying; tourist needs; travel;
restaurants; hotel; sports;
relationships; pastimes

past subjunctive; conditional; *if*-clause
sentences; subjunctive with certain
conjunctions

TABLE OF CONTENTS

To the Student

Welcome to *Destinos: An Introduction to Spanish!* If you are reading this preface, you have already decided to study beginning Spanish. You probably know by now that an important portion of the instruction in the course will take place while you watch a series of fifty-two half-hour television shows. As you watch the shows, you will follow an unforgettable journey that has been designed to make learning Spanish enjoyable for you. We all like to follow the plot of a drama or television mystery show, and we eagerly await the next episode of a continuing story to find out what will happen. That sense of pleasurable suspense can be a powerful factor in helping you learn Spanish more easily. In addition, the *Destinos* series will allow you to experience, through the powerful medium of television, some of the many places in which Spanish is spoken (including the United States).

The Goals of *Destinos*

As you take this journey, keep one thing in mind at all times. The *Destinos* materials have been designed to make learning Spanish enjoyable, but they were also created to make it really possible for you to learn something about Spanish and how to use it. How many times have people told you that you get out of a course what you put into it? That adage is especially true with regard to language learning and to *Destinos*. What you will get out of the materials is directly related to, among other things, how much time you put into using them.

In addition to watching the series, if you use the Textbook along with the Workbook/Study Guides, and if you have access to and regularly use the audiocassette program, you can expect to accomplish a great deal with *Destinos*.

- By the end of the series, you should be able to understand most Spanish spoken at slower than normal pace and some Spanish spoken at normal pace. You will also have developed skills and coping strategies for filling in gaps when your comprehension of Spanish is not perfect. After all, you don't understand absolutely every word of what people say to you in English, and it isn't reasonable to expect that of yourself in Spanish.
- In terms of speaking, you should be able to ask and answer questions on a variety of everyday topics, describe people and places, talk about things that are happening in your life, and have some ability to talk about things that happened in the past. In the context of learning a second language, that is actually quite a lot to achieve.
- You will be able to interact with Spanish speakers in important ways: making phone calls, greeting and departing, and so on.
- You will be able to read Spanish materials that were written for you, a second language learner. And you will gain some experience reading materials written for the native-speaking reader. You will not understand every word of those materials, but you may be surprised by how much you *can* understand.
- The writing skills that you develop will, in many cases, be the same as the speaking skills, that is, the ability to describe and narrate in the present, and to some extent in the past, and so on.
- Finally, by the end of the series you will have seen and heard a great deal about the culture and history of places around the world where Spanish is spoken, and you will have many visual memories of those places. We hope that you will come to think of the Spanish-speaking world as a place that you would like to visit someday.

Using the Textbook and the Workbook/Study Guides

The Textbook and Workbook/Study Guides that accompany the *Destinos* series are designed so that you can work though them on your own. Of course, they can also be used in a classroom setting, but if you are studying Spanish independently or as a telecourse student you will be able to work with the materials on your own.

Just as there are fifty-two shows in the *Destinos* series, so there are fifty-two lessons in the Textbook and the Workbook/Study Guides. You will always start in the Textbook lesson with a special section that will prepare you to watch the show. Having watched the show, you will finish the rest of that lesson in the Textbook, then you will continue on with the corresponding lesson in the Workbook/Study Guide.

All lessons of the Textbook and the Workbook/Study Guides (with the exception of the review lessons) follow approximately the same format: You will very quickly become familiar with how the lessons are structured. The best news, however, is that you will always work through the materials sequentially, and you will be alerted to listen to the audiocassette tape when you see a cassette symbol in the margin. For all these reasons, you will find the lessons easy to follow.

However, just to be on the safe side, Lessons 1 and 2 and Lessons 27 and 28 in the Textbook and the Workbook/Study Guides are preceded by a separate "Study Guide" that outlines the steps necessary to work through each of the fifty-two lessons. Those pages are shaded (light blue in the Textbook, light gray in the Workbook), and they have a distinctive band in one margin to make them easy for you to spot. After Lessons 1 and 2, the Study Guide materials are integrated into the lessons; you will find them at the beginning and at the end of each lesson (as light-blue boxes in the Textbook, light-gray boxes in the Workbook). You will quickly see that all you need to do is to work through the materials sequentially.

The lessons of the Textbook and the Workbook/Study Guides are divided into repeating sections that appear in most lessons. Each time a section appears for the first time, its purpose will be explained to you in the textual materials. However, so that you have an overview of the materials before you start using them, here is a brief description of the major sections.

Textbook Lesson Formats

- Textbook lessons begin with a section called **Preparación** (*Preparation*). This section will help you get ready to view the upcoming show by previewing information and conversations from that show as well as reviewing important information from previous shows.
- In **¿Tienes buena memoria?** (*Do You Have a Good Memory?*) sections, you can "test" yourself about what you remember from the episode. If you can answer most of the questions in the activities in this section, you will have understood enough of the show . . . even though you may not have understood every word.
- In **Vocabulario del tema** (*Thematic Vocabulary*) sections, you will practice vocabulary useful for talking about everyday topics. You will practice vocabulary first by using it in the context of the television series, then by using it to talk about yourself and others.
- In **Conversaciones** (*Conversations*) sections, which appear in most but not all chapters, you will practice everyday conversational skills: answering the phone, saying thank you, and so on.
- The **Un poco de gramática** (*A Bit of Grammar*) sections are "previews" of grammar that you will learn more about in the Workbook/Study Guide.
- A **Nota cultural** (*Cultural Note*) ends each lesson. In it you will learn interesting information about some aspect of Hispanic culture relevant to the current episode. Furthermore, there are additional **Notas culturales** in other parts of the lessons as well.
- At the end of every lesson there is a reference **Vocabulario** (*Vocabulary*), a list of words that are important for that lesson.

At the back of the Textbook you can find the following reference materials:

- an answer section for you to check your answers to many Textbook activities (Appendix 1)
- charts featuring the Spanish verb system (Appendix 2)
- a complete Spanish-English end vocabulary that you can use with the Textbook and with the Workbook/Study Guides
- a brief reference index of the major characters in the series
- an index of the content of the Textbook.

WORKBOOK/STUDY GUIDES LESSON FORMATS

- Most Workbook/Study Guide lessons begin with **Más allá del episodio** (*Beyond the Episode*) sections, which contain either a reading or a listening passage (sometimes both) that give you more information about the characters and events in the series. These sections explore motivations, important events that shaped a character's personality, and other background information that takes you beyond what you see and hear on the screen.
- The sequentially numbered sections in **Gramática** (*Grammar*) expand on the grammar point that was previewed in the Textbook lesson. Then a series of activities gives you the chance to work with the grammar. In most cases you will not actually produce the grammar item at first. You will generally see and hear the grammar in a context (usually about the characters), then use it to talk about yourself or people you know. In addition to expanding on the grammar point from the Textbook lesson, most Workbook/Study Guide lessons also present one or two secondary grammar items.

Some lessons contain **Notas culturales**, as needed, and many lessons end with a **Vocabulario** list of additional vocabulary that you should review in addition to that in the corresponding Textbook lesson.

At the back of the Workbook/Study Guides you can find the following reference materials:

- an answer section for you to check your answers to many Workbook/Study Guide activities (Appendix 1)
- charts featuring the Spanish verb system (Appendix 2)
- an index of the content of each Workbook/Study Guide, integrated with that of the Textbook.

DIFFERENCES BETWEEN WORKBOOK/STUDY GUIDE I AND II

The following sections appear only in Workbook/Study Guide I, which corresponds to Lessons 1–26:

- Cognate study sections called **¡Aumenta tu vocabulario!** (*Expand your Vocabulary*) that will help you learn to recognize and use words that are similar but not identical in Spanish and in English.
- **Pronunciación** (*Pronunciation*) sections that will introduce you to the ways in which Spanish is pronounced throughout the world, as well as give you practice in hearing and producing the sounds of Spanish.

The following sections appear only in Workbook/Study Guide II, which corresponds to Lessons 27–52:

- **¡A leer!** (*Let's Read!*) sections with guided activities that will help you read materials excerpted from authentic sources, that is, magazines and newspapers published in the Spanish-speaking world for native speakers of Spanish.
- **Repaso** (*Review*) sections that will give you the chance to work with past tenses to describe and narrate events, an important goal in most beginning Spanish language courses.

Review Lessons

In the Textbook and the Workbook/Study Guides, review lessons follow a simpler and shorter format. The Textbook will help you prepare to watch the review episode and test your memory of it, as well as sum up what you remember about the shows included in the review. In the Workbook/Study Guides you will put together, in review fashion, the grammar and vocabulary you have learned in preceding lessons. Most review lessons in the Workbook/Study Guides also contain a guided writing activity called **Para escribir** (*For Writing*).

Some Additional Hints About Using the Materials

Worksheet Activities

In many sections of the Workbook/Study Guide, specific activities have been selected to be torn out and turned in to your instructor if he or she wishes you to do so. Those activities have the word *Worksheet* in parentheses at the end of the direction lines. The reference is to a section at the back of the Workbook/Study Guide that has a Worksheet page for each lesson. You will need to flip to the back of the Workbook/Study Guide to find these sections. They have been placed there to allow you to tear them out and still keep the other sections of the Workbook/Study Guide intact for future study or reference.

In most other cases you will have room to do a particular activity directly on the Workbook/Study Guide page. If you need more space, use additional paper. The assignments in the writing sections (**Para escribir**) should always be done on a separate sheet of paper.

Self-Tests

For all lessons except the review lessons, a brief Self-Test is provided with the Worksheet page. These quizzes give you a chance to evaluate what you have learned about the story of *Destinos* and about vocabulary and grammar presented in the lesson. It is a good idea to take the Self-Test after you finish each lesson.

Answers

As you work through the materials in the Textbook and the Workbook/Study Guide, you will find that answers are generally provided either on tape or in Appendix 1. Sometimes, however, answers are provided in both places so that you can check your answers in print if you have trouble catching something on the tape, or so that you can be doubly certain of the answers.

Some activities, however, do not have right or wrong answers. For example, you may be asked to give your opinion about a character or venture a guess about someone's past or future. Don't worry about whether you are answering those kinds of questions correctly or incorrectly. As long as you are answering with a real opinion and using the best Spanish that you know how, you are doing just fine!

Following Directions

In general, as long as you follow the directions for each activity, you will be doing exactly what you need to do in a beginning Spanish language course. If you follow the guided steps (**Pasos**) you will stay on target and should have no problems, even when a listening passage or an authentic reading seems challenging, or a composition topic seems daunting. Of course, as in any other learning situations, you should always consult with your instructor if you are uncertain about how to proceed or just want more information or guidance.

Accent Marks

Finally, there is a minor difference between the Spanish you will see on-screen in the TV shows and that in your Textbook and Workbook/Study Guides. Accent marks (´) are used on capital letters in the textual materials but not on-screen. The use of accents on capital letters is optional in Spanish. Some Spanish speakers use them when they write; others do not. Accents are used on capitals in your texts to help you learn when to use them, but the capabilities of the system used to produce the on-screen graphics did not permit their use in the series. Because Spanish is spoken in so many parts of the world, there are bound to be vocabulary, rules, and usage variations such as this.

* * * * * *

And now it's time to begin the series. If you have not yet seen the first show, turn to page 1 of your Textbook, look at the unit opener, scan through the Study Guide for **Lección 1,** then do the **Preparación** section in that lesson. Then, after you have finished, watch the first show. Here is how the story begins.

> An old man has retired to his hacienda outside a small town close to Mexico City. With the wealth he has accumulated since leaving Spain at the end of its bloody Civil War, he is restoring the hacienda to its original sixteenth-century splendor. But his health has begun to fail, and now he hopes to live out the remainder of his years peacefully, in the tranquillity of the Mexican countryside.
>
> Then a letter arrives—a letter in which a woman from Spain makes claims about the old man's past . . . .

S T U D Y   G U I D E

L E C C I Ó N
. . . .

1

Follow these simple steps as you work your way through **Lección 1** in the materials that accompany *Destinos*: the Textbook and the Workbook.

. . . .

STEP 1 USING THE TEXTBOOK

BEFORE VIEWING . . .

Be sure to complete the preview section (called **Preparación**) in **Lección 1** before viewing **Episodio I** (the video segment that corresponds to **Lección 1**). Check off the preview section here after you have completed it.

_____ **Preparación**

AFTER VIEWING . . .

The rest of the materials in **Lección 1** of the Textbook and the Workbook will help you better understand the video episode you have just seen and take you beyond it, giving you additional information about places and characters in the series. The Textbook will also help you to develop skill in using the Spanish language. In this lesson you will learn

- about cognates (words that look alike in English and Spanish and mean the same thing)
- about some simple Spanish verb forms.

Be sure to work through all parts of the lesson. When you see a cassette symbol in the margin, listen to the tape for **Lección 1**. Answers or hints for many activities are given in Appendix 1. Be sure to check your answers for each activity before going on to the next one.

Check off the following sections of the lesson here as you complete them.

_____ **¿Tienes buena memoria?**

_____ **Vocabulario del tema**

_____ **Un poco de gramática**

Now scan the words in the **Vocabulario** list to be sure that you understand the meaning of most of them.

STEP 2 USING THE WORKBOOK

Now turn to the Workbook and complete all the activities for **Lección 1**. Whereas the materials in the Textbook all had to do with the video episode, the materials in the Workbook will help you expand your knowledge of the Spanish language in general, as well as give you opportunities for self-expression in Spanish. In this lesson you will learn

- more about **ser** (one Spanish verb that means *to be*)
- more about cognates (how to pronounce them) and about false cognates.

Remember to listen to the tape for **Lección 1** when you see the cassette symbol, and to check your answers in Appendix 1.

Check off the following sections of the lesson here as you complete them.

_____ **Más allá del episodio**

_____ **Gramática**

_____ **Pronunciación**

_____ **¡Aumenta tu vocabulario!**

Now scan the words in the **Vocabulario** list to be sure that you understand the meaning of most of them.

STEP 3 WRAPPING THINGS UP

Now that you have worked through Steps 1–2, here are some of the things you have accomplished in Spanish.

- You can recognize many cognates, and you are aware that not every Spanish word that looks like an English word has exactly the same meaning.
- You know some basic information about one Spanish verb, **ser.**
- You have listened to, seen, and understood some spoken and written Spanish—in the video episode and on the cassette tape—and you have a sense of how much you are expected to understand when working with the *Destinos* materials.

After you have followed these steps in working your way through **Lección 1,** you will be ready to continue on with **Lección 2** in the Textbook.

1

LA CARTA

OBJETIVOS

Whereas the materials in the Textbook all had to do with the video episode, the materials in the Workbook will help you expand your knowledge of the Spanish language in general, as well as give you opportunities for self-expression in Spanish. In this lesson you will learn

- more about **ser** (one Spanish verb that means *to be*)
- more about cognates (how to pronounce them) and about false cognates.

Remember to listen to the tape for **Lección 1** when you see the cassette symbol, and to check your answers in Appendix 1.

MÁS ALLÁ DEL EPISODIO

The information you will learn in these repeating sections of *Destinos* will help to "round out" the personalities and the background of characters and places in the series. The activities will also give you additional practice in reading Spanish. In this section, as when you were watching **Episodio 1**, you do not have to understand every word in the readings and activities.

Actividad A.   La Gavia

In **Episodio 1** of *Destinos*, you saw a number of scenes shot at La Gavia, the hacienda of the Castillo Saavedra family. What else can you *guess* or *infer* about the hacienda? Here is a series of statements about aspects of La Gavia. Based on what you know now, decide whether the following statements are **Cierto** (*True*) or **Falso** (*False*). Before doing this activity, you might want to look at the photographs that accompany the reading.

C F   1. Don Fernando Castillo Saavedra es el propietario actual (*current*) de La Gavia.
C F   2. La Gavia es una hacienda moderna.
C F   3. La Gavia es una hacienda pequeña (*small*).

Ⓒ F 4. En la hacienda hay (*there is*) una biblioteca muy grande (*a large library*).
C F 5. La religión no tiene importancia en la historia de La Gavia.

The answers you have given are based completely on the very small amount of information about La Gavia that you have at this point. The following reading passage offers more information. Read it and see whether you wish to change any answers.

Don't be intimidated by the reading. Scan through it once, getting what you can; then go through it a second time and check your answers against **Actividad A** in Appendix 1. And relax! You will have a chance to work through the reading again later on in this lesson of the Workbook.

La entrada de La Gavia

La capilla de la familia Castillo Saavedra

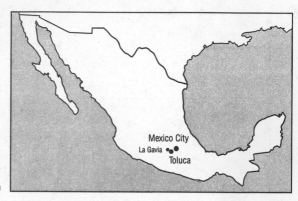

La Gavia es el nombre de una hacienda mexicana. Es la residencia principal de don Fernando Castillo Saavedra, el patriarca de la familia Castillo. Es una hacienda de la época colonial. Está situada [1] al suroeste de la Ciudad de México, cerca de [2] la ciudad industrial de Toluca.

Don Fernando compró [3] La Gavia en ruinas con la idea de restaurar la hacienda. Es un lugar histórico, pero también es muy importante para don Fernando.

La Gavia es una hacienda muy grande. Tiene una entrada majestuosa y una capilla muy bonita. En la hacienda hay también un patio muy agradable y una biblioteca impresionante.

[1] Está... *It is located* [2] cerca... *close to* [3] *bought*

 Actividad B. Los lugares de La Gavia
Follow along as the speaker on the tape lists places, and indicate the ones you would expect to find at La Gavia based on what you now know about it. You should be able to recognize the meaning of all of the place names, which are preceded by **un** or **una** (Spanish words for *a* or *an*).

1. ✓ un patio
2. ___ un hospital
3. ✓ una capilla
4. ✓ una biblioteca
5. ___ un aeropuerto
6. ✓ una entrada
7. ___ un restaurante
8. ✓ un establo
9. ___ una farmacia
10. ___ un hotel
11. ___ un garaje
12. ___ un supermercado

....

Gramática

This repeating section of the Workbook presents more detailed explanations of the structures you have heard in the video episode and used in the Textbook. The grammar topics are sequentially numbered throughout the Workbook for ease of reference.

1. *YO SOY...*: THE VERB *ser*

RAQUEL: Soy abogada. Don
    Fernando es mi cliente.
RAMÓN: Carlos, Juan y yo **somos**
    hijos de don Fernando.

RAQUEL: *I'm a lawyer. Don*
    Fernando is my client.
RAMÓN: *Carlos, Juan, and*
    I are don Fernando's sons.

Forms

Ser is one Spanish verb that means *to be* in English. The forms of this Spanish verb do not follow a regular pattern.

SINGULAR		PLURAL	
soy	I am	somos	we are
eres	you are	sois	you are
es	you are	son	you are
	he/she/it is		they are

Note in particular the four different Spanish equivalents for *you are.* One of the reasons for this phenomenon is that Spanish uses a different word for *you* in formal and informal situations. Another reason is that, as you can see, Spanish verbs also differ for singular *you* and plural *you* (the equivalent of English *you all*). You will learn more about these aspects of Spanish in upcoming lessons.

Uses

Forms of **ser** are used . . .

* to equate one thing with another

    Raquel **es** abogada.   Raquel = abogada
    Don Fernando **es** cliente.   don Fernando = cliente

* to tell where someone or something is from, with **de** (*from*)

    Raquel **es de** los Estados Unidos.
    Don Fernando **es de** España.

Actividad A.   ¿Quién habla? (*Who is speaking?*)

Which of the following *Destinos* characters is describing himself or herself? Follow along in the Workbook as you listen to the tape. Choose characters from this list: don Fernando, Mercedes, Raquel, Ramón.

1. _____ Soy abogada. Don Fernando es mi cliente.
2. _____ Soy de España. Ahora (*Now*) soy propietario de La Gavia.
3. _____ Mercedes y yo somos miembros de la familia Castillo.
4. _____ Soy hija (*daughter*) de don Fernando.
5. _____ Carlos, Juan y yo somos hijos de don Fernando.

Actividad B. ¿Quiénes son?

Complete the following descriptions with the appropriate forms of the verb **ser**. The first item has been done for you. Then identify the characters described.

(Yo) <u>Soy</u> ¹ de México. Vivo (*I live*) en La Gavia. Don Fernando <u>es</u> ² mi padre.

Carlos, Juan y yo <u>somos</u>³ hijos de don Fernando. Soy...

(Yo) <u>Soy</u> ⁴ abogada. (Yo) <u>Soy</u> ⁵ de Los Ángeles y <u>soy</u> ⁶ mexicoamericana. Don Fernando <u>es</u> ⁷ mi cliente en un caso especial. Soy...

Actividad C. ¿Y tú? (*And you?*)

Describe yourself briefly by completing the following description with the appropriate forms of the verb **ser** and the necessary information. (Worksheet)

(Yo) <u>Soy</u> estudiante de español. (Yo) <u>Soy</u> de <u>Canadá</u> (lugar). Vivo (*I live*) ahora en <u>Nanaimo</u> (lugar).

PRONUNCIACIÓN: PRONOUNCING COGNATES

Even though Spanish and English cognates look alike, they do not usually sound alike. If you have heard cognates, you will be better able to identify them when you see them. For this reason, this section and the section that follows provide pronunciation practice with cognates. At this point you will probably not understand why words are pronounced a certain way. The rules of Spanish pronunciation are explained in this section in the chapters that follow. For the moment, just try to imitate the pronunciation of the speaker you hear on the tape.

Actividad A. La serie *Destinos*

Listen to the following brief description of *Destinos*, the TV series. It contains many cognates and is based on Raquel's description of the story in this episode. Then the description will be repeated, with pauses for you to repeat what you have heard.

> *Destinos*... Es una historia muy interesante. Es una historia de aventuras... de secretos... y de amor. También es una historia muy importante para la familia Castillo.

Actividad B.

The following brief sentences containing cognates describe *Destinos*, the TV series. Repeat them after the speaker. Then, based on what you know about *Destinos* and on what you learned in **Actividad A**, indicate whether the sentences are **Cierto** (*True*) or **Falso** (*False*). Make educated guesses if you don't know.

C F 1. *Destinos* es una serie romántica.
C F 2. Es una serie complicada.
C F 3. No hay aventuras en *Destinos*.
C F 4. No tiene elementos misteriosos.

Now listen as the speaker gives you the correct answers. Do you hear additional cognates? (You can also check your answers in Appendix 1.)

¡Aumenta tu vocabulario!

This repeating section of the Workbook occurs only in the first five lessons. In it you will learn more about cognates (words that are similar in form and meaning in two languages) and recognizing cognate patterns. Developing confidence in your ability to make intelligent guesses will help you throughout your study of Spanish.

In Lección 1 you learned that Spanish and English have many cognates. But . . . ¡OJO! (*Watch out!*) Some words that look alike in Spanish and English are not cognates but, rather, false cognates. Here are some examples.

_____ means _____, not _____, which is _____ in Spanish

| la librería | = | *bookstore* | *library* | = | la biblioteca |
| el colegio | = | *high school* | *college* | = | la universidad |

In general, however, if a Spanish word looks or sounds like an English word, you can assume that it probably has the same meaning. You will learn the meanings of false cognates like librería as you progress through the Textbook and Workbook.

Actividad A.

Not all cognates are as close as those you have seen so far, but they are still "guessable," especially in context. Can you match the following definitions or synonyms with the indicated words?

una persona   información   una condición mental

1. Los hijos de don Fernando están muy **preocupados**.
2. Carmen, la **esposa** de don Fernando, ya está muerta (*dead*).
3. Raquel tiene unos **datos** importantes.

Actividad B.

Now that you know a great deal more about cognates, the reading passage on La Gavia with which you worked in the Workbook may seem easier to you. Here it is again, without the glosses but with a new section in the middle. Listen and follow along in your Workbook, circling the words you now think are cognates. The word **siglo** means *century*.

La Gavia, hacienda histórica

La Gavia es el nombre de una hacienda mexicana. Es la residencia principal de don Fernando Castillo Saavedra, el patriarca de la familia Castillo. Es una hacienda de la época colonial. Está situada al suroeste de la Ciudad de México, cerca de la ciudad industrial de Toluca.

La historia de La Gavia

Siglo XVI: Construcción de la hacienda.
Siglo XVII: Período de gran esplendor.
Siglo XVIII: Los jesuitas se instalan en La Gavia.
Siglo XIX: Centro importante en el movimiento de la Independencia Nacional.
Siglo XX: Destrucción parcial de La Gavia durante la Revolución Mexicana de 1910.

Don Fernando compró La Gavia en ruinas con la idea de restaurar la hacienda. Es un lugar histórico, pero también es muy importante para don Fernando.

La Gavia es una hacienda muy grande. Tiene una entrada majestuosa y una capilla muy bonita. En la hacienda hay también un patio muy agradable y una biblioteca impresionante.

Have you completed the following sections of the lesson? Check them off here.

_____ **Más allá del episodio**	_____ **Pronunciación**
_____ **Gramática**	_____ **¡Aumenta tu vocabulario!**

Now scan the words in the **Vocabulario** list to be sure that you understand the meaning of most of them.

• •

VOCABULARIO

Note: This reference list supplements the list in the Textbook. It contains some words that appear frequently in **Lección 1** of the Workbook and that are important for understanding and discussing the lesson. Be sure that you can recognize all of them.

Las personas (People)
el cliente   client

Los verbos (Verbs)
ser   to be
  soy   I am
  eres   you are
  es   you are; he/she/it is

somos   we are
sois   you are
son   you are; they are

hay   there is

Las palabras adicionales (Additional Words)
yo   I

PALABRAS DEL TEXTO

la pronunciación	pronunciation
la serie	(TV) series
¡aumenta tu vocabulario!	increase your vocabulary!
más allá	beyond
¡OJO!	be careful! pay close attention
¿Y tú?	And you? What about you?

Now that you have worked through the Textbook and the Workbook, here are some of the things you have accomplished in Spanish.

- You can recognize many cognates, and you are aware that not every Spanish word that looks like an English word has exactly the same meaning.
- You know some basic information about one Spanish verb, **ser.**
- You have listened to, seen, and understood some spoken and written Spanish—in the video episode and on the cassette tape—and you have a sense of how much you are expected to understand when working with the *Destinos* materials.

You are now ready to continue on with **Lección 2** in the Textbook.

S T U D Y   G U I D E

L E C C I Ó N
· · · · · · · · · · · · · · · · · · · ·

2

Follow these simple steps as you work your way through **Lección 2** in the materials that accompany *Destinos*: the Textbook and the Workbook.

· ·
_____

STEP 1 USING THE TEXTBOOK

▭— BEFORE VIEWING . . .

Be sure to complete the preview section (called **Preparación**) in **Lección 2** before viewing **Episodio 2** (the video segment that corresponds to **Lección 2**). Check off the preview section here after you have completed it.

_____ **Preparación**

▭— AFTER VIEWING . . .

The rest of the materials in **Lección 2** of the Textbook and the Workbook will help you better understand the video episode you have just seen and take you beyond it, giving you additional information about places and characters in the series. The Textbook will also help you to develop skill in using the Spanish language. In this lesson you will learn

- vocabulary to express family relationships
- greetings to people in Spanish
- ways to express possession (what belongs to you).

You will also learn information about Hispanic families and about the Spanish Civil War.

Be sure to work through all parts of the lesson. When you see a cassette symbol in the margin, listen to the tape for **Lección 2**. Answers or hints for many activities are given in Appendix 1. Be sure to check your answers for each activity before going on to the next one.

Check off the following sections of the lesson here as you complete them.

_____ **¿Tienes buena memoria?**		_____ **Conversaciones**
_____ **Vocabulario del tema**		_____ **Un poco de gramática**

Now scan the words in the **Vocabulario** list to be sure that you understand the meaning of most of them.

• •

STEP 2 USING THE WORKBOOK

Now turn to the Workbook and complete all the activities for **Lección 2**. Whereas the materials in the Textbook all had to do with the video episode, the materials in the Workbook will help you expand your knowledge of the Spanish language in general, as well as give you opportunities for self-expression in Spanish. In this lesson you will learn

- how to express *a/an* and *the* in Spanish
- about the Spanish noun gender system
- more about expressing possession
- how to pronounce the letters of the Spanish alphabet
- more about cognates.

Remember to listen to the tape for **Lección 2** when you see the cassette symbol, and to check your answers in Appendix 1.

Check off the following sections of the lesson here as you complete them.

_____ **Más allá del episodio**   _____ **Pronunciación**
_____ **Gramática**   _____ **¡Aumenta tu vocabulario!**

Now scan the words in the **Vocabulario** list to be sure that you understand the meaning of most of them.

• •

STEP 3 TAKING THE SELF-TEST

Now that you have completed the Textbook and Workbook for **Lecciones 1** and **2**, take the Self-Test for those lessons. Remember to use the tape when you see the cassette symbol and to check your answers.

_____ **Self-Test**

• •

STEP 4 WRAPPING THINGS UP

Now that you have worked through Steps 1–3, here are some of the things you have accomplished in Spanish.

- You can use some basic greetings in Spanish.
- You can now talk simply about your own family and the families of others.
- You can give definite and indefinite articles for a variety of nouns, as well as their plural forms, and you know that all nouns in Spanish are either masculine or feminine.
- You know about several ways to express possession.
- You are familiar with the Spanish alphabet.
- You can recognize more common cognates.
- You have continued to work on listening skills with the video episode and the cassette tape, and you are comfortable focusing on what you do understand even when you don't comprehend every word.

After you have followed these steps in working your way through **Lección 2**, you will be ready to continue on with **Lección 3** in the Textbook.

LECCIÓN

2

EL SECRETO

OBJETIVOS

Whereas the materials in the Textbook all had to do with the video segment, the materials in the Workbook will help you expand your knowledge of the Spanish language in general, as well as give you opportunities for self-expression in Spanish. In this lesson you will learn

- how to express *the* and *a/an* in Spanish
- about the system of gender that nouns have in Spanish
- how to pronounce the letters of the Spanish alphabet
- more about cognates.

Remember to listen to the tape for **Lección 2** when you see the cassette symbol, and to check your answers in Appendix 1.

MÁS ALLÁ DEL EPISODIO

Actividad A.   Juan y Pati, una relación tumultuosa

You have met and learned a little about the principal characters of *Destinos*. But, as the saying goes, there is often more to something than meets the eye. What do you really know about Juan and Pati? What might you *guess* or *infer* about them? Here is a series of statements about Juan and Pati. Choose from the following five responses to express your reaction.

a. Sé (*I know*) que es cierto.   d. Creo que es falso.
b. Creo (*I believe*) que es cierto.   e. Sé que es falso.
c. No sé. (*I don't know.*)

1. (uno)   c   Juan es el hijo favorito de don Fernando.
2. (dos)   c   Juan es profesor de literatura italiana. *e*
3. (tres)   c   Pati también es profesora, pero (*but*) de música. b
4. (cuatro)   c   Pati es la segunda (*second*) esposa de Juan.
5. (cinco)   c   Juan es el segundo esposo de Pati.

6. (seis) El matrimonio de Juan y Pati es muy estable y es un modelo para otras personas.

7. (siete) Juan y Pati viven en Nueva York.

The answers you have given are based solely on the very small amount of information about Juan and Pati that you have at this point. The following reading passage offers more information. Read it and see whether you wish to change any answers.

Juan Castillo, con Pati, su esposa

Juan y Pati son esposos. Viven en un apartamento en el Soho, un barrio[1] de la ciudad de Nueva York. Juan es profesor de literatura latinoamericana en la Universidad de Nueva York (NYU). Pati también es profesora en la Universidad de Nueva York, pero no de literatura. Su especialización es el teatro y ha sido[2] la directora de obras como[3] *Bodas de sangre* (*Blood Wedding*) (del dramaturgo español Federico García Lorca). El montaje[4] fue[5] de la compañía «Hispanic Theater of New York».

En este momento,[6] el matrimonio de Juan y Pati es inestable y tenso. Los dos trabajan[7] y las responsabilidades de sus respectivas carreras académicas aumentan la tensión entre ellos. También, sus personalidades están en conflicto: Los dos son muy ambiciosos y hay rivalidad entre ellos. El futuro de su matrimonio es incierto...

[1]*neighborhood, district* [2]*ha... has been* [3]*obras... works like* [4]*production* [5]*was* [6]*En... Right now, Currently* [7]*Los... Both of them work*

Actividad B.

Now return to statements 1–7 and make any changes in your answers that you feel are necessary. Which statements do you still have to guess at or answer **No sé**? Listen to the cassette tape, on which the speaker will give you some answers, then provide some more information.

• •

GRAMÁTICA

2. *EL HIJO, LA HIJA, LOS HIJOS*: ARTICLES AND NOUNS— GENDER AND NUMBER

A. Spanish, like English, has a system of articles. In English, the articles are *the* (the definite article) and *a, an, some* (the indefinite articles). In Spanish, however, each article must also reflect the gender and number of its noun (a person, place, thing, or concept). Here is an example.

> profesor = *male professor*   **el profesor** (*the professor*)
>   **un profesor** (*a professor*)
> profesora = *female professor*   **la profesora** (*the professor*)
>   **una profesora** (*a professor*)

Here are the plural forms; note the articles: **el profesor** becomes **los profesores** or **unos profesores**, and **la profesora** becomes **las profesoras** or **unas profesoras**. The paragraphs that follow will explain more about this system.

B. Gender in Spanish is purely a grammatical concept. All nouns have gender, whether they represent people, places, things, or concepts. Gender is either masculine or feminine, but it does not always mean that the noun is viewed as having masculine or feminine traits.

The nouns for all humans and most animals are assigned grammatical gender based on sexual gender. The nouns for most objects, things, and concepts have gender based on their word endings. As you are introduced to nouns, you should make a mental note of their gender. At different points throughout the Textbook and Workbook, you will also learn rules of thumb for determining gender.

C. In addition to gender, all nouns also have number; that is, they are singular or plural. Look at the following chart.

	MASCULINO		FEMENINO	
	singular	*plural*	*singular*	*plural*
definido	el secreto	los secretos	la carta	las cartas
indefinido	un secreto	unos secretos	una carta	unas cartas

D. It is unreasonable for you to expect to master the system of gender immediately or to always use the correct article, but here are some rules of thumb to get you started.

- Nouns that refer to male beings and most nouns that end in **-o** are masculine in gender: **el hombre, el hermano, el concepto.** Can you think of any other examples from this lesson or from **Lección 1**?
- Nouns that refer to female beings and almost all nouns that end in **-a, -ión,** and **-d** are feminine: **la mujer, la hermana, la compañía, la relación, la universidad.** What other words from this lesson or from **Lección 1** follow the same rule?
- Nouns that have other endings and that do not refer to either males or females may be masculine or feminine. Their gender must be memorized: **el español, la serie,** and so on. Of course, most rules have exceptions. Two words that you have already seen are exceptions to the "most nouns that end in **-a**" rule: **el patriarca, el idioma.**

E. You have probably noticed that for some nouns that refer to people, if the masculine ends in **-o**, the feminine ends in **-a**.

el hijo → la hija
el esposo → la esposa

What other word pairs of this kind appear in the lesson?

For other nouns that refer to people, if the masculine ends in a consonant, the feminine has a final **-a**.

un profesor → una profesora
un director → una directora

Many other nouns that refer to people have a single form. Gender is indicated by the article: **el/un estudiante, la/una estudiante.**

F. Nouns that end in a vowel form their plural by adding **-s**: **hijo → hijos.** Nouns that end in a consonant form their plural by adding **-es**: **profesor → profesores.** Note the following accent pattern for nouns that end in **-ión**: **lección,** but **lecciones.**

Actividad A. ¿Masculino o femenino?
Give the correct definite article (**el, la, los, las**) for these nouns.

MODELO: hijo → el hijo

Personas
1. hombre — el/un
2. mujer — la/una
3. estudiante (*male*) — el/un
4. estudiante (*female*) — la/una
5. tíos — los/unos
6. tías — las/unas
7. director — el/un
8. directora — la/una
9. clientes (*male*) — los/unos
10. abogadas — las/unas

[handwritten margin notes:]
hombre/hombres
mujer/mujeres
estudiantes
tío/tía
directores/directoras
cliente   abogada

Lugares

11. compañía — la / una 13. oficinas — las / unas 15. hacienda — la / una
12. universidad — la / una (14.) ciudades — las / unas

Cosas

16. cartas — las / unas 18. memoria — las / una
17. columna — la / una 19. modelos — los / unos

Conceptos

20. futuro — el / uno 22. relaciones — los / unos
(21.) tensión — la / una (23.) rivalidad — la / una

Now go back and give the correct indefinite articles for the same nouns.

MODELO: hija → **una** hija

Now go back and change singular nouns to plural and plural nouns to singular.

MODELO: hija → hijas

Actividad B.   Definiciones

Listen as the speaker on the cassette tape gives a series of definitions. You will not under-stand every word of the definitions. Just listen and try to catch the word defined and the gist of the definition. Then write the words defined in the appropriate column: **Personas, Lugares, Cosas, Conceptos.** Be sure to write an article with each word. (Worksheet)

3. *MI HIJO, MIS HIJOS*: EXPRESSING POSSESSION (PART 1)

DON FERNANDO: Tengo[1] una familia muy grande. **Mis** cuatro (4) hijos viven en distintas partes del mundo. **Mi** hija Mercedes, vive en La Gavia. No tiene hijos. **Mi** hijo Ramón también vive en La Gavia, con[2] **su** esposa, Consuelo, y **su** hija, Maricarmen. **Mi** hijo Carlos vive en Miami, con **su** esposa Gloria, y **sus** dos (2) hijos, Juanita y Carlitos. **Mi** hijo Juan vive en Nueva York con **su** esposa, Pati. No tienen hijos. **Mi** esposa, Carmen, ya murió; está muerta.

[1]*I have* [2]*with*

The preceding paragraph, written from don Fernando's point of view, shows how words like **mi (mis)** and **su (sus)** are used in Spanish. You know that **su (sus)** can mean *his, her,* or *their,* and you can guess that **mi (mis)** means *my.*

The words **mi (mis)** and **su (sus)** are similar to the articles that accompany nouns in Spanish in that they must agree with the nouns in number. You will learn more about words such as these in later chapters of *Destinos.*

Actividad A.   ¿Quién es?

Identify the person described in each group.

¿Quién habla? (*Who is talking?*)

Gloria   Juan
don Fernando Raquel
Mercedes   Ramón

1. _____ «Mis hijos se llaman Carlos, Juan, Ramón y Mercedes. Su madre ya no vive; está muerta.»
2. _____ «Mi esposa se llama (*is named*) Consuelo. Mi hija se llama Maricarmen. Mi padre es don Fernando y mi tío es Pedro.»
3. _____ «Yo soy de los Estados Unidos. Mi profesión es muy importante para mí.»
4. _____ «Mi esposo se llama Carlos. Su secretaria se llama Ofelia. Mis hijos son Juanita y Carlitos.»

¿De quién se habla? (*Who is being talked about?*)

los hijos de don Fernando   Mercedes   Carlos   Juan   Raquel

5. _____ Su esposa se llama Pati. Su padre vive en La Gavia. Tiene tres hermanos.

6. _____ Su esposa es Gloria. Tiene tres hermanos. Sus dos hijos viven en Miami.

7. _____ Su padre es don Fernando y su madre es Carmen. Viven en La Gavia, en Miami y en Nueva York.

8. _____ Sus hermanos son Juan, Ramón y Carlos. Su padre vive en La Gavia y su madre ya no vive; está muerta.

Actividad B.   La familia de don Fernando

Return to the paragraph with which Section 3 begins, don Fernando's description of his family. Read through the paragraph, changing words as needed to make the paragraph describe don Fernando's family from your perspective. Here is the beginning of the paragraph done for you. (Worksheet)

Don Fernando tiene una familia muy grande. **Sus** cuatro (4) hijos viven...

Actividad C.   ¿Y tú?

Describe your family by completing the appropriate sentences from this list. (Worksheet)

Mi familia es...   (muy) grande
                    (muy) pequeña (*small*)
                    regular
Mi madre se llama...   Vive en...
Mi padre se llama...   Vive en...
Tengo (uno, dos, tres, cuatro, cinco, seis...) hermanos.
    (No tengo hermanos.)
Mi hermano/a _____ vive en...
Tengo (uno, dos, tres, cuatro, cinco, seis...) hijos.
    (No tengo hijos.)

• •

PRONUNCIACIÓN: EL ALFABETO ESPAÑOL

The Spanish and English alphabets are similar but not identical. Listen as the speaker on the cassette tape pronounces each letter of the Spanish alphabet, along with a name that contains the letter. Then pronounce the letter and name after you hear them.

a	Antonio	h	Héctor	ñ	España	u	Agustín
b	Blanca	i	Inés	o	Olivia	v	Víctor
c	Cecilia	j	José	p	Pablo	w	Oswaldo
ch	Chile	k	(Kati)	q	Raquel	x	Félix
d	Dolores	l	Luis	r	Clara	y	Yucatán
e	Elena	ll	Guillermina	rr	Monterrey	z	Zaragoza
f	Felipe	m	Manuel	s	Sara		
g	Gloria	n	Nicaragua	t	Tomás		

Four letters in the Spanish alphabet are different from those in the English alphabet. Which ones are they? You will want to keep them in mind when looking up words in a Spanish dictionary, since they affect alphabetical order. Words that begin with **ch, ll,** or **ñ** are in their own sections of the dictionary, after the **c, l,** and **n** sections, respectively. And the word **coche** comes *after* coco in an alphabetical list.*

---

*The **Real Academia Española de la Lengua** (Royal Spanish Academy of Language), located in Spain, recently decided that **ch** should no longer be considered a separate letter. As of this writing, it is difficult to predict what effect this decision may have on Spanish throughout the world.

¡Aumenta tu vocabulario!

In **Lección 1** you learned about cognates: words that look alike in both Spanish and English. Beginning in this lesson, you will learn some common cognate patterns that will help you recognize many Spanish words, even if you have never seen them before. In many instances these cognate patterns can also help you come up with the correct word in Spanish if you know the English word.

Here are three pairs of suffixes (word endings) that make up some of the most common cognate groups. Note that most Spanish nouns that end in these suffixes are feminine. The spoken stress falls on the end of the Spanish words.

SPANISH SUFFIX		ENGLISH EQUIVALENT	
-ción	nación	-tion	nation
	preparación		preparation
-sión	tensión	-sion	tension
	expresión		expression
-dad	vitalidad	-ty	vitality
	ciudad		city

Actividad A.

By using the suffix patterns given in this section, you should be able to understand the indicated words. Repeat the sentences after the speaker the second time you hear them. Then indicate whether the sentences are **Cierto** or **Falso**.

C F 1. ¿Cuál es la **profesión** de Juan? Es profesor en la **universidad**.
C F 2. Hay mucha **tensión** entre las **naciones** del mundo (*world*).
C F 3. En la ciudad de Los Ángeles, no hay una **comunidad** de mexicoamericanos.
C F 4. En una **conversación**, hay **comunicación** entre (*between*) dos personas.
C F 5. Hay programas interesantes en la **televisión**.
C F 6. La **opresión** de unos grupos por (*by*) otros grupos no tiene **solución**.

Actividad B.

The following paragraph is adapted from a reading passage you worked with in **Más allá del episodio**. Complete it using words from the list.

rivalidad	universidad	especialización	presiones
profesión	personalidades	tensión	

En este momento,ᵃ el matrimonio de Juan y Pati es inestable y tenso. Los dos trabajanᵇ en la _____ ¹ y su _____ ² es muy importante. Juan es profesor de literatura, y la _____ ³ de Pati es el teatro. Las _____ ⁴ de sus respectivas carreras académicas aumentan la _____ ⁵ entre ellos. También, sus _____ ⁶ están en conflicto: Los dos son muy ambiciosos y hay _____ ⁷ entre ellos. El futuro de su matrimonio es incierto....

ᵃ En... *Right now*   ᵇ Los... *Both of them work*

Have you completed the following sections of the lesson? Check them off here.

_____ **Más allá del episodio**   _____ **Pronunciación**
_____ **Gramática**   _____ **¡Aumenta tu vocabulario!**

Now scan the words in the **Vocabulario** list to be sure that you understand the meaning of most of them.

VOCABULARIO

Los lugares (Places)

la ciudad	city
el mundo	world
la oficina	office
la universidad	university

Los verbos (Verbs)

se llama	(he/she) is called, named
tengo	I have

Las palabras adicionales (Additional Words)

mi/mis	my

Now that you have completed the Textbook and Workbook for **Lecciones** 1 and 2, take the Self-Test for those lessons. (It is on page 246.) Remember to use the tape when you see the cassette symbol and to check your answers.

_____ **Self-Test**

Now that you have worked through the Textbook and the Workbook and taken the Self-Test, here are some of the things you have accomplished in Spanish.

- You can use some basic greetings in Spanish.
- You can now talk simply about your own family and the families of others.
- You can give definite and indefinite articles for a variety of nouns, as well as their plural forms, and you know that all nouns in Spanish are either masculine or feminine.
- You know about several ways to express possession.
- You are familiar with the Spanish alphabet.
- You can recognize more common cognates.
- You have continued to work on listening skills with the video episode and the cassette tape, and you are comfortable focusing on what you do understand even when you don't comprehend every word.

You are now ready to continue on with **Lección 3** in the Textbook.

LECCIÓN

3

EL COMIENZO

OBJETIVOS

Whereas the materials in the Textbook all had to do with the video segment, the materials in the Workbook will help you expand your knowledge of the Spanish language in general, as well as give you opportunities for self-expression in Spanish. In this lesson you will learn

- the use of the word **hay**
- several uses of **estar** (another Spanish verb that means *to be*)
- more about describing what others are doing
- pronunciation of the Spanish vowels
- more about cognates.

Remember to listen to the tape for **Lección 3** when you see the cassette symbol and to check your answers in Appendix 1.

MÁS ALLÁ DEL EPISODIO

Actividad A.   La familia Ruiz

In this episode you meet some members of the Ruiz family for the first time, and you learn of the existence of others. Here is a series of statements about Elena, her husband, Miguel, and their two sons, Miguel and Jaime. Choose from the following five responses to express your reaction.

a.   Sé (*I know*) que es cierto.
b.   Creo (*I believe*) que es cierto.
c.   No sé. (*I don't know.*)

d.   Creo que es falso.
e.   Sé que es falso.

As you read, remember to guess the meaning of words when you can and skip over those that you don't know. When you see the phrase **le gusta**, the sentence is about something that someone likes—or doesn't like—to do.

18

1. _____ Elena Ramírez tiene mucho trabajo (*work*) con dos hijos.
2. _____ Miguel Ruiz, el padre, trabaja (*works*) en la universidad de Sevilla.
3. _____ Jaime es el hijo mayor (*older*).
4. _____ Miguel no es muy buen estudiante.
5. _____ Los dos hermanos no se llevan muy bien (*get along very well*).
6. _____ Elena y Miguel padre no se llevan muy bien.
7. _____ Teresa Suárez visita a la familia con frecuencia.

The answers you have given are based solely on the very small amount of information you have at this point about the Ruiz family. The following reading passage offers more information. Read it and see whether you wish to change any answers.

Elena y Miguel, con sus dos hijos

Elena Ramírez es la madre de Miguel y Jaime, los dos chicos que Raquel conoce[1] en la calle Pureza. Con dos hijos, Elena tiene mucho trabajo. Jaime, especialmente, le da problemas.

Jaime es un niño con mucha energía. Es el menor[2] de los dos hijos y le gusta ser el centro de atención. No es muy buen estudiante y Elena habla con frecuencia con su maestro[3] y el director de su escuela. Este año,[4] Jaime tiene muchas dificultades en la clase de matemáticas.

En cambio,[5] Miguel es un hijo modelo y Elena está muy orgullosa[6] de él. Miguel es inteligente, estudioso... y sus maestros hablan muy bien de él. Como hermanos típicos, a veces Jaime y Miguel no se llevan bien... y Elena tiene que intervenir en sus peleas.[7]

¿Y el padre de los chicos? ¿Cómo es él? ¿Y cómo es la relación que tiene con Elena, Jaime y Miguel?

[1]*meets* [2]*younger* [3]*teacher* [4]*Este... This year* [5]*En... On the other hand* [6]*proud* [7]*fights*

 Actividad B.

Now return to statements 1–7 and make any changes in your answers that you feel are necessary. Which statements do you still have to guess at or answer **No sé**? Listen to the cassette tape, on which the speaker will give you some answers and provide some more information.

• •

GRAMÁTICA

 ## 4. ¿QUÉ HAY EN... ?: USING *hay*

Use the verb form **hay**, which you learned in **Lección 1**, to express both *there is* and *there are* in Spanish. **No hay** means *there is not* and *there are not*. ¿**Hay**... ? asks *Is there . . . ?* or *Are there . . . ?* Unlike other verb forms you have learned, **hay** does not change form.

En Sevilla **hay** muchos[1] mercados y tiendas.[2] Pero **no hay** muchas fábricas.[3] **Hay** pocas[4] industrias en el sur de España. ¿Qué **hay** en tu ciudad? ¿**Hay** mucha industria? ¿**Hay** muchas tiendas?

[1]*many* [2]*stores* [3]*factories* [4]*few*

Actividad A. ¿Qué hay en Sevilla?

Based on what you have read and heard about Sevilla, is the content of the following sentences **Cierto** or **Falso**? Try to make logical guesses. If you really don't know yet, answer **No sé** (*I don't know*).

C F 1. Hay muchas industrias.
C F 2. Hay muchos mercados.
C F 3. No hay muchas iglesias.

C F 4. Hay muchas cerámicas.
C F 5. No hay muchas tradiciones religiosas.

 ## Actividad B. Una familia española

Listen as the speaker on the cassette tape asks some questions about this family. Begin your answers with **Hay...** or **No hay...** , as appropriate.

1. ... 2. ... 3. ... 4. ... 5. ...

 ## Actividad C. ¿Y tú?

¿Qué hay donde tú vives? Are the following sentences **Cierto** or **Falso** for the city in which you live?

C F 1. Hay muchas industrias.
C F 2. No hay muchas iglesias.
C F 3. Hay muchos mercados.

C F 4. Hay muchos hoteles.
C F 5. No hay muchas plazas.
C F 6. Hay muchas personas de habla española (*Spanish-speaking*).

 ## 5. ¿CÓMO ESTÁS?: THE VERB *estar*

As you read the following conversation that might have taken place in **Episodio 2**, try to determine what two topics are being discussed.

CARLOS: Tío Pedro, mucho tiempo sin verte. ¿Cómo estás?
PEDRO: Sí, sí, Carlos, bien. ¿Cómo estás?
CARLOS: Bien, bien, tío.
PEDRO: Y Gloria, ¿dónde está?
GLORIA: Aquí, tío Pedro.
PEDRO: ¿Y dónde están Carlitos y Juanita?

Forms

Estar is another verb that means *to be* in Spanish. Its forms do not follow a completely regular pattern. Here are its third-person forms: **está, están.**

In **Lección 1** you learned the forms of **ser**, along with a few of its uses. You will learn additional verb forms and more about the differences between **ser** and **estar** in **Lección 10**.

Uses

Forms of **estar** are used to talk about how someone is feeling. You have probably noticed the use of forms of **estar** as members of the Castillo family greet one another and talk about don Fernando. For example, when Juan asks Ramón how he is, "**¿Cómo estás?**", Ramón answers, "**Yo, bien, pero papá está muy mal.**"

To find out how someone is feeling, one of two different questions is used.

¿Cómo **está** usted?   used in formal situations or to show respect
¿Cómo **estás** (tú)?   used in informal situations or with people you know well

Both of these questions correspond to the English *How are you?* Note the two different ways to say *you* (**usted, tú**) and the two different verb forms used.

You will learn more about this system in **Lección 4** to tell where someone or something is located. Here is an example.

África **está** al sur de España. Francia y el mar Cantábrico **están** al norte de España. No **están** al sur.

Actividad A. ¿Cómo está usted? ¿Cómo estás?

Which question from the title of this activity is appropriate in each of the following situations?

1. Carlos, speaking to his secretary
2. Ofelia, his secretary, speaking to him
3. Pedro, speaking to Raquel
4. Raquel, speaking to Pedro
5. you, speaking to your Spanish instructor

 ### Actividad B. ¿Dónde está... ?

Show what you have learned about Spanish geography by selecting the correct answer to the questions you hear.

1. en África / en Europa / en Asia
2. al sur de España / al norte de España / al este de España
3. al sur / al oeste / al este
4. al norte / al este / al oeste
5. en Sevilla / en Madrid / en Barcelona

Actividad C. ¿Quién... ?

Indicate where the following characters from *Destinos* are or whom they are with by matching the names with the descriptions. Use **está** or **están**, as appropriate. Create as many different sentences as you can. (Worksheet)

1.	Raquel	en La Gavia, en su habitación (*room*)
2.	don Fernando	en el patio de La Gavia
3.	Elena y Raquel	en el mercado de Triana
4.	los hijos de don Fernando	en la calle Pureza
5.	Raquel y los chicos	en la plaza
6.	los chicos	en el barrio de Triana

con Elena
con el taxista
con Raquel
con los chicos
con sus hermanos

Actividad D.   ¿Y tú?

Describe the following people and places with which you are familiar. Create as many sentences as you can. Select only those items from the left-hand column that are appropriate for you. Use **no** as needed. (Worksheet)

mi padre/mi madre	(no) está	bien
mis padres	están	mal
mis hijos		en (ciudad)
mi abuelo/mi abuela		en casa (*at home*)
mis abuelos		en la calle _____
mi universidad		en clase
mis amigos		en ¿_____?

 ## 6.   *RAQUEL HABLA CON...* : THIRD-PERSON FORMS OF REGULAR VERBS (PRESENT TENSE)

Forms

As you have learned, third-person verb forms are used to talk about other people. When you and I speak of someone else, we are talking about a "third" party.

Note that the third-person verb forms correspond to the following subject pronouns.* As you will see, the Spanish pronouns indicate gender.

he	él habla, explica
she	ella escribe, vive
they (male)	ellos hablan, explican
they (female)	ellas escriben, viven

The preceding verb forms are called "regular" because their endings follow predictable patterns: -a or -e for singular, -an or -en for plural.

---

*The subject of a sentence is its topic, what it is about: "*Raquel* lives in Los Angeles. *Fernando's children* live in Mexico." Subject pronouns take the place of subject nouns: "*She* lives in Los Angeles. *They* live in Mexico."

Uses

The present-tense forms of Spanish verbs have the following English equivalents. Note also the position of **no** (before the verb).

Raquel explica la historia.   *Raquel explains (is explaining) the story.*

Raquel **no** explica el misterio.   *Raquel doesn't explain the mystery.*

When the context makes meaning clear, subject pronouns are not used with these verb forms. In the following brief paragraphs, you can easily identify the subject of the verbs because it is indicated at the beginning and the context is obvious.

Elena Ruiz vive en Sevilla. No trabaja en una oficina. Tiene esposo y dos hijos. **Don Fernando** vive en La Gavia. Ya no trabaja. Tiene cuatro hijos, pero no tiene esposa.

 Actividad A. ¿De quién se habla? (*Who is being talked about?*)

¡OJO! There is more than one possible answer for some items. First, take a few seconds to scan the list of characters.

Raquel   Teresa Suárez   Miguel y Jaime
don Fernando   Raquel y el taxista   Ramón y Mercedes

1. _____ Escribe una carta.
2. _____ Viaja a Sevilla.
3. _____ Busca a Rosario.
4. _____ Hablan con Raquel en la calle.
5. _____ Viven en La Gavia, con su padre.
6. _____ Entran en el barrio de Triana en taxi.
7. _____ Cree que Rosario está en España.
8. _____ Llega al mercado de Triana con dos chicos.
9. _____ Investiga el secreto de don Fernando.
10. _____ Revela un secreto a su familia.

Actividad B. Los personajes de *Destinos*

Compare the activities of different characters in the series by finishing these sentences.

1. Carlos trabaja en Miami. Ramón y Mercedes no...
2. Pati viaja con frecuencia. Mercedes y don Fernando no...
3. Juan y Pati visitan a don Fernando en La Gavia. Carlos también...
4. Don Fernando toma muchas medicinas. Sus hijos no...
5. Raquel explica la historia. Miguel y Jaime no...
6. Miguel y Jaime no preguntan dónde vive Teresa Suárez. Raquel...

Actividad C. ¿Y tú?

Tell about the members of your family and your acquaintances. Create as many sentences as you can. Select only those items from the left-hand column that are appropriate for you. Use **no** as needed. (Worksheet)

mi madre/mi padre   vive(n) en _____ (lugar) _____
mis padres   habla(n) mucho por teléfono
mi hermano/mi hermana   habla(n) inglés/español
mis hermanos   habla(n) otra lengua
mi esposo/mi esposa   trabaja(n) mucho/poco
mi hijo/ mi hija   viaja(n) con frecuencia (a _____)
mis hijos   escribe(n) muchas cartas/muchos reportes
mi profesor(a) de español   toma(n) muchas/pocas medicinas
mi amigo _____   tiene(n) muchas clases/muchos pacientes
mis amigos   trabaja(n) en una oficina/en la universidad
mi doctor   ¿____?
mi ¿____?
mis ¿____?

Actividad D.   ¿Y tú?

How do the activities of your family and acquaintances compare with those of the *Destinos* characters? Use the names of other people as appropriate. (Worksheet)

Note: **tu, tus** = *your* (with people you know well).

1. Ramón y Mercedes viven con su padre. ¿Con quién viven tus amigos? ¿tus hijos? ¿tus abuelos?
2. Pati trabaja en un teatro, en Nueva York. ¿Dónde trabaja tu padre? ¿tu madre?
3. Carlos escribe muchos reportes. También escribe muchas cartas. ¿y tus amigos? ¿y tus padres?

7.   *RAQUEL NECESITA HABLAR CON...* : INFINITIVES AND THEIR USE

Forms

In English the infinitive is the verb form indicated by the word *to*: *to talk, to work, to be,* and so on. In Spanish, all infinitives end in **-r: -ar, -er, -ir.** You have already learned two Spanish infinitives, **ser** and **estar,** that are irregular; that is, their forms are unpredictable. Here are the infinitives of the regular third-person verbs you have worked with so far. You should understand the meaning of all of them. If not, look them up in the **Vocabulario** at the end of this lesson.

REGULAR **-ar** VERBS		REGULAR **-er** VERBS	REGULAR **-ir** VERBS
buscar	necesitar	creer	escribir
entrar (en)	preguntar		vivir
explicar	revelar		
hablar	tomar		
investigar	trabajar		
llegar	viajar		
	visitar		

Uses

Some verb forms are created from infinitives by conjugating. To conjugate a Spanish infinitive, it is necessary to substitute a personal ending for the **-ar, -er,** or **-ir** of the infinitive. You have already used the personal endings **-a, -e, -an,** and **-en.** They are indicated in the following chart.

Infinitive	hablar	creer	vivir
Verb Stem	habl-	cre-	viv-
él/ella	habla	cree	vive
ellos/ellas	hablan	creen	viven

A few Spanish verbs can be followed directly by the infinitive form of another verb. Verbs that can be followed by infinitives include **desear** (*to want, wish*), **deber** (*should, must*), and **necesitar.** As you will notice in the following examples, sometimes this usage corresponds to English, but not always.

Raquel **debe hablar** con Miguel Ruiz. Ella **desea encontrar** a Rosario y **necesita saber** dónde vive la señora Suárez.	*Raquel should speak with Miguel Ruiz. She wants to find Rosario and she needs to know where Mrs. Suárez lives.*

Actividad. Obligaciones y deseos

Indicate what the following people need or want to do by combining elements from each column. Use **no** as appropriate. (Worksheet)

1. Raquel   debe(n)   hablar con Teresa Suárez / con Pedro
    Miguel y Jaime   Castillo / con Elena Ramírez
                      necesita(n)   buscar a Rosario / a su madre en el
                                        mercado / al otro hijo de don Fernando*
                      desea(n)   visitar a su abuela*
                                     visitar los monumentos históricos de Sevilla
                                     estudiar mucho

2. mi _____   debe(n)   trabajar más (*more*) / menos (*less*)
    mis _____   necesita(n)   hablar más / menos (por teléfono)
                      desea(n)   viajar más / a ____
                                     estudiar más / menos

· ·

Pronunciación: Las vocales—*a, e, i, o, u*

Unlike English vowels, which can have many different pronunciations or be silent, Spanish vowels are always pronounced,† and they are almost always pronounced in the same way. Spanish vowels are always short and tense. They are never drawn out with a *w* or *y* glide as in English: Spanish **lo** is not pronounced *low*, and **de** is not pronounced *day*.

Actividad A.

Listen to the description of how Spanish vowels are pronounced; then repeat the example words you hear on the tape. Try to imitate the speaker's pronunciation as closely as you can. Note that when you see an accent mark (´) over a vowel, it is stressed. You will learn more about this aspect of Spanish in upcoming lessons.

a: pronounced like the *a* in *father*, but short and tense

    padre   carta   gata

e: pronounced like the *e* in *they*, but without the *y* glide

    Pepe   trece   bebé

i: pronounced like the *i* in *machine*, but short and tense

    Mimi   Trini   Pili

o: pronounced like the *o* in *home*, but without the *w* glide

    como   poco   somos

u: pronouced like the *u* in *rule*, but short and tense

    Lulú   tutú   gurú

---

*Throughout this lesson of the Textbook and Workbook, you have seen the word **a** used before the names of people or nouns that refer to specific persons. You will learn more about this use of **a** in Lección 5. This **a** has no equivalent in English. For now, just be sure to use it when you see it.

---

†As you will learn later, there are a few exceptions to this rule. One is the silent **u** in the **que** or **qui** combinations. You are already familiar with the **que** combination in the name **Raquel**.

¡OJO! As you listened and repeated, did you notice how each vowel was carefully pronounced, even when it did not receive the spoken stress? In English, unstressed vowels are pronounced *uh* (a sound called a schwa), as in these words: c*a*nal, mot*o*r, An*a*. The schwa does not exist in Spanish. Note how each vowel is distinctly pronounced in these identical cognates: **canal, motor, Ana.**

 ### Actividad B.
Pronounce the following words and phrases, paying special attention to the vowel sounds.

1. habla   trabaja   cree   preguntan   deben   escribe
2. mamá   papá   hermano   esposa   abuelos   amigos
3. número   secreto   oficina   director   abogado
4. Está en España.   Está muy bien.   Es mi hermano.   Vive en Madrid.

NOTA CULTURAL: SPANISH IN SPAIN

You have probably noticed a difference between the Spanish you heard in the first two episodes and that spoken in **Episodio 3** by the people who live in Sevilla. Compared to the Spanish spoken by don Fernando and his family and by Raquel, this Spanish is more rapid, and you may perceive that individual words are heard less distinctly. In addition, the letters **z** and (in some positions) **c** are pronounced with a "soft" *th* sound. You can most easily listen for this sound by comparing the way Raquel says numbers in this episode with the way Jaime, the hotel clerk, and others say them.

• •

¡AUMENTA TU VOCABULARIO!

In **Lección 2** you learned about the cognate suffixes **-ción, -sión,** and **-dad.** Here are three more useful endings that will help you recognize additional cognate groups.

SPANISH SUFFIX		ENGLISH EQUIVALENT	
-oso	famoso	-ous	famous
	riguroso		rigorous
-ía*	filosofía	-y	philosophy
	teoría		theory
-mente	frecuentemente	-ly	frequently
	rápidamente		rapidly

It is also helpful to know that many words that begin with Spanish **es** + consonant are equivalent to English cognates that begin with *s* + consonant.

escuela	school	**estudiante**	student
estatua	statue	**España**	Spain

 ### Actividad A.
By using the suffix patterns given in this section, you should be able to understand the indicated words. Repeat the sentences after the speaker the second time you hear them. Then match them with the appropriate drawing.

---

*Almost all nouns that end in -ía are feminine. The spoken stress falls on the accented *i.*

Lección 3 El comienzo

a.
b.
c.
d.
e.

1. En Sevilla hay estatuas **maravillosas**.
2. En la religión árabe, hay muchas **profecías**.
3. Para Jaime, las matemáticas son **especialmente** difíciles.
4. En España, la **cortesía** es muy importante.
5. La **economía** del norte de España se basa en la industria.

Actividad B.

The following paragraph is about Jaime and Miguel. Complete it using words from the list.

> estudioso biología especialmente escuela teorías
> estudiar fantasías totalmente estudiante realmente

Miguel y Jaime son los hijos de Miguel y Elena Ruiz. Miguel es un chico muy _____.¹

Le gusta la _____² y es un buen _____.³ Tiene mucho interés en las

_____⁴ de las ciencias naturales, _____⁵ la _____.⁶

Jaime es _____⁷ diferente. No le gusta _____;⁸ estudia _____⁹

muy poco. Pero tiene muchas _____¹⁰ y una en particular: ¡desea tener² un perro!

²*to have*

Have you completed the following sections of the lesson? Check them off here.

_____ **Más allá del episodio**   _____ **Pronunciación**

_____ **Gramática**   _____ **¡Aumenta tu vocabulario!**

Now scan the words in the **Vocabulario** list to be sure that you understand the meaning of most of them.

VOCABULARIO

Los verbos

buscar	to look for	investigar	to investigate
creer	to think, believe	llegar	to arrive
deber (+ *inf.*)	should, must (*do something*)	necesitar (+ *inf.*)	to need (*to do something*)
desear (+ *inf.*)	to wish, want (*to do something*)	preguntar	to ask (*a question*)
entrar (en)	to enter	revelar	to reveal
escribir	to write	tomar	to take (*transportation*); to drink
explicar	to explain	trabajar	to work
hablar	to speak; to talk	viajar	to travel

visitar	to visit	**Las palabras adicionales**	
vivir	to live	él/ella	he/she
		ellos/ellas	they (*masculine/feminine*)
estar	to be		
está	he/she is	bien	well
están	they are	con frecuencia	frequently
		¿dónde?	where?
hay	there is, there are	mal	badly, not well
		mucho*	a lot
		muchos/muchas*	many
Los lugares		poco*	little, not much
el barrio	neighborhood, district	pocos/pocas*	few
la calle	street	¿qué?	what?
la iglesia	church		
el mercado	market		

Más saludos

¿Cómo está usted?	How are you? (*formal*)
¿Cómo estás?	How are you? (*informal*)

Now that you have completed the Textbook and Workbook for **Lección 3,** take the Self-Test for that lesson. (It is on page 248.) Remember to use the tape when you see the cassette symbol and to check your answers.

_____ **Self-Test**

Now that you have worked through the Textbook and the Workbook and taken the Self-Test, here are some of the things you have accomplished in Spanish.

- You can use some additional greetings in Spanish.
- You can use and understand some numbers.
- You can use a variety of verb forms to talk about what people are doing, where people and things are located, and how people are.
- You know how Spanish vowels are pronounced.
- You can recognize more common cognates.
- You have continued to work on listening skills.

You are now ready to continue on with **Lección 4** in the Textbook.

---

*Don't be confused by the different forms in this section of the vocabulary list. Just learn to recognize the meaning of these words in context. You will learn to use them in upcoming chapters.

L E C C I Ó N
. . . .

4

PERDIDO

OBJETIVOS

Whereas the materials in the Textbook all had to do with the video segment, the materials in the Workbook will help you expand your knowledge of the Spanish language in general, as well as give you opportunities for self-expression in Spanish. In this lesson you will learn

- more about describing what you and others are doing
- more about addressing others in Spanish
- more about descriptions
- about two aspects of Spanish pronunciation, diphthongs and linking
- more about cognates.

Remember to listen to the tape for **Lección 4** when you see the cassette symbol and to check your answers in Appendix 1.

MÁS ALLÁ DEL EPISODIO

Actividad A.   Raquel Rodríguez

You may have speculated about what Raquel is like and about other details of her life. Here is a series of statements about Raquel. Choose from the following five responses to express your reaction.

a. Sé (*I know*) que es cierto.   d. Creo que es falso.
b. Creo que es cierto.   e. Sé que es falso.
c. No sé.

1. _____ Los padres de Raquel viven en California.
2. _____ Raquel y Pedro Castillo son buenos amigos.
3. _____ A Raquel le gustan mucho los animales.
4. _____ Raquel está casada (*married*).
5. _____ Raquel tiene un hijo.
6. _____ Es impaciente y arrogante.

7. ____ Trabaja en San Diego.
8. ____ Viaja con frecuencia a España.

The answers you have given are based solely on the very small amount of information you have at this point about Raquel. The following reading passage offers more information. Read it and see whether you wish to change any answers. As you read, note that one paragraph starts out in the past; it is a safe bet that other verb forms in that paragraph will also be in the past.

Raquel usa
su computadora
con frecuencia.

Raquel Rodríguez es una abogada mexicoamericana. Es soltera.[1] Es una mujer muy inteligente. Es sensible,[2] sincera y generosa con sus amigos y colegas. También tiene mucha imaginación. A veces,[3] es un poco impaciente. En sus ratos libres,[4] le gusta ir de compras[5] y leer novelas. Los padres de Raquel viven en Los Ángeles. Están jubilados.[6] Raquel es hija única[7] y su madre se mete mucho[8] en su vida. Las dos se pelean[9] con frecuencia. Pero Raquel quiere[10] mucho a sus padres y los visita regularmente. Raquel también tiene familia en México.

Raquel conoció[11] a Pedro Castillo en México. El bufete[12] donde Raquel trabaja tiene una sucursal[13] allí. Pedro ha tenido[14] mucho contacto con esa oficina y siempre ha admirado[15] el trabajo de Raquel. Por eso, Pedro se puso en contacto con Raquel cuando don Fernando reveló el secreto de la carta. Ella aceptó el caso inmediatamente.

Raquel está muy emocionada[16] porque éste es su primer viaje a España. Pero, ¿va a encontrar[17] a Teresa Suárez, la mujer que le escribió una carta a don Fernando? ¿y a Rosario, la primera esposa de don Fernando?

[1]*single* [2]*sensitive* [3]*A... Sometimes* [4]*ratos... free time* [5]*ir... to go shopping* [6]*ya no trabajan* [7]*hija... no tiene hermanos* [8]*se... gets very involved* [9]*se... fight* [10]*loves* [11]*met* [12]*law office* [13]*branch office* [14]*ha... has had* [15]*ha... has admired* [16]*excited* [17]*va... is she going to find*

 Actividad B.
Now return to statements 1–8 and make any changes in your answers that you feel are necessary. Which statements do you still have to guess at or answer **No sé?** Listen to the cassette tape, on which the speaker will give you some answers and then provide some more information.

• •

GRAMÁTICA

 8. *BUSCO A LA SRA. SUÁREZ:* **FIRST-PERSON SINGULAR FORMS OF REGULAR VERBS (PRESENT TENSE)**

RAQUEL: Tengo un caso interesante que investigar. **Busco** a una señora, Teresa Suárez. **Creo** que vive en España. **Necesito** hablar con ella por mi cliente, don Fernando.

Forms
In **Lección 3** you learned to talk about the actions of others by adding **-a/-an** or **-e/-en** to the stem of regular verbs. To talk about your own actions, add **-o** to the verb stem. These forms, called "first person," refer to "I," the first person in the I-you dialogue.

Infinitive	hablar	creer	vivir
Verb Stem	habl-	cre-	viv-
yo	hablo	creo	vivo

Uses

Note the English equivalents of the first-person singular verb forms in this paragraph. As you will see, the subject pronoun yo is not generally used, since the -o ending makes it clear who the subject is. Note also the position of no.

MIGUEL: Estudio mucho. Este semestre, saco buenas notas. Algún día, deseo ser científico. No deseo ser guía.

MIGUEL: *I study a lot. This semester, I'm getting good grades. Some day I want to be a scientist. I don't want to be a guide.*

Actividad A. ¿Quién habla?

You have learned a great deal about Raquel, Pati (Juan's wife), and Elena Ramírez. Indicate whether the following statements would be made by Raquel (R), by Pati (P), or by Elena (E). Don't be misled by the voice you hear on the tape.

R (P) E 1. Vivo en Nueva York, con mi esposo.
(R) P E 2. Acepto el caso porque es muy interesante.
(R) P (E) 3. Viajo a España.
R P (E) 4. Vivo en Sevilla, con mi esposo y mis dos hijos.
R (P) E 5. Trabajo en un teatro.
(R) P E 6. Necesito hablar con una señora.
R P (E) 7. Visito a* la abuela de mis hijos con frecuencia.
(R) P E 8. Escribo muchos reportes.

Actividad B. Miguel Ruiz Ramírez habla de sus actividades

In the following paragraph Miguel talks about himself and his life. Complete the paragraph with the appropriate verb forms. It may be possible to use some forms more than once, and there are extra verbs.

deseo soy debo creo necesito tengo
saco estudio escribo camino visito trabajo

Estoy en octavo (*8th*) grado. Mi colegio se llama San Fernando de Paula y está en Sevilla. Yo

_____¹ al colegio—¡no hay autobuses! _____² mucho y siempre*

_____³ buenas notas. A veces _____⁴ con mi hermano Jaime, pero no

_____⁵ sus lecciones.

_____⁶ el mercado de los animales con frecuencia porque _____⁷tener un

pájaro. Pero mi mamá cree que no _____⁸ tener uno porque _____⁹

irresponsable a veces. Yo _____¹⁰ que _____¹¹ hablar con ella. También es

posible hablar con papá, a ver si él decide el caso....

always

Actividad C. ¿Y tú?

Now it's time to give some information about yourself. Create as many sentences as you can about the following subjects. (Worksheet)

- Where you live and with whom
- Where you are studying and what subjects you are studying
- If you work and, if so, where
- What you write (¿muchos reportes? ¿muchas cartas?)
- Whom you speak with in Spanish (en español)

---

*Once again, and throughout this chaper, note the use of the word a before names or nouns that refer to specific people. This a has no equivalent in English. You will learn more about it in **Lección 5**.

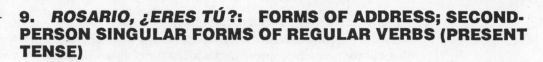

9. *ROSARIO, ¿ERES TÚ?*: FORMS OF ADDRESS; SECOND-PERSON SINGULAR FORMS OF REGULAR VERBS (PRESENT TENSE)

> RAQUEL: Jaime, ¿y tú? ¿En qué año estás?
> JAIME: Estoy en el primer año.
>
> ELENA: ¿Por qué no pasamos por **usted** a las diez de la mañana? ¿Vale?
> RAQUEL: Perfecto.

Forms of Address

In **Lección 3** you learned two questions to ask others how they are feeling: **¿Cómo está usted?**, **¿Cómo estás (tú)?** These questions show two of the subject pronouns used to express English *you* in Spanish: **usted** (often abbreviated Ud.) and **tú**.

- Use **usted** with people you do not know well or with people to whom you wish to show deference or respect.
- Use **tú** with people of your own age or those younger than you, or with people you know well.

The use of these pronouns varies widely throughout the Hispanic world and among different circles of friends or acquaintances. Note in the preceding models that Raquel addresses Jaime with **tú** and that Elena uses **usted** with Raquel. In *Destinos* Miguel and Elena address Raquel as **usted**, because they have just met. However, they all speak to the children using **tú** forms. This is a very common pattern observed by many Spanish speakers. Young children often address all adults with **tú** until they learn to be more deferential. As you watch future episodes of *Destinos*, note in what contexts people use **tú** or **usted**.

NOTA CULTURAL: FORMS OF ADDRESS

Language is a process. It is forever changing, whether we like it or not. An example of language change noted by many experts during recent years is the almost exclusive use of **tú** by Spaniards, particularly young people. Some theorists have suggested that the use of **tú** forms coincides with the emergence of Spain as a democratic nation after the long and repressive Franco dictatorship.

Second-Person Singular Forms of Regular Verbs

Forms

"Second person" is the term used to refer to a person to whom you are speaking directly. It is the "you" in the I-you dialogue. Because there are two ways in Spanish to express *you* (singular), there are also two verb forms that correspond to those pronouns.

For **tú**, add **-as** or **-es** to the verb stem. The **usted** forms add **-a** or **-e,** as do the third-person forms you have already learned.

Infinitive	hablar	creer	vivir
Verb Stem	habl-	cre-	viv-
tú	hablas	crees	vives
usted	habla	cree	vive

Uses

The subject pronoun **tú** is not always used, because the -as or -es ending makes meaning clear. When you hear **tú**, it is often to express *and you?* (¿y tú?) or for emphasis, as in **Rosario, ¿eres tú?** The pronoun **usted** is frequently used to clarify meaning, because its verb forms are the same as those for **él** and **ella**.

Actividad A. Las preguntas de Jaime

Match the following questions Jaime might ask Raquel* with her answers. Pay particular attention to the question words with which many of Jaime's questions begin. You have heard all of them in the video episodes of *Destinos*. You will hear only the questions on the cassette tape. Listen to all of them first; then do the activity.

1. _d_ ¿Dónde vives? ¿en México?
2. _g_ ¿Viajas con frecuencia?
3. _a_ ¿A quién buscas en Sevilla?
4. _e_ ¿Cuándo tomas el tren? ¿mañana?
5. _c_ ¿Visitas a tus padres con frecuencia?
6. _b_ ¿A quién debes llamar ahora?
7. _f_ ¿Qué escribes? ¿una carta?

a. Busco a la señora Suárez, tu abuela.
b. Debo llamar a Pedro, el hermano de mi cliente.
c. Sí, y también me gusta hablar con ellos por teléfono.
d. No. Vivo en Los Ángeles, en los Estados Unidos.
e. No. Tomo el tren pasado mañana.
f. No. Escribo un reporte, para don Fernando.
g. No, no mucho. Pero me gusta viajar. Es una contradicción, ¿no?

Actividad B. Miguel Ruiz habla con su hijo

In the following paragraph Miguel Ruiz talks directly to his son, Jaime. Complete the paragraph with the appropriate verb forms. It may be possible to use some forms more than once, and there are extra verbs.

dehes sacas buscas llamas llevas deseas crees eres hablas escribes visitas viajas

Jaime... Jaime... ¿Qué vamos a hacer contigo?ª _____¹ estudiar más, ¿no _____²? _____³ mucho con tus amigos y no _____⁴ las lecciones. No _____⁵ a la abuela Teresa, pero sí _____⁶ a todos tus amigos por teléfono y luegoᵇ _____⁷ tus juguetesᶜ a sus casas. Y a veces _____⁸ desobediente.

Si no _____⁹ buena nota en el examen de matemáticas pasado mañana, yo no teᵈ compro el perro que _____.¹⁰ Si _____¹¹con tu mamá, dileᵉ que yo decido el caso.

ª¿Qué... *What are we going to do with you?* ᵇ*then* ᶜ*toys* ᵈ*for you* ᵉ*tell her*

Actividad C. Más preguntas para Raquel

Here are the questions Jaime asked Raquel in **Actividad A**. Use them as the basis for asking her the same questions, but address her with **usted** forms. You will hear the correct question on the tape. Use the pronoun **usted** in the first questions.

MODELO: (*you see*) ¿Dónde vives? ¿en México? →
(*you say*) ¿Dónde vive usted? ¿en México?

1. ¿Dónde vives? ¿en México?
2. ¿Viajas con frecuencia?
3. ¿A quién buscas en Sevilla?
4. ¿Cuándo tomas el tren? ¿mañana?
5. ¿Visitas a tus padres con frecuencia? (¡OJO! a sus padres)
6. ¿A quién debes llamar ahora?
7. ¿Qué escribes? ¿una carta?

---

*Jaime should not really address her as **tú**, but, as you know, Jaime's behavior often presents problems.

10. *MIGUEL Y JAIME SON BUENOS CHICOS*: USING ADJECTIVES (PART 1)

From the first episode of *Destinos*, you have been hearing examples of the adjective agreement described in the **Un poco de gramática** section of your Textbook. Although it is a relatively simple concept to grasp, adjective agreement takes time and practice to bring under control when speaking Spanish. Therefore, be patient with yourself as you move through the *Destinos* materials.

This is the first of several sections of the Workbook that deal with adjectives and how to use them. Compare the use of adjectives in the following paragraphs. The one on the left is a description of Osito. The other is a description of an imaginary female cat.

> El perro de Jaime se llama Osito porque es pequeño y negro. Osito es un perro inteligente y cariñoso.

> La gata de un amigo de Jaime se llama Osita porque es pequeña y negra. Osita es una gata inteligente y cariñosa.

As you probably noticed, adjectives normally follow the noun they modify in Spanish. Note the following additional characteristics of Spanish adjectives, which are similar to those of Spanish nouns.

Singular adjectives

- Adjectives that end in -o have a feminine form: **pequeño/pequeña, cariñoso/cariñosa.**
- Adjectives that end in -e or in most consonants have only one singular form: **inteligente, fiel.**

Plural adjectives

- Adjectives of either gender that end in a vowel add -s to form the plural: **pequeño → pequeños, cariñosa → cariñosas.**
- Most adjectives that end in a consonant add -es to form the plural: **fiel → fieles.**

 ### Actividad. Miguel y Jaime: ¡Dos hermanos diferentes!

Listen as the speaker on the cassette tape reads the following incomplete paragraph with all of the adjectives in place, in their proper form. Then complete the paragraph yourself, using the adjectives from the right-hand column.

Miguel es un chico muy _serio_¹ y es un estudiante muy _bueno_.² Siempreª saca _buenos_³ notas. Le gustan todas las asignaturas, pero su asignatura _favorita_⁴ es ciencias _naturales_.⁵ Algún díaᵇ desea ser un científico _famoso_.⁶ Cree que los científicos hacenᶜ contribuciones _importantes_⁷ a la sociedad.

En cambio,ᵈ Jaime es un chico realmente _desobediente_.⁸ No le gusta estudiar y siempre saca notas _mediocres_.⁹ Su materia _favorita_¹⁰ es educación _física_.¹¹ Le gustan mucho los animales _domésticos_,¹² especialmente los perros. Cree que los perros son _fieles_¹³ y _cariñosos_.¹⁴

serio
bueno, bueno
favorito, natural
famoso
importante

desobediente
mediocre, favorito
físico, doméstico
fiel
cariñoso

ªAlways ᵇAlgún... *Some day* ᶜ*make* ᵈEn... *On the other hand*

PRONUNCIACIÓN: DIPHTHONGS AND LINKING

You already know that Spanish vowels are pronounced with a short, "crisp" sound. Two vowels occuring next to each other are sometimes pronounced as a single sound, forming what is called a diphthong. Spanish diphthongs are formed by combinations of the vowels **a, e,** and **o** with the vowels **i** or **u,** in any order, or by the vowels **i** or **u** in any order.

Actividad A.
Repeat the following words that contain common diphthong patterns.

1. (ia) materia estudiar patriarca
2. (ie) también siete tiene
3. (io) episodio idioma matrimonio
4. (ua) Eduardo lengua cuatro
5. (ue) abuelo nueve bueno
6. (ei) seis veinte veintiuno

Actividad B.
Diphthongs can also occur between words, causing the words to be "linked," pronounced as one long word. Listen to the following phrases and sentences; then repeat them, imitating the speaker on the tape. The second time you hear them, write the missing words.

1. Miguel y _Elena_
2. Raquel _y_ _el_ taxista
3. _Pati_ es la _esposa_ de Juan.
4. No _esta_ _ahora_ en Madrid.
5. _Vive_ ahora _en_ Los Ángeles.

Actividad C.
Another type of linking occurs when two identical vowels appear next to each other. Repeat the following phrases and sentences, noting in particular how the indicated vowel sounds are reduced to one.

1. la clase de español
2. el hermano de Ernesto
3. ¿Dónde está Alicia?
4. una lengua antigua

¡AUMENTA TU VOCABULARIO!

Here are some additional cognate suffixes that will enable you to recognize cognate groups.

SPANISH SUFFIX		ENGLISH EQUIVALENT	
-ismo	comunismo	-ism	communism
	racismo		racism
-ista	artista	-ist	artist
	optimista		optimist
-or	director	-er, -or	director
	constructor		builder, manufacturer

IGNACIO M. ROZAS

Constructor de Guitarras

CALLE MAYOR, 66   MADRID 28013   Tfno. (91) 542 69 21

Note that nouns that end in **-ista** can refer to males or to females; the article indicates gender: **el artista, la artista.** Adjectives that end in **-ista** do not vary when they modify masculine nouns. The plural adds **-s:**

Raquel es optimista al principio; cree que va a encontrar a (*is going to find*) Rosario. ¿Y Pedro? ¿Es optimista? ¿Son pesimistas Ramón y Carlos?

Words that end in **-or** are masculine. Their feminine form ends in **-ora: el profesor, la profesora.**

Actividad A.

Listen to the following groups of cognates; then select the word that does not belong in the group.

1. comunismo, egoísmo, fascismo
2. artista, muralista, dentista
3. instructor, programador, profesor
4. organista, realista, violinista
5. actor, director, pintor

Actividad B.

You will hear a series of descriptions of people, including some characters from *Destinos* and some people from the real world. Listen carefully and indicate who is being described, selecting names from the list below. Remember that the word **fue** means *he was* or *she was.* That word will give you an important hint. Listen, in addition, for cognates that end in the patterns you have just learned.

Mercedes Castillo   Pablo Picasso
Carlos Castillo   Carlos Marx

1. ...   2. ...   3. ...   4. ...

Have you completed the following sections of the lesson? Check them off here.

_____ **Más allá del episodio**   _____ **Pronunciación**
_____ **Gramática**   _____ **¡Aumenta tu vocabulario!**

Now scan the words in the **Vocabulario** list to be sure that you understand the meaning of most of them.

• •

VOCABULARIO

Los verbos
sacar   to get, receive (*grades*)

Las cosas
la nota   grade (*academic*)

Las palabras adicionales
a veces   at times
con frecuencia   frequently
siempre   always
tú   you (*informal*)
usted (Ud.)   you (*formal*)

Now that you have completed the Textbook and Workbook for **Lección 4,** take the Self-Test for that lesson. (It is on page 250.) Remember to use the tape when you see the cassette symbol and to check your answers.

_____ **Self-Test**

Now that you have worked through the Textbook and the Workbook and taken the Self-Test, here are some of the things you have accomplished in Spanish.

- You can introduce people to each other in Spanish.
- You know the names of many academic subjects and of some domestic animals.
- You can use a variety of verb forms to talk directly to others and to tell what you are doing.
- You know more about how Spanish vowels are pronounced and how words are joined when they are pronounced.
- You can recognize more common cognates.
- You have continued to work on listening skills.

You are now ready to continue on with **Lección 5** in the Textbook.

LECCIÓN

5
LA DESPEDIDA

OBJETIVOS

Whereas the materials in the Textbook all had to do with the video segment, the materials in the Workbook will help you expand your knowledge of the Spanish language in general, as well as give you opportunities for self-expression in Spanish. In this lesson you will learn

- more about using Spanish verbs to talk about what you and others are doing
- more about addressing others in Spanish and talking about people
- several uses of the Spanish verb **Ir** (*to go*): how to talk about where you are going and about future actions
- about the written and spoken accent in Spanish words
- more about cognates.

Remember to listen to the tape for **Lección 5** when you see the cassette symbol and to check your answers in Appendix 1.

MÁS ALLÁ DEL EPISODIO

Actividad A.   Don Fernando Castillo Saavedra

You have already met don Fernando and know some of the details of his secret. But you really don't know much about him as a person yet. Here is a series of statements about him. Choose from the following five responses to express your reaction.

a. Sé que es cierto.
b. Creo que es cierto.
c. No sé.
d. Creo que es falso.
e. Sé que es falso.

1. _____ Don Fernando vive en la Ciudad de México.
2. _____ Es español.
3. _____ Es muy religioso.
4. _____ Tiene poca influencia sobre su familia.
5. _____ Habla mucho de su pasado (*past*).

6. ____ Cuando era joven (*he was young*), don Fernando era duro (*hard*) y ambicioso.
7. ____ Carmen, su segunda esposa, nunca supo (*found out*) nada de Rosario.
8. ____ Don Fernando y Rosario tienen un hijo.

The answers you have given are based solely on the very small amount of information you have at this point about don Fernando. The following reading passage offers more information. Read it and see if you wish to change any answers.

The first and last paragraphs are written largely in the past tense. You should be able to recognize the verbs, however, and to guess their meaning in the past.

Don Fernando recuerda[1] a Rosario, su primera esposa.

Para su familia, don Fernando es una persona buena y generosa. Pero cuando era joven, era un hombre muy duro y ambicioso. Cuando llegó a México, después de[2] la Guerra Civil española, no tenía nada. En pocos años se convirtió en un gran industrial, pero... hay muchas personas que no tienen precisamente buenos recuerdos[3] de él.

Don Fernando adora a su familia. También le gusta mucho su papel[4] de patriarca de la familia. Tiene gran influencia sobre sus hijos.

Es curioso, pero don Fernando nunca habla de su pasado. Nace[5] en Bilbao, una ciudad en el norte de España. Se casa[6] muy joven con Rosario. Después de la boda, los dos viven en Guernica. Cuando comienza la Guerra Civil, Fernando es soldado del ejército[7] republicano. Después del bombardeo de Guernica, busca desesperadamente a Rosario, pero no la encuentra. Cree que Rosario está muerta. Por eso se va a Madrid y al final de la Guerra toma un barco con destino a México.

Don Fernando nunca le habló de Rosario a Carmen, su segunda esposa, ni[8] al resto de su familia. Pero Carmen siempre creyó que él tenía un gran secreto—¿un gran amor?—en España. Los hijos no sospechaban nada. Cuando don Fernando recibió una carta de España, decidió buscar a Rosario. Así[9] comenzó la búsqueda[10] de Raquel.

[1] *remembers* [2] *después... after* [3] *memories* [4] *role* [5] *He is born* [6] *Se... He marries* [7] *army* [8] *nor* [9] *Thus, In that way* [10] *search, quest*

 Actividad B.

Now return to statements 1–8 and make any changes in your answers that you feel are necessary. Which statements do you still have to guess at or answer **No sé**? Listen to the cassette tape, on which the speaker will give you some answers and then provide some more information.

GRAMÁTICA

11. ¡BUSCAMOS A JAIME POR TODAS PARTES!: FIRST-PERSON PLURAL FORMS OF REGULAR VERBS (PRESENT TENSE)

RAQUEL: **Vamos** al mercadillo de los animales, **compramos** un perro, el perro se pierde, **buscamos** al perro—¡y a Jaime!—por todas partes, **encontramos** al niño, **visitamos** el Alcázar pero no **entramos, cenamos** en un restaurante elegante... ¡Qué día hemos pasado!

Forms

In **Lección 4** you learned to talk about your own actions by adding **-o** to the stem of regular verbs. To talk about yourself and another person (or others), add **-amos, -emos,** or **-imos** to the verb stem. These forms, called "first-person" plural, correspond to English *we.*

Infinitive	hablar	creer	vivir
Verb Stem	habl-	cre-	viv-
nosotros/nosotras	hablamos	creemos	vivimos

Uses

The subject pronoun **nosotros/nosotras** is not generally used with these verb forms, since the **-mos** ending makes it clear who the subject is.

Actividad A. ¿Quién habla?

You will hear a series of statements that could be made by characters from *Destinos.* Indicate who is the most likely speaker, choosing from the characters shown here.

1. _____   2. _____   3. _____   a. Carlitos   b. Jaime   c. Ramón

Actividad B. Miguel habla de su clase de geografía

In the following paragraph, Miguel Ruiz talks about his geography class. Complete the paragraph with the appropriate verb forms. It may be possible to use some forms more than once, and there are extra verbs.

usamos   deseamos   comprendemos   estudiamos   escribimos
somos   sacamos   buscamos   llevamos   investigamos

Este año en mi clase de geografía _____¹ geografía mundial:ᵃ las naciones de Europa y de los otros continentes también. _____² muchos mapas y globos, en donde _____³ las regiones y los nombres de los ríos y ciudades más importantes. También _____⁴ la economía de las naciones del mundo. _____⁵ saberᵇ cuáles son sus productos principales. Mis amigos y yo _____⁶ muchos trabajosᶜ y en esta clase generalmente _____⁷ buenas notas. Claro,ᵈ también _____⁸ mucho más acerca del mundo.ᵉ ¡_____⁹ estudiantes excelentes!

ᵃworld ᵇto know ᶜschool papers, reports ᵈOf course ᵉacerca... about the

Actividad C.   ¿Qué haces (*What do you do*) y con quién?

Here is a list of activities that college students often participate in. Do you do any of them? with whom? on what day of the week? Make as many sentences as you can, being as specific as you can. (Worksheet)

MODELO: El lunes mis amigos y yo cenamos en McDonald's.
El viernes mi amiga Susie y yo estudiamos historia.

Actividades: estudiar _____, ir a la iglesia (sinagoga, mezquita), caminar (en el parque), correr (en la calle _____), tomar algo (en la cafetería), cenar, trabajar, visitar (a _____), hablar (con_____), llamar (a _____), escribir ejercicios

12.   ¿QUÉ CREEN UDS.?: FORMS OF ADDRESS; SECOND-PERSON PLURAL FORMS OF REGULAR VERBS (PRESENT TENSE)

Forms of Address

In previous lessons you learned that two Spanish subject pronouns express English *you* (singular): **tú** and **usted**. Spanish also has plural *you* forms, similar in concept to the "you all" used by some English speakers to directly address more than one person. The plural *you* forms used by Spanish speakers are different depending on which part of the Spanish-speaking world they are from.

Raquel and the members of the Castillo family, like Spanish speakers in most of the world, use **ustedes** (Uds.) to speak to more than one person. Thus, when Raquel wants to know what all of her viewers think about something, she asks them, "¿**Qué creen ustedes**?" Note that no differentiation is made between deferential versus informal usage, as happens with the singular pronouns.

tú → Uds.   Ud. → Uds.

Spanish speakers from Spain, however, do differentiate between formal and informal usage for *you* plural. Here are the forms used by members of the Ruiz family.

tú → vosotros/vosotras   Ud. → Uds.

Which plural pronoun should you use to address others in Spanish? That decision is entirely up to you and your instructor. Raquel will use **ustedes**, because that is culturally and linguistically appropriate for her. The Textbook and Workbook for *Destinos* will also adopt the **ustedes** form of address, when necessary.

Second-Person Plural Forms of Regular Verbs

Forms
As you know, "second person" is the term used to refer to persons to whom you are speaking directly, equivalent to English *you all*. Because there are two ways in Spain to express *you* (plural), there are also two verb forms that correspond to those pronouns. Only one form is used in the rest of the Spanish-speaking world.

For **vosotros/vosotras**, add -áis, -éis, or -ís to the verb stem. The **ustedes** forms add -an or -en, as do the third-person plural forms you have already learned.

Infinitive	hablar	creer	vivir
Verb Stem	habl-	cre-	viv-
vosotros/vosotras	habláis	creéis	vivís
ustedes	hablan	creen	viven

Uses

The subject pronoun **vosotros/vosotras** is rarely used, because the endings make meaning clear. The pronoun **ustedes** is more frequently used to clarify meaning, because its forms are the same as those for **ellos** and **ellas**. Compare the following questions addressed to the Ruiz boys by Elena and Raquel.

ELENA: ¿Dónde deseáis cenar hoy?
RAQUEL: ¿Dónde desean cenar hoy?

ELENA: ¿Creéis que Rosario está en Madrid?
RAQUEL: ¿Creen que Rosario está en Madrid?

Actividad A.   ¿Quién habla?

Listen to the following statements and questions, which are addressed to the Ruiz children. Then indicate who is speaking in each case, Elena (**E**) or Raquel (**R**). Both the content of the questions and the verb forms used will help you in some cases.

E R 1. ¿Desean tener un gato también?
E R 2. ¿Deseáis cenar en un restaurante hoy?
E R 3. ¿Viajan a Madrid con frecuencia?
E R 4. ¡Sois irresponsables!
E R 5. ¿Creéis que Rosario está en Madrid?
E R 6. Son buenos estudiantes, ¿no?

Actividad B.   Roberto García, el taxista, habla con Miguel y Jaime

In the following paragraph Roberto García asks the Ruiz children a series of questions. Complete the paragraph with the appropriate verb forms. It may be possible to use some forms more than once, and there are extra verbs.

comprendéis   vivís   debéis   creéis

¡**C**hicos, necesito hablar con vosotros! ¿Dónde _____,¹ en la Calle Pureza?...
¿_____² que la señora Suárez está en casa hoy?... ¿Cómo?ª ¿Ya no vive aquíᵇ? Pues,ᶜ
_____³ decirle a vuestra madreᵈ que esta señorita desea hablar con ella.
¿_____?⁴... Gracias.

ªWhat do you mean?   ᵇhere   ᶜWell   ᵈdecirle... tell your mother

¡Un desafío! Can you give the answers Miguel would give, speaking for himself and for his brother?

Actividad C.   ¿Qué deseas saber?

You now know a good deal about Elena Ramírez and Miguel Ruiz, but you probably would like to know more about their lives and their opinions. Using the cues provided, form questions to find out more information from them. Use the **vosotros** or **ustedes** form, as appropriate. You will hear both questions on the cassette tape. After you have worked through all of the questions, match the questions with the appropriate answers and identify who has given the answer.

Preguntas

MODELO: (*you see*) hablar francés
(*you say*) ¿Habláis francés?
or ¿Hablan francés?

1. hablar inglés
2. cenar con frecuencia en restaurantes
3. viajar mucho
4. comprar muchos cupones de la lotería
5. escribir muchas cartas
6. visitar a Teresa Suárez con frecuencia
7. desear tener (*to have*) más hijos
8. creer que Rosario está en Madrid

Respuestas

MODELO: No, no hablamos francés.

a. _____ No sabemos nada de esta situación.
b. _____ No, pero llamamos a Madrid con frecuencia.
c. _____ Miguel sí compra cupones de la lotería, pero yo no.
d. _____ Sí, cenamos en restaurantes con frecuencia.
e. _____ Deseamos viajar mucho, pero desgraciadamente no lo hacemos (*we don't do it*).
f. _____ Elena sí habla un poco de inglés, pero yo no.
g. _____ Sí, escribimos muchas, especialmente a la abuela.
h. _____ ¡No! Ya tenemos a Jaime y Miguel...

13. *BUSCO A LA SRA. SUÁREZ*: USING *a* WITH PEOPLE

Use the word **a** whenever a specific person or persons are the direct object of a verb.
(A direct object answers the question *what?* or *whom?* after the verb.)

Raquel visita España. Va a visitar **a** Teresa Suárez.

Raquel is visiting Spain. She is going to visit Teresa Suárez.

Teresa Suárez desea ver **a** Raquel en Madrid. No ve la necesidad de ir **a** Sevilla.

Teresa Suárez wants to see Raquel in Madrid. She doesn't see the need to go to Sevilla.

The word **a**, called the personal **a**, has no equivalent in English. It is also often used with pets: Jaime busca a Osito. *Note:* a + the article el = al.

Actividad. Los personajes de *Destinos*
Complete the following paragraphs with the personal **a** (or with **al**) whenever it is needed.

Jaime y Miguel llaman _____¹ su abuela con frecuencia. Los domingos visitan _____² una tía que vive en Sevilla. Generalmente Elena y Miguel acompañan _____³ sus hijos. Este domingo Jaime desea llevar _____⁴ Osito también. Elena cree que no es buena idea llevar _____⁵ el perro a la casa de la tía. Vamos a ver... .ᵃ

Al comienzo de *Destinos*, Raquel busca _____⁶ la calle Pureza. Realmente busca _____⁷ la Sra. Suárez, la persona que le escribió _____⁸ una carta a don Fernando. Miguel, el hijo de la Sra. Suárez, no sabe nada de la carta y no comprende_____⁹ la situación. Por esoᵇ llama _____¹⁰ su madre, que está en Barcelona. La Sra. Suárez desea ver _____¹¹ Raquel, pero en Madrid. Raquel necesita llamar _____¹² Pedro para decirleᶜ que va a Madrid. Pedro habla con don Fernando y probablemente llama _____¹³ los otros miembros de la familia Castillo.

ᵃVamos... *We'll see* . . .   ᵇPor... *That's why*   ᶜpara... *in order to tell him*

14. ¡VOY A HABLAR CON LA SRA. SUÁREZ! : THE VERB *ir*

ELENA: Chicos, Raquel **va** a Madrid mañana, en tren. Tu papá y yo **vamos a** llevarla a la estación. **Vais** con nosotros, ¿no?

Forms

The verb **ir** means *to go*. Whereas the verb follows a regular pattern, it is not the one you would expect.

SINGULAR		PLURAL	
voy	I go	vamos	we go
vas	you go	vais	you go
va	you go	van	you go
	he/she/it goes		they go

Note in particular the four different Spanish equivalents for *you go*. Can you match the verb forms with their corresponding pronouns?

tú _____   Ud. _____

vosotros _____   Uds. _____

Uses

Forms of **ir** are used

- to tell where someone is going

  Voy a Madrid en tren.   *I'm going to Madrid by train.*
  ¿Por qué no **vamos al*** Alcázar? *Why don't we go to the Alcázar?*

- to express future actions: **ir + a + infinitive.**

  Voy a buscar a la señora Suárez. *I'm going to look for Mrs. Suárez.*

Actividad A. Un repaso del Episodio 5

Listen to Raquel's story review as you follow along in the Workbook. Then complete the paragraph with the following forms of ir: voy, va, vamos, ir.

Bueno, ahora _____¹ a Madrid. La señora Suárez no vive en Sevilla y yo tengo que _____² a Madrid para hablar con ella personalmente. Bueno, estos últimos días en Sevilla han sido inolvidables, ¿no creen? ¿Recuerdan Uds. el episodio con el perro, Osito? Osito se escapa y uno de los hijos de Miguel y Elena lo _____³ a buscar y se pierde. Lo buscamos por todas partes. Por fin yo lo encuentro. A las once y media, Jaime y yo _____⁴ a la Catedral a buscar a sus padres, pero Jaime se pierde otra vez. Por fin encuentro a la familia de Jaime enfrente de la Catedral y _____⁵ a un lugar histórico. Y eso es todo. Mañana, si tengo suerte, _____⁶ a ver a la señora Suárez.

Actividad B. ¿Adónde van?

Indicate where the following people will go, based on what they want to do. Answer using yo forms. (Worksheet)

MODELO: (*you see*) CARLOS: Deseo hablar con papá.
    (*you answer*) Voy a La Gavia.

_____
*Remember: a + the article el = al.

1. Raquel: Deseo investigar este caso.
2. Elena: Necesito comprar pan (*bread*) y café.
3. Jaime: Deseo comprar un perro.
4. Carlos: Necesito escribir un reporte.
5. Miguel, padre: Elena y yo deseamos cenar a solas (*alone*), sin los niños.
6. Jaime: Miguel y yo deseamos ver al ciego.
7. Raquel: Necesito tomar el tren.

Lugares: la estación, Madrid, el mercadillo de los animales, la Plaza de las Tres Cruces, el mercado de Triana, un restaurante elegante, la oficina

Actividad C.   Voy a...

What do you think the following characters from *Destinos* are likely to do in the near future? Create as many sentences as you can, using **ir** + **a** + phrases from the right-hand column. (Worksheet)

MODELO: Raquel va a hablar con don Fernando.

1. Raquel	llamar al médico
2. Jaime y Miguel	hablar con don Fernando
3. Miguel y Elena	viajar a Madrid en tren
4. Mercedes	ir a la escuela el lunes
5. el ciego	correr con Osito
6. Miguel hijo	vender cupones de la lotería
	sacar buenas notas
	ver a la señora Suárez
	visitar a su tía el domingo
	cenar en un restaurante, con sus hijos

Now describe what you are likely to do if the following situations are true.

MODELO: (*you see*)   Deseas ir a una fiesta. →
          (*you answer*) Voy a llamar a un amigo.

7. Hay un examen mañana.	buscar un teléfono
8. Una persona vende cupones de la lotería.	ir a un restaurante
9. Necesitas llamar a un amigo.	comprar un cupón
10. Deseas tomar una Coca-Cola.	estudiar mucho
11. Deseas tener un animal en casa.	comprar un pez tropical
	¿____?

Actividad D.   ¿Y tú?

What do you know about your activities for next week? Create as many sentences as you can about your activities, and those of your friends and family members if you wish. Add the time if you know it. (Worksheet)

MODELOS: El jueves voy a ver «L.A. Law» a las diez.

           El lunes voy a llegar a la universidad a las ocho de la mañana.

           El sábado mis amigos y yo vamos a un partido de fútbol americano.

           El domingo mi padre no va a salir de casa.

Frases útiles: salir (*to leave*) de casa, ver una película (*movie*), ir a una fiesta, ir a un partido de fútbol americano, ir a la casa de _____

PRONUNCIACIÓN: STRESS AND WRITTEN ACCENT MARKS

 It is quite easy to learn to pronounce and spell Spanish words correctly. Three simple rules will help you determine whether a written accent is necessary and which syllable to stress when speaking in most cases. Pronounce the words in each section after the speaker on the tape.

Three Simple Rules

Rule 1: If a word ends in a vowel, -n, or -s, stress normally falls on the next-to-the-last syllable.

> hijo   fascinante   Sevilla   Fernando   cenan   examen   Mercedes   abuelos

Rule 2: If a word ends in any other consonant, stress normally falls on the last syllable.

> preguntar   actividad   director   universidad   Raquel   Miguel   español   cultural

Rule 3: Any exception to Rules 1 and 2 will have a written accent mark on the stressed vowel.

> sábado   inglés   matemáticas   religión   Suárez   Ramón   tradición   también

Actividad A.

Pronounce the following words, which follow Rules 1 and 2. You will hear the correct pronunciation after you say the words.

Rule 1

> Castillo   hermana   escribes   hablamos   arte   literatura   creen   vamos

Rule 2

> correr   cenar   hotel   español   contabilidad   doctor   profesor   Madrid

Actividad B.

The speaker on the tape will pronounce the following words. Each will be said twice. Listen carefully and write an accent mark on the appropriate vowel. Then repeat the word.

> esta   musica   miercoles   Rodriguez   tambien   conversacion   quimica   informatica

Words with Diphthongs

In a word containing a diphthong, a written accent on the vowel **i** or **u** will break the diphthong, causing it to be pronounced as two separate syllables. Note in particular the stress pattern on words that end in -**ía**. When **a**, **e**, and **o** are paired in any combination, they also result in two separate syllables. Pronounce the words after the speaker on the tape.

> psicología   sociología   Andalucía   desafío
> aeropuerto   reorganizar   caos   paella

¡AUMENTA TU VOCABULARIO!

Here are two more important suffix patterns that will help you identify the Spanish equivalents of many English words.

SPANISH SUFFIX	ENGLISH EQUIVALENT
-ante, -ente	-ent, -ant, -ing
interesante	interesting
inteligente	intelligent
dominante	dominant
-ura	-ure
literatura	literature
figura	figure

Actividad.

The following paragraph is based on information you worked with in the Textbook. Complete it using words from the list.

> fascinante cultura dominante pintura
> arquitectura escultura tolerante figura

Por muchos siglos[a] los árabes formaban la cultura _____[1] en la Península Ibérica. Todavía se puede[b] ver esta influencia árabe en la _____[2] de los monumentos históricos de ciudades como Sevilla y Córdoba. Los árabes no permitían la representación de la_____[3] humana en el arte. Por eso no estudiamos ejemplos de la _____[4] y la _____[5] de esa época. El arte árabe se representa primariamente por complicados diseños geométricos.

Otro aspecto _____[6] de la _____[7] árabe es que era bastante[c] _____[8] de diferentes religiones. Por eso convivían en las ciudades del sur de España cristianos, judíos y árabes, cada[d] una con su cultura única.

[a]Por... *For many centuries* [b]se... *one can* [c]*relatively* [d]*each*

Have you completed the following sections of the lesson? Check them off here.

_____ **Más allá del episodio**	_____ **Pronunciación**
_____ **Gramática**	_____ **¡Aumenta tu vocabulario!**

Now scan the words in the **Vocabulario** list to be sure that you understand the meaning of most of them.

• •

VOCABULARIO

Los verbos

ir	to go
voy, vas, va	
vamos, vais, van	
ver*	to see

Las palabras adicionales

nosotros/nosotras	we
ustedes (Uds.)	you (*formal*)
vosotros/vosotras	you (*informal*)
ir + a (+ *inf.*)	to be going to (*do something*)

---

*The first-person singular of ver is irregular: veo. You will learn to use ver and other irregular verbs in **Lección 6**.

Now that you have completed the Textbook and Workbook for **Lección 5,** take the Self-Test for that lesson. (It is on page 252.) Remember to use the tape when you see the cassette symbol and to check your answers.

_____ **Self-Test**

Now that you have worked through the Textbook and the Workbook and taken the Self-Test, here are some of the things you have accomplished in Spanish.

- You can use some parting words in Spanish.
- You know the days of the week and you can tell time in Spanish.
- You can use a variety of verb forms to talk about what people are doing, where people are going, and what they will do.
- You know something about written accent marks.
- You can recognize more common cognates.
- You have continued to work on listening skills.

You are now ready to continue on with **Lección 6** in the Textbook.

6

¿MAESTRA?

OBJETIVOS

Whereas the materials in the Textbook all had to do with the video segment, the materials in the Workbook will help you expand your knowledge of the Spanish language in general, as well as give you opportunities for self-expression in Spanish. In this lesson you will review

- what you have learned about the present tense of regular Spanish verbs and a few irregular verbs
- numbers and telling time
- vocabulary groups—names for members of the family, academic subjects, and so on.

Remember to listen to the tape for **Lección 6** when you see the cassette symbol, and to check your answers in Appendix 1.

GRAMÁTICA

15. *RESUMEN*: PRESENT-TENSE FORMS OF REGULAR VERBS

Here are the endings for the regular verbs with which you have worked so far. Can you complete the table?

Infinitive	buscar	creer	vivir
Verb Stem	busc-	cre-	viv-
yo	-o	-o	___
tú	___	-es	-es
él, ella, Ud.	-a	___	-e
nosotros/nosotras	___	-emos	
vosotros/vosotras	-áis	-éis	-ís
ellos, ellas, Uds.	-an	___	-en

¡OJO! Spanish has a full range of verb forms for talking about different points in time: the present, the past, the future, what one might do, and so on. You have already heard a variety of Spanish verb tenses in the episodes of *Destinos*. Different past and future forms will continue to be used by the characters in the series. But you are not expected to learn these forms until you study them in the Textbook and Workbook.

Actividad A.   ¿Qué pronombre?

Match the subject pronouns on the right with the sentences on the left. ¡OJO! More than one pronoun may be appropriate for some sentences.

1. ____ Llegamos al restaurante a las diez.   a. yo
2. ____ Viajo a Europa para investigar el caso.   b. tú
3. ____ Hablas con tu abuela con frecuencia.   c. él, ella
4. ____ Comprenden el episodio.   d. nosotros/nosotras
5. ____ Vives en La Gavia.   e. vosotros/vosotras
6. ____ Conversan con su tío.   f. ellos, ellas
7. ____ Descubrimos el secreto de don Fernando.   g. Ud.
8. ____ Estudiáis ciencias naturales.   h. Uds.
9. ____ Escribe muchas cartas... y una carta en particular.
10. ____ Debéis estudiar más.

Actividad B.   ¿Qué pronombre?

Continue to indicate the subject pronouns for the following groups of sentences. This time, you will only hear the sentences, and some irregular verbs will be used.

Who is being spoken *to* in these sentences?

1. tú   Ud.   Uds. (vosotros)   2. tú   Ud. (Uds.) vosotros

Who *is speaking* in these sentences?

3. (yo) nosotros   4. yo (nosotros)

Who is being spoken *about* in these sentences?

5. (él) ellos   6. ella (ellas)

16.   ¿QUIÉN... ?: INTERROGATIVE WORDS

Throughout the first episodes of *Destinos*, you have heard and read interrogative words, words used to ask questions. You will learn more about asking questions in **Lección 8**. For now, here is a list of the interrogatives with which you have worked so far. Be sure that you understand their meaning.

¿quién?	*who?*	¿Quién es Raquel?
¿dónde?	*where?*	¿Dónde está Sevilla?
¿cuál?	*what? which one?*	¿Cuál es el hijo de don Fernando?
¿cómo?	*how?*	¿Cómo estás?
¿qué?	*what?*	¿Qué busca Raquel?

Note the use of the inverted question mark before each of the questions and the use of a written accent mark on the interrogative words.

Actividad. Preguntas sobre *Destinos*

Listen to the following brief questions about *Destinos* and answer them. If you like, use the phrases below in your answers. You will hear a possible answer on the tape, and you may want to repeat it.

muy mal abogada una carta en España

1. ... 2. ... 3. ... 4. ...

• •

UN POCO DE TODO

Actividad A. Oraciones originales

Create as many original sentences as you can in each group. Don't be limited to the verbs and verb phrases given here. (Worksheet)

Grupo 1

1. Raquel	escribir	por las calles
2. Jaime	viajar	ciencias naturales
3. Teresa Suárez	estudiar	a Madrid en tren
4. a Miguel le gusta	correr	una carta a don Fernando

Grupo 2

5. Raquel	necesitar	hablar con Teresa
6. Miguel	ir a	la escuela de San Francisco de Paula
7. Miguel y Jaime	deber	ser científico
8. don Fernando	desear	saber (*to know*) dónde vive Rosario

Actividad B. ¿Y tú?

Create as many sentences as you can about yourself. Don't be limited to the verbs and verb phrases given here. (Worksheet)

1. Yo... 2. Voy a... 3. Debo... 4. Deseo...

comprender los episodios
vivir en / con...
estudiar...
viajar a...

escribir muchos trabajos / muchas cartas
hablar por teléfono con...
sacar buenas / malas notas
comprar muchos cupones de la lotería

 Actividad C. Números... y más números

Can you provide the numbers contained in each of the following excerpts from *Destinos*?

1. Buenos días. Tengo que ir a la calle Pureza, número _veinte uno_ .

2. Si desea visitar algunos lugares interesantes e históricos, mire, aquí el número _trece_ es el mercado. El número _catorce_ es la Capilla de la Esperanza de Triana. Y la Iglesia de Santa Ana está aquí, en el número _quince_ .

3. Tengo que llamar a México. —Muy bien. ¿Adónde? —A la Ciudad de México. El número es _221_ - _3_ - ___ - _12_ .

4. Éste es el compartimiento _quince_ , en el vagón número _____ .

¡Un desafío! Can you go back and identify the person who is speaking in each case? Can you tell to whom they are speaking?

Actividad D. El calendario de Raquel

This page from Raquel's notebook outlines the events of the last few days.

lunes 14	lunes 21	*tren*
martes 15	martes 22	
miércoles 16	miércoles 23	
jueves 17	*Pedro*	jueves 24
viernes 18	*Sevilla*	viernes 25
sábado 19	*la familia Ruiz*	sábado 26
domingo 20	*mercadillo*	domingo 27

Paso 1

Scan Raquel's notes; then look at the verb phrases listed here and give their yo form. (Worksheet)

1. hablar con Pedro, aceptar el caso
2. ir a Sevilla, llegar al hotel
3. ir al Barrio de Triana, hablar con la familia, descubrir que Teresa Suárez ya no vive en Sevilla
4. acompañar a la familia al mercadillo, correr por las calles, buscar a Jaime, visitar el Alcázar, cenar con la familia
5. ir a la estación, tomar el tren

Paso 2

Now put the verb phrases together with Raquel's calendar and create a summary of what Raquel has done so far, from her perspective. Add any details that you can. (Worksheet)

Actividad E. Día de un estudiante típico

In previous lessons you have heard about a typical day for Raquel. Listen as a typical student talks about a day in his life. As you listen, complete the following chart with the missing details.

6.30 : a la universidad   *1:00* : en la cafetería

8:00 : *química*   3:30 : *casa*

9:30 : inglés   6:00 : *cena*

10:45 informática

Actividad F. ¿Y tú?

Now give a few details about a typical day in your life. Answer the brief questions you will hear based on the following cues.

1. Voy a la universidad a la(s)... *8*
2. A la(s)... tengo clase de.... A la(s)... voy a la clase de....
3. A la(s)... voy a casa.
4. Ceno (con...) a la(s)...

Have you completed the following sections of the lesson? Check them off here.

_____ **Gramática**   _____ **Un poco de todo**

There is no Self-Test for this lesson of the Textbook and Workbook. In preparation for a unit test or just as a general review, it would be a good idea to scan back over the Self-Tests in the previous four lessons. Then you will be ready to continue on with Lección 7 in the Textbook.

7

LA CARTERA

MÁS ALLÁ DEL EPISODIO

Actividad A.   Alfredo Sánchez

You have seen Raquel meet and talk with Alfredo Sánchez, a young TV reporter. But you really don't know much about him as a person yet. Here is a series of statements about him. Choose from the following five responses to express your reaction.

a. Sé que es cierto.
b. Creo que es cierto.
c. No sé.

d. Creo que es falso.
e. Sé que es falso.

1. _____ Alfredo es muy curioso.
2. _____ Desea hacer un reportaje sobre Raquel.
3. _____ Cree que Madrid es la ciudad perfecta para un reportero.
4. _____ A Alfredo le gusta mucho Raquel.
5. _____ Alfredo busca un ascenso (*promotion*).
6. _____ Es casado (*married*).
7. _____ Desea cambiar de (*change*) profesión.
8. _____ Le gustan los deportes (*sports*).

The answers you have given are based solely on the very small amount of information you have at this point about Alfredo. The following reading passage offers more information. Read it and see whether you wish to change any answers.

Un reportero que tiene grandes ambiciones

Alfredo Sánchez trabaja para la televisión española. Tiene todas las cualidades necesarias para ser un buen reportero: es una persona dinámica y ambiciosa... ¡y además[1] es muy curioso! Está siempre en busca de[2] un nuevo caso.

      Alfredo es madrileño[3] y, para él, Madrid es la ciudad ideal para un reportero. Allí viven muchas personas importantes en la vida[4] política y artística de España. Siempre es posible encontrar algún escándalo o alguna intriga para hacer un buen reportaje.

      A Alfredo le gusta mucho el periodismo,[5] pero en estos momentos se siente un poco frustrado en su vida profesional. Según[6] él, no avanza lo suficientemente de prisa[7] en su carrera. Su jefe[8] le ha prometido[9] un ascenso si puede conseguir una entrevista exclusiva con la maestra que ganó un premio en la lotería. Por otra parte, la revista[10] *¡Hola!* también desea una entrevista exclusiva....

      Alfredo tiene mucho interés en Raquel, en su viaje, en su cliente y en la persona que ella busca. Cuando ve el nombre Fernando Castillo en el sobre[11] que tiene Raquel, llama inmediatamente a un contacto que tiene. Desea saber más acerca de este señor Castillo. Ahora tiene un poco de información: Don Fernando Castillo Saavedra, un poderoso industrial mexicano que busca a una persona en España... ¿Será[12] una persona de su pasado? ¿una historia de amor? ¿una intriga internacional? Alfredo está seguro de que aquí hay algo interesante.... Pero ¿a quién le dará[13] su exclusiva, a la televisión o a la revista *¡Hola!* ?

[1] *besides* [2] *en... in search of* [3] *de* Madrid [4] *life* [5] *journalism* [6] *According to* [7] *no... he's not getting ahead quickly enough* [8] *boss* [9] *le... has promised him* [10] *magazine* [11] *envelope* [12] *Could it be* [13] *will he give*

Actividad B.

Now return to statements 1–8 and make any changes in your answers that you feel are necessary. Which statements do you still have to guess at or answer **No sé**? Listen to the cassette tape, on which the speaker will give you some answers then provide some more information.

• •

GRAMÁTICA

17. *NECESITO SABER DÓNDE VIVE ROSARIO*: THE VERBS *saber* AND *conocer*

RAQUEL: Ando buscando a una señora... la Sra. Teresa Suárez. ¿La **conocen**?
MIGUEL: Sí. Es mi abuela.
RAQUEL: ¿Vive con Uds.?
MIGUEL: Ya no.
RAQUEL: ¿Y dónde vive ahora?
MIGUEL: Ahora vive en Madrid.
RAQUEL: Y... ¿**saben** Uds. su dirección en Madrid?
MIGUEL: No. Pero la **sabe** mi madre.

Forms

Spanish has two verbs, **saber** and **conocer**, that both express *to know*, depending on the context. Here are the full conjugations of these verbs. Notice that the **yo** form of each is irregular; that is, it does not follow the usual pattern.

saber		conocer	
sé	sabemos	conozco	conocemos
sabes	sabéis	conoces	conocéis
sabe	saben	conoce	conocen

Uses

Saber means *to know facts or pieces of information*. When followed by an infinitive, **saber** means *to know how to do something*.

Sé por qué Raquel viaja a Madrid.   *I know why Raquel is traveling to Madrid.*

Alfredo no **sabe** quién es el Sr. Díaz.   *Alfredo doesn't know who Mr. Díaz is.*

Raquel **sabe** usar una computadora.   *Raquel knows how to use a computer.*

Conocer means *to know* or *to be acquainted (familiar) with a person, place, or thing*. It can also mean *to meet someone for the first time*. Note the personal **a** used before a specific person.

Teresa Suárez no **conoce** a Raquel   *Teresa Suárez doesn't know Raquel yet.*
todavía. La va a **conocer** pronto.   *She's going to meet her soon.*
Raquel ahora **conoce** Sevilla y Madrid.   *Raquel now knows (is acquainted with) Sevilla and Madrid.*

Actividad A. ¿Quién habla?

Listen to the following statements and indicate who might have said each of them. ¡OJO! More than one person may be appropriate for each statement.

1. Conozco muy bien la ciudad de Los Ángeles.
2. No conozco a don Fernando personalmente.
3. Voy a conocer a la abogada de California esta noche (*tonight*).
4. Conocemos muy bien Sevilla.
5. No conozco a la Sra. Suárez pero sé quién es.

Teresa Suárez
Federico Ruiz
Miguel y Jaime
Raquel Rodríguez

Actividad B.   Las preocupaciones de Teresa Suárez

In the following paragraph Teresa Suárez thinks about the details of her upcoming conversation with Raquel. Indicate the appropriate verb forms.

No (sé/conozco¹) mucho acerca de Raquel Rodríguez... sólo que desea (saber/conocer²) más de Rosario del Valle, mi buena amiga. Mi hijo y su eposa (saben/conocen³) a esta abogada y dicen que es simpática. No (sé/conozco⁴)... pero laª voy a (saber/conocer⁵) pronto.

Tengo muchos recuerdosᵇ de Rosario. ¿Qué (sabe/conoce⁶) el Sr. Castillo de Rosario? No (sé/conozco⁷) a este primer esposo de Rosario. Sólo (sé/conozco⁸) que vive en México ahora, y que tiene otra familia, otra vida... ¿Cuáles son sus motivos? ¿Desea (conocer/saber⁹) al hijo que tuvo con Rosario? ¿O desea ocultarᶜ la historia de su primer matrimonio? Todo es posible....

ª*her* (la voy a... = *I'm going to meet her*) ᵇ*memories* ᶜ*to hide*

Now check your answers by listening to the cassette tape.

Actividad C. ¿Y tú?

Describe your experience with Spanish so far, choosing the appropriate verb in each sentence. Make sentences negative if you must do so to tell the truth.

1. Sé/Conozco a mi profesor(a) de español.
2. Ya sé/conozco mucho español.
3. Sé/Conozco que España está en la Península Ibérica.
4. Sé/Conozco el nombre de la capital de España.
5. Sé/Conozco un poco de la historia y geografía españolas.
6. Sé/Conozco la región de Andalucía.

Actividad D.   Personas importantes

Whom do you know well? Who would you like to meet? Complete each of the following sentences. (Worksheet)

> MODELO: Conozco muy bien a mi amigo Étienne. Es una persona interesante porque es de Francia y sabe hablar muchas lenguas.
>
> Conozco muy bien a.... Es una persona interesante porque....
>   Me gustaría conocer a... porque....

18.   *¿ALFREDO? NO LO VEO*: PRESENT-TENSE FORMS OF IRREGULAR VERBS (PART 1)

Forms
The following verbs have irregular yo forms. Otherwise they are conjugated just like the regular verbs you have already learned. Can you complete their conjugations?

hacer	*to make; to do*	dar	*to give*	traer	*to bring*
hago	_____	doy	damos	traigo	traemos
haces	hacéis	das	_____	traes	traéis
hace	hacen	da	dan	trae	_____
salir	*to leave*	poner	*to put; to place*	ver	*to see*
salgo	salimos	pongo	ponemos	veo	_____
sales	salís	_____	ponéis	ves	veis
_____	salen	pone	ponen	ve	ven

Uses
Salir means *to leave a place*. When the place is specified, it is preceded by **de: El reportero sale del hotel.**

Remember to use the personal **a** with **ver**, when appropriate: **No veo a Alfredo en ninguna parte** (*anywhere*).

Use **traer** to indicate that someone is bringing something to where you are. **Llevar** is used when someone is taking something to somewhere else.

Hacer un viaje means *to take a trip*. **Hacer las maletas** means *to pack one's suitcases*. **Antes de** (*before*) **hacer un viaje, hago las maletas.**

Actividad.   ¿Quién lo dice?
Read the following statements, which could be made by the characters in **Episodio 7.** Then indicate who is speaking in each case. ¡OJO! Some of the statements are appropriate for more than one character.

Teresa Suárez   el recepcionista   Alfredo Sánchez
el Sr. Díaz   Raquel Rodríguez   el botones

1. _____ Hago este viaje para buscar a la mujer que le escribió una carta a don Fernando.
2. _____ Veo a todos los clientes que entran en este hotel.
3. _____ ¡Dios mío! ¡No veo el taxi en donde dejé (*I left*) la cartera!
4. _____ Salgo del hotel para buscar la cartera perdida.
5. _____ Ayudo (*I help*) a los clientes con las maletas y ellos me dan una propina (*tip*).

6. _____ Pongo toda la ropa en la cama (*bed*). No sé si tengo suficiente ropa...

7. _____ No salgo de mi apartamento esta noche. Espero a la abogada aquí (*here*), en casa.

8. _____ Perdone Ud. Hay un error. Veo aquí que la reserva está a nombre de una señora.

Note: There are more activities with these verb forms in Section 19.

19. *ENTONCES, TENGO QUE IR A MADRID*: PRESENT-TENSE FORMS OF IRREGULAR VERBS (PART 2)

Forms

The following verbs have irregular **yo** forms, as well as changes in the stem of some forms. Note that the endings are the same as those you have already learned for regular verbs.

decir	*to say, tell*	**tener**	*to have*	**oír**	*to hear*	**venir**	*to come*
digo	decimos	**tengo**	tenemos	**oigo**	oímos	**vengo**	venimos
dices	decís	tienes	tenéis	oyes	oís	vienes	venís
dice	dicen	tiene	tienen	oye	oyen	viene	vienen

Pay particular attention to the pattern of change in the verb stem in the conjugations of each of these verbs. You will learn more about verbs of this style—called stem-changing verbs—in **Lección 8**.

Uses

Use forms of **tener** + **que** + infinitive to express obligation.

RAQUEL: Entonces, **tengo que ir** a Madrid.

RAQUEL: *Then I have to go to Madrid.*

Decir and **dar** are generally used with special pronouns—**me, le,...**—that indicate the person being addressed or the person to whom something is given.

TERESA: ¿Qué le voy a decir a la abogada?

TERESA: *What am I going to say to the lawyer?*

RAQUEL: ¿Qué me va a **decir** la señora Suárez? ¿Me va a **dar** algo para don Fernando?

RAQUEL: *What is Mrs. Suárez going to say to me? Is she going to give me something for don Fernando?*

You will learn more about these pronouns in upcoming lessons of the Textbook and Workbook.

Actividad A. ¿Quién lo dice?

Again, read the following statements, which could be made by the characters in **Episodio 7**. Then indicate who is speaking in each case. ¡OJO! Some of the statements are appropriate for more than one character.

Teresa Suárez	el recepcionista	Alfredo Sánchez
el Sr. Díaz	Raquel Rodríguez	Federico Ruiz

1. _____ Buenas tardes. Tengo una habitación reservada para esta noche.

2. _____ Les digo el número de su habitación a todos los clientes.

3. _____ Lo siento, pero no tengo mi cartera en este momento.

4. _____ Tengo la información que la señorita Rodríguez busca. Pero no sé si desea oír lo que (*what*) voy a decir.

5. _____ Creo que tengo que comprar más ropa para el resto de mi viaje.

6. _____ Vengo al hotel en busca de una abogada norteamericana que no conozco.

7. _____ No veo a Alfredo en ninguna parte.

8. _____ Bueno, voy a ver si Federico tiene ropa para mañana.

Actividad B.   Las aventuras de Raquel

Paso 1

Listen to Raquel's story review, spoken in the living room of the Suárez home. Pay particular attention to the sequence of events, and note the use of the phrase **no está** to mean *he or she is out, not there.*

Paso 2

Now complete the following summary of Raquel's story review with the appropriate verb forms. ¡OJO! Some forms may be used more than once, and there are extra forms.

vengo   tengo   digo   hago   veo   salgo
viene   tiene   dice   hacen   ven   salen

Cuando llego al hotel, no _____¹ mi cartera. Voy al taxi a buscarla, pero el taxi no está. El reportero y su asistente _____² a buscar el taxi. En mi habitación, _____³ una llamada a Pedro, pero no está. Alfredo me llama y _____⁴ que _____⁵ mi cartera; _____⁶ al hotel para dármela.

Bajoª a buscar a Alfredo y encuentro a Federico Ruiz. Acepto la invitación de su madre a cenar en su casa. Pero primero _____⁷ que encontrar a Alfredo. Desgraciadamente no lo _____⁸ en ninguna parte (*nowhere*). Por eso le dejo una nota y _____⁹ aquí, con Federico, a la casa de la señora Suárez.

ª*I go downstairs*

Paso 3

Now, using the following brief cues, retell Raquel's story.

MODELO: (*you see*)   Raquel: llegar al hotel
          (*you say*)   Raquel llega al hotel.
          (*you hear*)   Raquel llega al hotel.

1. Raquel: llegar al hotel
2. no tener la cartera
3. buscar la cartera en el taxi
4. hacer una llamada a Pedro
5. hablar con Alfredo
6. Alfredo: tener la cartera
7. Raquel: esperar a Alfredo
8. ver a Federico Ruiz
9. aceptar la invitación de su madre
10. buscar a Alfredo
11. no ver al reportero
12. salir con Federico

Actividad C.   ¿Y tú?

Create sentences that accurately describe you and your habits. (Worksheet)

MODELO: (no) decir siempre la verdad (*truth*) →
          No digo siempre la verdad.

1. (no) decir siempre la verdad
2. (no) hacer siempre las lecciones de español
3. (no) salir todos los viernes por la noche
4. (no) tener secretos
5. (no) ver telenovelas (*soaps*) con frecuencia
6. (no) ver con frecuencia la televisión

Actividad D.   ¿Y tus amigos?

Now create as many statements as you can about the habits of your friends. You can also describe family members if you like. (Worksheet)

¿Quién... ?

hace muchos viajes. ¿adónde?
ve con frecuencia las telenovelas

hace muchas llamadas de larga distancia
siempre tiene muchas tarjetas de crédito
sale con muchas personas diferentes
dice estupideces (*dumb things*)
da dinero ($$) para causas políticas
nunca tiene mucho dinero

• •

PRONUNCIACIÓN: *d*

 The Spanish **d** has two pronunciations. At the beginning of a phrase or sentence and after **n** or **l**, it is pronounced like English *d*, as in *dog*.

diez   dos   ¿dónde?   venden   el día   el doctor

In all other cases, it is pronounced like the English sound *th* in *another*.

adiós   usted   ¿adónde?   todo   buenos días   la doctora

Actividad.
Repeat the following sentences, imitating the speaker.

1. ¿Dónde está la ciudad de Madrid?
2. Don Julio es el doctor de don Fernando.
3. Dos más diez son doce.
4. Buenos días, Alfredo. ¿Adónde vas?
5. ¿Podría pagar con tarjeta de crédito?

Have you completed the following sections of the lesson? Check them off here.

_____ **Más allá del episodio**   _____ **Pronunciación**
_____ **Gramática**

Now scan the words in the **Vocabulario** list to be sure that you understand the meaning of most of them.

• •

VOCABULARIO

Los verbos

conocer (conozco)	to know (*a person*); to be familiar with (*a place*)
dar (doy)	to give
decir (digo)	to say; to tell
hacer (hago)	to make; to do
oír (oigo)	to hear
poner (pongo)	to put, place
saber (sé); + *inf.*	to know (*information*); to know how to (*do something*)
salir (salgo) (de)	to leave (*a place*)
tener (tengo)	to have
traer (traigo)	to bring
venir (vengo)	to come

Repaso: ver (veo)

Las palabras adicionales

hacer un viaje	to take a trip
tener que (+ *inf.*)	to have to (*do something*)
aquí	here
esta noche	tonight
pronto	soon
sólo	only

Now that you have completed the Textbook and Workbook for **Lección 7,** take the Self-Test for that lesson. (It is on page 256.) Remember to listen to the tape when you see the cassette symbol and to check your answers.

_____ **Self-Test**

Now that you have worked through the Textbook and the Workbook and taken the Self-Test, here are some of the things you have accomplished in Spanish.

- You can express requests politely in Spanish.
- You can use and understand more numbers.
- You can use more verb forms to talk about what people do.
- You know how Spanish **d** is pronounced.
- You have continued to work on listening skills.

You are now ready to continue on with **Lección 8** in the Textbook.

L E C C I Ó N
·············

8
EL ENCUENTRO

OBJETIVOS

Whereas the materials in the Textbook all had to do with the video segment, the materials in the Workbook will help you expand your knowledge of the Spanish language in general, as well as give you opportunities for self-expression in Spanish. In this lesson you will learn

- additional ways to ask questions in Spanish
- the use of stem-changing verbs and reflexive constructions to talk about others
- the pronunciation of Spanish **b** and **v**.

Remember to listen to the tape for **Lección 8** when you see the cassette symbol and to check your answers in Appendix 1.

MÁS ALLÁ DEL EPISODIO

Actividad A.   Rosario del Valle Iglesias

You have heard Rosario's name many times since the first episode of *Destinos*. But you really don't know much about her as a person yet. Here is a series of statements about her. Choose from the following five responses to express your reactions.

a. Sé que es cierto.
b. Creo que es cierto.
c. No sé.

d. Creo que es falso.
e. Sé que es falso.

1. _____ Rosario era (*was*) muy buena amiga de Teresa Suárez.
2. _____ Cree que Fernando murió en Guernica.
3. _____ Ángel no es hijo de don Fernando.
4. _____ Rosario no amaba (*loved*) a don Fernando.
5. _____ Cree que hay más oportunidades para su hijo en otro país (*country*).
6. _____ Se casó de nuevo por (*because of*) su hijo.
7. _____ Tuvo (*She had*) otro hijo.
8. _____ Rosario ya murió; está muerta.

The answers you have given are based solely on the very small amount of information you have at this point about Rosario. The following reading passage offers more information. Read it and see if you wish to change any answers.

As in previous **Más allá del episodio** sections, portions of this reading are in the past tense. You should be able to recognize the verbs, however, and to guess their meaning.

«**R**osario, ¿eres tú?» Don Fernando recuerda[1] a una joven y hermosa mujer... la persona con quien se casó hace muchos años.[2] Para Teresa Suárez, Rosario es una compañera... la buena amiga de su juventud[3]... la amiga que perdió después de la Guerra Civil.

Después del bombardeo de Guernica, Rosario buscó a Fernando desesperadamente por todas partes, pero no lo encontró. La casa, la oficina del banco, las casas de los amigos... casi todo el pueblo fue destruido. Finalmente tuvo que aceptar que Fernando murió.

¿Qué podía hacer? La ciudad estaba en ruinas y la Guerra Civil continuaba. Rosario estaba sola, embarazada,[4] sin familia ni amigos. Decidió alejarse[5] de Guernica y comenzó un largo y difícil viaje. Llegó a Sevilla y encontró una pequeña casa en el barrio de Triana. Allí conoció a Teresa Suárez, su vecina,[6] y se hicieron buenas amigas.

El hijo de Fernando que esperaba nació unos meses[7] después. Llamó al niño Ángel, por ser un rayo de esperanza en medio de su dolor.[8] Al terminar[9] la guerra, la vida[10] era muy difícil y Rosario no tuvo fuerzas para esperar tiempos mejores.[11] Decidió alejarse de nuevo, para olvidar el gran amor de su vida y la tragedia de su país. Y, lo más importante de todo, para empezar una nueva vida por su hijo. Pero... ¿adónde ir?

Rosario, la primera esposa de don Fernando

[1] *remembers* [2] *hace... many years ago* [3] *youth* [4] *pregnant* [5] *to go far away* [6] *neighbor* [7] *unos... several months* [8] *por... because he was a ray of hope in the midst of her pain* [9] *Al... When ... was over* [10] *life* [11] *tiempos... better times*

 Actividad B.

Now return to statements 1–8 and make any changes in your answers that you feel are necessary. Which statements do you still have to guess at or answer **No sé**? Listen to the cassette tape, on which the speakers will give you some answers; then provide some more information.

• •

GRAMÁTICA

 ## 20. *¿CÓMO?*: ASKING QUESTIONS

Questions with Interrogative Words

You have already learned the most important Spanish interrogatives. Note the following information about using them.

Some interrogatives are used with the words **a, de,** and **para** to pose additional questions. Here are some examples.

¿adónde?	*where to?*	¿Adónde va Raquel ahora?
¿de dónde?	*where from?*	¿De dónde es Raquel?
¿a quién?	*to whom?*	¿A quién habla Raquel en Madrid?
¿de quién?	*whose?*	¿De quién es la cartera perdida?
	about whom?	¿De quién hablan?
¿para quién?	*for whom?*	¿Para quién es el mensaje?

The interrogatives ¿cuál? and ¿quién? have plural forms. The interrogative ¿cuánto? has masculine and feminine, singular and plural forms. The use of these forms depends on the topic of the question.

¿Quién es Elena Ramírez?   ¿Quiénes son Miguel y Jaime?

¿Cuánto tiempo va a estar Raquel en Madrid?

¿Cuántos hijos tiene Teresa Suárez?   ¿Cuántas maletas tiene Raquel?

Use ¿cómo? to ask someone to repeat something that you didn't hear or didn't understand.

¿Cómo? No comprendo.   *What? I don't understand.*

Use ¿qué? to mean *what?* when you are asking for a definition or an explanation. ¿Qué? directly followed by a noun expresses *what?* or *which?*

Definition:

¿Qué es un certificado de nacimiento?   *What is a birth certificate?*

Explanation:

¿Qué necesitas?   *What do you need?*
¿Qué dices?   *What are you saying?*

¿Qué + *noun:*

¿Qué tren vas a tomar?   *What (Which) train are you going to take?*

Use ¿cuál? to express *what?* or *which?* in all other situations.

¿Cuál es tu número de teléfono?   *What is your phone number?*
¿Cuál es la casa de Teresa Suárez? *Which is Teresa Suárez's house?*

Other Kinds of Questions

It is also possible to ask questions without using any of the interrogative words.

A rising intonation in Spanish (an upturn in the level of the voice at the end) can turn a statement into a question.

Statement:

Teresa Suárez conoce a Rosario.   *Teresa Suárez knows Rosario.*

Question:

¿Teresa Suárez conoce a Rosario?   *Does Teresa Suárez know Rosario?*

Note that Spanish does not have the auxiliary ("helping") verb *do/does* in questions.

Sabes la dirección.   *You know the address.*
¿Sabes la dirección?   *Do you know the address?*

Questions can also be formed by inverting the usual subject-verb word order.

Question:

¿Conoce Teresa Suárez a Rosario?   *Does Teresa Suárez know Rosario?*

Because word order in Spanish is extremely flexible—much more so than in English—questions are formed in a variety of ways. When you are listening and conversing, listen for the rising intonation that signals a question formed without interrogative words. When you are reading, watch for the inverted question mark (¿) that signals the beginning of a question.

Actividad A. ¿Qué oyes?

As you listen to the speaker on the cassette tape, indicate whether what she says is a statement (S) or a question (Q). Remember that questions can be formed in a variety of ways.

1. S Q   3. S Q   5. S Q   7. S Q
2. S Q   4. S Q   6. S Q   8. S Q

Actividad B. La respuesta correcta

Choose the logical answer for each of the following questions.

1. _____ ¿Quién busca a Rosario?
2. _____ ¿Qué necesita Raquel de Elena?
3. _____ ¿Cuándo se fue Rosario de España?
4. _____ ¿Dónde vive Teresa Suárez?
5. _____ ¿A quién le deja Raquel un mensaje en el hotel?
6. _____ ¿Cuál es el número de teléfono de Pedro?
7. _____ ¿Cuántos hijos tienen Rosario y Fernando?
8. _____ ¿Adónde se fue a vivir Rosario?
9. _____ ¿Por qué la señora Suárez le escribió a don Fernando?
10. _____ ¿De dónde viene Raquel cuando llega a Madrid?
11. _____ ¿De quién hablan Teresa y Raquel?
12. _____ ¿Cómo se llama el hijo de Rosario y don Fernando?

a. El 2-31-56-42.
b. A Alfredo Sánchez, el reportero.
c. En Madrid.
d. De Sevilla.
e. Raquel Rodríguez, abogada norteamericana.
f. A la Argentina.
g. Después de la Guerra Civil.
h. El certificado de nacimiento de Ángel.
i. De don Fernando y Rosario.
j. Ángel.
k. Porque tiene información acerca de Rosario.
l. Sólo uno.

Actividad C. Una entrevista (interview)

You would like some information about a young Spanish woman who is studying at your university. Complete the following groups of questions with the appropriate interrogative words from the column to the right.

1. ¿_____ᵃ eres? ¿_____ᵇ vives ahora? ¿_____ᶜ vives allí? ¿_____ᵈ tiempo vas a estar en los Estados Unidos? ¿_____ᵉ otras ciudades quieres conocer? ¿_____ᶠ vas a España, en junio?

¿cuál?
¿cuándo?
¿cuánto?
¿de dónde?
¿dónde?
¿por qué?
¿qué?

2. ¿_____ᵃ estudias en esta universidad? ¿_____ᵇ clases tienes en total? ¿_____ᶜ estudias inglés? ¿_____ᵈ es tu profesor de inglés? ¿_____ᵉ es tu clase favorita?

¿cuál?
¿cuántas?
¿dónde?
¿por qué?
¿qué?
¿quién?
¿a quién?

3. ¿_____ᵃ vas a hacer esta noche? ¿_____ᵇ vas a llamar? ¿_____ᶜ vas a salir? ¿_____ᵈ vais? ¿_____ᵉ vas a hacer el domingo? ¿_____ᶠ es tu número de teléfono?

¿a quién?
¿adónde?
¿con quién?
¿cuál?
¿cuándo
¿dónde?
¿qué?

Actividad D. ¿Y tú? Datos personales

Answer the following questions with appropriate information about yourself. (Worksheet)

1. ¿Cuáles son tus apellidos?
2. ¿Cuál es tu nombre?
3. ¿Cuándo (¿En qué año) naciste (*were you born*)?
4. ¿Dónde naciste?
5. ¿Dónde vives ahora?
6. ¿Cuál es tu número de teléfono?
7. ¿Cuántas lenguas hablas?
8. ¿Por qué estudias español?

 21. *LA SRA. SUÁREZ EMPIEZA A CONTAR LA HISTORIA*: THIRD-PERSON FORMS OF STEM-CHANGING VERBS (PRESENT TENSE)

> En Madrid, Raquel **encuentra** más información sobre Rosario, pero está segura de que don Fernando **quiere** saber más. Por eso Raquel **sigue** con la investigación. Pero... la abogada **empieza** a preocuparse. ¿Y si don Fernando **muere**, antes de saber la verdad? Eso no **puede** ser....

Forms

In Lección 7 you worked with a series of verbs that have some changes in the stem in the present tense: **decir, tener, venir.** And you have learned other verb forms—**pierde, puede,** and so on—that have similar vowel combinations in the stem.

Various Spanish verb groups have vowel stem changes that follow patterns similar to those you have seen in **decir, tener,** and **venir.** The group is called the stem-changing verbs. These verbs fall into three groups, based on the type of vowel change they undergo. Here are the third-person singular and plural forms for the three patterns, along with some frequently-used verbs in each group.

INFINITIVE		STEM	él/ella	ellos/ellas
Group 1:	e in the infinitive stem → ie in the conjugated stem			
empezar	*to begin*	empiez-	empieza	empiezan
pensar	*to think*	piens-	piensa	piensan
perder	*to lose*	pierd-	pierde	pierden
querer	*to wish, want*	quier-	quiere	quieren
Group 2:	e in the infinitive stem → i in the conjugated stem			
pedir	*to ask for*	pid-	pide	piden
seguir	*to follow*	sigu-	sigue	siguen
Group 3:	o in the infinitive stem → ue in the conjugated stem			
contar	*to tell*	cuent-	cuenta	cuentan
encontrar	*to find*	encuentr-	encuentra	encuentran
morir	*to die*	muer-	muere	mueren
poder	*to be able to, can*	pued-	puede	pueden
recordar	*to remember*	recuerd-	recuerda	recuerdan
volver	*to return*	vuelv-	vuelve	vuelven

You will learn the other forms of these verbs in **Lecciones 9** and **10.**

Stem-changing verbs are indicated in vocabulary lists with the stem change in parentheses: **empezar (ie), pedir (i), poder (ue).**

Uses

The English equivalents of present-tense stem-changing verbs follow the same patterns as other verbs.

Raquel no quiere ser una molestia.	*Raquel doesn't want to be a bother.*
Alfredo encuentra la cartera de Raquel.	*Alfredo finds Raquel's wallet.*

When used before another infinitive, **pensar** means *to plan or intend.*

Raquel piensa ir a la Argentina.	*Raquel plans (intends) to go to Argentina.*

Also note the use of **pensar** with **en** and **que.**

Don Fernando piensa mucho en Rosario. Piensa que murió en Guernica.	*Don Fernando thinks about Rosario a lot. He thinks that she died at Guernica.*

Querer can also mean *to love.*

Teresa quiere a sus hijos.	*Teresa loves her children.*

Pedir and **contar,** like **dar** and **decir,** are often used with special pronouns. You will learn more about them in **Lección 10.**

Raquel le pide a Miguel la dirección de su madre.	*Raquel asks Miguel for his mother's address.*

Actividad A. ¿Cierto o falso?

Paso 1

Complete the following statements that describe events that have happened so far in *Destinos.* (Or have they?)

empieza   pide   vuelve   quiere   recuerda
muere   sigue   pierde   piensan   pueden

1. Raquel habla con la Sra. Suárez porque _____ saber algo más de Rosario.
2. La Sra. Suárez no _____ adónde se fue a vivir Rosario.
3. Federico y su madre _____ que Raquel es entrometida (*nosey*).
4. Don Fernando _____ muy mal, muy enfermo.
5. Raquel le _____ a Teresa la dirección de Rosario.
6. Raquel _____ su pasaporte.
7. La investigación _____ a ser aburrida (*boring*) para Raquel.
8. Raquel _____ a Sevilla mañana.
9. Alfredo y su asistente no _____ encontrar la cartera de Raquel.
10. Don Fernando _____ en el hospital.

Paso 2

Listen to the completed statements on the cassette tape, check your answers, and indicate whether the statements are true (Cierto) or false (Falso).

Actividad B. Teresa, Federico, Jaime

Create as many sentences as you can about these members of three generations of the Ruiz family. Use the written cues as a guide. You will hear a possible answer on the tape.

¿Quién... ?

1. pide caramelos
2. quiere mucho a sus hijos
3. piensa que los perros son una molestia
4. cuenta una historia trágica
5. vuelve a su casa con Raquel
6. pierde a su perro
7. sigue a su perro por las calles
8. encuentra una foto de don Fernando en un periódico (*newspaper*)
9. quiere ver a Raquel mañana
10. empieza a meterse (*meddle*) en la vida de sus hijos

Actividad C. ¿A quién conoces que... ?

Who do you know that fits the following descriptions? Think about people in your family or in your circle of friends, or even about famous people or people in the news. If you don't know anyone who fits the description, answer with **nadie** (*no one*).

1. Siempre pierde(n) las cosas.
2. Piensa(n) viajar a Europa.
3. Quiere(n) comer la comida de los demás (*others*).
4. Recuerda(n) con nostalgia otra época de su vida.
5. Siempre pide(n) algún favor.
6. Empieza(n) a estudiar en la universidad muy pronto.
7. Siempre encuentra(n) algún motivo para criticar.
8. Sigue(n) la misma rutina todos los días (*every day*).

22. *ROSARIO SE CASÓ DE NUEVO*: THIRD-PERSON REFLEXIVE PRONOUNS

> RAQUEL: Sí, es cierto, Pedro. Después de la Guerra, Rosario **se va** a vivir a la Argentina. Allí **se casa** de nuevo. Pero nunca **se olvida** de don Fernando.

Forms

Some Spanish verbs are usually conjugated with pronouns that are called reflexive pronouns.* That pronoun is the same for third-person singular and plural verb forms: **se**.

El hijo de Rosario y don Fernando **se llama** Ángel.	*Rosario and don Fernando's son is called Ángel.*
Raquel y la Sra. Suárez **se sientan** para hablar.	*Raquel and Mrs. Suárez sit down to talk.*

Here is a list of verbs that are conjugated with reflexive pronouns. The **-se** attached to the infinitive indicates that the verb is always conjugated in this way. Note that some of these verbs are also stem-changing.

---

*You will learn why they are called "reflexive" in **Lección 13** of the Workbook.

acordarse (ue) (de)*	*to remember*	se acuerda	se acuerdan
casarse (con)*	*to get married*	se casa	se casan
llamarse	*to be called, named*	se llama	se llaman
olvidarse (de)*	*to forget*	se olvida	se olvidan
sentarse (ie)	*to sit down*	se sienta	se sientan
sentirse (ie)	*to feel*	se siente	se sienten

Uses

The pronoun **se** precedes conjugated verb forms. It generally follows and is attached to an infinitive. Note the position of the word **no** (before the word **se**).

Don Fernando **no se olvida** de Rosario.	*Don Fernando doesn't forget Rosario.*
Don Fernando no quiere **olvidarse** de Rosario.	*Don Fernando doesn't want to forget Rosario.*

Se can be used to change the meaning of some verbs slightly; for example, **va** (*goes*) versus **se va** (*goes away*), **fue** (*went*) versus **se fue** (*went away*). Learn to recognize the meaning of verbs such as these as they occur.

Actividad A. Una cuestión de lógica

Match the names on the left with the phrases on the right to form complete sentences that accurately describe some of the *Destinos* characters. ¡OJO! Some phrases are appropriate for more than one character.

1. Raquel
2. la Sra. Suárez
3. Rosario y Martín Iglesias
4. don Fernando
5. Raquel y la Sra. Suárez
6. el hijo de Rosario y don Fernando
7. Rosario

se casa dos veces
no se siente bien
se sientan a hablar
se acuerda de Rosario con nostalgia
se casan en Buenos Aires
se sienta al lado de (*next to*) la Sra. Suárez
no se olvida de llamar a Elena
se va a la Argentina
se llama Ángel

Actividad B. ¿A quién conoces que... ?

Who do you know that fits the following descriptions? Think about people in your family or in your circle of friends, or even about famous people or people in the news. If you don't know anyone who fits the description, answer with **nadie** (*no one*).

1. Se casa(n) con frecuencia. (¡Piensa en Hollywood!)
2. No se siente(n) bien ahora.
3. Siempre se siente(n) estupendamente.
4. Se va(n) a vivir a otro estado (otro país) pronto.
5. Siempre se olvida(n) de algo o de hacer algo.
6. Se acuerda(n) de una guerra.

Actividad C. ¿Y tú?

Give a few details about your parents, your grandparents, or any other member of your family (or a friend's family). Use the following paragraph as a model. (Worksheet)

---

*Note the prepositions used with these verbs when they are followed by an object (a person, a place, and so on). These prepositions do not appear in the English equivalents.

Fernando se casó con Rosario.	*Fernando married Rosario.*
Teresa Suárez se acuerda de Rosario.	*Teresa Suárez remembers Rosario.*

Mi abuelo se llama _____. Es de _____. Se casó con

_____, mi abuela, en _____ (año). Ahora viven en _____.

(_____ murió en _____ [año].)

PRONUNCIACIÓN: *b* AND *v*

In most dialects of Spanish, the consonants **b** and **v** are pronounced exactly the same way.

At the beginning of a phrase, or after **m** or **n**, **b** and **v** are pronounced like the English *b*, as a stop; that is, no air is allowed to escape through the lips. This sound is represented in this way: [b].

In all other positions, **b** and **v** are fricatives; that is, they are produced by allowing some air to escape through the lips. There is no equivalent for this sound in English. The sound is represented in this way: [ƀ].

Actividad.

Listen and repeat as the speaker on the tape pronounces the following words and phrases. Note that the type of **b** sound you will hear is marked at the beginning of each series.

1. [b] blusa barrio biología vestido venden viajar Barcelona Valencia
   hombre miembro Alhambra investigar investigación
2. [ƀ] hablar trabajar contabilidad todavía sábado habitación revela Sevilla
3. [b/ƀ] bueno / es bueno viaje / el viaje va / se va bien / muy bien en Venezuela
   / de Venezuela

Have you completed the following sections of the lesson? Check them off here.

_____ **Más allá del episodio**   _____ **Pronunciación**

_____ **Gramática**

Now scan the words in the **Vocabulario** list to be sure that you understand the meaning of most of them.

VOCABULARIO

Los verbos

acordarse (ue) (de)	to remember
casarse (con)	to marry
contar (ue)	to tell
empezar (ie)	to begin
encontrar (ue)	to find
llamarse	to be called, named
morir (ue)	to die
olvidarse (de)	to forget
pedir (i)	to ask for

pensar (ie)	to think
perder (ie)	to lose
poder (ue)	to be able (to), can
querer (ie)	to wish, want; to love
recordar (ue)	to remember
seguir (i)	to follow; to continue
sentarse (ie)	to sit down
sentirse (ie)	to feel
volver (ue)	to return
se fue	he/she went away

Las personas

nadie   no one

Los conceptos

la vida   life

Las palabras interrogativas

¿adónde?   where to?
¿de dónde?   where from?

Las palabras adicionales

allí   there
empezar a + *inf.*   to begin to (*do something*)
pensar + *inf.*   to intend to (*do something*)
pensar en   to think about
pensar que   to think that

Now that you have completed the Textbook and Workbook for **Lección 8,** take the Self-Test for that lesson. (It is on page 258.) Remember to use the tape when you see the cassette symbol and to check your answers.

_____ **Self-Test**

Now that you have worked through the Textbook and the Workbook and taken the Self-Test, here are some of the things you have accomplished in Spanish.

- You can thank someone and acknowledge thanks in Spanish.
- You can ask and understand questions formed in a number of ways.
- You have learned more about Spanish verbs and can use them to talk about what others are doing.
- You know how Spanish **b** and **v** are pronounced.
- You have continued to work on listening skills.

You are now ready to continue on with **Lección 9** in the Textbook.

LECCIÓN
9
ESTACIONES

OBJETIVOS

Whereas the materials in the Textbook all had to do with the video segment, the materials in the Workbook will help you expand your knowledge of the Spanish language in general, as well as give you opportunities for self-expression in Spanish. In this lesson you will learn

- the use of stem-changing verbs and reflexive constructions to talk about your own activities and those of people you address directly
- more ways to express possession, that is, to talk about things that are yours and people who are associated with you
- ways to point out people or things
- the pronunciation of Spanish **j** and **g**.

Remember to listen to the tape for **Lección 9** when you see the cassette symbol and to check your answers in Appendix 1.

MÁS ALLÁ DEL EPISODIO

Actividad A.   Teresa Suárez
You have already met Teresa Suárez and have seen her interact with others. But you really don't know much about her as a person yet. Here is a series of statements about her. Choose from the following five responses to express your reaction.

a. Sé que es cierto.
b. Creo que es cierto.
c. No sé.
d. Creo que es falso.
e. Sé que es falso.

1. __C__ Teresa Suárez es divorciada.
2. __C__ Vive ahora en Madrid, pero es de Andalucía.
3. __E__ No tiene título (*degree*) universitario.
4. __C__ Le gusta mucho hablar con sus amigas.

5. __C__ Lo que (*What*) más recuerda de Rosario es su alegría (*happy nature*) y espontaneidad.
6. __d__ A Teresa le gusta mucho preparar cenas deliciosas, especialmente para su familia.
7. __C__ Trabajó en un hospital después de la Guerra Civil.
8. __c__ Espera recibir una recompensa (*reward*) de don Fernando.

The answers you have given are based solely on the very small amount of information you have at this point about Teresa Suárez. The following reading passage offers more information. Read it and see whether you wish to change any answers.

This reading, like many previous readings, is written largely in the past. You should be able to recognize the verbs, however, and to guess their meanings.

La mujer que le escribió una carta a don Fernando

ESPAÑA

Sevilla
Jerez de la Frontera

Teresa Suárez conoció a Rosario en Sevilla. Las dos vivían en el barrio de Triana. Se hicieron[1] amigas rápidamente. Teresa estaba recién casada[2] y podía comprender muy bien el dolor[3] de su amiga, que pensaba mucho en su esposo muerto. Con frecuencia cuidó al[4] pequeño Ángel mientras Rosario trabajaba.

Teresa nació[5] en Jerez de la Frontera, pero sus padres se trasladaron[6] a Sevilla cuando era pequeña. En Sevilla, conoció a Juan Ruiz, se casaron y tuvieron tres hijos. Teresa no estudió en la universidad y nunca trabajó fuera de[7] casa. Siempre se dedicó a la familia. Su esposo murió hace años[8] y desde entonces vive en Madrid.

Ahora que sus hijos son grandes,[9] su vida ha cambiado bastante.[10] Ya no ve con frecuencia a Julio, el hijo que vive en Barcelona. Desgraciadamente, Teresa no se lleva bien con[11] su esposa. A ella le gusta meterse en los asuntos de sus hijos, y eso no le gusta mucho a la esposa de Julio.

El hijo menor de Teresa, Federico, todavía vive con ella. Esto le gusta mucho porque Federico es su hijo favorito. También quiere mucho a Miguel y a su familia y los visita con frecuencia. Miguel y Jaime adoran a su abuela. Sobre todo les gustan las cenas deliciosas que les prepara: una paella exquisita, una tortilla de patatas sabrosa....

---
[1]Se... *They became* [2]recién... *recently married* [3]*pain* [4]cuidó... *took care of* [5]*was born* [6]se... *moved* [7]fuera... *outside of* [8]hace... *some years ago* [9]*grown* [10]ha... *has changed a great deal* [11]no... *she doesn't get along with*

 Actividad B.

Now return to statements 1–8 and make any changes in your answers that you feel are necessary. Which statements do you still have to guess at or answer **No sé?** Listen to the cassette tape, on which the speaker will give you some answers and then provide some more information.

GRAMÁTICA

—▪▪— **23. *QUIERO SABER QUIÉN ES DON FERNANDO*: FIRST- AND SECOND-PERSON SINGULAR FORMS OF STEM-CHANGING VERBS (PRESENT TENSE)**

ALFREDO: Empiezo a sentir más curiosidad sobre el cliente misterioso de Raquel. Si no encuentro a la maestra de primaria, puedo escribir una historia para la televisión acerca del industrial mexicano.

Forms

In **Lección 8** you learned the third-person singular and plural forms of a group of verbs that have a change in the stem vowel. Here are the first-person singular (**yo**) and second-person singular (**tú**) forms of those verbs. The changes are identical to those forms. As happens with regular verbs, the form used with **Ud.** is identical to the third-person singular form.

INFINITIVE	STEM	**yo**	**tú**	**Ud.**
Group 1	e in the infinitive stem → ie in the conjugated stem			
empezar	empiez-	empiezo	empiezas	empieza
Other verbs in this group: pensar, perder, querer.				
Group 2	e in the infinitive stem → i in the conjugated stem			
pedir	pid-	pido	pides	pide
Other verbs in this group: seguir.*				
Group 3	o in the infinitive stem → ue in the conjugated stem			
contar	cuent-	cuento	cuentas	cuenta
Other verbs in this group: encontrar, morir, poder, recordar, volver.				

Actividad A. El plan de Alfredo

Paso 1

Taking Alfredo's point of view, complete the following description of his plan of attack for the stories he wants to write. ¡OJO! Some verbs may be used more than once.

pienso	quiero
empiezo	puedo
sigo	tengo
pido	encuentro

---

*Note the first-person singular form of seguir: sigo (*but* sigues, sigue).

ALFREDO: Esto es lo que voy a hacer. _____Tengo_____ ¹ la cartera de Raquel, pero no _____pienso_____ ²
dejársela* en la recepción. En realidad, _____empiezo_____ ³ otros motivos. _____pido_____ ⁴ hablar
con ella porque _____encuentro_____ ⁵ saber más sobre el caso de Fernando Castillo. _____sigo_____ ⁶
a perder un poco la paciencia, ¿sabes? Le _____quiero_____ ⁷ información a Raquel, pero ella no
quiere contarme nada. Mientras tanto, _____quiero_____ ⁸ buscando a la maestra de primaria. Si no
la _____sigo_____, ⁹ _____pienso_____ ¹⁰ escribir la historia de Fernando Castillo. Ahora que lo
_____tengo_____, ¹¹ ¿por qué no _____empiezo_____ ¹² escribir las dos historias?

* *Leave it for her*

Paso 2

Now listen as the contact person whom Alfredo called in **Episodio 6** asks him about what
he plans to do. Then select the correct answer for each question, based on the preceding
paragraph, and say it.

MODELO: (*you hear*) Hola, Alfredo.
(*you see*) Hasta luego, Julio. / Buenas tardes, Julio.
(*you say*) Buenas tardes, Julio.

1. Creo que sí. / Espero que no.
2. Sí, claro. / No, no la dejo allí.
3. No, no es necesario. / Sí. Tengo muchas preguntas.
4. No. Ahora no la busco. / Sí, ¡y pienso encontrarla!
5. No, no escribo su historia. / Sí, pienso escribir su historia.
6. Sí, quiero escribir su historia también. / No. Su historia no me interesa.
7. ¡Qué idea fatal! / ¡Excelente idea!

Actividad B. ¿Y tú?

Paso 1

Complete the following statements with the yo form of the indicated infinitives. Then
decide whether the statements are true for you. If not, change them to make them accurate.

1. _____Seguirn_____ la misma rutina todos los días. (seguir)

2. ¡A veces _____contarn_____ historias exageradas! (contar)

3. _____pensarn_____ viajar a España en el futuro. (pensar)

4. _____perdern_____ la paciencia a veces. (perder)

5. _____Seguirn_____ una telenovela (*soap opera*) en la televisión. (seguir)

6. _____empezarn_____ a comprender más cuando veo los episodios de *Destinos*. (empezar)

7. _____recordarn_____ muy bien a todos mis maestros de primaria. (recordar)

8. _____querern_____ saber más acerca de Raquel y Federico. (querer)

Paso 2

Now, using the same sentences as a guide, give the questions you would use to ask a friend
about the same information. (Worksheet)

24. ¿CÓMO TE LLAMAS? —ME LLAMO JAIME : FIRST- AND SECOND-PERSON SINGULAR REFLEXIVE PRONOUNS

Forms

In **Lección 8** you learned to use the pronoun **se** with the third-person singular and plural forms of some verbs. The first-person singular (**yo**) and second-person singular (**tú**) forms of those same verbs are used with the pronouns **me** and **te**, respectively. As happens with regular verbs, the form used with **Ud.** is identical to the third-person singular form: **se.** Here are some examples.

	yo	tú	Ud.
casarse	me caso	te casas	se casa
acordarse	me acuerdo	te acuerdas	se acuerda
sentarse	me siento	te sientas	se sienta

Other verbs used with these pronouns: **llamarse, olvidarse, sentirse.**

TERESA SUÁREZ: **Me acuerdo** muy bien de Rosario.

MERCEDES: Papá, **te sientes** muy triste cuando piensas en Rosario, ¿verdad?

TERESA SUÁREZ: *I remember Rosario very well.*

MERCEDES: *Papa, you feel very sad when you think about Rosario, don't you?*

Uses

Remember that the pronoun precedes conjugated verb forms and generally follows and is attached to an infinitive: **Quiero sentarme a hablar con Teresa Suárez.**

A number of verbs that describe one's daily routine are used with these pronouns. Here are some of them, listed in a logical sequence.

despertarse (ie)	to wake up	**acostarse (ue)**	to go to bed
levantarse	to get up	**dormirse (ue)**	to fall asleep
vestirse (i)	to get dressed		

 ### Actividad A.   La rutina diaria (*daily*) de la Sra. Suárez

Listen as the narrator repeats the details of Teresa Suárez's daily routine. Check off her activities on the following list. Take a few seconds to scan the list.

1. _____ correr
2. _____ caminar a la plaza
3. _____ ir a la farmacia
4. _____ leer (*to read*) algo
5. _____ ir al mercado
6. _____ trabajar
7. _____ comprar un cupón de lotería
8. _____ ver la televisión

Now listen as the speaker adds some more details about what Sra. Suárez does every day. Compare them with the following statements made by Sra. Suárez. Are the statements you hear on the tape true (**Cierto**) or false (**Falso**)?

C F 1. Me despierto a las ocho.
C F 2. Me levanto en unos minutos, a las ocho y cuarto.
C F 3. Desayuno (*I have breakfast*) y preparo el desayuno de Federico a las ocho y media.
C F 4. Me visto después de desayunar.
C F 5. Me acuesto temprano, a las diez generalmente.
C F 6. Me duermo inmediatamente.

Actividad B. ¿Quién habla?

You know that Federico lives with his mother, and you know a few details about their lives. Indicate whether the following statements would most likely be made by Federico (F) or by his mother, Teresa Suárez (T).

F (T) Siempre me acuerdo de mi buena amiga Rosario.
(F) T Creo que me caso este verano.
(F) T Vuelvo a casa muy tarde (*very late*) y me acuesto muy tarde.
(F) T A veces me olvido de decirle adiós a mamá.
F (T) No me caso otra vez. ¡Imposible!
F (T) Todos los días me levanto, me visto y voy al taller.

Actividad C. ¿Y tú?

For each group of activities, indicate the order (1–6) in which you do them on a typical class day. Provide the time when appropriate.

Grupo 1

____ Llego a la universidad a las...   ____ (No) Me levanto inmediatamente.
____ Me despierto a las...   ____ Desayuno.
____ Me visto.   ____ Salgo a la calle a las...

Grupo 2

____ Vuelvo a casa a las...   ____ Estudio un poco o veo la televisión.
____ Hablo con... (Llamo a... por teléfono.)   ____ Me acuesto a las...
____ Ceno a las...   ____ (No) Me duermo inmediatamente.

Actividad D. Preguntas para un amigo

Using the following phrases as a guide, ask the appropriate questions to get the following information.

> MODELO: (*you see*) ¿cómo? / llamarse
> (*you say*) ¿Cómo te llamas?
> (*you hear*) ¿Cómo te llamas?

1. ¿cómo? / llamarse
2. ¿dónde? / vivir
3. ¿a qué hora? / levantarse, generalmente
4. ¿a qué hora? / llegar a la universidad
5. ¿a qué hora? / volver a casa
6. ¿a qué hora? / acostarse
7. dormirse inmediatamente

Actividad E. ¿Y tú? Información personal

You have given some general information about your routine. This activity asks you to provide more details. Complete each group of sentences, giving as much information as you can. (Worksheet)

1. Los días que tengo clases, me despierto a las... Los sábados, me despierto a las... Y los domingos, me despierto a las...
2. Los días que tengo clases, me acuesto a la(s)... Los viernes, me acuesto a la(s)... Los sábados, me acuesto a la(s)... (¿A veces no te acuestas?)
3. Cuando me acuesto, generalmente (no) me duermo inmediatamente. En vez de (*Instead of*) dormirme, ... (leo una novela, veo la televisión, hablo con...)
4. Cuando no puedo dormirme, ...

25. *NUESTRO HIJO, NUESTROS HIJOS*: EXPRESSING POSSESSION (PART 2)

TERESA: Juan y yo nos casamos después de la Guerra Civil. **Nuestros** tres hijos nacieron en Sevilla. En **nuestra** casa siempre había paz y tranquilidad, pues Juan era un hombre pacífico y quería mucho a **sus** hijos. **Nuestro** hijo Miguel es como su padre. Por eso me gusta visitar la casa **de Miguel**. Me recuerda otra época de la vida... .

Possessive Adjectives

Forms

In Lección 2 you learned the possessive adjectives **su/sus** and **mi/mis**. Now that you have learned about Spanish adjectives in general, you probably understand more about how the possessive adjectives "work." Here is the complete set.

mi, mis	my
tu, tus	your (*sing., fam.*)
su, sus	his, her, their
	your (*sing.* and *pl., form.*)
nuestro, nuestra, nuestros, nuestras	our
vuestro, vuestra, vuestros, vuestras*	your (*pl., form.*)

The following patterns of agreement for possessive adjectives will seem similar to you, because they are identical to those for other adjectives.

Like all adjectives that end in -o, **nuestro** and **vuestro** have four forms. The adjective must agree in number (singular or plural) and gender (masculine or feminine) with the noun it modifies. Note the agreement of the **nuestro** forms in the following sentences. The speaker is Miguel the son.

> **Nuestro** perro se llama Osito.
> **Nuestra** abuela vive en Madrid.
> **Nuestros** padres son Miguel y Elena.
> ¿Y **nuestras** tías? Tenemos sólo una, que vive en Barcelona.

The other possessive adjectives have only two forms: singular and plural. Here is a description of an outfit Raquel will wear in an upcoming episode of *Destinos*.

> **Su** falda es azul, y **su** chaqueta también.
> **Su** blusa es blanca.
> **Sus** zapatos son negros, y **sus** medias son blancas.

Uses

Just as you must choose the appropriate subject pronoun and verb form to use when you address someone, you must select an appropriate possessive adjective. Here is the same question, "What is your family like?", as it would be asked of four different persons or groups of people.

> Y tú, Federico, ¿cómo es **tu** familia?
> Y Ud., don Fernando, ¿cómo es **su** familia?
> Y vosotros, Jaime y Miguel, ¿cómo es **vuestra** familia?
> Y Uds., Ramón y Mercedes, ¿cómo es **su** familia?

---

*The **vuestro** forms are generally used only in Spain, like the **vosotros** forms of verbs. In Latin America **su** and **sus** are preferred, just as ustedes is preferred.

Expressing Possession with *de*

Possession can also be expressed with a *de* + noun (or pronoun) phrase.

Los pantalones de Federico son pardos.   *Federico's pants are brown.*
El conjunto de Raquel es de color   *Raquel's outfit is salmon-colored.*
salmón.

This construction is often used when the meaning of **su(s)** is not completely clear. Here is an example. The phrase **su hijo** can mean *his son, her son, their son,* or *your son,* depending on the context. Meaning can be made clear by using a **de** + pronoun phrase.

su hijo = el hijo **de él** (de Miguel Ruiz)
            = el hijo **de ella** (de Elena)
            = el hijo **de Ud.**
            = el hijo **de ellos** (de Miguel y Elena)
            = el hijo **de Uds.**

Note: As you know, **de** + **el** = **del.** However, the words **de** + **él** do not form a contraction.

Actividad A. Los comentarios de la Sra. Suárez

Is it probable (P) or improbable (IMP) that Teresa Suárez would make the following statements?

1. _____ Mi hijo Miguel tiene dos hijos.
2. _____ Mis otros hijos viven en Madrid y Granada.
3. _____ Mi hijo Federico vive conmigo (*with me*).
4. _____ Nuestro apartamento es pequeño (*small*), pero tiene suficiente espacio para nuestras cosas.
5. _____ ¡Ay, Federico! ¿Por qué dejas tu ropa en el suelo (*floor*)?
6. _____ Jaime y Miguel, ¿por qué no traéis vuestro perro cuando venís a Madrid?

Actividad B. La vida de Miguel y Jaime

Paso 1

Taking the point of view of Miguel and Jaime, create as many sentences as you can that describe aspects of the life of Teresa's grandchildren. (Worksheet)

nuestro	abuela	van a la misma (*same*) escuela
nuestra	perro	está en el Barrio de Triana
nuestros	padres	vive en Madrid con nuestro tío, Federico
nuestras	escuela	se llama el Colegio de San Francisco de Paula
	calle	todavía piensan mucho en Raquel
	amigos	se llama Osito

Paso 2

Now, using the middle column as a guide, ask Miguel or Jaime as many questions as possible about these aspects of their lives. It is likely that you would use **tú** with them, because they are children. The possessive forms you use will depend on whether you have decided to learn the **vosotros** forms. (Worksheet)

MODELO: ¿Dónde vive vuestra abuela?
          ¿Dónde vive su abuela?

Actividad C. El caso de Raquel

Given what you know about Raquel's investigation, you should be able to complete her description of it with the appropriate forms of **mi** or **su**. After you have completed the description, give the English equivalent for each form of **su** that you have used.

RAQUEL: Mi vida es un poco complicada ahora porque investigo un caso interesante. _____¹ cliente, don Fernando, es un industrial mexicano. _____² primera esposa murió en el bombardeo de Guernica... o por lo menos así creía él^a hasta que^b recibió una carta de una amiga de _____³ esposa. Ay, pobre don Fernando. _____⁴ cuatro hijos no sabían nada^c de la primera esposa de _____⁵ padre... . Y ahora también es posible que tengan^d otro hermano, el hijo de _____⁶ padre con _____⁷ primera esposa.

^a por... *at least that's what he thought*   ^b hasta... *until*   ^c no... *didn't know anything*   ^d *they have*

Actividad D.   ¿Y tú?

Paso 1
Are the following statements true for you? If not, change the details to make them accurate.

1. Mis padres (abuelos) son de los Estados Unidos.
2. Mi familia vive ahora en este estado.
3. Mi estación favorita es el otoño.
4. Mi color favorito es el azul.
5. Nuestra universidad es famosa.
6. Nuestro semestre (trimestre) empieza en agosto.

Paso 2
Now, using the same sentences as a guide, create the questions you would use to ask a friend about the same information. (Worksheet)

26. *ÉSTE ES MI HERMANO JAIME*: USING DEMONSTRATIVES TO POINT OUT SPECIFIC NOUNS

Quiero ver este... esa... y aquellos...

In Lección 4 you learned to use the phrase Éste es... and others like it (**ésta, éstos, éstas**) to make introductions. Those words are demonstratives. In Spanish, as in English, demonstrative adjectives are used to point out the location or indicate the presence of a specific noun. Like all Spanish adjectives, the demonstratives agree with the nouns they modify in gender and number.

There are three groups of demonstratives in Spanish. Demonstratives are used to indicate nouns that are

- near to the speaker

this	**este** suéter	**esta** camisa
these	**estos** suéteres	**estas** camisas

- not near to the speaker; usually, close to the person addressed

that	**ese** vestido	**esa** bufanda
those	**esos** vestidos	**esas** bufandas

- even farther away.

that (over there)	**aquel** zapato	**aquella** falda
those (over there)	**aquellos** zapatos	**aquellas** faldas

You will hear and use demonstratives throughout the rest of the *Destinos* materials. For now, try to get a sense of the meaning they convey.

Actividad. En la tienda de ropa

You will hear and read parts of Raquel's interaction with a salesclerk in a clothing store. Before beginning this activity, you may wish to review the phrases you learned in **Lección 7** for making polite requests.

Paso 1

Listen to the questions the salesclerk might ask Raquel about the clothing she wants to try on or buy.

Las preguntas de la vendedora

1. ¿Desea ver aquellas blusas que están en el escaparate (*display window*)?
2. ¿Busca también un vestido?
3. ¿Le gusta ese sombrero? Es muy elegante, ¿no cree?
4. ¿Quisiera ver estos zapatos negros?
5. ¿No quiere ver también aquella chaqueta blanca? Es ideal para la primavera.
6. ¿Necesita medias? Ésas son muy económicas.
7. ¿Va a comprar también esta falda negra?

Paso 2

Match the questions you have just heard with the appropriate answer. Then indicate whether Raquel is talking about something that is close to her (C), not close to her (NC), or even farther away (F).

C NC F _____ a. Creo que esos azules van mejor (*better*) con la ropa que tengo.
C NC F _____ b. No, gracias, no necesito blusas. Pero sí necesito una camiseta. Esa camiseta, de color salmón, es bonita...
C NC F _____ c. No, tengo muchas faldas. Quisiera ver aquellos pantalones blancos, por favor.
C NC F _____ d. No. Éstas de aquí me gustan más. ¿Me permite verlas?
C NC F _____ e. Si, y éste es elegante también. Pero no necesito sombrero.
C NC F _____ f. Sí. ¿Ve Ud. aquel vestido rojo? ¿No lo tiene en rosado?
C NC F _____ g. ¡Qué buena idea! Sólo tengo esta chaqueta gruesa (*heavy*).

PRONUNCIACIÓN: *j* AND *g*

Spanish **j** never has the sound of English *j*, as in *Jane* or *John*. In some dialects of Spanish it is pronounced like the English *h*; in others it has a rougher, more fricative sound that is produced in the back part of the mouth, just about where you would make a [k] sound: taco/Tajo, carro/jarro.

The sound of the letter **j**, represented phonetically as [x], can also be written in Spanish with the letter **g** when **g** appears in front of **e** or **i** (**ge, gi**). Note the difference in the pronunciation of these words.

Spain:	Jorge	jueves	genial	álgebra
Latin America:	Jorge	jueves	genial	álgebra

Actividad A.

Repeat the following words and phrases, imitating the speaker.

1. Jaime   junio   julio   jersey   extranjero   mujer   hijo
2. general   inteligente   geografía   religión   psicología   sociología
3. un colegio religioso   un hijo generoso   una mujer extranjera

When Spanish g appears anywhere else (other than before e or i), it is pronounced like the g in English *go* [g]. Spanish g has the [g] sound at the beginning of a phrase or sentence or after n. The [g] sound is written as gu before e and i.*

In all other positions the g in these letter combinations (ga, go, gu, gue, gui, gr, gl) represents a fricative sound [ǥ], produced by allowing some air to escape when it is pronounced. There is no exact equivalent for this sound in English.

Actividad B.
Repeat the following words and sentences, imitating the speaker.

1. [g] gato   gusto   guerra   guitarra
        gracias   gris   tengo   vengo
2. [ǥ] el gato   el gusto la guerra   la guitarra
        abogado   agosto   mucho gusto hasta luego
        sigo   sigues   sigue   seguir
3. Hasta luego, Gerardo.
   El gusto es mío, doña Julia.

Have you completed the following sections of the lesson? Check them off here.

_____ **Más allá del episodio**   _____ **Pronunciación**
_____ **Gramática**

Now scan the words in the **Vocabulario** list to be sure that you understand the meaning of most of them.

• •

VOCABULARIO

Los verbos

acostarse (ue)	to go to bed
desayunar	to have breakfast
despertarse (ie)	to wake up
dormirse (ue)	to fall asleep
levantarse	to get up
vestirse (i)	to get dressed

Los adjetivos demostrativos (Demonstrative Adjectives)

este, esta	this (*near to the speaker*)
estos, estas	these (*near to the speaker*)
ese, esa	that (*near the person spoken to*)
esos, esas	those (*near the person spoken to*)
aquel, aquella	that (*even farther away*)
aquellos, aquellas	those (*even farther away*)

Los adjetivos posesivos (Possessive Adjectives)

tu, tus	your (*familiar*)
su, sus	your (*formal*)
nuestro, nuestra, nuestros, nuestras	our
vuestro, vuestra, vuestros, vuestras	your (*familiar*)

Repaso: mi(s); su(s) (his, her, their)

Las palabras adicionales

inmediatamente	immediately, right away

---

*Note the *wa* sound of the gua combination: lengua, igualmente.

Now that you have completed the Textbook and Workbook for **Lección 9**, take the Self-Test for that lesson. (It is on page 260.) Remember to listen to the tape when you see the cassette symbol and to check your answers.

_____ **Self-Test**

Now that you have worked through the Textbook and the Workbook and taken the Self-Test, here are some of the things you have accomplished in Spanish.

- You can agree with a suggestion someone has made.
- You can express colors, the months, and the seasons in Spanish.
- You have learned more verb forms for talking about what you and others do or are doing.
- You can describe daily routines for yourself and others.
- You can point things out and indicate in a variety of ways what belongs to you and others.
- You know how Spanish **j** and **g** are pronounced.
- You have continued to work on listening skills.

You are now ready to continue on with **Lección 10** in the Textbook.

10
CUADROS

OBJETIVOS

Whereas the materials in the Textbook all had to do with the video segment, the materials in the Workbook will help you expand your knowledge of the Spanish language in general, as well as give you opportunities for self-expression in Spanish. In this lesson you will learn

- more about using adjectives to describe people and things in Spanish
- the use of stem-changing verbs and reflexive constructions to talk about activities you engage in with others
- more about expressing *to be* in Spanish
- the pronunciation of Spanish **c** and **qu**.

Remember to listen to the tape for **Lección 10** when you see the cassette symbol and to check your answers in Appendix 1.

MÁS ALLÁ DEL EPISODIO

Actividad A. Manuel Díaz

You have seen and listened to Manuel Díaz since meeting him on the train to Madrid in **Episodio 6.** But you really don't know much about him as a person yet. Here is a series of statements about him. Choose from the following three responses to express your reactions.

a. Es probable.   c. Es improbable.
b. No sé.

1. ____ Manuel Díaz es una persona reservada y muy metódica.
2. ____ Vive en un pequeño apartamento, con su madre.
3. ____ El Sr. Díaz tiene muchas manías. Una de ellas es la puntualidad.
4. ____ Es intelectual.
5. ____ Sus pintores favoritos son Picasso y Dalí.

6. _____ Le gusta mucho la ópera, especialmente *Aída* y *La Bohème*.
7. _____ Ahora que tiene un poco de dinero, piensa viajar mucho.
8. _____ Va a la Argentina en el mismo vuelo (*flight*) que Raquel.

The answers you have given are based solely on the very small amount of information you have at this point about Manuel Díaz. The following reading passage offers more information. Read it and see whether you wish to change any answers.

Manuel Díaz, el maestro ganador del premio de la lotería

Manuel Díaz es un maestro como muchos otros. Lleva una vida ordenada y sencilla.[1] Vive en un pequeño apartamento, con un gato muy viejo que se llama Tigre. Sigue desde hace años[2] la misma rutina y detesta las situaciones inesperadas.[3]

El Sr. Díaz es una persona muy reservada. No le gusta hablar de sí mismo.[4] Cuándo está con personas que no conoce bien, prefiere hablar de temas generales. Vive solo[5] y tiene muchas manías. Su ropa, por ejemplo, tiene que estar siempre bien planchada,[6] y no soporta[7] la música moderna. Pero a pesar de[8] esas manías, es muy simpático, especialmente cuando se le conoce bien.[9]

A Manuel le gusta mucho la literatura. Ha leído[10] casi todos los clásicos por lo menos dos veces. También es apasionado del arte, especialmente de la pintura clásica. Sus pintores favoritos son Goya y Velázquez.

Hasta ahora, su único lujo[11] ha sido[12] la ópera. No se pierde ni[13] una representación. Ahora que tiene un poco de dinero, va a poder realizar finalmente uno de sus sueños:[14] visitar los grandes teatros del mundo, como la Escala de Milán, el Metropolitano de Nueva York o el teatro Colón de Buenos Aires. ¿Ya tiene el viaje planeado? ¿Va a ver a Raquel en la Argentina?

[1]*simple* [2]*desde... for many years* [3]*unexpected* [4]*de... about himself* [5]*alone* [6]*ironed* [7]*no... he can't stand* [8]*a... in spite of* [9]*se... you get to know him well* [10]*Ha... He has read* [11]*luxury* [12]*ha... has been* [13]*No... He never misses even* [14]*dreams*

 Actividad B.

Now return to statements 1–8 and make any changes in your answers that you feel are necessary. Which statements do you still have to answer **no sé**? Listen to the cassette tape, on which the speaker will give you some answers and then provide some more information.

● ●

GRAMÁTICA

 27. *SOY MEXICOAMERICANA*: USING ADJECTIVES (PART 2)

You have heard adjectives used in conversation and narration since the first episode of *Destinos*. In **Lección 4** you learned some patterns according to which adjectives change their form to agree with the noun they modify. In subsequent lessons you worked with specific types of adjectives—possessive, demonstrative—that also agree in number and gender. In this section you will learn more about adjective agreement and practice using adjectives to describe people.

Here is some review and new information about the patterns by which adjectives agree with nouns.

● Remember that adjectives that end in **-ista** have only a singular form and a plural form (**-istas**).

Velázquez fue un pintor **realista**. Pintó la realidad.

Raquel es **optimista**. Cree que va a encontrar a Rosario en la Argentina.

The same is also true for any adjective whose singular form ends in -a, for example, **hipócrita.**

- Adjectives of nationality that end in -o have four forms. Adjectives of nationality that end in a consonant also have four forms.

	MASCULINE	FEMININE	MASCULINE	FEMININE
Singular	mexicano	mexicana	español	española
Plural	mexicanos	mexicanas	españoles	españolas

- When an adjective modifies both a masculine noun and a feminine noun, the form of the adjective is masculine.

> Ramón y Mercedes son **mexicanos.**
> Miguel Ruiz y Elena Ramírez son **españoles.**

Actividad A. ¿De quién se habla?

Indicate who is being described in each of the descriptions you will hear. ¡OJO! Many of the adjectives you will hear end in -a because they agree with the word **persona,** which is feminine. Don't assume that a woman is being described.

1. Rosario/don Fernando
2. Teresa Suárez/Manuel Díaz
3. Miguel Ruiz padre/Elena Ramírez

Actividad B. ¿Cómo son?

Complete each sentence with all of the appropriate adjectives. Pay attention to the adjective endings as well as to the meaning of the adjectives.

1. Raquel es... inteligente / alto / jóvenes / guapa
   Tiene... pelo rubio / pelo castaño / ojos muy oscuros / ojos claros
2. La señora Suárez es... grandes / vieja / bonito / baja / simpático / un poco gordita
   Tiene... pelo negro / pelo blanco
3. Alfredo Sánchez es... pequeños / curioso / ambicioso / persistente
   Tiene... pelo largo / pelo corto / barba

Now check your answers on the cassette tape.

Actividad C. ¿De dónde son?

Match the characters on the left with the ethnic descriptions on the right. Only one match is possible for each. Pay attention to the adjective endings as well as to the meaning of the adjectives.

1. _b_ Raquel es...
2. _h_ Ramón, Carlos y Juan Castillo son...
3. _f_ Mercedes es...
4. _g_ Teresa Suárez es...
5. _a_ Miguel Ruiz y Elena Ramírez son...
6. _e_ El segundo esposo de Rosario es...
7. _c_ Jaime Ruiz es...
8. _d_ Juanita y Maricarmen son...

a. españoles
b. mexicoamericana
c. español
d. mexicanas
e. argentino
f. mexicana
g. española
h. mexicanos

Actividad D. ¿Y estas otras personas famosas?

Now the people are historical figures from around the world. Can you find their nationalities? Once again, only one match is possible for each.

Scan the list of nationalities first. All of them are close cognates with English except one, **alemán**. The following sentence contains information that will help you guess its meaning: **En la Segunda Guerra mundial, Alemania, Italia y el Japón lucharon contra Francia, Inglaterra, la Unión Soviética y los Estados Unidos.** Now can you guess what **alemán** means?

The adjectives of nationality listed in this activity are not considered active vocabulary that you must memorize. Just learn those that are useful to you for describing your family, spouse, friends, and so on.

1. Madame Curie	portugués
2. el rey Enrique VIII (octavo) y la reina Elizabeth I (primera)	chino
3. el zar Nicolás y la zarina Alejandra	rusos
4. Clara Barton y Carry Nation	francesa
5. el explorador Vasco da Gama (¡OJO! Es de la Península Ibérica, pero no es español.)	norteamericanas alemanes
6. el filósofo Nietzsche y el compositor Beethoven	japonés
7. el pintor y escultor Miguel Ángel (¿Reconoces su nombre? Miguel = *Michael*. Pintó una capilla muy famosa en el Vaticano.)	italiano ingleses
8. el gran filósofo Confucio	
9. el famoso director de cine Kurosawa	

Actividad E. ¿Y tú?

Think about someone you know well—male or female—and that you would like to describe. Use the following questions as a guide for your description. (Worksheet)

HOMBRE

1. ¿Es alto, bajo o de estatura mediana?
2. ¿Tiene pelo largo? ¿pelo corto? ¿de qué color?
3. ¿Tiene ojos claros? ¿ojos oscuros?
4. ¿Es delgado? ¿gordito?
5. ¿Es joven? ¿viejo?
6. ¿Es guapo? ¿inteligente? ¿optimista? ¿simpático? ¿____?
7. ¿Es norteamericano? ¿____?
8. Es mi _____.

MUJER

1. ¿Es alta, baja o de estatura mediana?
2. ¿Tiene pelo largo? ¿pelo corto? ¿de qué color?
3. ¿Tiene ojos claros? ¿ojos oscuros?
4. ¿Es delgada? ¿gordita?
5. ¿Es joven? ¿vieja?
6. ¿Es guapa? ¿inteligente? ¿optimista? ¿simpática? ¿____?
7. ¿Es norteamericana? ¿____?
8. Es mi _____.

28. ¿CÓMO ESTÁS? ¿QUIÉN ERES?: EXPRESSING *ser*; MORE ABOUT THE VERB *estar*

As you listen to the following summary of aspects of *Destinos*, think about the ways in which the verbs **ser** and **estar** are used in it.

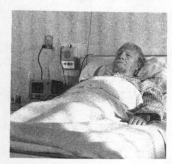

Raquel Rodríguez **es**[1] abogada. **Es**[2] de los Estados Unidos, de Los Ángeles, y **es**[3] mexicoamericana. **Está**[4] en España ahora porque investiga un caso.... El caso **es**[5] el secreto de su cliente.

Don Fernando Castillo Saavedra **es**[6] el cliente de Raquel. **Es**[7] un hacendado mexicano que **está**[8] muy mal. **Está**[9] en el hospital. ¿Y el secreto? **Es**[10] sobre su primera esposa.... Para don Fernando, **es**[11] muy importante encontrar a Rosario.

Después de su investigación en España, Raquel ya sabe muchos detalles del caso. Va a la Argentina ahora y lleva una carta. La carta **es**[12] de la señora Suárez; **es**[13] para Rosario. **Son**[14] las cinco y el vuelo de Raquel sále en quince minutos. ¿Va a encontrar a Rosario? Raquel **es**[15] persistente... ¡y **es**[16] muy curiosa!

Forms

In previous lessons of *Destinos* you have learned information about how **ser** and **estar**, two Spanish verbs that express *to be*, are used. Here are the complete present-tense conjugations of both verbs. Some of the forms of **estar** will be new to you.

ser		estar	
soy	somos	estoy	estamos
eres	sois	estás	estáis
es	son	está	están

Uses

You have used **ser** and **estar** so far to perform the following functions. Look back at the two paragraphs at the beginning of this section and indicate which function they demonstrate by writing the numbers in the appropriate blank.

- Uses of **ser**

  a. _____ to identify people and things (*noun = noun*)
  b. _____ with adjectives, to describe basic, inherent characteristics (*noun = adjective*)
  c. _____ to express nationality (*noun = adjective of nationality*)
  d. _____ with **de**, to express origin (**de** + *place*)
  e. _____ with **para**, to tell for whom something is intended (*noun* = **para** _____)
  f. _____ to tell time (**es/son la[s]**...)
  g. _____ with **de**, to express possession (*noun* = **de** _____)
  h. _____ to form many generalizations (**es** + *adjective*)

- Uses of **estar**

  a. _____ with **en**, to tell where someone or something is located (*noun* + **está** + **en** _____)
  b. _____ to talk about how someone is feeling (_____ **está bien/mal**)

- ¡OJO! Remember that *there is/there are* is expressed in Spanish with **hay**.

Hay un secreto. El secreto está en una carta.	*There is a secret. The secret is in a letter.*
Hay un problema. Teresa Suárez ya no está en Sevilla.	*There is a problem. Teresa Suárez is no longer in Sevilla.*

Actividad A.   ¿Tienes buena memoria?

Here are brief descriptions of some of the *Destinos* characters. You haven't heard or seen some of them much recently. Match the descriptions with the characters.

1. _____ Es viejo y está muy mal.
2. _____ Es abogado y está con don Fernando, en el hospital.
3. _____ Es mexicoamericana y está en Madrid ahora.
4. _____ Es artesano—fabrica guitarras—y es joven.
5. _____ Es maestro, pero no está con sus estudiantes ahora.
6. _____ Es reportero y es muy curioso y persistente, especialmente cuando hay un misterio.
7. _____ Es guía turístico y está en Sevilla, donde hay muchos monumentos históricos.
8. _____ Es hombre de negocios. Es de México pero está en Miami.
9. _____ Es de Jaime y es negro.
10. _____ Es de Nueva York, pero su esposo es de México.

a. Pati
b. Alfredo Sánchez
c. Osito
d. don Fernando
e. Raquel
f. Pedro Castillo
g. Manuel Díaz
h. Miguel Ruiz
i. Federico
j. Carlos

Actividad B.   Lección de geografía

Combine elements from each column to form logical statements. There is more than one possible answer for some items. (Worksheet)

1. España y Portugal	es	la capital de España
2. Andalucía	son	en la Península Ibérica
3. El Alcázar	está	dos lenguas

4. El Prado y el Parque del Retiro — están — en Madrid
5. el catalán y el gallego — en el sur de España
6. Madrid — una comunidad autónoma
en Sevilla
un monumento de gran interés histórico

Actividad C.   Estereotipos

Stereotyping is generally not encouraged, but it is acceptable in this activity. Form as many sentences as you can about the following groups of people. You will be describing what you feel to be the basic, inherent characteristics of people who belong to the group. Be sure to make each adjective agree with the noun you are describing. (Worksheet)

1. los políticos
2. los abogados
3. los hombres de negocios
4. las mujeres de negocios
5. los artistas
6. los atletas
7. los científicos
8. los actores y las actrices

valiente, materialista, idealista, hipócrita, popular, cruel, realista, temperamental, sensible (*sensitive*), ¿____? honesto, serio, cómico, sincero, vicioso, guapo, agresivo, mentiroso (*lying*), bueno, cariñoso, ¿____?

 ## Actividad D.   ¿Y tú?

Paso 1

The speaker on the tape will ask you a series of questions. But first, listen as the speaker asks another person the same questions. Listening carefully to the answers will help you when the speaker addresses you directly.

1. ¿Cómo te llamas?
2. ¿De dónde eres? (nación, ciudad)
3. ¿Cuál es tu nacionalidad?
4. ¿Eres estudiante? ¿de qué?
5. ¿Dónde (¿En qué universidad) estudias?
6. ¿Cómo eres? (= ¿Qué tipo de persona eres?)
7. ¿Cómo estás hoy?
8. ¿Dónde estás en este momento?

Now indicate the statement that best describes the person who answered the questions.

a. ____ Es un estudiante norteamericano, de Los Ángeles, que estudia en México.
b. ____ Es un estudiante mexicano, de la capital, México, D. F., que estudia en California.

Paso 2

Now the speaker will ask you the same questions. Answer with real information about yourself, and try not to look back at the questions.

29. ¡NOS ACOSTAMOS TARDE Y NOS LEVANTAMOS TARDE!: FIRST- AND SECOND-PERSON PLURAL FORMS OF STEM-CHANGING VERBS (PRESENT TENSE) AND REFLEXIVE PRONOUNS

Aquí en esta universidad estudiamos mucho. Pero los sábados y domingos, los días del fin de semana, nuestra rutina es diferente. Los sábados **nos levantamos** muy tarde. Estudiamos un poco por la tarde, pero luego, por la noche, salimos a la calle o vamos a fiestas. **Nos acostamos** tarde y al día siguiente **nos despertamos** tarde.

Forms

Here are the first-person plural (**nosotros**) and second-person plural (**vosotros**) forms for the stem-changing verbs and reflexive pronouns with which you have been working since **Lección 8**. Note that the stem vowel does not change in these forms; it is identical to the stem vowel of the infinitive, just as in regular verbs. The pronouns used with these forms are **nos** and **os**, respectively.

As happens with regular verbs, the form used with **Uds.** is identical to the third-person plural form, where the stem change does occur. In the following chart the stem given is for first- and second-person plural forms.

INFINITIVE	STEM	**nosotros**	**vosotros**	**Uds.**
Group 1	e in the infinitive stem = e in the conjugated stem			
empezar	empez-	empezamos	empezáis	empiezan
despertarse	despert-	nos despertamos	os despertáis	se despiertan

Other verbs in this group: **pensar, perder, querer, sentarse.**

Group 2	e in the infinitive stem = e in the conjugated stem			
pedir	ped-	pedimos	pedís	piden
sentirse	sent-	nos sentimos	os sentís	se sienten

Other verbs in this group: **despedirse, seguir, vestirse.**

Group 3	o in the infinitive stem = o in the conjugated stem			
contar	cont-	contamos	contáis	cuentan
dormirse	dorm-	nos dormimos	os dormís	se duermen

Other verbs in this group: **acordarse, acostarse, encontrar, morir, poder, recordar, volver.**

Other verbs used reflexively that you have learned so far and that are *not* stem-changing include **casarse, levantarse, llamarse,** and **olvidarse.**

Uses

- Remember that the pronoun precedes conjugated verb forms and may follow and be attached to an infinitive.

> TERESA: ¿Cuándo **os** casáis, por fin?
> FEDERICO: Mamá, ya lo sabes. **Nos** gustaría casar**nos** este verano. A mí me gustaría casar**me** más pronto.

Actividad A. ¿Quién habla?

Who might make each of the following statements?

1. _____ Fernando y yo seguimos la investigación de Raquel con mucho interés.
2. _____ Mi esposo y yo pensamos ir a Madrid para la Navidad.
3. _____ Nos casamos más pronto si encontramos un apartamento que nos guste (*is pleasing*) a los dos.
4. _____ Jaime y yo siempre le pedimos dinero a papá para ir al cine.
5. _____ Pedro y yo siempre recordamos nuestra infancia (*childhood*) en España.
6. _____ Nunca nos olvidamos de mi mamá.

a. don Fernando
b. Miguel hijo
c. Pedro
d. Miguel padre
e. Elena Ramírez
f. Federico

Actividad B. Pati y Juan

Complete the following description of a typical day in the life of this Castillo family couple, taking the perspective of Pati. Infinitives appear to the right of the line on which they are used.

Juan y yo vivimos muy ocupados. Ésta es nuestra rutina. _____¹ temprano,ᵃ a las siete, y   **despertarse**

_____² inmediatamente. ¡No hay tiempo que perder! _____³ rápidamente. No es   **levantarse, vestirse**

necesario _____⁴ con elegancia para ir a la universidad... .   **vestirse**

    Generalmente _____⁵ juntos,ᵇ pero un desayuno muy ligero.ᶜ Yo tomo café y Juan toma café   **desayunar**

con leche, nada más. Hablamos poco... yo por lo menosᵈ hablo poco—no me gusta _____⁶ y   **levantarse**

generalmente estoy de mal humor hasta las nueve o las nueve y media. En cambio,ᵉ Juan... . Pero ésa es

otra historia.

    Salimos a la calle y _____.⁷ Juan va a la universidad en autobús y yo tomo el metro para llegar   **despedirse**

al teatro. Trabajamos en diferentes partes de la ciudad, desgraciadamente. _____⁸ buscar un   **querer**

apartamento más céntrico para los dos, pero... no hay tiempo.

    No _____⁹ a casa hasta la noche, más o menos a las siete. Nos gusta tomar algo para   **volver**

relajarnos—un tequila o ron—y nos _____¹⁰ los detalles del día. Luego _____¹¹ a cenar   **contar, sentarse**

juntos.

    Después _____¹² a preparar las cosas para el día siguiente. Vemos la televisión y luego   **empezar**

_____,¹³ a las diez y media o a las once. _____¹⁴ inmediatamente—¡en eso somos   **acostarse, dormirse**

igualesᶠ! Pero por las mañanas, ¡ay!

ᵃ*early*   ᵇ*together*   ᶜ*light*   ᵈpor... *at least*   ᵉEn... *On the other hand*   ᶠ*the same*

 Now check your answers by listening to the cassette tape.

Actividad C. ¿Y tú?

What is the daily routine in your family, at your house or apartment where you live, or in your dorm? Is your routine like Juan and Pati's? Listen to the questions you hear on the tape and answer them, using **nosotros** forms, to express what generally happens where you live. The answer you hear will always be different from what Juan and Pati do. Use the answer to check the verb form you used.

MODELO: (*you hear*)   Juan y Pati tienen una rutina muy ocupada. ¿Y Uds.?
             (*you say*)   Nosotros tenemos una rutina muy ocupada también.
             (*or*)   Nosotros no tenemos una rutina muy ocupada.
             (*you hear*)   Nosotros no tenemos una rutina muy ocupada.

1. ...　2. ...　3. ...　4. ...　5. ...　6. ...　7. ...　8. ...

• •

PRONUNCIACIÓN: *c* AND *qu*

The Spanish [k] sound is like English [k], but it is not aspirated; that is, no puff of air accompanies its pronunciation. Compare the following pairs of English words in which the first [k] sound is aspirated and the second is not.

      can/scan   cold/scold   kit/skit

Spanish [k] is always written as **qu** before **e** and **i**. In all other cases it is written as **c**. The letter **k** appears only in words that are borrowed from other languages.

Actividad A.
Repeat the following words, imitating the speaker.

1. ¿qué? ¿quién? aquí porque quiero queremos quisiera
2. casa corto castaño curioso comprar
   recuerda oscuro busca acuesta doctor
3. kilo kilogramo kerosén kilómetro karate

Actividad B.
Repeat the following sentences, imitating the speaker. Pay close attention to intonation.

1. ¿Quién quiere correr en el parque?
2. ¿De qué color es tu corbata?
3. Ricardo tiene pelo castaño y corto.
4. Carmen tiene ojos oscuros.

Have you completed the following sections of the lesson? Check them off here.

_____ **Más allá del episodio**   _____ **Pronunciación**
_____ **Gramática**

Now scan the words in the **Vocabulario** list to be sure that you understand the meaning of most of them.

• •

VOCABULARIO

Los verbos
estar (estoy)   to be

Los adjetivos
simpático/a   nice, pleasant

Las palabras adicionales
tarde   late
temprano   early

Now that you have completed the Textbook and Workbook for **Lección 10**, take the Self-Test for that lesson. (It is on page 262.) Remember to listen to the tape when you see the cassette symbol and to check your answers.

_____ **Self-Test**

Now that you have worked through the Textbook and the Workbook and taken the Self-Test, here are some of the things you have accomplished in Spanish.

• You can wish someone a pleasant trip in Spanish.
• You can use a variety of words and phrases to describe people.
• You have reviewed what you have learned so far about expressing *to be* in Spanish.
• You can describe what you and others do together.
• You know how to spell the Spanish [k] sound.
• You have continued to work on listening skills.

You are now ready to continue on with **Lección 11** in the Textbook.

11
LA DEMORA

OBJETIVOS

Whereas the materials in the Textbook all had to do with the video segment, the materials in the Workbook will help you expand your knowledge of the Spanish language in general, as well as give you opportunities for self-expression in Spanish. In this lesson you will review

• stem-changing and reflexive Spanish verbs, as well as more irregular verbs
• the use of numbers and adjectives
• ways to ask questions
• vocabulary groups such as clothing, colors, months, and seasons.

Remember to listen to the tape for **Lección 11** when you see the cassette symbol and to check your answers in Appendix 1.

GRAMÁTICA

30. *RESUMEN:* PRESENT-TENSE FORMS OF STEM-CHANGING VERBS

As you know, the stem vowel of some Spanish verbs changes in the present tense. The change occurs in a predictable pattern, always when the stem vowel receives the stress (emphasis in speaking). Think about where (in which persons of the present-tense conjugation) the stem change occurs and indicate the change with an X in the following chart.

yo form	_____	**nosotros/as** form	_____
tú form	_____	**vosotros/as** form	_____
Ud. form	_____	**Uds.** form	_____
él/ella form	_____	**ellos/ellas** form	_____

Here are the forms of the stem-changing verbs with which you have worked so far. Can you complete the table?

INFINITIVE	STEM	CHANGE	COMPLETE CONJUGATION	
empezar	empez-	e → ie	empiezo	empezamos
			emp_ie_zas	emp_E_záis
			emp_ie_za	empiezan
pedir	ped-	e → i	p_ue_do	p_o_dimos
			pides	pedís
			p_i_de	piden
contar	cont-	o → ue	cuento	c_o_ntamos
			cuentas	contáis
			c_ue_nta	c_ue_ntan

31. *RESUMEN*: REFLEXIVE PRONOUNS

Here are the forms of two verbs generally used with reflexive pronouns. Can you complete the table with the appropriate pronouns?

casarse		acostarse	
me caso	nos casamos	_me_ acuesto	_nos_ acostamos
te casas	_vosotros_ casáis	_te_ acuestas	os acostáis
ud el ella casa	se casan	se acuesta	_se_ acuestan

Remember that a verb can be both stem-changing and used reflexively, such as **acostarse**. When a verb is used with the reflexive pronouns, it will be given in vocabulary lists with **-se: casarse**. You will learn more about verbs of this type in **Lección 13**.

32. *RESUMEN*: PRESENT-TENSE FORMS OF VERBS WITH IRREGULARITIES

You have already learned the present-tense forms of most common verbs in Spanish that have irregularities. Review what you know by supplying the indicated forms in the following chart. Can you also give the meaning of each infinitive?

conocer	yo	conozco	él	conoce
dar	yo	day	Uds.	dan
decir	yo	digo	nosotros	decimos
estar	yo	estoy	ellos	estan
hacer	yo	hago	vosotros	haaes
ir	yo	voy	nosotros	vamos
oír	yo	oyo	Ud.	oye
poner	yo	pongo	ella	pone
saber	yo	se	tú	sabes
salir	yo	salgo	nosotros	salimos

ser	yo	_Soy_		ellos	_Son_
tener	yo	_Tengo_		Ud.	_Tiene_
traer	yo	_Traego_		tú	_Traes_
venir	yo	_Vengo_		Uds.	_Vienen_
ver	yo	_Veo_		nosotros	_Vemos_

Note in particular that the yo forms of all of these verbs are irregular; other forms may or may not be irregular, depending on the verb. If you wish to review the complete conjugations, look them up in Appendix 2.

Actividad A.   ¿Qué pronombre?

Match the subject pronouns on the right with the sentences on the left. ¡OJO! More than one pronoun may be appropriate for some sentences.

1. _d_ Nos despedimos en la Plaza Mayor, después de cenar.
2. _cg_ Se acuesta y se duerme en seguida en su habitación del hotel.
3. _a_ Veo los cuadros de los maestros de la pintura española en el Prado.
4. _hf_ Quieren casarse pronto... este verano, si es posible.
5. _a_ No estoy muy bien. Por eso estoy en el hospital.
6. _b_ ¿Quieres venir mañana a mi taller?
7. _cg_ Tiene muchas preguntas que hacerme sobre el premio.
8. _a_ Voy a darle a esta abogada una carta para Rosario.
9. _fh_ ¿Por qué no se sientan a hablar?
10. _cg_ Trae un jerez para las dos señoras.

a. yo
b. tú
c. él, ella
d. nosotros/nosotras
e. vosotros/vosotras
f. ellos, ellas
g. Ud.
h. Uds.

¡Un desafío! Can you tell who might have made each of the preceding statements or whom they are about?

Actividad B.   La tarjeta de Raquel

Seated on a bench in the Parque del Retiro during her last day in Madrid, Raquel started to write a postcard to her parents and talked to you about aspects of her trip. Listen again to what she said and wrote; then complete the following version of her words as if you were Raquel. Choose the appropriate verb from the two given. Don't be distracted by unfamiliar verb forms; try to find the verb stem and determine the meaning from the context.

Queridos mamá y papá,

Aquí me (acostar/encontrar) _____[1] en un banco pensando[a] en otro viaje que (deber/tener) _____[2] que hacer. Esta vez, es a la Argentina.

No (esperar/poder) _____[3] creer que salga para la Argentina. Me gustaría (pasar/contar) _____[4] unos días más en Madrid. ¡Hay tanto que ver! Hoy fui[b] al Museo del Prado. Fue una verdadera experiencia. Vi[c] algunas obras de tres artistas españoles... . En el Museo del Prado vi al señor Díaz y también a Alfredo.

Ahora (ser/estar) _____[5] aquí en este hermoso parque. Bueno. (Volver/Deber) _____[6] terminar de escribir mis tarjetas. (Sacar/Salir) _____[7] para la Argentina a las cinco. Ojalá pueda[d] encontrar a Rosario y a su hijo en Buenos Aires.

[a]_thinking_   [b]_I went_   [c]_I saw_   [d]Ojalá... _I hope I can_

33. *RESUMEN*: USING ADJECTIVES

In the first eleven chapters of *Destinos* you have learned to understand and use Spanish adjectives of many different kinds: descriptive, demonstrative, possessive. Review what you know by completing the following chart.

	SINGULAR		PLURAL	
	Masculine	*Feminine*	*Masculine*	*Feminine*
rojo	rojo	roja	rojos	rojas
azul	azul	*azule*	azules	*azules*
realista	*rlsto*	realista	*realistas*	realistas
mexicano	mexicano	mexicana		
español	español			españolas
mi		mi	mis	
nuestro	nuestro			nuestras
este	este			estas

Actividad. Personas y lugares

Complete the following descriptions of people and places you have seen in the video segments.

Adjetivos: atractivo, educado, feo, imposible, posible

1. la señora Suárez, hablando[a] con Raquel: Una señorita como Ud. ... tan[b] ___atractiva___, bien ___educada___ ... ¡y abogada! Eso era casi[c] ___imposible___ cuando yo tenía su edad. Y ahora es tan corriente.[d]

Adjetivos: medieval, moderno, musical, secundario, típico, universitario

2. Las tunas son grupos ___musicales___ formados por estudiantes ___universitarios___. Las tunas[e] se visten con trajes ___medievales___ ... y tocan música ___típica___ de la España ___medieval___.

Adjetivos: bonito, expresivo, feo, pequeño

3. la señora Suárez, hablando de Osito: ¡Qué feo! No tiene los ojos ___bonitos expresivos___. A mí me gustan los perros con los ojos ___bonitos___ ... ojos ___expresivos___ .... Es ___feo___, es un perro ___feo___.

Adjetivos: grecorromano, grande, gris, neoclásico, pequeño

4. El Museo del Prado es un edificio de color ___gris___ ... de estilo ___neoclásico___ con figuras ___grecorromanas___ en las paredes[f] y con ___grandes___ columnas en la entrada.[g]

[a]*speaking* [b]*so* [c]*Eso... That was almost* [d]*common, usual* [e]*Las... The members of a tuna* [f]*walls* [g]*entrance*

Now check your answers by listening to the cassette tape.

UN POCO DE TODO

Actividad A. Oraciones originales

Create as many original sentences as you can in each group. If a subject is not appropriate for you, don't use it. Don't be limited to the verbs and verb phrases given here, and vary the days and seasons as appropriate. Use **no** as needed. (Worksheet)

Grupo 1: En mi familia / casa / apartamento / residencia (*dorm*)...

1. mi padre/madre	se levanta(n)	tarde/temprano
2. mi esposo/a	se acuesta(n)	juntos (*together*)
3. mi compañero/a	se duerme(n)	a la(s)...
4. mis compañeros	desayuna(n)	
5. mis hijos	cena(n)	

Grupo 2: ¿Y tú?

6. los lunes	quisiera	levantarme	(más) tarde
7. los sábados	me gustaría	acostarme	(más) temprano
8. los domingos	tengo que	dormirme	
	es mi costumbre	desayunar	pronto
	me gusta	cenar	otra vez

Actividad B. Lencería

Here is a laundry/cleaning form from Raquel's hotel in Madrid. Although the original form is in Spanish, French, and English—so as to accommodate the needs of the international clientele the hotel enjoys—only the Spanish portions of the form are given here. Scan them, trying not to focus on words and phrases that are unfamiliar to you. You may be surprised by how many words you can recognize. Then answer the questions that follow.

1. Find the Spanish equivalents for *women's clothing* and *men's clothing*. (*Hint:* Look for *women's clothing* first.)
2. Find the Spanish equivalents for the following:
   cleaning and pressing (*Hint:* Two phrases express this; one of them appears several times.)
   pressing (*Hint:* If you can find the equivalent for *cleaning and pressing*, you have found *pressing*.)
3. According to this form, how does one say *man's sweater* in Spain? *woman's sweater*?
4. Find the Spanish equivalents for the following:
   handkerchief (*Hint:* This word appears on both the men's and women's lists.)
   nightgown
   pajamas

ROPA DE CABALLERO	ROPA DE SEÑORA
Camisa	Sueter ....
Camiseta	Camisa de noche ....
Calzoncillo	Camiseta ....
Calcetines	Bragas ....
Pañuelo	Pañuelo ....
Pijama	Blusa, lavado o plancha.
Corbata, limpiar y plan- char	Medias ....
Pantalón, planchar	Bata ....
Pantalón, limpiar y plan- char	Pijama ....
Chaqueta, planchar	Sujetador ....
Chaqueta, limpiar y plan- char (o cazadora)	Combinación ....
	Vestido, planchar ....
Traje completo, planchar.	Pantalón o falda, lavar ...
Traje completo, limpiar y planchar	Pantalón o falda limpiar y planchar ....
Pantalón corto	Vestido, limpiar y plan- char ....
Jersey	Traje chaqueta, planchar.
	Traje chaqueta, limpiar y planchar ....

Los vestidos se lavarán bajo la responsabilidad del cliente. No somos responsables de
la ropa de color ni de la ropa que se encoja.

Las ropas deterioradas o manchadas, se lavarán sin responsabilidad alguna.

Actividad C. Recomendaciones del guía

Paso 1

Listen as a guide from a travel agency recommended by the Hotel Príncipe de Vergara describes a number of events that take place annually in Spain. Some—but not all—of them will be familiar to you. Give the month or season when each event takes place. ¡OJO! One holiday is not mentioned by the guide.

1. el Día de los Reyes Magos
2. la noche de San Juan
3. la fiesta de San Fermín
4. la feria de Sevilla

5. el Día de los Enamorados
6. el Día del Año Nuevo
7. la Navidad
8. la Semana Santa

Paso 2

Now it is your turn to play guide. Listen again to the descriptions of Madrid and Sevilla and of Castilla and Andalucía that you heard at the beginning of Episode 8. Then form as many sentences as you can about those two cities and regions, using information you have just heard or any other information you remember about them. Use the phrases given here as a guide. You may want to scan the **Nota cultural** on Sevilla in **Lección 4** before beginning this activity. (Worksheet)

Madrid	es	una ciudad moderna
Sevilla	está	en Andalucía
Castilla	tiene	una ciudad de muchas plazas
Andalucía	hay	la capital de España
en Madrid		muchas iglesias
en Sevilla		muchos monumentos históricos
en Castilla		el Barrio de Santa Cruz
en Andalucía		pueblos medievales
		vastos terrenos cultivados
		edificios modernos
		¿____?

Actividad D. La familia de Carlos IV (cuarto)

Here is a reproduction of Goya's painting of the family of Carlos IV, which you saw briefly in Episode 10. Using all of the words and phrases you know to describe people, create as many sentences as you can about this royal family. (Worksheet)

Actividad E. ¿Y tú?

What can you say about your own family? Select one member of your family and describe him/her as fully as you can. Use these questions and phrases as a guide. (Worksheet)

1. ¿Cómo se llama? ¿Dónde vive? ¿Con quién?
2. ¿Es joven o viejo? (¿Cuántos años tiene? [*How old is he/she?*])
3. ¿Cómo es físicamente?
4. ¿Cómo es su personalidad?
5. ¿Trabaja? ¿Dónde? ¿Le gusta trabajar?
6. ¿Cuál es su rutina diaria?

PARA ESCRIBIR

In this repeating section of the Workbook you will practice writing. You will narrate events (at first, in the present and, eventually, in the past), describe people and events, and express opinions about many things.

In this activity you will write a short narration in which you describe your daily routine to someone who is not familiar with it. You want to tell the reader as much as you can about what you do and also include some interesting information about yourself. Your narration should be no fewer than 150 and no more than 250 words long.

Thinking About What You Will Write

In order to write this narration, the first thing you must do is to think about what daily activities you will include. A good place to begin is in your Textbook and Workbook.

Look over the sections that have to do with verbs in **Lecciones 7–10** and the review sections in this lesson. You may also want to scan the **Vocabulario** sections in both your Textbook and Workbook. As you scan all of these sections, make a list of verbs that have to do with your daily routine. You will not necessarily use them all in your narration, but that is O.K. For the moment, you are just trying to create a bank of ideas from which to draw.

It may also be helpful to look back at **Actividad C** (page 76 of the Workbook). In that activity, you put events in order for a typical class day and noted the time that it took you to do some activities. Some of the work you did there may be useful to you as you work on this narration.

Organizing Your Thoughts

Now think about the order in which you will present your daily routine. You will probably choose a chronological order. What kind of day will you describe? A week-day on which you go to the university or to work? A Saturday or Sunday on which your routine may be substantially different from that of weekdays?

Drafting

Paso 1

Now draft your narration. At this stage, your should not worry about grammar and spelling. Your goal is to get your ideas down on paper.

Paso 2

After you have completed your draft, look over what you have done. Are you still satisfied with the activities you selected? Do you want to add some and delete others? Do you want to go into more detail about some aspects of your routine? Have you included at least one interesting detail about yourself or your life? Keep in mind that you are writing for someone who doesn't know anything about you.

Finalizing Your Narration

If you are satisfied with the information contained in your draft, it is time to look it over for language and style.

Paso 1

First, look at your narration, for style. Does the narration flow, or is it disjointed and choppy? Does it contain words and phrases that connect events, or is it mostly an accumulation of sentences?

Here is a list of words and phrases that can help make your narration flow more smoothly.

también	also		**por eso**	that's why; therefore
pero	but		**y**	and

These words and phrase can help you express the sequence of events in your routine smoothly.

primero	first		**después**	later (on)
luego	then, next		**por fin**	finally
por la mañana	in the morning		**por la noche**	in the evening
por la tarde	in the afternoon			

Paso 2
Review your composition for the following language elements as well.

_____ gender of nouns
_____ adjective agreement
_____ agreement of subjects and verbs

Paso 3
Prepare a clean copy of the final version of your narration for your instructor.

Have you completed the following sections of the lesson? Check them off here.

_____ **Gramática**   _____ **Para escribir**

_____ **Un poco de todo**

There is no Self-Test for this lesson of the Textbook and Workbook. In preparation for a unit test or just as a general review, it would be a good idea to scan back over the Self-Tests in the previous four lessons. Then you will be ready to continue on with **Lección 12** in the Textbook.

12
REVELACIONES

MÁS ALLÁ DEL EPISODIO

Actividad A.   Martín Iglesias

You know that, according to Teresa Suárez, Rosario married **un gran hacendado**. But you really don't know much about him yet. Here is a series of statements about Rosario's second husband, Martín Iglesias. Express your reactions by choosing from the following statements.

a. Es probable.   c. Es improbable.
b. No sé.

1. ____ Martín Iglesias era el dueño (*owner*) de una gran estancia cerca de Buenos Aires.
2. ____ Rosario conoció a Martín en Buenos Aires.
3. ____ Ella se enamoró de (*fell in love with*) él inmediatamente.
4. ____ Martin ayudó a Rosario a encontrar trabajo en Buenos Aires.
5. ____ Ángel no tuvo (*didn't have*) problemas en aceptar a Martín como su padre.
6. ____ Rosario se fue de Buenos Aires por razones políticas.

The answers you have given are based solely on the very small amount of information about Martín Iglesias that you have at this point. The following reading passage offers more information. Read it and see whether you wish to change any answers. As you read, you will probably note many preterite tense verb forms as well as other past tenses. Not all of these forms are glossed for you. Pay attention to the verb stem and try to let the stem and context determine meaning.

Martín Iglesias tenía[1] una estancia próspera en su país, la Argentina. Cuando terminó la Guerra Civil española, Martín era joven y muy trabajador.[2] Vio en España una gran oportunidad. Pensó que los productos de su estancia tendrían[3] un buen mercado allí. Por eso se fue a España, primero a Madrid y luego a Barcelona.

Martín tenía también otro motivo para viajar a España. Quería buscar a una hermana de su madre que vivía en Sevilla. Sólo tenía una vieja dirección y el nombre del hospital en que su tía trabajaba antes de la guerra. Llegó a la casa de la dirección, pero nadie conocía a esa señora. Uno de los vecinos[4] le dio la dirección del hospital. Fue allí, en ese mismo hospital, donde Martín conoció a Rosario.

Rosario ayudó a Martín a buscar a la hermana de su madre. Desde el principio[5] a Rosario le gustó mucho la manera de ser del argentino. También comprendió muy bien su búsqueda.[6] ¡Ella sabía mucho de búsquedas imposibles! Desgraciadamente, después de varios días, descubrieron que la tía de Martín había muerto. Su familia vivía ahora en el sur de Francia.

Martín ya no tenía motivos para estar más tiempo en Sevilla. Empezaba a hacer los preparativos para regresar a la Argentina. Y pasaba mucho tiempo—todo el tiempo que podía—con Rosario.

Martín era muy serio y algo estricto, pero tenía un gran corazón. Rosario le habló de sus cosas, de su pasado,[7] de su hijo... y Martín la escuchó con atención. Comprendió que el corazón de su amiga estaba lleno de dolor.[8] Ella no podía olvidar... todavía. Pensó que un gran cambio[9] sería una buena idea. Martín le habló mucho de su país y de su familia. Trató de[10] convencerla. «Estoy seguro[11] de que podés rehacer[12] tu vida en la Argentina» le repetía varias veces. «Te vas a sentir como en casa.»

Por fin Martín tuvo que volver. Rosario pensó mucho en las cosas que Martín le había dicho.[13] Por fin decidió irse a la Argentina, con su hijo. Le escribió una larga carta a Martín y se embarcó. Cuando llegó a Buenos Aires, Rosario no pudo contener las lágrimas[14] cuando vio a Martín. Por primera vez en mucho tiempo lloraba de alegría.[15] Pero ¿cómo reaccionó Ángel? ¿Le gustó la Argentina? ¿Aceptó a Martín?

Martín Iglesias, poco antes de morir

[1]*had* [2]*hardworking* [3]*would have* [4]*neighbors* [5]*Desde... From the beginning* [6]*search, quest* [7]*past* [8]*estaba... was filled with pain* [9]*change* [10]*Trató... He tried to* [11]*sure* [12]*remake, make over* [13]*le... had told her* [14]*no... couldn't hold back her tears* [15]*lloraba... she was crying for joy*

 Actividad B.

Now return to statements 1–6 in **Actividad A** and make any changes in your answers that you feel are necessary. Which statements do you still have to answer with **No sé**? Listen to the speaker on the cassette tape, who will give you some answers and provide additional information.

● ●

GRAMÁTICA

34. *ÁNGEL NUNCA VOLVIÓ A BUENOS AIRES*: THIRD-PER-SON FORMS OF REGULAR VERBS (PRETERITE TENSE)

En Buenos Aires, Raquel **conoció** a Arturo, el medio hermano de Ángel. Según Arturo, Ángel **abandonó** sus estudios y se **dedicó** a la pintura. Luego se **embarcó** como marinero y **salió** de Buenos Aires. Los dos **perdieron** contacto hace muchos años.

Forms

In Spanish two simple tenses,* the preterite and the imperfect, are used to talk about the past. You have already heard and seen examples of both of them in the video, the Textbook, and the Workbook. For now, don't worry about the differences between the two tenses. In this and the next five lessons you will learn the forms and uses of the preterite. Then you will learn how to form and use the imperfect as well as how to use the two tenses together.

The preterite forms of regular verbs all have the primary stress on the ending, unlike present-tense forms. Here are the third-person preterite forms of some regular verbs. As with present-tense forms, the third-person endings are used with **Ud.** and **Uds.** as well.

INFINITIVE	STEM	él/ella/Ud.		ellos/ellas/Uds.	
contestar	contest-	-ó	contestó	-aron	contestaron
perder	perd-	-ió	perdió	-ieron	perdieron
vivir	viv-	-ió	vivió	-ieron	vivieron

Notice that the endings for **-er** and **-ir** verbs are identical.

Most stem-changing verbs, like **perder** in the preceding chart, do not show the stem change in the preterite, since the stress is on the ending. Here are some additional examples: **pensar: pensó, pensaron; volver: volvió, volvieron.** The **-ir** stem-changing verbs, however, do have changes in the preterite; you will learn about them in **Lección 17.**

A few verbs have spelling changes in some of their preterite forms. When the conjugated stem of an **-er** or **-ir** verb ends in a vowel, the third-person preterite forms usually change the **i** of the ending to a **y.** This is a spelling convention that does not affect the pronunciation of these regular verbs in the preterite. You have learned two verbs in this category.

INFINITIVE	STEM	él/ella/Ud.	ellos/ellas/Uds.
creer	cre-	creyó	creyeron
oír	o-	oyó	oyeron

Uses

- The preterite-tense forms of Spanish verbs usually correspond to the English verb form that ends in *-ed* or to the compound past tense formed with *did:*

  contestó = he/she/it/you answered, did answer
  vivieron = they/you lived, did live

  Remember, however, that many English verbs are irregular in the past, so the English equivalent may not always end in *-ed:*

  perdió = he/she/it/you lost, did lose

- Preterite forms are often used to express actions or events that happened once in the past as well as events that happened a specified number of times.

  ARTURO: Ángel **abandonó** sus estudios y **empezó** a pintar.

  ARTURO: *Ángel abandoned his studies and started to paint.*

  ARTURO: Un día **llegó** una carta para mi madre.

  ARTURO: *One day a letter arrived for my mother.*

---

*Simple tenses have only one verb form: (*I*) *am, speak, run.* Compound tenses have more than one verb form: (*I*) *have been, had spoken, did run.*

Can you give the English equivalents of the verbs in the brief paragraph with which this section begins?

Actividad A.   ¿Qué pasó?

Can you match the actions with the characters? ¡OJO! More than one answer is possible for some items.

1. ____ El recepcionista del hotel
2. ____ Raquel
3. ____ Raquel y el chofer
4. ____ En la estancia, un joven
5. ____ Cirilo

6. ____ Rosario y su hijo
7. ____ El doctor Iglesias
8. ____ Arturo Iglesias y Raquel
9. ____ Ángel Castillo
10. ____ A Martín Iglesias

a. le contó a Raquel que Rosario se mudó a Buenos Aires
b. vivieron en la calle Gorostiaga, según Cirilo
c. viajaron desde Buenos Aires a la estancia Santa Susana
d. contestó cordialmente las preguntas de Raquel
e. visitaron la tumba de Rosario y Martín Iglesias
f. le informó a Raquel que Rosario murió hace años (*years ago*)
g. abandonó sus estudios y se dedicó a pintar
h. buscó otra habitación para Raquel
i. no le gustó la decisión de su hijo
j. llegó al hotel y subió a su habitación

Actividad B.   La vida sigue en La Gavia

You will hear a series of sentences about activities that might have happened or might be happening at La Gavia. Indicate whether the action is Past or Present.

1. Past   Present
2. Past   Present
3. Past   Present
4. Past   Present
5. Past   Present

6. Past   Present
7. Past   Present
8. Past   Present
9. Past   Present
10. Past   Present

Actividad C.   ¿Recuerdas quién... ?

Listen to the actions described on the cassette tape and match them with the person(s) on the list who performed them. The items become progressively more challenging.

a. ____ Sean Penn y Madonna
b. ____ unos generales argentinos
c. ____ Martin Luther King
d. ____ Agatha Christie
e. ____ Cristóbal Colón

f. ____ Ronald y Nancy Reagan
g. ____ Huckleberry Finn
h. ____ Thomas Jefferson
i. ____ Pablo Picasso
j. ____ Rip Van Winkle

Actividad D.   La historia de Ángel

Complete the following version of Arturo's story of Ángel in Buenos Aires with the correct form of the verbs in the preterite.

Ángel y su madre Rosario (salir) _____[1] de España después de

la Guerra Civil. (Llegar) _____[2] a la Argentina y, dentro de poco,ᵃ

Rosario (casarse) _____[3] con Martín Iglesias. Los tres (vivir)

_____[4] en la estancia Santa Susana.

Pasaron los años y Ángel se fue a vivir a Buenos Aires. (Empezar) _____[5]

ᵃdentro... *very soon*

a estudiar Ciencias Económicas, como lo quería[b] su padrastro. Pero, Ángel pronto

(abandonar) _____[6] sus estudios y (dedicarse)

_____[7] a pintar.

    Una vez los padres de Ángel lo (visitar) _____[8] en Buenos Aires.

Martín (enterarse[c]) _____[9] de que lo que estaba haciendo.[d] Esa

noche Martín (sufrir) _____[10] un ataque cardíaco. Después de la

muerte de su esposo, Rosario (mudarse) _____[11] a Buenos Aires

con su hijo Arturo. Éste[e] nunca (perdonar) _____[12] a su hermano y,

por fin, los dos (perder) _____[13] contacto con él.

[b]como... *as wanted* [c]*to find out* [d]lo... *what he (Ángel) was doing* [e]*The latter*

Actividad E. ¿A quién conoces que... ?

Who do you know that fits the following descriptions? Think about people in your family or in your circle of friends, or even about famous individuals or people in the news. Then write complete sentences, with the verb in the preterite. If you don't know anyone who fits the description, answer with **No conozco a nadie** (*no one*). (Worksheet)

> MODELO: Una vez mi madre compró algo muy caro (*expensive*)... un reloj Cartier.

1. comprar algo muy caro
2. revelar un secreto importante
3. recibir una carta que cambió su vida
4. visitar a la Casa Blanca
5. viajar a otro estado/otro país (*country*)
6. conocer a una persona famosa
7. oír algo que le causó muchos problemas
8. dejar su país para vivir en otro lugar
9. perder algo importante
10. ver un partido (*game*) de la Serie Mundial

35. ¿UD. LA CONOCE? —CLARO QUE LA CONOZCO: TELLING WHOM OR WHAT: THIRD-PERSON DIRECT OBJECT PRONOUNS

A direct object is the first recipient of the action of a verb. What are the direct objects in these sentences?

> I see Tom.

> I gave Joe the money.

In the first sentence, *Tom* is the direct object. In the second, *money* is the direct object (=the *first* recipient of the action of the verb*).

    In the following brief dialogues the direct object nouns are replaced in the answers with direct object pronouns. This can be done because the direct object noun has already been mentioned.

> Do you see Tom? —Yes, I see *him*.

> Did you give Joe the money? —Yes, I gave *it* to him.

_____

*Note that *Joe* is not the direct object. In this sentence, *Joe* is the second recipient of the action of the verb *give*. First, I must get the money and only then can I give it to Joe.

Forms

In Spanish, the third-person direct object pronouns have forms that reflect both the number and gender of the noun to which they refer. These forms express the third-person English pronouns *him/her/it/them*, referring to people, places, or things.

SINGULAR		PLURAL	
Masculine	*Feminine*	*Masculine*	*Feminine*
lo	la	los	las

Tengo una *suite*.	*I have a suite.*
—Está bien. **La** tomo.	—*All right. I'll take it.*
EL CHOFER: Yo tengo un amigo en Los Ángeles. Se llama Carlos López. Claro, usted no **lo** conocerá, ¿no?	CHAUFFEUR: *I have a friend in Los Angeles. His name is Carlos López. Of course, you probably don't know him, do you?*
¿Las revelaciones de Raquel? Arturo **las** creyó después de leer la carta.	*Raquel's revelations? Arturo believed them after reading the letter.*

The third-person pronouns also express *you* when the **usted** form of address is used. When they mean *you*, they agree in number and gender with the person spoken to.

¿Usted busca a la señora Rosario?	*You're looking for Rosario?*
—Sí. ¿Usted **la** conoce?	—*Yes. Do you know her?*
—Claro que **la** conozco.	—*Of course I know her.*
¿Los padres de los niños? Raquel **los** quiere conocer. (Raquel quiere conocer**los**.)	*The children's parents? Raquel wants to meet them.*

Uses

- In the preceding examples, note that direct object pronouns follow the same rules of placement as reflexive pronouns. Direct object pronouns

  precede conjugated verb forms
  come in between **no** and a conjugated verb form
  may follow and be attached to an infinitive.

- Note in particular that, although the word *it* has no gender in English, it does in Spanish, so you must make it agree with the word it refers to in the sentence. The same is true when *them* (the plural of *it*) refers to things.

¿Usted sabe su nueva dirección?	*Do you know her new address?*
—Tal vez Cirilo **la** sepa.	—*Maybe Cirilo knows it.*
¿Sus estudios? Ángel **los** abandonó.	*His studies? Ángel abandoned them.*

- The pronoun **lo** often is used to refer back to an idea or concept that was previously mentioned. You have already heard this use of **lo** and will continue to hear it often in the video episodes.

¿A qué hora regresa el doctor?	*When will the doctor return?*
—No **lo** sé.	—*I don't know.*

Note in the preceding sentence that the word **lo** does not have an English equivalent.

Actividad A. ¿Qué pasó?

Paso 1

Answer the following questions about **Episodio 12** by indicating the appropriate direct object pronoun.

1. En el hotel, ¿tiene el recepcionista la reserva de Raquel?
   —No, no lo/la tiene.
2. En la estancia, ¿encontró Raquel a Rosario y Ángel?
   —No, no los/las encontró allí.
3. ¿Recordó Cirilo la nueva dirección de Rosario?
   —Sí, lo/la recordó, en parte.
4. ¿Creyó Arturo la historia de don Fernando?
   —Sí, lo/la creyó.
5. ¿Raquel conoció a los padres de Arturo?
   —No, no los/las conoció.
6. ¿Cuándo perdió Arturo a sus padres?
   —Los/Las perdió hace muchos años (*many years ago*).
7. ¿Adónde llevó Arturo a Raquel?
   —Lo/La llevó al cementerio, para ver la tumba de sus padres.
8. ¿Estudió Ángel la literatura española?
   —No, no lo/la estudió. Ángel estudió economía.
9. ¿Arturo perdonó a Ángel?
   —No, no lo/la perdonó.

Paso 2

Now listen while the speaker on the cassette tape asks you the questions. Read your answer, then listen to the correct answer.

Actividad B. ¡Un desafío!

What do the direct object pronouns refer to in these brief excerpts from **Episodio 12**?

1. RAQUEL: Está bien. **La** tomo.
2. JOVEN: Tal vez Cirilo **la** sabe.
3. CIRILO: Para mí es un gusto conocer**la**.
4. RAQUEL: ¿Usted **la** conoce?
   CIRILO: Claro que **la** conozco.
5. ARTURO: ¿En qué puedo servir**la**?
6. ARTURO: Yo nunca **lo** perdoné.

Actividad C. ¿Qué hace Raquel?

You will hear a series of questions on the cassette tape; here are the answers. Write the number of each question next to the appropriate answer. It is a good idea to scan the answers before you begin this activity.

a. _____ Sí, lo recuerda.
b. _____ Sí, los conoció.
c. _____ Sí, lo quiere encontrar.
d. _____ Sí, la toma.

e. _____ Sí, va a recordarlos.
f. _____ Sí, quiere encontrarla.
g. _____ No, no los conoció.

Actividad D. Hablando con Cirilo

You have already heard Raquel's conversation with Cirilo. Here is another version of it. Can you complete the conversation with the appropriate direct object pronouns?

RAQUEL: ¿Conoce usted a Rosario del Valle?

CIRILO: Sí, _____¹ conozco muy bien. Es muy buena persona.

RAQUEL: Necesito encontrar_____.²

CIRILO: Ah, se mudó a la capital y vive allí con su hijo.

RAQUEL: ¿Dónde _____³ puedo buscar? ¿Sabe usted la dirección de ellos?

CIRILO: No _____⁴ sé. El hijo es médico...

RAQUEL: ¿Sabe el nombre del hijo?

CIRILO: No, señorita, no _____⁵ sé. Déjeme*ª* pensar... Era*ᵇ* una casa blanca... en la calle Gorostiaga.

RAQUEL: Muchas gracias, señor. Mucho gusto en conocer_____.⁶

CIRILO: El gusto es mío, señorita.

ªLet me ᵇIt was

Actividad E. ¿Y tú?

Answer the following questions based on your own experiences or with your own opinions. Use direct object pronouns when possible in your answers. (Worksheet)

1. ¿Cómo practicas el español? ¿Cuándo lo practicas? ¿Lo hablas a veces con unos amigos?
2. ¿Hay un canal (*channel*) de televisión en español en tu ciudad? ¿Lo ves con frecuencia?
3. ¿Cuándo ves televisión? ¿por (*in*) la mañana? ¿por la tarde? ¿por la noche? ¿La ves con frecuencia? ¿demasiado (*too much*)?
4. ¿Dónde ves los episodios de *Destinos?* ¿en casa? ¿en clase? ¿en el laboratorio? ¿Los ves con alguien?
5. En el libro de texto, ¿siempre haces la sección que se llama **Preparación?** ¿Cuánto tiempo (*time*) necesitas para completar esa sección?
6. ¿Admiras a Raquel? ¿Te gustaría conocerla? ¿A quién más admiras en la serie? ¿A quién más te gustaría conocer?

NOTA CULTURAL: LOS PRONOMBRES *LE* Y *LO*

In Spain the pronoun **le** is often used instead of **lo** when referring to a male person. Thus, the sentence *I see him* can be expressed in two ways: **Le veo. Lo veo.** You have already heard this usage in the video episodes that took place in Spain, and you will occasionally hear it in upcoming shows as well. The preference for using **le** instead of **lo** is called **leísmo.**

You should also be aware that in natural, unedited speech many speakers of Spanish are not very exact in their use of object pronouns. It is best to try to determine the meaning of pronouns from context rather than analyze the specific pronouns used.

36. *MUY BUEN HOMBRE*: USING ADJECTIVES (PART 3)

Shortened Forms of Some Adjectives

When they come before a noun, the masculine singular forms of these adjectives drop the final -o: **bueno (buen), malo (mal), primero (primer), tercero (tercer)** (*third*). In all other positions the usual endings appear.

Arturo va a ser un **buen** amigo para Raquel.   *Arturo is going to be a good friend for Raquel.*

No es **mala** idea pero puede tener un **mal** resultado.   *It's not a bad idea but it can have a bad result.*

El **primer** esposo de Rosario fue don Fernando.

Rosario's first husband was don Fernando.

Buenos Aires es el **tercer** lugar que Raquel visita. Es decir, es la **tercera** ciudad.

The third place Raquel visits is Buenos Aires. That is, it's the third city.

As you learned in **Lección 10**, when the adjective **grande** precedes any singular noun, masculine or feminine, it too is shortened, to **gran**. Unlike the adjectives just presented, however, its meaning changes, to *great*. When **grande** follows the noun, it means *large* (referring primarily to size).

Buenos Aires es una **gran** ciudad pero también es una ciudad **grande**.

Buenos Aires is a great city but it is also a large city.

Adjectives and Adverbs

Note the difference betweeen these groups of words. The adjectives agree in gender and number with the nouns they modify. The adverbs are invariable in form.

ADJETIVOS	ADVERBIOS
buen(o), buena, buenos, buenas	bien
mal(o), mala, malos, malas	mal
mucho, muchas, muchos, muchas	mucho
poco, poca, pocos, pocas	poco

Actividad A. ¿Qué oyó Raquel?

Listen again to two brief segments of conversation from **Episodio 12**. Indicate the response you hear, then answer the questions.

1. CIRILO: Vea, moza... Ella vivía con el hijo, el doctor...

    RAQUEL: ¿El hijo es médico?

    CIRILO: _____

    a. ¡Claro, y muy bueno!
    b. ¡Claro, y muy buen hombre!

    c. ¡Claro, y muy gran hombre!

    What is Cirilo saying?

    a. Rosario's son is a big guy!

    b. Rosario's son is a great guy!

2. ARTURO: Señorita, usted está hablando de mi madre y de mi hermano.

    RAQUEL: ¿Su hermano?

    ARTURO: Sí, Ángel. Bueno, quiero decir, es mi medio hermano. Lleva el apellido de su padre, pero _____.

    a. el primer hijo de mi madre murió
    b. el tercer esposo de mi madre murió
    c. el primer esposo de mi madre murió

    What is Arturo saying?

    a. My mother's first son died.

    b. My mother's first husband died.

Actividad B. ¿Y tú?

Answer according to your own experience or your own opinions.

Da (*Give*) el nombre

1. de un buen restaurante en esta ciudad
2. de un mal programa de televisión
3. de una gran mujer de la historia mundial (*world*)
4. del primer hijo de Rosario
5. del tercer país de la serie *Destinos*
6. de dos libros muy buenos
7. de dos películas (*movies*) muy malas
8. de algo que haces mucho
9. de algo que haces poco
10. de algo que haces muy bien
11. de algo que haces muy mal

PRONUNCIACIÓN: *p* AND *t*

Like the Spanish [k] sound, the Spanish [p] and [t] are similar to English [p] and [t], but they are not aspirated. Compare the following pairs of English words in which the first [p] or [t] sound is aspirated and the second is not.

pin/spin   pan/span   tan/Stan   top/stop

Actividad A.
Repeat the following words, imitating the speaker.

1. padre   paciente   profesor   esperar   España   esposo
2. tarde   temprano   trabajar   estudio   historia   actividad

Actividad B.
Repeat the following sentences, imitating the speaker. Pay close attention to intonation.

1. Su primer esposo es pintor.
2. Piden poco por la pintura.
3. ¿Tienes que trabajar en el taller?
4. Estudian temas históricos.
5. También investigan teorías matemáticas.

Have you completed the following sections of the lesson? Check them off here.

_____ **Más allá del episodio**   _____ **Pronunciación**

_____ **Gramática**

Now scan the words in the **Vocabulario** list to be sure that you understand the meaning of most of them.

VOCABULARIO

Los verbos
abandonar   to abandon
dedicarse   to dedicate oneself

Los lugares
el país   country

Los adjetivos
mal(o), mala   bad
tercer(o), tercera   third

Las palabras adicionales
una vez   once

Now that you have completed the Textbook and Workbook for **Lección 12**, take the Self-Test for that lesson. (It is on page 266.) Remember to listen to the tape when you see the cassette symbol and to check your answers.

_____ **Self-Test**

Now that you have worked through the Textbook and the Workbook and taken the Self-Test, here are some of the things you have accomplished in Spanish.

- You know more about forms of address in different parts of the Spanish-speaking world.
- You can use and understand more numbers.
- You have begun to learn how to talk about past events in Spanish.
- You know how to express words such as *it, him, them*, and so on, in Spanish.
- You have learned more about using Spanish adjectives to describe people, places, and things.
- You know how Spanish **p** and **t** are pronounced.
- You have continued to improve your listening skills.

You are now ready to continue on with **Lección 13** in the Textbook.

13
LA BÚSQUEDA

OBJETIVOS

Wheras the materials in the Textbook all had to do with the video episode, the materials in the Workbook will help you expand your knowledge of the Spanish language in general, as well as give you opportunities for self-expression in Spanish. In this lesson you will learn

- more about using verbs to talk about what you and people you know well have done
- more about direct object pronouns, including some that refer only to people
- more about when to use reflexive pronouns and when not to
- how to pronounce Spanish **s, z, ce,** and **cl.**

Remember to listen to the tape for **Lección 13** when you see the cassette symbol and to check your answers in Appendix 1.

MÁS ALLÁ DEL EPISODIO

Actividad A.   Ángel Castillo

You know that Ángel is Rosario and don Fernando's child. But you really don't know much about him yet. Here is a series of statements about Ángel. Express your reactions by choosing from the following statements.

a.   Es probable.   c.   Es improbable.
b.   No sé.

1. __a__ Martín y Ángel nunca se llevaron (*got along*) bien.
2. __c__ Rosario nunca fue severa con su primer hijo.
3. __b__ Ángel fue un estudiante mediocre, pero siguió con sus estudios.
4. ____ Ángel frecuentaba (*used to spend a lot of time in*) el centro de la ciudad porque le fascinaban los edificios altos y los grandes monumentos.
5. ____ Se fue de Buenos Aires después de la muerte de Martín.
6. __a__ Se sintió culpable de (*felt guilty about*) la muerte de Martín.
7. __b__ Tuvo mucho éxito (*He had a lot of success*) en vender sus pinturas y dibujos (*drawings*).
8. __b__ Se casó poco después de salir de Buenos Aires.

The answers you have given are based solely on the very small amount of information about Ángel Castillo that you have at this point. The following reading passage offers more information. Read it and see whether you wish to change any answers. As you read, you will probably note many preterite-tense verb forms as well as other past tenses. Not all of these forms are glossed for you. Pay attention to the verb stem and try to let the stem and context determine the meaning.

Ángel Castillo, el hijo de don Fernando y Rosario

Ángel era[1] muy pequeño cuando su madre se casó con Martín Iglesias. Para el niño, la transición a la Argentina fue muy difícil: abandonar a sus amigos españoles, el largo viaje, la llegada a Buenos Aires, tener que adaptarse a otras costumbres...

Además[2] Ángel ya no era el único[3] rey de la casa. Nunca aceptó por completo a su nuevo padre. Martín era muy ordenado y algo estricto. Verdaderamente quiso[4] ser un buen padre, pero muchas cosas los separaba. Desde pequeño[5] Ángel fue muy inquieto y poco disciplinado. El nacimiento de su nuevo hermano fue otra cosa difícil de aceptar. Rosario no fue severa con él. Pensaba que sólo era cuestión de tiempo. Además... Ángel le recordaba a[6] su padre, a su primer esposo... ¡a Fernando!

Rosario y Martín tenían grandes planes para Ángel. El muchacho, sin embargo,[7] nunca fue un buen estudiante. La única materia que le gustaba era el dibujo. Pasaba horas y horas en la estancia pintando. Un día hizo un retrato[8] muy bonito de Cirilo tocando la guitarra. Todos admiraban su talento, pero para sus padres la pintura sólo era un pasatiempo.[9] Tenía que comenzar una carrera seria.

Ángel empezó entonces a estudiar Ciencias Económicas en la Universidad de Buenos Aires. Rápidamente se aburrió de[10] los estudios y volvió a su pasión, la pintura. Empezó a frecuentar el medio[11] artístico de la ciudad y a llevar una vida bohemia. Pintó mucho en esa época, especialmente las calles pintorescas de La Boca y el puerto. Los barcos le fascinaban. Trató de[12] vender sus cuadros, pero sin mucho éxito. Un día su familia descubrió su engaño.[13] Después de una violenta pelea[14] su padrastro murió. ¿Qué hizo entonces Ángel? ¿Es cierto lo que[15] cree Arturo?

[1]was [2]Besides [3]only [4]he tried [5]Desde... From a very young age [6]le... reminded her of [7]sin... nevertheless [8]hizo... he did a portrait [9]hobby [10]se... he got bored with [11]environment, culture [12]Trató... He tried to [13]deception [14]fight [15]lo... what

Actividad B.

Now return to statements 1–8 in **Actividad A** and make any changes in your answers that you feel are necessary. Which statements do you still have to answer with **No sé**? Listen to the speaker on the cassette tape, who will give you some answers and provide additional information.

• •

GRAMÁTICA

37. *ARTURO VOLVIÓ A SU CASA Y YO REGRESÉ AL HOTEL:* FIRST- AND SECOND-PERSON SINGULAR FORMS OF REGULAR VERBS (PRETERITE TENSE)

RAQUEL: **Llegué** a Buenos Aires y **tomé** un taxi a mi hotel. **Resolví** el problema con mi habitación y **subí** a una *suite*. **Descansé** y, al día siguiente, **salí** para la estancia Santa Susana.

Forms

You already know that the third-person preterite forms of regular verbs are formed by adding **-ó/-ió** for the singular and **-aron/-ieron** for the plural. Here are the endings for the first- (**yo**) and second-person (**tú**) preterite forms for regular verbs. Note that the **-ir** and **-er** verbs have the same endings. The Ud. forms are also given.

	contest*ar*	reconoc*er*	decid*ir*
	contest-	reconoc-	decid-
yo	contesté	reconocí	decidí
tú	contestaste	reconociste	decidiste
Ud.	contestó	reconoció	decidió

Some verbs undergo spelling changes when the -é ending (for first-person singular -**ar** verbs) is added; this is done to maintain the original sound of the stem's final consonant. There are three groups of -**ar** verbs that encounter such a change. As you read about them, remember the following:

Spanish [k] is written as **qu** before **e** or **i**
Spanish [g] is written as **gu** before **e** or **i**

• Verbs ending in -**car** change to -**qué**.

buscar: bus**qué**, buscaste, buscó...

• Verbs ending in -**gar** change to -**gué**.

llegar: lle**gué**, llegaste, llegó...

• Verbs ending in -**zar** change to -**cé**.

almorzar: almor**cé**, almorzaste, almorzó...

Here is a complete list of the verbs you already know that fall into these groups. Be sure you understand their meaning.

-**car:** buscar, dedicarse, explicar, sacar
-**gar:** investigar, llegar
-**zar:** almorzar, comenzar, empezar

Uses
Remember that preterite forms are often used to express actions or events that happened once in the past (as compared to repeated or habitual actions).

Empecé la búsqueda de Ángel con Arturo.	*I started the search for Ángel with Arturo.*
Yo **volví** al hotel y tú **volviste** a casa. Luego **llamé** a México.	*I returned to the hotel and you returned home. Then I called Mexico.*
¿**Encontraste** a Héctor?	*Did you find Héctor?*

Actividad A. ¿Quién lo dijo?
Did Raquel (R) or Arturo (A) make the following statements in **Episodio 13**?

R Ⓐ 1. Encontré esto entre las cosas de mi madre.
R Ⓐ 2. La última vez que vi a mi hermano, fue allí.
R Ⓐ 3. Estoy buscando a mi hermano con el cual (*whom*) perdí contacto hace muchos años.
R A 4. ¿Alguna vez probaste (*did you try*) la parrillada?
Ⓡ A 5. Después Arturo volvió a su casa y yo regresé al hotel.
Ⓡ A 6. Llamé a México y hablé con Pedro.

Actividad B. Antes de la búsqueda
The following sentences indicate what happened to Raquel in Argentina until the start of the search with Arturo, but they are out of order. Can you put them in chronological order, from 1 to 10?

a. _____ Conocí a Arturo y le expliqué la historia.
b. _____ Por la mañana, salí para la estancia Santa Susana.
c. _____ Subí a mi *suite* y comencé a contar (*count*) mi dinero.
d. _____ Le pregunté a Cirilo dónde vivía (*lived*) Rosario.
e. _____ Llegué a Buenos Aires y tomé un taxi a mi hotel.
f. _____ Busqué la dirección en la calle Gorostiaga.
g. _____ Descansé en la *suite* y dormí muy bien por la noche.
h. _____ Volví a la ciudad con el chofer.
i. _____ Él decidió ayudarme.
j. _____ El recepcionista me buscó otra habitación.

Now check your answers on the cassette tape.

Actividad C. ¿Qué pasó?

Paso 1

The following are questions that Pedro might have asked Raquel when she called to tell him the results of her investigation so far. Can you match them with the most logical answers?

1. _e_ ¿Cuándo llegaste a Buenos Aires?
2. _g_ ¿Cómo comenzaste la investigación?
3. _a_ ¿Con quién hablaste en la estancia?
4. _b_ ¿Volviste a Buenos Aires en seguida?
5. _f_ ¿Encontraste la casa fácilmente (*easily*)?
6. _d_ ¿Conociste al hijo en seguida?
7. _c_ ¿Le explicaste la situación a Arturo?

a. Hablé con Cirilo, un gaucho.
b. Sí, claro. Volví inmediatamente.
c. Le expliqué todo y me escuchó con atención.
d. Sí, entré y hablé con él inmediatamente.
e. Llegué ayer por la tarde.
f. La encontré, pero no fácilmente.
g. Viajé a la estancia Santa Susana.

Paso 2

Now check your answers on the cassette tape. First, ask each question, then listen to the correct question-and-answer sequence on the tape.

Actividad D. ¿Y tú?

You will hear a series of questions about what you did yesterday (**ayer**) and last night (**anoche**). Listen carefully and write down the best answer according to what you did. You will hear each question twice. (Worksheet)

MODELO: (*you hear*) ¿Estudiaste anoche o viste la televisión?
(*you write*) Estudié y también vi* la televisión anoche.

1. ... 2. ... 3. ... 4. ... 5. ... 6. ...

---

*Note that the singular forms of ver do not take accents in the preterite: **vi, viste, vio.**

38. ¡JOSÉ! TE BUSCAN: TELLING WHOM OR WHAT (FIRST- AND SECOND-PERSON SINGULAR DIRECT OBJECT PRONOUNS)

Forms

	SUBJECT	OBJECT	
First person:	yo	me	*me*
Second person:	tú	te	*you*
	Ud.	lo, la	*you*

As you know, the third-person singular direct object pronouns (**lo, la**) have separate masculine and feminine forms. The first-person (**me**) and second-person familiar (**te**) pronouns do not show gender.

Uses

RAQUEL: Arturo **me** ha invitado a cenar.	RAQUEL: *Arturo has invited me to dinner.*
¿No **me** invitas a pasar?	*(to Arturo) Aren't you going to invite me to come in?*
MARINERO: ¡José! **Te** buscan.	SAILOR: *José! Someone is looking for you.*
ARTURO: ¿En qué puedo servir**la**?	ARTURO: *(to Raquel): How may I help you?*

- The first- and second-person pronouns refer only to people: to you or to a person to whom you are speaking.
- The third-person forms are used when speaking to someone you address as **Ud.** Because these forms reflect gender, use **la** when speaking to a woman and **lo** when speaking to a man.
- These pronouns, like all object pronouns, precede conjugated verb forms, come in between **no** and a conjugated verb form, and may follow and be attached to an infinitive.

Actividad A.   ¿Quién lo dijo?

Who made the following statements, Raquel (R), Arturo (A), or another character (Otro personaje = O)? Can you name the other character?

Ⓡ A O 1. Un chofer me llevó a la estancia.
R A Ⓞ 2. La señora Rosario me trató muy bien, pero se mudó para la capital.
R Ⓐ O 3. Si querés, yo te llevo otra vez al cementerio.
R Ⓐ O 4. Nadie me va a reconocer en este barrio, pero pueden conocer a mi hermano.
R Ⓐ O 5. Te invito a probar una parrillada en mi casa.
R A Ⓞ 6. José, te buscan. Es tu mujer. Ya sabe de tus escapadas.
R A Ⓞ 7. Te conocí hace unos días y ya sé que tu hermano es muy importante para ti.
R Ⓐ O 8. ¿Me vas a ayudar a buscar a Ángel?

Actividad B.   ¿Quién la ayudó?

Paso 1

Here are Raquel's descriptions of some of the people who have helped her so far. Can you match the descriptions with the following names?

a. Arturo   c. el chofer   e. el ama de casa (*housekeeper*)
b. Mario   d. José

1. __c__ Me dejó en casa de Arturo.
2. __a__ Me recibió en casa de Arturo.
3. __a__ Me buscó en el hotel, con una foto de Ángel.
4. __a__ Me llevó al barrio de La Boca.
5. _____ Me llevó a la casa de José, y a su barco.
6. _____ Me invitó a almorzar.
7. _____ También me invitó a cenar.

 Paso 2

Now check your answers on the cassette tape. First, ask each question, then listen to the correct question-and-answer sequence on the tape.

> MODELO: (*you see*) Me dejó en casa de Arturo.
> (*you say*) ¿Quién te dejó en casa de Arturo?
> (*you hear*) ¿Quién te dejó en casa de Arturo? —El chofer.

Actividad C. ¿Y tú?

Complete these sentences with the name of someone you know who fits the bill. If you can't think of anyone, answer with **nadie**.

1. _____ me invita a comer con frecuencia.
2. _____ me conoce muy muy bien.
3. _____ me busca cuando necesita dinero.
4. _____ me llama por teléfono y habla y habla y habla.
5. _____ me invita a salir con él/ella los sábados.
6. _____ me quiere mucho.
7. _____ me cree siempre, no importa lo que diga (*no matter what I say*).
8. _____ nunca (*never*) me comprende.

 Actividad D. ¿Y tú?

You will hear a series of questions about people you know. Listen carefully and write down the best answer you can think of. If no one occurs to you, begin your answer with **Nadie...** . You will hear each question twice. (Worksheet)

1. ...   2. ...   3. ...   4. ...   5. ...   6. ...

 ## 39. *SE LLAMA ÁNGEL CASTILLO*: VERBS USED BOTH REFLEXIVELY AND NONREFLEXIVELY

Using Reflexive Pronouns

Forms
You have already learned the reflexive pronouns (**me, te, se, nos, os, se**) and a number of verbs commonly used with them. Verbs of this type are indicated in vocabulary lists with **-se: despertarse, sentirse,** and so on.

Uses
The reflexive pronouns are used with the following groups of verbs.

Category 1: actions that one does to oneself

With these verbs, the subject of the sentence and the object (the reflexive pronoun) refer the same person. This category includes the following verb that you already know: **llamarse** (lit. *to call oneself*), **vestirse (i)**.

Category 2: actions that "happen" to someone without anyone in particular doing the action

This category includes verbs such as: **acordarse (ue)**, **acostarse (ue)**, **casarse**, **dedicarse**, **despedirse (i)**, **despertarse (ie)**, **levantarse**, **olvidarse**, **sentarse (ie)**, **sentirse (ie)**

Note that the meaning of verbs in these two categories is sometimes expressed with *get* in English: *to get dressed/up/married*, and so on.

Note also that many of these verbs can be used without the reflexive pronouns. In that case, the action is not done to or does not involve oneself, but rather another person or thing. Compare the following sentences.

El teléfono **despertó** a Raquel a las seis.   *The telephone woke Raquel up at six.*
Raquel **se despertó** a las seis.   *Raquel woke up at six.*

Elena **vistió** a Jaime y después **se vistió**   *Elena dressed Jaime and afterward she*
también.   *also got dressed.*

Category 3: certain verbs that change meaning when used with reflexive pronouns

Some verbs, when used reflexively, have a slightly different English equivalent than when used nonreflexively. Here are some that you already know; they are frequently used in Spanish.

dormir (ue) *to sleep* ir *to go*	dormirse (ue) *to fall asleep* irse *to go away; to leave (for a place)*

Raquel y Arturo **se** miran.

Expressing Reciprocal Actions

Reflexive pronouns can also express reciprocal actions. This usage only occurs in the plural, when two or more subjects do something to each other.

Raquel y Pedro **se llaman** por teléfono   *Raquel and Pedro call each other by*
con frecuencia.   *phone often.*

¿Crees que Raquel y Arturo **se**   *Do you think that Raquel and Arturo*
comprenden?   *understand each other?*

Learn to recognize this use of the reflexives when you see or hear it. Many Spanish verbs can be used in this way.

Actividad A. ¿Cierto o falso?
Based on what you know about them up to now, are the following statements about these characters probably **Cierto (C)** or **Falso (F)**?

C F 1. Raquel siempre se duerme en los vuelos internacionales.
C Ⓕ 2. Arturo siempre se viste con ropa muy formal.
Ⓒ F 3. Cirilo se acuerda de Rosario con afecto.
C F 4. Rosario se casó otra vez después de la muerte de Martín Iglesias.
C F 5. Arturo se olvidó por completo de su hermano Ángel.

Actividad B. El comienzo de la búsqueda
Can you complete the following paragraphs, which summarize aspects of Raquel's first days in Buenos Aires?

En su *suite*, Raquel (sentó/se sentó)[1] en la cama y contó su dinero. Se sintió más tranquila al saber[a] que, de momento,[b] tenía[c] suficiente. (Acostó/Se acostó)[2] muy temprano y (durmió/se durmió)[3] en seguida.

Al día siguiente Raquel salió muy temprano para la estancia Santa Susana. Habló con Cirilo y (despidió/se despidió)[4] de él muy contenta, porque tenía la dirección de Rosario. En una casa en la calle Gorostiaga, un ama de casa la dejó entrar y (se sentó/la invitó a sentarse)[5] en un sofá. Conoció al doctor... el hijo de Rosario.

Los dos (nos contamos/se contaron)[6] sus historias y (nos escuchamos/se escucharon)[7] con atención. Al día siguiente, Arturo y Raquel (fueron/se fueron)[8] a La Boca. De momento, sólo la búsqueda de Ángel los unía.[d]

[a]al... *when she knew* [b]de... *for the moment* [c]*she had* [d]*was uniting*

Now check your answers on the cassette tape.

Actividad C. ¿Y tú?

Do the following statements describe you? Answer the first group based on your own experience, the second group based on your experience and that of others.

Primer grupo

Sí No 1. Me duermo fácilmente.
Sí No 2. Despierto a todo el mundo los domingos por la mañana.
Sí No 3. Me gusta sentarme en el suelo (*floor*) para ver la televisión.
Sí No 4. Siempre me levanto antes de las once de la mañana.
Sí No 5. Nunca me acuerdo de los cumpleaños (*birthdays*) de mis amigos.
Sí No 6. Creo que es un error casarse muy joven.
Sí No 7. Me siento muy flojo/a (*sluggish*) los lunes por la mañana.

Segundo grupo

Sí No 8. Mis padres y yo nos visitamos con frecuencia.
Sí No 9. Mi mejor amigo/a y yo nos vemos con frecuencia.
Sí No 10. Mi (¿ ?) y yo nos escribimos con frecuencia.

• •

PRONUNCIACIÓN: *s, z, ci,* AND *ce*

In Spanish the [s] sound can be written in several different ways: with **s, z,** or **c** (before **e** or **i**). It also has several variant pronunciations, depending on the country or region of origin of the speaker.

Actividad A.

Listen to the differences between these pronunciations of the [s] sound in two distinct Spanish-speaking areas of the world.

Spain: Vamos a Santa Susana este lunes.
Latin America: Vamos a Santa Susana este lunes.

Spain: El ciego reconoce la voz de Jaime Ramírez.
Latin America: El ciego reconoce la voz de Jaime Ramírez.

Spain: Dicen que hay una buena merluza para el almuerzo.
Latin America: Dicen que hay una buena merluza para el almuerzo.

Actividad B.

Listen as the speaker pronounces these sentences that contain the [s] sound. Note that his pronunciation reflects a usage common in informal speech in the Hispanic world: the [s] sound is aspirated at the end of a word or syllable.

1. Los mejillones son fabulosos, y también el arroz con calamares.
2. Todos los pescados y mariscos que hay por aquí están frescos.
3. Es mi hermano. Perdimos contacto hace muchos años.

Actividad C.
Repeat the following words and sentences, imitating the speaker.

1. búsqueda ostras mariscos langostas miércoles
2. ciudad cierto cenar conocer hacienda
3. arroz azul conozco otra vez empiezo
4. estación dirección preparación lección conversación
5. Cirilo busca a cinco o seis gauchos.
   Sus zapatos son azules y sus calcetines son rosados.
   Reconozco la necesidad de decidir en seguida.

Have you completed the following sections of the lesson? Check them off here.

_____ **Más allá del episodio**   _____ **Pronunciación**

_____ **Gramática**

Now scan the words in the **Vocabulario** list to be sure that you understand the meaning of most of them.

VOCABULARIO

Los verbos

contar (ue)	to count
dormir (ue)	to sleep
invitar	to invite
irse	to go away; to leave (*for a place*)
probar (ue)	to try, taste (*food*)

Las cosas

el dinero	money

Las palabras adicionales

anoche	last night
ayer	yesterday
fácilmente	easily
nunca	never

Now that you have completed the Textbook and Workbook for **Lección 13**, take the Self-Test for that lesson. (It is on page 268.) Remember to listen to the tape when you see the cassette symbol and to check your answers.

_____ **Self-Test**

Now that you have worked through the Textbook and the Workbook and taken the Self-Test, here are some of the things you have accomplished in Spanish.

- You have learned how to make direct requests in a store.
- You can use and understand vocabulary related to seafood.
- You have learned more about narrating in the past in Spanish.
- You know how to express words such as *me* and *you* in some contexts in Spanish.
- You have learned more about using Spanish reflexive pronouns to talk about different kinds of actions.
- You know how Spanish **s**, **z**, **ce**, and **ci** are pronounced.
- You have continued to improve your listening skills.

You are now ready to continue on with **Lección 14** in the Textbook.

14

EN EL EXTRANJERO

OBJETIVOS

Whereas the materials in the Textbook all had to do with the video episode, the materials in the Workbook will help you expand your knowledge of the Spanish language in general, as well as give you opportunities for self-expression in Spanish. In this lesson you will learn

- more about the preterite tense
- more about direct objects that refer to people
- about Spanish prepositions and how they are used
- how to pronounce Spanish **r** and **rr.**

Remember to listen to the tape for **Lección 14** when you see the cassette symbol and to check your answers in Appendix 1.

MÁS ALLÁ DEL EPISODIO

Actividad.   Arturo Iglesias

You have seen and listened to Arturo Iglesias since meeting him in **Episodio 12**. In this video episode you learned a little more about him, along with Raquel. But you really don't know much about him as a person yet. Here is a series of statements about him. Express your reactions by choosing from the following statements.

a.   Es probable.   c.   Es improbable.
b.   No sé.

1. _____ Las relaciones entre Arturo y Rosario eran muy especiales.
2. _____ Arturo nunca tuvo (*had*) relaciones muy buenas con Ángel, su medio hermano.
3. _____ Arturo sufrió mucho con la muerte de su padre.
4. _____ Arturo quería (*wanted to*) estudiar Ciencias Económicas, pero su padre lo obligó a estudiar siquiatría.
5. _____ Conoció a su primera esposa en el Perú.

6. ____ Arturo y su esposa tuvieron un hijo.
7. ____ Tuvieron problemas desde el primer día de casados (*as a married couple*).
8. ____ Arturo quiere casarse otra vez.

The answers you have given are based solely on the very small amount of information about Arturo Iglesias that you have at this point. The following reading passage offers more information. Read it and see whether you wish to change any answers. As you read, you will probably note many preterite-tense verb forms as well as other past tenses. Not all of these forms are glossed for you. Pay attention to the verb stem and try to let the stem and context determine meaning.

Arturo Iglesias, el hijo de Rosario y Martín

Dos cosas marcaron profundamente la personalidad de Arturo. Primero, la relación muy especial que existía entre su madre y Ángel, el hijo de su primer esposo. Arturo se sentía totalmente excluido de aquellas relaciones. Segundo, la muerte de su padre cuando Arturo era[1] todavía un niño. Para él, Ángel era el único culpable.[2] Durante muchos años Arturo trató de[3] olvidar a Ángel y por eso, nunca hizo[4] nada para encontrarlo.

Desde pequeño, Arturo siempre tuvo un carácter mucho más reflexivo que su medio hermano. Le gustaba mucho la sicología. Ya de adolescente decidió ser psiquiatra. Le gustaba la idea de ayudar a los demás,[5] pero no era ésta la única razón. Por sus propios conflictos internos en cuanto a[6] su hermano, le interesó mucho la cuestión de «la vida interior» del ser humano.

Arturo fue un buen estudiante. Terminó sus estudios de psiquiatría siendo el número uno de su clase. Rosario estaba muy orgullosa[7] de él. Le regaló[8] una cámara fotográfica y un viaje a Europa, ¡el sueño[9] de Arturo desde siempre! Así descubrió sus dos pasatiempos favoritos, la fotografía y los viajes.

Unos años más tarde, cuando Arturo era ya un psiquiatra de cierto prestigio en Buenos Aires, viajó a Lima para un Congreso.[10] En una conferencia,[11] conoció a Estela Vargas, la amiga de un colega y en aquella época estudiante de sicología. Fue una atracción muy fuerte.[12] Arturo regresó a Buenos Aires pero él y Estela se escribían y se telefoneaban con frecuencia. Vivieron unas relaciones muy intensas a pesar de[13] la distancia. Todo era muy romántico, breves estancias[14] en el Perú o la Argentina, flores, mensajes, regalos... Pronto decidieron casarse. La boda[15] fue en Lima con una ceremonia muy bonita. Los novios se fueron a Italia de luna de miel.[16]

El primer año todo fue muy bien. Pero poco a poco las relaciones se deterioraron. Entre su consulta y las clases en la universidad, Arturo tenía poco tiempo para su esposa. Llegó a estar obsesionado con su trabajo. Ella, por su parte, no trabajaba—nunca terminó su carrera—y no tenía muchos amigos en Buenos Aires. Se sentía muy sola. Además, extrañaba[17] mucho a su familia. Al cabo de cinco años de matrimonio, se divorciaron. ¿Crees que Arturo todavía piensa mucho en Estela?

[1] *was*   [2] *responsible*   [3] *trató... tried to*   [4] *did*   [5] *los... others*   [6] *en... about*   [7] *estaba... was very proud*   [8] *Le... She gave him as a gift*   [9] *dream*   [10] *Convention*   [11] *lecture*   [12] *strong*   [13] *a... in spite of*   [14] *stays*   [15] *wedding*   [16] *de... for a honeymoon*   [17] *she missed*

Actividad B.

Now return to statements 1–8 in **Actividad A** and make any changes in your answers that you feel are necessary. Which statements do you still have to answer with **No sé**? Listen to the speaker on the cassette tape, who will give you some answers and then provide additional information.

GRAMÁTICA

40. *DESPUÉS DE LA CENA, TOMAMOS UN POCO DE CAFÉ*: FIRST- AND SECOND-PERSON PLURAL FORMS OF REGULAR VERBS (PRETERITE TENSE)

Forms

Here are the endings for the first- (**nosotros/as**) and second-person (**vosotros/as**) plural preterite forms for regular verbs. Note that the **-er** and **-ir** verbs have the same endings. The **Uds.** forms are also given.

	invit**ar**	aprend**er**	sal**ir**
	invit-	aprend-	sal-
nosotros/as	invitamos	aprendimos	salimos
vosotros/as	invitasteis	aprendisteis	salisteis
Uds.	invitaron	aprendieron	salieron

Note that the **nosotros** forms of **-ar** and **-ir** verbs are identical to their corresponding present-tense forms. Context will normally clarify which meaning, present or past, is intended.

Note that the **vosotros** forms are the same as the **tú** forms with **-is** added to the end: **invitaste → invitasteis.**

Uses

Remember that, as with the present tense, the **vosotros** form is used primarily in Spain. Raquel and Arturo do not use it. In Latin America the **ustedes** form is used for both formal and familiar address. In other words, it is the plural form of both **tú** and **usted.**

Ángel y yo **viajamos** mucho juntos.	*Ángel and I traveled a lot together.*
Arturo y yo **comimos** en su casa anoche.	*Arturo and I ate at his house last night.*
Miguel, ¿ya **estudiasteis** tú y Jaime?	*Miguel, have you and Jaime studied already?*
Teresa, ¿**vivisteis** tú y tu hijo en Sevilla antes?	*Teresa, did you and your son live in Sevilla before?*

Actividad A. ¿Qué pasó?

Do the following statements, made by Raquel, accurately express what she and Arturo have done together?

Sí No 1. Comenzamos la búsqueda en la zona universitaria.
Sí No 2. Encontramos a José en el barco donde trabaja.
Sí No 3. Probamos una parrillada en el restaurante El Barco.
Sí No 4. Comimos unas brochetas anoche en casa de Arturo.
Sí No 5. Por la noche, llegamos al Piccolo Navio en busca de Héctor.
Sí No 6. Héctor vio la foto de Ángel y claro que lo reconoció.
Sí No 7. Acompañamos a Héctor a su casa.
Sí No 8. Le escribimos una carta a Ángel a Puerto Rico.
Sí No 9. Subimos con Héctor a hablar con su esposa.
Sí No 10. Comprendimos que Ángel salió en un barco hacia el Caribe.

Actividad B.   Hace muchos años

As you know, Rosario and a friend corresponded for a while after Rosario went to Argentina. How would Rosario have responded to these questions the friend might have asked about Rosario's life in a new country with a new family?

Preguntó la amiga:

1. __d__ ¿Os reconocisteis Martín y tú en seguida cuando llegasteis a Buenos Aires?
2. __i__ ¿Cuándo y dónde os casasteis?
3. __j__ ¿Dónde vivisteis?
4. _____ ¿Perdisteis contacto Ángel y tú?
5. __h__ ¿Y no os visteis frecuentemente?
6. _____ ¿No os escribisteis algunas veces (*a few times*)?
7. __c__ ¿Continuasteis Arturo y tú viviendo (*living*) en la estancia?
8. _____ ¿Encontrasteis a Ángel después, tú y Arturo?
9. __g__ Pero, por fin empezasteis a recibir cartas de Ángel, ¿no?
10. __e__ ¿Buscasteis a los amigos de Ángel, para saber dónde estaba él (*where he was*)?

Contestó Rosario:

a. Sí, pues... él se mudó a Buenos Aires, a estudiar.
b. Sí, claro, nos escribimos todas las semanas.
c. No, no lo vimos otra vez después de la muerte de Martín.
d. ¡Claro que nos reconocimos!
e. Sí, una amiga y yo buscamos a sus amigos, pero no los encontramos.
f. No. Nos mudamos a Buenos Aires, donde Arturo estudió medicina.
g. Sí, recibimos una carta de él.
h. Bueno, nos vimos cuando Martín y yo visitamos Buenos Aires.
i. Nos casamos el diez de mayo, en Buenos Aires.
j. Vivimos en la estancia Santa Susana.

Actividad C.   ¿Cómo pasaron el tiempo?

Indicate whether you and another person recently did any of the things you will hear described on the cassette tape.

1. Sí No   3. Sí No   5. Sí No   7. Sí No   9. Sí No
2. Sí No   4. Sí No   6. Sí No   8. Sí No   10. Sí No

Actividad D.   ¿Qué hicieron Uds. la semana pasada?

Write four sentences that describe some things you did last week with friends or family. (Worksheet)

Frases útiles: ver una película (*film*) buena, almorzar en un restaurante interesante, mudarnos de una casa a otra, desayunar juntos, invitar a unos amigos a comer, despedirnos de un buen amigo

41. *HÉCTOR NOS LLEVÓ A SU CASA:* TELLING WHOM OR WHAT (FIRST- AND SECOND-PERSON PLURAL DIRECT OBJECT PRONOUNS)

Forms

	SUBJECT	OBJECT	
First person:	nosotros/as	nos	*us*
Second person:	vosotros/as	os	*you*
	Uds.	los, las	*you*

As you know, the third-person plural direct object pronouns (**los, las**) have separate masculine and feminine forms. The first-person (**nos**) and second-person familiar (**os**) pronouns do not show gender.

Uses

José **nos** buscó en el restaurante.	*José looked for us in the restaurant.*
Quiero invitar**os** a cenar en mi casa.	*I want to invite you (all) to dine at my house.*
Vamos, **los** llevo a la cantina.	*Let's go; I'll take you (all) to the bar.*

- Remember that, as with the **vosotros** verb forms, the second-person plural familiar pronoun **os** is used primarily in Spain. In Latin America, the plural of **te** is **los** or **las**. Since these forms reflect gender, use **las** when speaking to women and **los** when speaking to men.
- The first- and second-person pronouns refer only to people: to you and one or more persons, or to the persons to whom you are speaking.
- These pronouns, like all object pronouns, precede conjugated verb forms, come in between **no** and a conjugated verb form, and may follow and be attached to an infinitive.

Actividad A. ¿Qué nos pasó?

Arturo is describing what has happened to him and to Raquel so far during their search. Can you complete his sentences?

1. En una pescadería (*fish market*), un señor
   a. _____ nos reconoció en seguida
   b. ✓ no nos ayudó mucho, realmente
   c. _____ nos invitó a almorzar

2. Mario, el dependiente de una tienda de antigüedades,
   a. _____ se acordó de que nos conoció hace muchos años
   b. ✓ nos llevó a la casa de José
   c. _____ no nos vio en la puerta

3. José investigó dónde estaba Héctor y luego
   a. _____ nos encontró en un restaurante, El Barco
   b. ✓ nos llevó a un baile en el Piccolo Navio
   c. _____ nos esperó en su barco

4. Héctor
   a. _____ no nos comprendió completamente
   b. ✓ nos invitó a acompañarlo a casa
   c. _____ nos dejó en el Piccolo Navio

5. Héctor
   a. ✓ nos prometió (*promised*) buscar una carta de Ángel
   b. _____ no nos ayudó para nada
   c. _____ nos invitó a comer

 Now check your answers on the cassette tape. Read your answer and see whether it corresponds to the one you hear.

Actividad B. Las cartas de Rosario y una amiga

Now match these questions from a friend with Rosario's answers. The friend is asking about the period when Rosario and Arturo moved to Buenos Aires.

La amiga preguntó:

1. _a_ ¿Os visitaron con frecuencia los amigos de la estancia?
2. _d_ ¿Os ayudaron a estableceros (*get settled*) los amigos de la capital?
3. _c_ ¿Os invitaron a cenar?
4. _b_ ¿Os llamaron frecuentemente los parientes de Martín?

Rosario contestó:

a. Al principio (*at first*), sí. Pero después, nos llamaron menos.
b. Unos sí nos visitaron a veces, pero otros no.
c. Sí, nos invitaron a comer en su casa con frecuencia.
d. ¡Sí, mucho! Hay muchos detalles cuando uno se muda...

Actividad C.   ¿Y tú?

Paso 1

What does the word "friend" mean to you? Which of the following statements accurately describe what you think your friends do for you?

Sí	No	1.	Nos ayudan cuando necesitamos dinero.
(Sí)	No	2.	Nos escuchan cuando tenemos problemas.
Sí	No	3.	Nos aceptan sin condiciones.
(Sí)	No	4.	Nos visitan (si no vivimos con ellos).
Sí	No	5.	Nos critican a veces.
Sí	(No)	6.	Nos comparan con sus otros amigos.
(Sí)	No	7.	Nos llevan a comer en restaurantes.
Sí	No	8.	Nos quieren.
Sí	(No)	9.	Nos abandonan si no hacemos lo que ellos quieren.
Sí	No	10.	Nos comprenden mejor que nuestra familia.

Paso 2

Of the characteristics listed in **Paso 2**, which two are the most important to you? Which are the most annoying? Can you create one more sentence in each category that describes your family? (Worksheet)

Actividad D.   ¿Y tú?

Complete the following statements by indicating what each item does for us. (Worksheet)

Verbos útiles:

molesta(n)	bother, annoy	**hace(n) pensar**	make . . . think
divierte(n)	entertain	**imita(n)**	imitate
preocupa(n)	worry	**hipnotiza(n)**	hypnotize
fastidia(n)	"drive up a wall"	**horroriza(n)**	terrify

1. Los perros nos...
2. Los psiquiatras nos...
3. La televisión...
4. La ciencia-ficción...
5. Los gatos...
6. Los hermanos menores (*younger*)...
7. ¿____?

42. SÍ, MAMÁ, Y BESOS PARA PAPÁ: PREPOSITIONS

Arturo y yo comenzamos la búsqueda en La Boca. Es un barrio **cerca del** puerto. Al principio[1] nadie reconoció a Ángel. Luego un hombre que trabajaba **en** una tienda **de** antigüedades pensó que un tal[2] José podría[3] conocerlo. El hombre nos llevó **a la casa de** José, que estaba[4] **al lado de** su tienda. Pero José estaba **en** el barco donde trabajaba.[5]

José pensó que Héctor podía conocer a Ángel. Nos dijo que podríamos[6] encontrarlo esa noche en una cantina que no estaba **lejos del** puerto. **Después de** cenar **en casa de** Arturo, salimos **para** la cantina.

[1]*Al... At first* [2]un... *a guy named* [3]*might* [4]*was* [5]*he worked* [6]*we would be able to*

Prepositions are words that express the relationship between two elements of the sentence. For example, these may be relationships of time, place, means, or purpose.

You have already learned the simple (one-word) prepositions **a, de, con, en,** and **para.** You have used the simple prepositions **por** in phrases such as **por teléfono/fin** and **hasta** in phrases such as **hasta luego/mañana.** You have also learned the compound (multiple word) prepositions **acerca de** and **después de.**

More About Prepositions and Their Uses

Forms
Here are some additional prepositions that you will see and hear frequently.

sin	without	al lado de	beside, next to
sobre	about	entre	between, among
		junto a	next to
antes de	before	cerca de	near (to)
durante	during	lejos de	far from

Uses

Después de vestirse, Raquel fue a la casa de Arturo.	*After getting dressed, Raquel went to Arturo's house.*
Arturo preparó brochetas, pero **antes de** servirlas, probaron unos quesos deliciosos.	*Arturo prepared brochettes, but before serving them, they tried some delicious cheeses.*
Tome. —No, no, no. Es **para** Ud. Es **de** su hermano.	*Here. —No, no, no. It's for you. It belongs to your brother.*
Es muy importante **para** mí.	*It's very important for me.*

- Prepositions do not show gender or number. Remember that **de** and **a** (which form parts of some compound prepositions) combine with the definite article **el** to form **del** and **al,** respectively.
- Spanish prepositions always have expressed objects—a noun, pronoun, or verb. The object directly follows the preposition.
- When the object of a preposition is a verb, it will always be the infinitive form. (The English verb equivalent is usually the -*ing* form.) Objects of the infinitive are attached to the infinitive.
- When the object of a preposition is a pronoun, the subject pronouns are used in all but two cases. The pronouns corresponding to **yo** and **tú** are **mí** and **ti. Mí** has a written accent to distinguish it from the possessive **mi** which means *my.* **Mí** and **ti** combine with the preposition **con** to form **conmigo** (*with me*) and **contigo** (*with you*).

One-Word Spanish Verbs that Express English Verbs With Prepositions

Some Spanish verbs contain within their basic meaning a concept that English expresses with a verb + preposition combination. For example, you know that **buscar** means *to look* *for* and **escuchar** means *to listen to.* Here are two additional verbs of this type: **mirar** (*to look at*) and **esperar** (*to wait for, to hope, to expect*).

Todos **miran** la foto de Ángel, pero no lo reconocen.	*Everyone looks at the photo of Ángel, but no one recognizes him.*
Raquel y Arturo **esperan** a Héctor en el Piccolo Navio.	*Raquel and Arturo wait for Héctor at the Piccolo Navio.*

Actividad A.   Detalles de la investigación

Which of the following statements would Raquel include in her description of the investigation so far? Indicate with **sí** those that are factual.

Sí No 1. Arturo trabaja lejos de su casa.
Sí No 2. José vive cerca de la tienda de Mario.
Sí No 3. Héctor vive al lado de mi hotel.
Sí No 4. Durante la búsqueda hablamos con muchas personas.
Sí No 5. Después de almorzar, Arturo y yo regresamos a su casa.
Sí No 6. Regresamos de La Boca sin encontrar a Ángel.
Sí No 7. Antes de cenar, Arturo y yo tomamos un poco de vino.
Sí No 8. Entre Arturo y yo hay unos sentimientos... interesantes.

Actividad B.   La vida de José

José lives in an area of Buenos Aires called La Boca. Complete the following description of his life and where he lives with prepositions from this list.

lejos de   al lado de   entre   sin   antes de   durante
cerca de   para   en   con   junto a

José vive _____*en*_____¹ el barrio de La Boca. Está ___*cerca de*___² el puerto[a] de Buenos Aires. Vive ___*con*___³ su esposa, doña Flora, _____⁴ la tienda de antigüedades de Mario. También vive _____⁵ el barco donde trabaja.

Todos los días, _____⁶ ir al barco, José desayuna en casa. Camina _____⁷ la casa y el trabajo, y _____⁸ el día regresa a casa a comer. José cree que es bueno no vivir _____⁹ donde él trabaja porque puede llegar al barco _____¹⁰ levantarse muy temprano.

[a]*port*

Now check your answers by listening to the cassette tape.

Actividad C.   ¿Y tú?

Complete as many of the following sentences as you can according to your own experiences. (Worksheet)

1. Cerca de donde yo vivo, hay...
2. No salgo de casa sin...
3. ...practica/estudia español conmigo.
4. Miro la televisión...
5. Yo creo que entre Raquel y Arturo...
6. En *Destinos,* espero ver...

PRONUNCIACIÓN: *r* AND *rr*

The letter **r** has two pronunciations in Spanish.*

- the trilled **r**, written as **rr** between vowels and as **r** at the beginning of a word
- the flap **r**, written as **r** in all positions. This sound does not occur at the beginning of a word.

The flap **r** is similar to the sound of *tt* or *dd* in the English words *Betty* and *ladder*, respectively.

petty/**pero**   sadder/**Sara**   motor/**moro**

Many pairs of words are distinguished only by the difference in these two sounds, so it is important to pronounce them accurately. For example, **pero** = but, **perro** = dog.

Actividad A.

Repeat the following words, phrases, and sentences, imitating the speaker.

1. para   gracias   pero   vivir   traer   tarde   muerto
2. rojo   revelar   retrato   rubio   rosado   repaso   real
3. barrio   correr   arroz   guerra   perro   marrón   error
4. Mi perro corre rápidamente.
5. Tenemos unos riñones ricos (*delicious*).
   Estos errores son raros.
   Recibieron el contrato temprano.
   Fernando, Martín y Rosario.

Actividad B.   ¿*r* o *rr*?

You will hear a series of words and phrases. Indicate the word or phrase you hear.

1. a. Ahora, gasolina.   b. Ahorra (*It saves*) gasolina.
2. a. ¿Hay coral aquí?   b. ¿Hay corral aquí?
3. a. Pero... no.   b. Perro, no.
4. a. Un arador (*plowman*).   b. Un narrador.

Actividad C.   Trabalenguas

Listen to the following tongue twister, then repeat it, imitating the speaker.

R con R, guitarra.
R con R, barril.
Mira qué rápido corren
los carros del ferrocarril (*railroad*).

Have you completed the following sections of the lesson? Check them off here.

_____ **Más allá del episodio**   _____ **Pronunciación**
_____ **Gramática**

Now scan the words in the **Vocabulario** list to be sure that you understand the meaning of most of them.

---

*Many dialectical variations exist in the pronunciation of **r**. There are individual preferences as well.

VOCABULARIO

Los verbos

esperar	to wait (for); to hope; to expect
mirar	to look (at)

Las preposiciones

al lado de	beside, next to
antes de	before
cerca de	near (to)
durante	during
entre	between, among
hasta	until
junto a	next to
lejos de	far from
sin	without
sobre	about

Los pronombres preposicionales

mí, conmigo	me, with me
ti, contigo	you, with you

Now that you have completed the Textbook and Workbook for **Lección 14**, take the Self-Test for that lesson. (It is on page 270.) Remember to listen to the tape when you see the cassette symbol and to check your answers.

_____ **Self-Test**

Now that you have worked through the Textbook and the Workbook and taken the Self-Test, here are some of the things you have accomplished in Spanish.

- You have learned some strategies for managing difficult conversational patterns.
- You can use and understand vocabulary related to meats and other foods.
- You have learned more about narrating in the past in Spanish.
- You know how to express words such as *us* and *you* (*all*) in some contexts in Spanish.
- You have learned more about using Spanish prepositions.
- You know how Spanish **r** and **rr** are pronounced.
- You have continued to improve your listening skills.

You are now ready to continue on with **Lección 15** in the Textbook.

LECCIÓN

15

CULPABLE

OBJETIVOS

Whereas the materials in the Textbook all had to do with the video epidode, the materials in the Workbook will help you expand your knowledge of the Spanish language in general, as well as give you opportunities for self-expression in Spanish. In this lesson you will learn

- how to form the irregular preterite tense of some Spanish verbs
- how to tell to whom or for whom something is done
- how to talk about what other people like or dislike, and what bothers or annoys them
- how to pronounce Spanish n and ñ.

Remember to listen to the tape for **Lección 15** when you see the cassette symbol and to check your answers in Appendix 1.

MÁS ALLÁ DEL EPISODIO

Actividad A. Héctor Condotti

You have been hearing about Héctor for several video episodes, and you have heard him speak with his friends, with his wife, and with Raquel and Arturo. But you really don't know much about him as a person yet. Here is a series of statements about him. Express your reactions by choosing from the following statements.

a. Es probable.   c. Es improbable.
b. No sé.

1. __b__ Héctor conoció a Ángel en la universidad.
2. __a__ A Héctor le cayó bien (*Héctor liked*) Ángel en seguida.
3. __a__ Héctor y Ángel eran (*were*) muy similares en todo.
4. __b__ Ángel encontró trabajo en un barco gracias a Héctor.
5. __b__ Ángel era un marinero excelente.
6. __b__ Héctor conoció (*met*) a su futura esposa por Ángel.

The answers you have given are based solely on the very small amount of information about Héctor Condotti that you have at this point. The following reading passage offers more information. Read it and see whether you wish to change any answers.

Héctor Condotti, la persona que reconoció la foto de Ángel

Héctor conoció a Ángel en el puerto de Buenos Aires. Ángel estaba pintando.[1] Héctor sintió curiosidad y fue a mirar el cuadro. ¡Era su pequeño barco! «¿Cómo puede un barco viejo y feo ser bonito en una pintura?» se preguntó Héctor. El cuadro le gustó mucho e[2] invitó a Ángel a tomar un café.

Los dos hablaron mucho aquel día. Ángel le habló de su viaje desde España que aún no había olvidado.[3] Desde entonces[4] los barcos siempre fueron algo muy especial para él. También le habló de la estancia de su padrastro. Héctor le preguntó: «¿Qué hace un niño rico[5] en este barrio?» Y Ángel le contó con detalle los últimos problemas que tuvo con Martín y su decisión de no depender de nadie.

Pronto los dos se hicieron[6] buenos amigos. Héctor le ayudó a su joven amigo a encontrar trabajo. Lo recomendó al capitán de su barco. Ángel estaba encantado,[7] pero, como sospechó Héctor, Ángel no tenía ni idea sobre el trabajo a bordo.[8] ¡Tampoco nadaba muy bien![9] Pero era feliz.[10]

Ángel le dio a Héctor más de un dolor de cabeza.[11] Por ejemplo, nunca aprendió a hacer un buen nudo.[12] Y la disciplina... «Ángel, ¡que tienes que seguir el reglamento[13]!» ¡Cuántas veces le repitió Héctor lo mismo[14]! También pasaron ratos[15] estupendos y se divirtieron[16] mucho juntos. Pero Ángel nunca perdía ninguna ocasión para sacar sus lápices[17] y ponerse a dibujar. Después de unos años surgió[18] un viaje especial al Caribe y Ángel se embarcó sin su amigo.

¿Va a encontrar Héctor la carta de Ángel? ¿Por qué guardó Héctor la carta? ¿Vive Ángel todavía en la dirección que le dio a su amigo?

[1]estaba... *was painting* [2]y [3]aún... *he still hadn't forgotten* [4]Desde... *From then on* [5]*rich* [6]se... *became* [7]estaba... *was in seventh heaven* [8]no... *he didn't have a clue about what you did on board* [9]¡Tampoco... *Nor was he a particularly good swimmer!* [10]contento [11]dolor... *headache* [12]*knot* [13]*rules* [14]lo... *the same thing* [15]*periods of time* [16]se... *they had a good time* [17]*pencils* [18]*came up*

Actividad B.

Now return to statements 1–6 in **Actividad A** and make any changes in your answers that you feel are necessary. Which statements do you still have to answer with **No sé?** Listen to the speaker on the cassette tape, who will give you some answers and provide additional information.

• •

GRAMÁTICA

43. *PRIMERO ANDUVIMOS EN MATEO... FINALMENTE TUVIMOS UN PICNIC:* VERBS WITH IRREGULARITIES IN THE PRETERITE (PART 1)

Although most verbs are regular in the preterite, a few very common verbs have irregular preterite forms. You have seen and heard many of the preterite forms of **traer, decir, estar, tener, andar,** and **dar** in the video episodes.

Forms
Here are all of the preterite forms of these verbs. Although they have irregularities, you will notice some patterns of similarity.

Two of these verbs have a **-j-** in the preterite stem.

decir: dij-		traer: traj-	
dije	dijimos	traje	trajimos
dijiste	dijisteis	trajiste	trajisteis
dijo	dijeron	trajo	trajeron

Other verbs have -uv- in the stem.

andar: anduv-		estar: estuv-		tener: tuv-	
anduve	anduvimos	estuve	estuvimos	tuve	tuvimos
anduviste	anduvisteis	estuviste	estuvisteis	tuviste	tuvisteis
anduvo	anduvieron	estuvo	estuvieron	tuvo	tuvieron

Note in particular the first- and third-person singular forms. They are unlike regular preterite forms in that they have unstressed endings. Note also that the same set of endings (-e, -iste, -o, -imos, -isteis, -[i]eron) is used regardless of whether the verb ends in -ar, -er, or -ir.

The preterite of **hay** (haber) is **hubo** (*there was/were*).

The preterite of **dar** is irregular in that it takes the regular endings for -er/-ir verbs. Its forms are unaccented, like those of **ver**.

di	dimos
diste	disteis
dio	dieron

Actividad A.   ¿Quién lo hizo?

Which character(s) did each of the following things?

a. Raquel
b. Arturo
c. Cirilo
d. Héctor
e. José
f. Ángel

1. _a,b_ Anduvieron por (*through*) el Rosedal y tuvieron un *picnic*.
2. _d_ Dijo que, hace años, recibió una carta de Ángel.
3. _b_ Trajo mucha fruta para el *picnic*.
4. _c_ Dijo que Rosario se mudó a Buenos Aires.
5. _d_ Dijo que Ángel se fue al Caribe.
6. _a,b_ Estuvieron en la calle Florida.
7. _e_ Le dio a Arturo el nombre de Héctor.
8. _b_ Tuvo un mal presentimiento.
9. _f_ Le dijo a su padre: «No quiero ser economista, quiero pintar.»
10. _d_ Trajo un cuadro de Ángel y le dio el cuadro a Arturo.

Actividad B.   «Una noche y un día interesantes»

Paso 1
Listen again to Raquel's review of what happened in this video episode. Try to focus on the sequence of the events rather than on details.

Paso 2
The following sentences and groups of sentences form a summary of the major events from Raquel's point of view, but they are out of order. Can you put them in chronological order, from 1 to 10?

a. _3_ Luego Arturo me llevó a mi hotel.
b. _6_ Luego nos separamos. Arturo volvió a su casa y yo seguí con mis compras.
c. _2_ Hablamos de Ángel, y Arturo me dijo que se sentía (*he felt*) culpable.
d. _7_ Más tarde (*Later*), cuando estuve otra vez en el hotel, Arturo me llamó.
e. _4_ Fuimos (*We went*) al Rosedal, donde anduvimos en mateo y en bote.
f. _5_ Allí entramos en varias tiendas. Yo compré una bolsa de cuero.

g. ___8___ No pudimos (*We couldn't*) hablar con Héctor hoy.

h. ___1___ Después de hablar con Héctor, Arturo y yo volvimos a su casa.

i. ___10___ Luego tuvimos un *picnic*. En total, lo pasamos muy bien.

j. ___4___ Al día siguiente estuvimos en la calle Florida por la mañana.

Actividad C. ¿Recuerdas quién... ?

Listen to the actions described on the cassette tape and match them with the person or persons on the list who performed them. The items will get progressively harder.

a. _____ George Washington
y sus soldados

b. _____ Neil Armstrong

c. _____ los europeos

d. _____ Cristóbal Colón

e. _____ la reina Isabel

f. _____ Evita Perón

g. _____ los Beatles

Actividad D. Una tarde en el Rosedal

Create as many sentences as you can about Raquel and Arturo's afternoon at the park. Base your sentences on the following photos, and use vocabulary from the list of **Frases útiles**. (Worksheet)

Frases útiles: andar por el parque/en mateo/en barco; comer fruta, pan y queso; estar en el Rosedal; pasar la tarde juntos; pasarlo muy bien; tener un *picnic*

Actividad E. ¿A quién conoces que... ?

Who do you know that fits the following descriptions? Think about people in your family or in your circle of friends, or even about famous people or people in the news. Do any of the descriptions fit you? Then write complete sentences, with the verb in the preterite. If you don't know anyone who fits the description, answer with **No conozco a nadie** (*no one*). (Worksheet)

1. tener un accidente cómico una vez   *mi hermana*
2. decir algo tonto (*silly*) en público
3. tener un problema serio con un profesor (una profesora)
4. estar contigo anoche
5. andar una vez por las playas (*beaches*) de Acapulco
6. traer a una persona muy rara a una fiesta
7. dar mucho dinero para causas políticas o sociales

44. *RAQUEL LE HABLÓ A SU MADRE DE SU NUEVO AMIGO, ARTURO*: TALKING ABOUT TO WHOM OR FOR WHOM SOMETHING IS DONE (THIRD-PERSON INDIRECT OBJECT PRONOUNS)

Le dijimos a Héctor que era[1] importante encontrar a Ángel. Le pedimos su ayuda y él no tuvo problema en ayudarnos.[2] Héctor **le** trajo a Arturo un cuadro de Ángel y **le** dimos las gracias. Dijo que **le** harían falta[3] un par de días para encontrar una carta que Ángel **le** había mandado[4] del extranjero.

[1] *it was*   [2] *helping us*   [3] **le**... *he would need*   [4] **había**... *had sent*

In **Lecciones 12–14** you learned the Spanish direct object pronouns (**me, te, lo, la, nos, os, los, las**). Another kind of verb object is the *indirect object.*

An indirect object is the second recipient of the action of a verb. It answers the question *to (for) whom?* in relation to the verb. Which are the indirect objects in these sentences?

> I gave the money to Paul.
> I lent Jane the car.

In the first sentence, *Paul* is the indirect object (to whom did "I" give the money? → to Paul). In the second, *Jane* is the indirect object (to whom did "I" lend the car? → to Jane). Note that the word *to* is not always expressed with the indirect object in English.

Here are the same sentences, with the indirect object nouns expressed with pronouns.

> I gave *him* the money.
> I lent *her* the car.

Forms

In Spanish, the third-person indirect object pronouns reflect number, but not gender. There are only two forms: **le** and **les**.

> singular: **le** = *to/for him, her, it*
> plural: **les** = *to/for them*

Arturo **le** regaló una campera.	*Arturo gave her a jacket* (as a gift).
Héctor **les** dijo que encontró la carta.	*Héctor told them that he found the letter.*
Héctor va a dar**les** la dirección de Ángel pero no **les** puede hablar hasta mañana.	*Héctor is going to give them Ángel's address, but he can't talk to them until tomorrow.*

Just as third-person verb forms also express the action performed by **Ud.** or **Uds.**, the third-person pronouns also express *to/for you* when the **usted** form of address is used. When they mean *you*, they agree in number with the person addressed.

¿Quién **le** dijo eso, señor?	*Who told you that, sir?*

Uses

- In the preceding examples, note that indirect object pronouns follow the same rules of placement as reflexive pronouns. Indirect object pronouns

  precede conjugated verb forms
  come in between **no** and a conjugated verb form
  may follow and be attached to an infinitive.

- Because the pronouns **le** and **les** have multiple meanings, it is sometimes necessary to clarify their meaning with a prepositional phrase beginning with **a: a él, a Raquel, a los amigos,** and so on.

Arturo **le** regaló una campera **a Raquel.**	*Arturo gave Raquel a jacket* (as a gift).
Héctor **les** dijo **a Arturo y Raquel** que encontró la carta.	*Héctor told Arturo and Raquel that he found the letter.*

Note that in Spanish the clarifying phrase is used in addition to, not instead of, the indirect object pronoun.

Lección 15 Culpable

- Note that, where English uses a prepositional phrase to express when something is done *for* (someone),* Spanish often uses the indirect object pronouns.

    Héctor **les** buscó la carta.   *Héctor looked for the letter for them.*

Actividad A.   ¿Quién... ?

Can you identify the following events from this and recent video episodes by indicating who performed each action and for whom? ¡OJO! More than one answer is possible for some items.

Who did it?	To or for whom?
a. Raquel →	Arturo
b. Arturo →	Raquel
c. Héctor →	Raquel y Arturo
d. Raquel y Arturo →	Héctor
e. Héctor →	Arturo
f. José →	Arturo
g. Raquel y Arturo →	las personas del barrio La Boca
h. Ángel →	Héctor

1. _b_ Le preparó brochetas en su casa.
2. _a_ Le explicaron por qué buscaban a Ángel.
3. _d_ Les preguntaron si reconocían a Ángel.
4. _e_ Les dijo que recibió una carta de Ángel.
5. _f_ Le dijo que Héctor conocía (*knew*) a todo el mundo.
6. ____ Le trajo un cuadro de Ángel.
7. _b_ Le regaló una campera de cuero.
8. _a_ Le contó la historia de Rosario y don Fernando.
9. _b_ Le dijo que no había (*there wasn't any*) motivo para sentirse culpable.
10. _h_ Le mandó (*sent*) una carta a Héctor.

Actividad B.   ¿Qué hicieron?

You will hear a series of questions about things that some *Destinos* characters have done. Answer the questions as completely as you can. Look at the list of useful phrases before beginning this activity and be sure you understand the meaning of all of them.

MODELO: (*you hear*) ¿Qué le mandó Teresa Suárez a don Fernando?
          (*you say*) Una carta. (Le mandó una carta.)
          (*you hear*) Le mandó una carta.

Frases útiles: el nombre de Héctor; una campera; fruta, pan y queso; una canasta; un cuadro; un barco; una historia; una dirección; una carta

1. ...   2. ...   3. ...   4. ...   5. ...   6. ...   7. ...   8. ...

Actividad C.   ¿Y tú?

What have you done to or for someone lately? Answer as many of the following questions as you can with real information. (Worksheet)

¿A quién(es) le(s)... ?

1. dijiste «buenos días» esta mañana
2. regalaste algo recientemente
3. dijiste algo horrible recientemente... sin querer (*without meaning to*)

---

*Note, however, that **para** (**mí, ti, él,** and so on) is used when the speaker wishes to express that something is to be given to someone. Compare these sentences.

   Esta campera es **para ti.**   *This jacket is for you.*
   Te compré esta campera.   *I bought this jacket for you.*

4. preparaste una cena especial
5. preguntaste ayer algo acerca del español
6. escribiste recientemente
7. revelaste un secreto íntimo
8. le compraste algo últimamente (*lately*)

 ## 45. *A ARTURO NO LE GUSTÓ LA IDEA*: TALKING ABOUT LIKES AND DISLIKES

The Verb *gustar*

Forms

You have already learned to use **le gusta** and **le gustan** to tell what someone likes.

A Raquel **le gusta** el parque.	*Raquel likes the park.*
Le gusta el parque.	*She likes the park.*
A Arturo **le gustan** las manzanas.	*Arturo likes apples.*
Le gustan las manzanas.	*He likes apples.*
A Raquel y Arturo **les gusta** la fruta.	*Raquel and Arturo like fruit.*
Les gusta la fruta.	*They like fruit.*

Uses

- The verb **gustar** means that something *is pleasing to* someone. In the preceding sentences, the subjects are **el parque, las manzanas,** and **la fruta.** Note that a singular or plural form of **gustar** is used depending on the number of the subject (which generally comes at the end of the sentence).

   The person to whom something is pleasing must be expressed with an indirect object pronoun. A prepositional phrase (**a** plus noun) is used if the person is named.

- When a verb or series of verbs is the subject of **gustar**, the singular form of **gustar** is used. The form of the other verbs is always the infinitive.

A Raquel **le gusta** estar al aire libre.	*Raquel likes to be outdoors.*
A Héctor **le gusta** bailar y cantar con sus amigos.	*Héctor likes to dance and sing with his friends.*

To express *he/she likes . . . more* (*better*), use **le gusta(n) más.**

A Héctor le gusta bailar pero le gusta **más** cantar.	*Héctor likes to dance but he likes to sing better.*

Other Verbs like *gustar*

A number of other verbs function like **gustar.**

- encantar = *to be especially pleasing**
- molestar = *to bother*

¿Le gustan las uvas rojas? —Claro. Le encantan.	*Does he like red grapes?* *—Of course. He loves them.*
A Raquel le molesta no poder concluir la investigación.	*Being unable to conclude the investigation bothers Raquel.*

---

*Note that **encantar** does not express *to love someone*. That is expressed with the verbs **querer** or **amar.**

Actividad A.   ¿Qué les gusta... o no les gusta... ?

Complete the phrases in the left-hand column with phrases from the right. ¡OJO! More than one answer is possible for some items.

1. _d_ A Raquel le gusta...
2. _k_ A Arturo le gusta...
3. _j b_ A Raquel le gustan...
4. _c_ A Arturo le gustan...
5. _e_ A Arturo le molesta...
6. _f h_ A Raquel no le gusta...
7. ____ A Raquel y Arturo les gusta...
8. ____ A Raquel y Arturo les molesta...
9. ____ A Raquel y Arturo les encantan...

a. las horas que pasan juntos
b. las brochetas que preparó Arturo
c. preparar brochetas para Raquel
d. la chaqueta que le compró Arturo
e. un sentimiento de culpabilidad
f. el ruido (*noise*) del Piccolo Navio
g. andar en mateo
h. no poder hablar con Héctor hoy
i. pensar en irse de Buenos Aires
j. las frutas que Arturo trajo al *picnic*
k. tener la tarde libre

Actividad B.   ¿Qué les gusta a Arturo y Raquel?

Paso 1

What likes and interests do Arturo and Raquel have? As you listen to a description of the things in which they are interested, check them on the following list. Write **A** for the things in which Arturo is interested or that he likes, and **R** for Raquel. Take a moment to scan the list before listening.

1. ____ ayudar a los demás (*others*)
2. ____ la sicología
3. ____ los problemas legales
4. ____ ir de compras
5. ____ viajar
6. ____ estar al aire libre
7. ____ los animales
8. ____ la fotografía
9. ____ comprarle regalos a la gente (*people*)
10. ____ su trabajo
11. ____ leer (*to read*) novelas

Paso 2

Now select someone you know well and compare that person to either Raquel or Arturo, based on the information you recorded in the list and on other things that you know about the characters. Begin by describing what the person you have selected likes (or doesn't like). Then give the comparison. (Worksheet)

A _____ le gusta _____, _____... y _____. Por

eso yo creo que se parece más a (*he/she most resembles*) _____.

Actividad C.   La televisión: Gustos y preferencias

Pick someone whose television viewing habits you know well and describe those habits. What kinds of shows does he/she like/not like to watch? What specific shows are his/her favorites? What specific shows does he/she not like at all (**no le gusta[n] para nada**)? Write at least four sentences. (Worksheet)

Frases útiles: el noticiero de las seis; los programas de detectives, de ciencia-ficción, los reportajes... ; los programas cómicos, románticos; las telenovelas, las *mini-series* dramáticas

• •

PRONUNCIACIÓN: *n* AND *ñ*

In Spanish the **n** is pronounced just as in English. The **ñ** is pronounced like the *ny* in the English word *canyon*, which comes from the Spanish word **cañón.** Remember that **ñ** is a separate letter in the Spanish alphabet; it comes after **n.**

Actividad A.

Repeat the following words and sentences, imitating the speaker.

1. año   señora   mañana   español   pequeño   compañera
2. cana/caña   sonar/soñar   mono/moño   cena/seña
3. La compañía del señor Muñoz está en España.
   Los niños pequeños hablan español.
   La señorita Ordóñez tiene veinte años.

Actividad B.

You will hear a series of words. Circle the word you hear.

1. pena   peña
2. una   uña
3. lena   leña

4. suena   sueña
5. tino   tiño

Have you completed the following sections of the lesson? Check them off here.

_____ **Más allá del episodio**   _____ **Pronunciación**

_____ **Gramática**

Now scan the words in the **Vocabulario** list to be sure that you understand the meaning of most of them.

• •

VOCABULARIO

Los verbos

encantar	to love, like something very much
gustar	to like; to be pleasing to
mandar	to send
molestar	to bother, disturb
pasarlo bien/mal	to have a good/bad time
regalar	to give (*as a gift*)
hubo	there was/were

Las palabras adicionales

estar al aire libre	to be outdoors
le gusta(n) más...	he/she likes . . . more (better); you (*form.*) like . . . more (better)
más tarde	later

Now that you have completed the Textbook and Workbook for **Lección 15**, take the Self-Test for that lesson. (It is on page 272.) Remember to listen to the tape when you see the cassette symbol and to check your answers.

_____ **Self-Test**

Now that you have worked through the Textbook and the Workbook and taken the Self-Test, here are some of the things you have accomplished in Spanish.

• You have learned some strategies for trying to get others to do things.
• You can use and understand vocabulary related to fruits.
• You have learned more about narrating in the past in Spanish.
• You know how to express phrases such as *to/for him* and *to/for them* in some contexts in Spanish.
• You have learned more about describing what others do and don't like.
• You know how Spanish **n** and **ñ** are pronounced.
• You have continued to improve your listening skills.

You are now ready to continue on with **Lección 16** in the Textbook.

LECCIÓN

16

CARAS

OBJETIVOS

Whereas the materials in the Textbook all had to do with the video episode, the materials in the Workbook will help you expand your knowledge of the Spanish language in general, as well as give you opportunities for self-expression in Spanish. In this lesson you will learn

- how to form the irregular preterite forms of more Spanish verbs
- more about how to tell to whom or for whom something is done
- how to use two object pronouns in the same sentence
- how to pronounce Spanish **ch.**

Remember to listen to the tape for **Lección 16** when you see the cassette symbol and to check your answers in Appendix 1.

MÁS ALLÁ DEL EPISODIO

Actividad A. Ángel Castillo

You have been hearing about Ángel since the first video episode of *Destinos*, and you learned a good deal about his early history in the **Más allá del episodio** section of **Lección 13.** You have also seen him through Héctor's eyes. Here is a series of statements about his life after meeting Héctor. Express your reactions by choosing from the following statements.

a. Es probable.
b. No sé.
c. Es improbable.

1. __b__ Ángel aceptó el trabajo que le encontró Héctor, pero la idea de ser marinero no le gustó.
2. __b__ De marinero, Ángel no pintó.
3. __c__ Se adaptó fácilmente a la vida de los marineros.
4. ____ De cada puerto, Ángel le mandó cartas a su madre.
5. ____ Cuando llegó a España, se sintió muy contento.
6. __b__ Fue a Sevilla, pero no habló con Teresa Suárez.

7. ____ En Puerto Rico se sintió verdaderamente libre (*free*).
8. ____ En Puerto Rico se convirtió en un pintor muy famoso.

The answers you have given are based solely on the very small amount of information about Ángel Castillo that you have at this point. The following reading passage offers more information. Read it and see whether you wish to change any answers. This passage, more than others you have read so far, contains unfamiliar verb tenses.

Ángel Castillo, un joven en busca de su destino

Para Ángel, conocer a Héctor fue como encontrar a su «hada madrina».[1] En aquella época no tenía dinero y debía varios meses de alquiler.[2] No lo dudó[3] cuando el capitán del barco donde trabajaba Héctor Condotti le ofreció trabajo. No sabía nada de barcos pero era joven y pensaba que aprendería rápidamente.

El barco en que Héctor y Ángel trabajaban era bastante grande y realizaba viajes transatlánticos. Por fin Ángel podía admirar nuevos horizontes. Siempre tenía a mano[4] algo con que dibujar. Su vocación por la pintura aumentaba con el paso del tiempo. A la vez,[5] su trabajo como marinero le resultaba más pesado.[6] Era una vida muy dura y algo monótona. Le molestaba mucho tener que abandonar un dibujo para cumplir[7] con sus obligaciones a bordo.

En uno de los viajes el barco llegó a España. Cuando Ángel llegó al puerto de Bilbao, se sintió muy confundido. Era su país, pero le pareció estar en un lugar desconocido. Quiso visitar Guernica, la ciudad donde murió su padre. Allí caminó durante horas. Trató de imaginar cómo era todo cuando sus padres vivían allí. Inconscientemente creía ver a su padre entre la gente[8] de las calles. La ciudad terminó por deprimirle.[9] Decidió, entonces, viajar a Sevilla. Allí tampoco encontró lo que buscaba. Pero ¿qué buscaba Ángel en España?

Poco tiempo después el barco hizo un viaje al Caribe. Llevaban una carga[10] para Puerto Rico. Ángel supo inmediatamente que se quedaría[11] allí. Había algo en aquel sol[12] y en aquella tranquilidad que no había visto en otros lugares. Allí, de repente, se sintió completamente libre. Sin duda era el lugar ideal para pintar. Estaba decidido. Dejó el trabajo y le escribió una larga carta a Héctor. En la carta le hablaba de cuánto le gustó la isla, de su necesidad de dedicarse totalmente a la pintura. También le daba las gracias por su ayuda.

Pero ¿encontró Ángel la felicidad en Puerto Rico? ¿Pudo vivir de su pintura? ¿Se hizo famoso?

[1]hada... *fairy godmother* [2]*rent* [3]*No... He didn't hesitate for a second* [4]*a... close by, at hand* [5]*A... At the same time* [6]*aburrido* [7]*to meet* [8]la... las personas [9]terminó... *ended up depressing him* [10]*load* [11]se... *he would stay* [12]Había... *There was something in that sun*

 Actividad B.

Now return to statements 1–8 in **Actividad A** and make any changes in your answers that you feel are necessary. Which statements do you still have to answer with **No sé**? Listen to the speaker on the cassette tape, who will give you some answers and provide additional information.

• •

Gramática

 ### 46. ¿ME PODÉS PERDONAR QUE NUNCA HICE NADA PARA BUSCARTE?: VERBS WITH IRREGULARITIES IN THE PRETERITE (PART 2)

Arturo **quiso** sacar una foto.	*Arturo wanted to (tried to) take a photo.*
Arturo no **pudo** sacar la foto.	*Arturo couldn't take the picture.*
¿Qué **hizo** Raquel con las verduras?	*What did Raquel do with the vegetables?*
¿Cuándo **vino** Raquel a la Argentina?	*When did Raquel come to Argentina?*
¿Por qué **se puso** enfadado Arturo?	*Why did Arturo become angry?*
No lo **supo** Arturo hasta más tarde.	*Arturo didn't find it out (know it) until later.*

Forms

Here are all of the preterite forms of some additional verbs that have irregularities in the preterite. Most of these verbs have the same endings as those in **Lección 15**: **-e, -iste, -o, -imos, -isteis, -ieron**. Although they have irregularities, you will notice some patterns of similarity.

These verbs have an **-i-** in the preterite stem.

querer: quis-		hacer: hic-		venir: vin-	
quise	quisimos	hice	hicimos	vine	vinimos
quisiste	quisisteis	hiciste	hicisteis	viniste	vinisteis
quiso	quisieron	hizo*	hicieron	vino	vinieron

These verbs have a **-u-** in the preterite stem.

poner: pus-		poder: pud-		saber: sup-	
puse	pusimos	pude	pudimos	supe	supimos
pusiste	pusisteis	pudiste	pudisteis	supiste	supisteis
puso	pusieron	pudo	pudieron	supo	supieron

The irregular forms for two verbs, **ser** and **ir**, are the same in the preterite.[†] Note that some of their endings are different from those above.

fui	*I went; I was*	fuimos	*we went; we were*
fuiste	*you went; you were*	fuisteis	*you went; you were*
fue	*you/he/she/it went; he/she/it was, you were*	fueron	*you/they went; you/they were*

Uses

Bueno, ¿adónde **fueron** Arturo y Raquel?	*Well, where did Arturo and Raquel go?*
Héctor y Ángel **fueron** amigos.	*Héctor and Ángel were friends.*

In the examples at the beginning of this section, note the English equivalents of the preterite forms of **querer** and **saber**. You will learn more about this aspect of the preterite of these verbs in **Lección 24**.

Actividad A.   ¿Quién lo dijo?

Which of the characters might have made the following statements, Raquel (R), Arturo (A), Arturo and Raquel (AR), or Otra(s) persona(s) (OP)?

1. _AR_ dijo: «Hice dos caras con verduras.»
2. _A_ dijo: «Quise sacar una foto de Raquel y yo juntos.»
3. _OP_ dijo: «En mi día libre, vine al puerto de Buenos Aires para pescar (*fish*).»
4. _____ dijo: «Me puse (*I put on*) la campera que me mandó Arturo.»
5. _____ dijo: «Al principio (*At first*) no pude sacar la foto porque no funcionó la cámara.»
6. _____ dijo: «Sí, yo fui amigo de Ángel en otra época.»
7. _____ dijeron: «Ayer no pudimos hablar con Héctor.»
8. _____ dijeron: «Fuimos al puerto a buscar a Héctor.»
9. _____ dijeron: «No pudimos ayudar a las personas que vinieron al barrio con la foto.»
10. _____ dijo: «No supe que Ángel se fue a vivir al Caribe.»

---

*The consonant **c** in the stem of **hacer** is pronounced [s]. The Spanish **c** when followed by **o** is pronounced [k]. Before the third-person **-o** preterite ending, the **c** in the stem (**hic-**) changes to a **z** to reflect the [s] sound of the infinitive.

†Context will indicate whether the **fui, fuiste...** forms are the preterite of **ir** or **ser**.

¡Un desafío! Can you give the name of the persons you have indicated with **Otra(s) persona(s)**?

Check your answers by listening to the cassette tape.

Actividad B. ¿Qué pasó?

Paso 1
Listen again to Raquel's review at the end of Episodio 16.

Paso 2
Can you complete the following summary of some of the things that have happened during Raquel's last two days? Many of the events were included in Raquel's review. ¡OJO! Some of the items may be used more than once.

quiso sacar una foto	le hice una sorpresa
vine a la casa	fui al hotel/a una tienda
tuvo un mal presentimiento	pudimos hablar con él
supo algo definitivo	fuimos allí
tuvimos noticias	se puso muy enfadado/muy pensativo

Héctor llamó a Arturo ayer, pero (nosotros) no _pudimos hablar con él._ [1] hasta hoy. (Yo) _Vine a la casa_ [2] de Arturo para esperar. Arturo _quiso sacar una foto_ [3] de nosotros dos. Desgraciadamente, la cámara no funcionó y Arturo _se puso muy enfadado_ .[4] Después de sacar la foto, _tuvimos noticas_ [5] de Héctor. Llamó para decir que quería[a] hablar con nosotros, en el puerto de Buenos Aires. (Nosotros) _fuimos allí_ [6] y Héctor le dio la carta a Arturo. Después de leer[b] la carta, Arturo _tuvo un mal presentimiento._ Por fin _tuvimos noticas_ [8] de Ángel, pero... al mismo tiempo[c] _____ .[9]

Hablamos de mi viaje a Puerto Rico y (yo) _____ .[10] Hablé con Ramón, quien también _____ [11] sobre Ángel. Luego Arturo llamó para invitarme a su casa, para revelar las fotos. Antes de ir a su casa, _____ [12] donde compré unas verduras. Luego, en casa de Arturo, _____ :[13] dos caras de verduras.

[a]*he wanted* [b]*reading* [c]*al... at the same time*

Actividad C. ¿Quién fue?
Name someone or something that matches the following situations. Think about people in the news as well as people from your family and circle of friends.

1. ¿Quién hizo el papel (*role*) principal en una película muy popular últimamente (*lately*)?
2. ¿Quién vino recientemente a visitar al presidente?
3. ¿Quién no pudo decir que no en una situación muy difícil?
4. ¿Qué película (*movie*) fue muy popular el año pasado?
5. ¿Quién quiso ser candidato a presidente en las últimas elecciones (pero no lo hizo)?
6. ¿Qué figura popular estuvo enfermo (*sick*) últimamente?
7. ¿Quién fue a un país extranjero últimamente?
8. ¿Cuál fue el último descubrimiento (*discovery*) científico importante?

Actividad D.   En este episodio

Create at least three sentences about two or three events in Raquel and Arturo's day together. Base your sentences on the following photos, but also include information about what happened before and after, if possible. Use vocabulary from the list of **Frases útiles**. Take a moment as well to scan back over previous activities and sections of **Lección 16** before beginning this activity. (Worksheet)

Frases útiles: ir al puerto/a la casa de Arturo/a la cocina (*kitchen*), ponerse enfadado/ pensativo/contento, darle/hacerle algo, pasarlo muy bien/mal, ver/leer algo

Actividad E.   ¿Y tú?

Answer at least five of the following questions about things you and people you know have or haven't done lately. (Worksheet)

1.   ¿Qué hiciste (hicisteis tus amigos y tú) el sábado pasado?
2.   ¿Qué hizo un pariente por ti últimamente?
3.   ¿Qué no quiso hacer por ti un amigo?
4.   ¿Adónde fuiste ayer? ¿Con quién fuiste?
5.   ¿Qué cosa no pudiste hacer recientemente?
6.   ¿Quiénes vinieron a tu casa la semana pasada?
7.   ¿Qué secreto supiste recientemente?
8.   ¿Cuál fue tu peor (*worst*) momento el año pasado?

47. ¿TE GUSTA?—¿QUE SI ME GUSTA? ¡PERO, POR SUPUESTO!: TALKING ABOUT TO WHOM OR FOR WHOM SOMETHING IS DONE (FIRST- AND SECOND-PERSON SINGULAR INDIRECT OBJECT PRONOUNS)

In Lección 15 you learned to use the third-person **le** and **les** (along with an **a** plus pronoun phrase) to indicate *to whom* or *for whom* the action of the verb is performed.

Forms

The first- and second-person singular indirect object pronouns are **me** and **te** (familiar). As usual, the form corresponding to **usted** is the third-person singular form, **le**.

Uses

*   Because **me** and **te** can have only one meaning, no clarifying phrase is ever needed with them. The prepositional phrases **a mí** and **a ti** are occasionally used for extra emphasis and/or contrast.

¿Cuándo **me** vas a decir lo que tienes en la canasta?	*When are you going to tell me what you have in the basket?*
¿Quién **te** dio la dirección?	*Who gave you the address?*
A mí **me** dio un regalo, no a ti.	*He gave me a gift, not you.*

- Remember that, because **le** has three possible meanings (*to/for him, her,* or *you*), it often needs to be clarified with **a él, a ella, a usted,** or **a** plus a noun.

    —Le hablé de mi nuevo amigo.   —*I told her about my new friend.*
    —¿A quién?   —*Told who(m)?*
    —A mi madre.   —*My mother.*

    Le voy a dar el cuadro **a Ud.**   *I'm going to give you the painting.*

- Remember that indirect object pronouns are used with verbs such as **gustar, encantar,** and **molestar.**

    La idea me gustó mucho.   *I liked the idea a lot.*

    ¿Qué pasa? ¿No te gusta?   *What? You don't like it?*

Actividad A.   ¿A quién?

Listen to the following conversations from **Episodio 16** and indicate the indirect object pronouns (**me, te, le,** or **les**) that you hear. Then, for each indirect object pronoun, indicate the meaning of the pronoun, with an **a** plus noun or pronoun phrase: **a mí, a Arturo,** and so on. For direct object pronouns (**lo, la, los, las**), indicate the noun to which the pronoun refers.

1. ARTURO: [La carta] Está fechada en San Juan de Puerto Rico. (Le/Les)ᵃ da las gracias por su recomendación. Dice que no es un verdadero marinero... y que sigue pintando.

    a. ___le___

2. ARTURO: Otra vez... este presentimiento. Algo (me/le)ᵃ dice que Ángel ya murió.

    a. ___me___

3. ARTURO: Hace unos pocos días que te conozco y parece como si hiciera muchos años.
   RAQUEL: Yo siento lo mismo.
   ARTURO: (Les/Te)ᵃ voy a extrañar.
   RAQUEL: Yo también a ti.
   ARTURO: Aunque... tal vez...
   RAQUEL: ¿Tal vez?
   ARTURO: Tal vez... yo podría ir a Puerto Rico y los dos continuar la búsqueda de Ángel...
   RAQUEL: ¿Quieres decir que irías a Puerto Rico?
   ARTURO: ¿(Me/Te)ᵇ gustaría?
   RAQUEL: ¡Claro que sí!

    a. ___Te___
    b. ___Te___

4. RAQUEL: (Le/Les)ᵃ conté a Ramón las últimas noticias. (Le/Te)ᵇ hablé de la carta de Ángel y del mal presentimiento de Arturo. Ramón (me/te)ᶜ dijo que él también tenía un mal presentimiento.

    a. ___les___   c. ___me___
    b. ___le___

5. ARTURO: ¿Qué pasó?
   RAQUEL: (Le/Te)ᵃ digo... Es una señal. Salgo mal en las fotos y la cámara (lo/la)ᵇ sabe.
   ARTURO: Raquel, basta ya de eso. Quiero una foto de nosotros y vamos a sacar(lo/la)ᶜ.

    a. ___Te___   c. ___la___
    b. ___la___

Actividad B. ¿Quién lo hizo?

Can you identify the person who carried out the activities you will hear on the cassette tape? ¡OJO! You will need to think back to previous video episodes.

a. Raquel
b. Arturo
c. Cirilo
d. don Fernando

e. Teresa Suárez
f. Arturo y Raquel
g. Héctor
h. José

1. ____   2. ____   3. ____   4. ____   5. ____   6. ____   7. ____   8. ____

Actividad C. ¿Y tú?

What gifts have you given or received recently? Complete as many of the following sentences as you can with real gifts and the names of real people. (Worksheet)

Para la Navidad (Chanuka)

yo le regalé a _____ _____ .

...mi _____ me regaló _____ .

Para mi cumpleaños (*birthday*), mi _____ me regaló _____ .

Para su cumpleaños, yo le regalé a _____ _____ .

Actividad D. ¿Y tú?

Paso 1

You have learned vocabulary useful for talking about a number of categories. Pick at least two categories from the following list and express your feelings about aspects of them. (Worksheet)

Categorías: las estaciones del año, los días de la semana, las materias, los programas de televisión (Lección 15, *Workbook*), los animales domésticos, la comida

    Me gusta(n)...
(No) Me encanta(n)...
    Me molesta(n)...

Paso 2

Now create at least four questions that you would use to ask a friend his/her feelings about some of the items you discussed in **Paso 1**. (Worksheet)

    (No) ¿Te gusta(n)... ?
          ¿Te gusta(n) más... o... ?
    (No) ¿Te molesta(n)... ?

48. *ESTE CUADRO ME LO DIO ÁNGEL:* USING TWO OBJECT PRONOUNS TOGETHER

Forms

A sentence can have both a direct object and an indirect object, and they may both be pronouns. The common combinations are limited, and the indirect object pronoun always comes first.

> me + lo, la, los, las
> te + lo, la, los, las

¿La carta? Me la dio Héctor.	*The letter? Héctor gave it to me.*
¿Las fotos? Te las traigo mañana.	*The photos? I'll bring them to you tomorrow.*

When the indirect object is the third person (**le** or **les**), **se** replaces it.

> le → se + lo, la, los, las
> les → se + lo, la, los, las

¿La dirección? Héctor *se* la dio a Arturo.	*The address? Héctor gave it to Arturo.*

se = le (a Arturo)
la = la foto

¿Las fotos? Arturo *se* las reveló a Raquel.	*The photos? Arturo developed them for Raquel.*

se = le (a Raquel)
las = las fotos

Uses

- Because **se** has several possible meanings, a prepositional phrase with **a** is often used for clarification, just as is done with **le** and **les**.

Va a traérselos a él.	*He's going to bring them to him.*
Se los van a mandar a Ud.	*They are going to send them to you.*
Se los van a dar a ellas.	*They are going to give them to them.*

- Note that both pronouns are always placed together. As with all other object pronouns, the double objects

precede conjugated verb forms
come in between **no** and a conjugated verb form
may follow and be attached to an infinitive.

When two pronouns precede a verb they are written as two words but when they are attached to the infinitive, the entire combination is written as one word. This combination requires a written accent to maintain the stress on the last syllable of the infinitive (as in the previous example of traérselos).

Actividad A.   Las preguntas de Raquel

Here are some questions that Raquel might have asked Arturo. Can you complete the answers as he would?

1. ¿Me preparaste las brochetas con pollo?
   No, ...te los/te las... preparé con riñones.
2. ¿Me muestras la carta de Ángel, por favor?
   Sí, claro que ...te lo/te la... muestro. Aquí la tienes.
3. ¿Me contaste toda la historia de tu familia?
   Sí, ...te las/te la... conté entera.
4. ¿Me revelaste todo tu mal presentimiento?
   Sí, ...te lo/te las... revelé todo. Ya no hay más.

5. Arturo, ¿cuándo me vas a decir lo que tienes en la canasta?
   Te lo/te los... voy a decir más tarde. Es una sorpresa.

Actividad B. ¿Eres buen(a) detective?

Here are the answers. Can you indicate *who* (the subject) and *what*?

> MODELO: Se la dio a Raquel en la estancia Santa Susana. →
> ¿Quién? Cirilo
> ¿Qué? la dirección de Rosario en Buenos Aires

Frases útiles: las brochetas, la campera, la canasta, las caras, la carta, el cuadro, el mal presentimiento, el mateo, el perro, el secreto de su pasado

1. Se lo contó a su familia... para su gran sorpresa.   _____

   _____

2. Se la compró a una mujer muy especial.   _____

   _____

3. Se la escribió a un señor que ahora vive en México.   _____

   _____

4. Se la mandó a un señor que todavía vive en la Argentina.   _____

   _____

5. Se las preparó con riñones a una persona que no las había probado (*had never tried*).   _____

   _____

6. Se lo reveló a una persona que no conoce muy bien todavía.   _____

   _____

7. Se las hizo a una persona para sorprenderla.   _____

   _____

8. Se lo dio a un pariente de la persona que lo hizo.   _____

   _____

Actividad C. ¿Y tú?

Answer as many of these questions as you can according to your own experience. Follow the model. (Worksheet)

> MODELO: ¿Quién te dio tu primera «A»? →
> Me la dio la profesora García.

¿Quién te... ?

1. dio tu primera nota mala
2. escribió la última carta que recibiste
3. dio tu primer trabajo
4. compró tu primer vestido/traje (*suit*)
5. recomendó la última película que viste
6. dio la sorpresa más importante que recuerdas

PRONUNCIACIÓN: *ch*

The Spanish ch is pronounced like the same letters in the word *church*. Remember that in Spanish the ch is considered a single letter; it comes after c in the alphabet.*

Actividad.
Repeat the following words, imitating the speaker.

1. mucho   champiñones   lechuga   chocolate
2. chico   chiles   chícharos   anoche
3. chorizo   chino   chuleta   chaqueta
4. Los muchachos escuchan a Charo.
   Chela es una chica chilena.

Have you completed the following sections of the lesson? Check them off here.

_____ **Más allá del episodio**   _____ **Pronunciación**

_____ **Gramática**

Now scan the words in the **Vocabulario** list to be sure that you understand the meaning of most of them.

VOCABULARIO

Los verbos

ponerse	to put on (*clothing*);
ponerse + *adj.*	to get, become (+ *adj.*)

Los adjetivos

enfadado/a	angry

Las palabras adicionales

últimamente	lately

Now that you have completed the Textbook and Workbook for **Lección 16**, take the Self-Test for that lesson. (It is on page 274.) Remember to listen to the tape when you see the cassette symbol and to check your answers.

_____ **Self-Test**

---

*As noted earlier, the Real Academia de la Lengua no longer considers ch to be a separate letter of the Spanish alphabet.

Now that you have worked through the Textbook and the Workbook and taken the Self-Test, here are some of the things you have accomplished in Spanish.

- You have learned some strategies for trying to get others to do things.
- You can use and understand vocabulary related to vegetables.
- You have learned more about narrating in the past in Spanish.
- You know how to express phrases such as *to/for me* and *to/for you* in some contexts in Spanish.
- You have learned more about describing what you and others do and don't like.
- You can use direct and indirect object pronouns together in the same sentences as well as understand their meaning.
- You know how Spanish **ch** is pronounced.
- You have continued to improve your listening skills.

You are now ready to continue on with **Lección 17** in the Textbook.

LECCIÓN

17
INOLVIDABLE

OBJETIVOS

Whereas the materials in the Textbook all had to do with the video episode, the materials in the Workbook will help you expand your knowledge of the Spanish language in general, as well as give you opportunities for self-expression in Spanish. In this lesson you will learn

- about a change that takes place in some preterite forms of **-ir** stem-changing verbs
- more about telling to whom or for whom something is done
- more about using two object pronouns in the same sentence
- how to pronounce Spanish **y** and **ll**.

Remember to listen to the tape for **Lección 17** when you see the cassette symbol and to check your answers in Appendix 1.

MÁS ALLÁ DEL EPISODIO

Actividad A. Luis, el ex novio de Raquel

In this video episode you heard Raquel talk a little about her past and in particular about an old boyfriend. But you really don't know much about him as a person yet. Here is a series of statements about him. Express your reactions by choosing from the following statements.

a. Es probable.   c. Es improbable.
b. No sé.

1. _____ El ex novio de Raquel era mexicoamericano.
2. _____ Luis estudió en la misma universidad que Raquel.
3. _____ Era un joven poco estudioso y sin ambiciones.
4. _____ Le ofrecieron un trabajo en Los Ángeles, pero no lo aceptó.
5. _____ Se fue a trabajar a San Francisco.
6. _____ Allí se enamoró de (*he fell in love with*) otra mujer.

The answers you have given are based solely on the very small amount of information about Luis that you have at this point. The following reading passage offers more information. Read it and see whether you wish to change any answers. As in previous readings, some unfamiliar verb forms will be used, but you should be able to guess meaning from context.

Luis, el antiguo[1] novio de Raquel

Raquel conoció a su ex novio en casa de unos amigos. Los dos eran estudiantes en la Universidad de California en Los Ángeles. Ella estudiaba Derecho[2] y él Administración de Empresas.[3] Además tenían otra cosa en común. Ella era mexicoamericana y él, mexicano.

Raquel se fijó[4] inmediatamente en Luis. ¿Por qué le gustó tanto[5] aquel muchacho? Era un joven muy inteligente y muy ambicioso. Tenía grandes planes para el futuro. Era muy simpático y extrovertido. Raquel también admiraba su dinamismo. Siempre tenía algo que hacer.

Desde aquella tarde en casa de sus amigos se vieron con relativa frecuencia en la universidad. Eran encuentros aparentemente espontáneos, entre las clases o en el almuerzo. Un sábado Luis invitó a Raquel a ir al cine. Desde ese día fueron inseparables. Raquel lo pasaba muy bien con él. Además, él era un gran estímulo para su propia carrera, ya que[6] era muy buen estudiante.

Los problemas entre ellos comenzaron durante los últimos meses antes de graduarse. La idea de terminar los estudios con buenas notas[7] y conseguir un buen puesto[8] consumía todo el tiempo de Luis. Raquel trató de comprenderlo. Sabía que aquello era muy importante para él. Había semanas en las que él no tenía ni cinco minutos para tomar una Coca-Cola con ella.

Llegó la época de los exámenes y ¡los dos salieron bien[9]! Especialmente Luis. Obtuvo el segundo puesto entre los estudiantes de su clase. Muchas empresas lo entrevistaron.[10] Por fin, aceptó un puesto en una empresa en Nueva York. Estaba muy contento con la decisión y se mudó tan pronto como[11] terminó el semestre.

¿Y su novia? Raquel decidió quedarse en California. Luis se graduaba pero a Raquel le faltaba un año más.[12] ¿Crees que las relaciones entre Raquel y Luis fueron serias? ¿Por qué no se mudó ella a Nueva York? ¿Y por qué se fue Luis a Nueva York?

[1]*former* [2]*Law* [3]*Administración... Business Administration* (empresas = *corporations*) [4]*se... noticed* [5]*so much* [6]*ya... since* [7]*grades* [8]*trabajo* [9]*salieron... passed* [10]*interviewed* [11]*tan... as soon as* [12]*a... Raquel had another year to go*

 Actividad B.

Now return to statements 1–6 in **Actividad A** and make any changes in your answers that you feel are necessary. Which statements do you still have to answer with **No sé?** Listen to the speaker on the cassette tape, who will give you some answers and provide additional information.

• •

GRAMÁTICA

 49. *YO PEDÍ PRIMERO Y LUEGO PIDIÓ ARTURO*: PRETERITE FORMS OF *-IR* STEM-CHANGING VERBS

ARTURO: Algún hombre habrá habido[1] en tu vida.

RAQUEL: Hubo uno. Nos conocimos en la Universidad de California. Él estudiaba administración de empresas.

ARTURO: ¿Y?

RAQUEL: Después de graduarse, **consiguió**[2] un buen trabajo en Nueva York y se fue a vivir allá.

ARTURO: ¿Y no se volvieron a ver?[3]

RAQUEL: Bueno. Yo también **conseguí** un puesto, pero en Los Ángeles. Con la distancia, nos fuimos alejando.[4]

[1]*habrá... there must have been* [2]*got (from* conseguir) [3]¿Y... *And didn't you see each other again?* [4]*nos... we grew apart*

You have learned the preterite forms of regular verbs and of a number of verbs that have irregularities in the preterite. You have also learned that stem-changing verbs* ending in -ar and -er have no changes in the preterite forms. However, verbs ending in -ir do show a change in the preterite.

Forms

Stem-changing -ir verbs have a stem change only in the third-person singular and plural of the preterite. There are two patterns of stem changes in the preterite: e → i and o → u.

e → i		o → u	
preferir		**morir**	
preferí	preferimos	morí	morimos
preferiste	preferisteis	moriste	moristeis
prefirió	prefirieron	murió	murieron
pedir			
pedí	pedimos		
pediste	pedisteis		
pidió	pidieron		

From this point on in the *Destinos* Textbook and Workbook, these preterite stem changes will be indicated in vocabulary lists with the stem change in parentheses, following the present-tense stem change: **preferir (ie, *i*); pedir (i, *i*); morir (ue, *u*).**

Here is a list of the verbs you already know in each group, along with some new ones.

e → i: despedirse, pedir, preferir, seguir, sentirse, vestirse

conseguir (*to get, obtain*), divertirse (ie,i), servir (*to serve*)

o → ue: dormir(se), morir

Note that the endings of these verbs (-í, -iste, -ió, -imos, -isteis, -ieron) are the regular -ir endings for the preterite tense.

Actividad A.   ¿Qué dijeron?

Here are some excerpts from this and recent video episodes. Can you complete them with the following verbs? ¡OJO! Some verbs are used more than once.

seguí, siguió   serviste, sirvió   murió   pedí, pidió, pedimos   conseguí, consiguió

1. ARTURO: Lleva el apellido de su padre, pero el primer esposo de mi madre

_____. Debe haber un error. Él _____ en la Guerra

Civil española y este señor de México no puede ser el padre de mi hermano.

2. RAQUEL: Al final compré una bolsa. Ésta. Es linda, ¿no creen Uds.? Después de la

tienda, Arturo y yo nos separamos. Él volvió a su casa y yo _____

haciendo mis compras.

3. RAQUEL: Finalmente tuvimos un *picnic* muy especial. Arturo _____ frutas

---

*Remember that there are three patterns of stem change in the *present* tense of -ar, -er, and -ir verbs.

Group 1: e → ie (pensar, perder...)
Group 2: e → i (pedir, seguir...)
Group 3: o → ue (contar, poder, morir...)

frescas: manzanas, melones, naranjas, bananas y uvas. Y también comimos pan y queso. ¡Lo pasé muy bien!

4. RAQUEL: Después de graduarse, _____ un buen trabajo en Nueva York y se fue a vivir allá.

ARTURO: ¿Y no se volvieron a ver?

RAQUEL: Bueno. Yo también _____ un puesto, pero en Los Ángeles. Con la distancia, nos fuimos alejando.

5. RAQUEL: En el jardín, les _____ a las estrellas que nos concedieran unos deseos. Yo _____ primero y luego _____ Arturo.

Now check your answers by listening to the cassette tape.

Actividad B. Los últimos (*last*) días

You will hear a series of questions about Raquel's last days in Buenos Aires. Answer them, beginning with a verb from the left-hand column followed by a phrase from the right. Take a moment to scan both columns before beginning.

siguió	algo para él... y también algo acerca de Raquel
sirvió	en su habitación, en el Hotel Alvear
se divirtieron	la dirección de Ángel en Puerto Rico
consiguieron	en unos lugares históricos y culturales de Buenos Aires
durmió	del recepcionista del hotel
les pidió	bailar (*to dance*) el tango
se despidió	una cena (*supper*) elegante
prefirió	al botones

1. ...   2. ...   3. ...   4. ...   5. ...   6. ...   7. ...

Actividad C. ¿Y tú?

What happened the last time you went out to the movies (**ir al cine a ver una película**), a show (**ir al teatro o a un espectáculo**), or a concert (**ir a un concierto**)? Answer as many of the following questions as apply to your experience. Add other details if you like. (Worksheet)

1. ¿Qué fuiste a ver?
2. ¿Quiénes fueron contigo? ¿unos amigos o parientes? ¿O fuiste solo/a?
3. ¿Cómo se vistieron todos para la función? ¿Llevaron ropa elegante? ¿o ropa de todos los días?
4. ¿Quién consiguió las entradas (*tickets*)? ¿Durmió en la cola (*line*) para poder comprarlas?
5. ¿Te pidió un amigo dinero para comprar su entrada?
6. ¿Se divirtieron todos? ¿Quién se divirtió más?
7. ¿Todos prefirieron las mismas (*same*) partes de la función?
8. ¿Sirvieron refrescos (*refreshments*) durante la función?
9. ¿A qué hora se despidieron todos después de la función?
10. ¿Cómo se sintieron al día siguiente?

50. *ADEMÁS, NOS VA A SERVIR PARA LA BÚSQUEDA:* TALKING ABOUT TO WHOM OR FOR WHOM SOMETHING IS DONE (FIRST- AND SECOND-PERSON PLURAL INDIRECT OBJECT PRONOUNS)

Una tarjeta postal

Queridos Elena, Miguel, Miguel y Jaime,
¡Buenas noticias! En Buenos Aires conocí
a un hijo de Rosario, Arturo. Ahora
tenemos una carta de Ángel, con su
dirección en Puerto Rico. (Nos la dio
Héctor, un amigo de Ángel). Por eso
voy ahora al Caribe.
  ¿Qué les parecen[1] las fotos, especialmente la del Rosedal? Les compré un
regalo en Buenos Aires. Voy a mandárselo
de Puerto Rico. ¡Me divertí mucho aquí!
  Abrazos,[2]
          Raquel

La Familia Ruiz
Calle Pureza, 21
Sevilla, España

[1]*¿Qué... What do you think about (of)*
[2]*Hugs.*

Forms

The first- and second-person plural indirect object pronouns are **nos** and **os** (familiar). As usual, the form corresponding to **ustedes** is the third-person plural form, **les**.

Uses

Héctor **nos** dijo que Ángel se fue a vivir a Puerto Rico. En el puerto, **nos** dio la carta que recibió de Ángel.	*Héctor told us that Ángel went to live in Puerto Rico. At the port he gave us the letter he got from Ángel.*
Chicos, Raquel **os** manda saludos en su tarjeta postal de Buenos Aires.	*Kids, Raquel sends you greetings in her postcard from Buenos Aires.*

- Since **nos** and **os** can have only one meaning, no clarifying phrase is ever needed with them. The prepositional phrases **a nosotros** and **a vosotros** are occasionally used for extra emphasis and/or contrast.
- The **os** form, which corresponds to the **vosotros** form of address, is used primarily in Spain. In Latin America the plural form used to refer to people with whom you use **tú**, such as a group of friends or family, is **les**.
- Remember that indirect object pronouns are required with verbs such as **gustar**, **encantar**, and **molestar**. Another useful verb that functions similarly to these verbs is **parecer** (*to seem, appear*).

Jaime y Miguel, ¿qué **os** parecen las fotos en la tarjeta postal que **os** mandó Raquel?	*Jaime and Miguel, what do you think of the photos on the postcard that Raquel sent (to) you?*
—Nos gustó el Rosedal. Nos pareció muy bonito.	*—We liked the Rosedal. It seemed very pretty to us.*

Note in particular the question **¿Qué te/le(s)/os parece(n)... ?**, used to ask someone's opinion.

- You may wish to review the rules for the placement of these object pronouns, which were explained in Lección 16 of the Workbook.

Actividad A.   Mientras tanto, en Sevilla

The Ruiz family has just received Raquel's postcard. On the cassette tape you will hear a series of questions that Jaime, who has not read the card yet, might ask about it. Can you find an appropriate answer that Elena might give? Take a moment to scan the possible answers before beginning.

a. Sí, nos contó un poco. Dice que va al Caribe.
b. A ver... (*Let's see . . .*) Dice que va a escribirnos de Puerto Rico.
c. Bueno, la investigación nos pareció muy importante.
d. No, no os mandó un regalo, pero sí os compró algo.
e. Sí, claro. Nos encantó conocerla.
f. No. Nos escribió una tarjeta postal.
g. Pues... nos habló de un hijo de Rosario, y luego de otro señor. Pero no está muy claro.

1. ____ 2. ____ 3. ____ 4. ____ 5. ____ 6. ____ 7. ____

Actividad B. La tarjeta de Raquel

Here is the text of the second paragraph from the postcard Raquel sent to the Ruiz family. Because she is of Mexican descent, Raquel uses **les** to express *you* (*plural*). If Raquel were Spanish, how would the paragraph read? ¡OJO!

> ¿Qué **les** parecen las fotos, especial-
> mente la del Rosedal? **Les** compré un
> regalo en Buenos Aires. Voy a mandár**selo**
> de Puerto Rico. ¡Me divertí mucho aquí!

 Now check your answers by listening to the cassette tape.

Actividad C. ¿Y tú?

Think about someone that you like to do things with on Saturdays or Sundays. It may be a good friend, a child of yours, your spouse, and so on. Then create at least four sentences that describe what you and that person do or don't like to do. (Worksheet)

MODELO: Los sábados/domingos, (no) nos gusta...

Frases útiles: cenar en restaurantes, ir al teatro/cine, bailar en una discoteca, leer novelas/revistas, despertarse tarde, trabajar en el jardín

Actividad D. ¿Y tú?

Now think of someone with whom you are generally in agreement about matters of taste. Then complete the following sentences, expressing your shared opinions. (Worksheet)

1. Un restaurante que a los dos nos parece fenomenal es...
2. Una película que nos gustó a los dos el año pasado fue...
3. Nos encanta ver _____ (programa de televisión).
4. La música moderna nos parece...

51. *HÉCTOR PROMETIÓ BUSCÁRNOSLA*: MORE ABOUT USING TWO OBJECT PRONOUNS TOGETHER

Forms

As with the singular forms, the plural indirect object pronouns **nos** and **os** can combine with direct object pronouns. Here are the common combinations. Remember that the indirect object pronoun always comes first.

> **nos** + lo, la, los, las
> **os** + lo, la, los, las

Remember that **le** and **les** change to **se**, producing these combinations: *se* + **lo, la, los, las.**

Uses

RAMÓN: Ángel está en Puerto Rico. **Nos lo** dijo Raquel.

RAMÓN: *Ángel is in Puerto Rico. Raquel told us (it).*

ELENA: Chicos, aquí hay una tarjeta postal de Raquel. **Os la** mandó desde Buenos Aires.

ELENA: *Kids, here's a postcard from Raquel. She sent it to you from Buenos Aires.*

RAQUEL: ¿Y las fotos de la tumba de Rosario? ¿Debo mandár**selas**, Ramón?

RAQUEL: *And the photos of Rosario's tomb? Should I send them to you, Ramón?*

RAMÓN: No, no es necesario. **Nos las** puedes dar cuando estés de vuelta.

RAMÓN: *No, it's not necessary. You can give them to us when you're back.*

You may wish to review the rules for the placement of these object pronouns, which were explained in **Lección 16** of the Workbook.

Actividad A.   Objetos importantes

The following things have changed hands during the first video episodes of *Destinos*. Read through the list and try to remember what people and actions were associated with them. Then match the statements with the items.

a.   la carta sobre Rosario
b.   el perro Osito
c.   la cartera de Raquel
d.   la foto de Jaime y Miguel
e.   la carta para Rosario

f.   el cuadro que pintó Ángel
g.   la tarjeta postal de Madrid
h.   el certificado de nacimiento de Ángel
i.   la carta de Ángel

1. ____ Raquel: «Me lo mandó Elena Ramírez a Madrid.»
2. ____ Jaime: «Papá nos lo compró en el mercadillo.»
3. ____ Los padres de Raquel: «Nuestra hija nos la escribió desde España.»
4. ____ Héctor: «Se lo di a Arturo Iglesias, el hermano de Ángel.»
5. ____ Raquel: «Teresa Suárez me la dio en Madrid.»
6. ____ don Fernando: «Teresa Suárez me la mandó.»
7. ____ Raquel: «Alfredo Sánchez me la encontró, gracias a Dios.»
8. ____ Héctor: «Se la di a Arturo Iglesias.»
9. ____ Teresa Suárez: «Me la trajo Raquel desde Sevilla.»

Actividad B.   La tarjeta de Raquel

Paso 1

Raquel tells the Ruiz family some things about her trip to Buenos Aires, but not everything. Read the postcard again, to be sure that you remember what she wrote.

> Queridos Elena, Miguel, Miguel y Jaime,
> ¡Buenas noticias! En Buenos Aires conocí a un hijo de Rosario, Arturo. Ahora tenemos una carta de Ángel, con su dirección en Puerto Rico. (Nos la dio Héctor, un amigo de Ángel). Por eso voy ahora al Caribe.
> ¿Qué les parecen las fotos, especialmente la del Rosedal? Les compré un regalo en Buenos Aires. Voy a mandárselo de Puerto Rico. ¡Me divertí mucho aquí!
> Abrazos,
> Raquel

> La Familia Ruiz
> Calle Pureza, 21
> Sevilla, España

 #### Paso 2

You will hear a series of questions about the content of Raquel's postcard. They are addressed to Miguel and Elena Ramírez; for that reason, the speaker will use the pronoun **os**. Can you find an appropriate answer for each question? Answer as if you were Miguel or Elena.

Sí, (No, no) nos lo dijo.
Sí, (No, no) nos lo explicó.
Sí, (No, no) nos lo contó.

1. ... 2. ... 3. ... 4. ... 5. ... 6. ...

Actividad C. ¿Y tú?

Who does the following things for you and your friends (or for you and your family)? Answer as many questions as you can based on your own experience. (Worksheet)

¿Quién(es)... ?

1. les da muchos problemas
2. les da consejos constantemente
3. les manda tarjetas de Navidad/Chanuka
4. les pide dinero con frecuencia
5. les recomienda nuevos restaurantes

• •

PRONUNCIACIÓN: *y* AND *ll*

The Spanish sound [y] is generally pronounced like the *y* in English *yo-yo* or *yellow*, although there are several slight regional variations that have no exact English equivalent. Especially at the beginning of a word, it is often pronounced more like the English *j* in *just*. In Argentina and Uruguay, as you have heard in Arturo's speech, it is pronounced more like the *s* in *measure* or the *z* in *azure*.

The letters *y* and *ll* are pronounced exactly the same by most Spanish speakers. Remember that in Spanish the *ll* is considered a single letter; it comes after *l* in the alphabet.

Actividad A.

Listen to the differences between these pronunciations of the [y] sound in different parts of the Spanish-speaking world.

el Caribe: Yolanda lleva una blusa amarilla. Yo, no.
Madrid: Yolanda lleva una blusa amarilla. Yo, no.
México: Yolanda lleva una blusa amarilla. Yo, no.
la Argentina: Yolanda lleva una blusa amarilla. Yo, no.

Now listen to these phrases.

la Argentina: Leyó un cuento en castellano.
México: Leyó un cuento en castellano.

Actividad B. ¿L o *ll*?

Indicate the letter used to spell each of the following words. Each word will be said twice.

1. ll l
2. ll l
3. ll l

4. ll l
5. ll l
6. ll l

Actividad C.

Repeat the following words and sentences, imitating the speaker.

1. llamar llevar llegar yo también ya no yoyó
2. ellas calle cebolla amarillo mayo leyó
3. Yolanda Carillo llegó de Castilla.
   Julio leyó la novela de Cela.
   Yo me llamo Guillermo.

Have you completed the following sections of the lesson? Check them off here.

_____ **Más allá del episodio**   _____ **Pronunciación**

_____ **Gramática**

Now scan the words in the **Vocabulario** list to be sure that you understand the meaning of most of them.

• •

VOCABULARIO

Los verbos

bailar	to dance
conseguir (i, i)	to get, obtain
divertirse (ie, i)	to have a good time
parecer	to seem, appear
servir (i, i)	to serve

Las cosas

la tarjeta postal	postcard

Los adjetivos

último/a	last

Las palabras adicionales

¿Qué te/os/le(s) parece(n)... ?	What do you think of . . . ?

Now that you have completed the Textbook and Workbook for **Lección 17**, take the Self-Test for that lesson. (It is on page 276.) Remember to listen to the tape when you see the cassette symbol and to check your answers.

_____ **Self-Test**

Now that you have worked through the Textbook and the Workbook and taken the Self-Test, here are some of the things you have accomplished in Spanish.

- You have learned more about greeting others and saying good-bye to them in Spanish.
- You can use and understand vocabulary related to writing and written materials.
- You have learned more about narrating in the past in Spanish.
- You know how to express phrases such as *to/for us* and *to/for all of you* in some contexts in Spanish.
- You have learned more about describing opinions you and others have.
- You can use direct and indirect object pronouns together in the same sentences as well as understand their meaning.
- You know how Spanish **y** and **ll** are pronounced.
- You have continued to improve your listening skills.

You are now ready to continue on with **Lección 18** in the Textbook.

18
ESTIMADA SRA. SUÁREZ

OBJETIVOS

Whereas the materials in the Textbook all had to do with the video episode, the materials in the Workbook will help you expand your knowledge of the Spanish language in general, as well as give you opportunities for self-expression in Spanish. In this lesson, you will review

- what you have learned about narrating in the past, using preterite verb forms
- the forms and uses of object pronouns of many kinds
- vocabulary groups such as words for meat, fish, fruits and vegetables, and other foods, as well as words for talking about writing and written materials.

Remember to listen to the tape for **Lección 18** when you see the cassette symbol and to check your answers in Appendix 1.

GRAMÁTICA

 ### 52. *RESUMEN*: PRETERITE-TENSE FORMS AND USES

You have learned the preterite forms for all types of Spanish verbs, and you have also learned the general uses of the preterite.

Regular Verbs

Can you complete the following table with the forms of verbs that are regular in the preterite tense?

cenar		correr		decidir	
cen____	cenamos	corrí	corr____	decid____	decidimos
cenaste	cen____	corr____	corristeis	decidiste	decid____
cen____	cenaron	corr____	corr____	decid____	decid____

Spelling Change Verbs

Remember that certain verbs have a spelling change in some preterite forms. Can you give the indicated preterite forms for these verbs?

-car: buscar: yo   _____
-gar: llegar: yo   _____
-zar: empezar: yo   _____

           leer: él   _____
           oír: ellos   _____

-Ir Stem-Changing Verbs

Remember that the stem vowel of -ir stem-changing verbs changes in the preterite tense. The change occurs in a predictable pattern. Think about where the stem change occurs (in which persons of the preterite-tense conjugation) and indicate the change with an X in the following chart.

yo form   _____   nosotros/as form   _____
tú form   _____   vosotros/as form   _____
Ud. form   _____   Uds. form   _____
él/ella form   _____   ellos/ellas form   _____

Here are the forms of two -ir stem-changing verbs. Can you complete the table?

INFINITIVE	STEM	CHANGE	COMPLETE CONJUGATION	
pedir	ped-	e → i	p____dí	p____dimos
			pediste	pedisteis
			p____dió	p____dieron
dormir	dorm-	o → u	d____rmí	d____rmimos
			dormiste	dormisteis
			d____rmió	d____rmieron

Verbs with Irregularities

You have already learned the preterite-tense forms of most of the Spanish verbs that have irregularities. Review what you know by supplying the indicated forms in the following chart.

andar: yo   _____   querer: Uds.   _____

decir: ellos   _____   saber: yo   _____

estar: Ud.   _____   ser: ellos   _____

hacer: él   _____   tener: vosotros   _____

ir: nosotros   _____   traer: ella   _____

poder: tú   _____   venir: tú   _____

poner: yo   _____

Uses

As you know, the preterite-tense forms of Spanish verbs usually correspond to the English verb form that ends in -ed or to the compound past tense formed with *did*. (However, many English verbs are irregular in the past, so the English equivalent will not always end in -ed.)

Preterite forms are often used to express actions or events that happened once in the past (as compared to repeated or habitual actions that occurred a number of times). The beginning of an action is also expressed with the preterite.

As you know, there is another simple past tense in Spanish, the imperfect. In the next six lessons you will learn the forms and uses of the imperfect, then learn how to use the preterite and the imperfect together.

Actividad A. En la Argentina I

Can you complete the following summary of the things that happened to Raquel early in her investigation? Provide the appropriate preterite form of the indicated verbs.

Cuando Raquel (llegar) _____[1] a Buenos Aires, (ir) _____[2] directamente a su hotel. A la mañana siguiente (salir) _____[3] para la estancia Santa Susana, la dirección que le (dar) _____[4] Teresa Suárez. En la estancia, (hablar) _____[5] con Cirilo, un gaucho que (acordarse) _____[6] de Rosario. Según Cirilo, Rosario (mudarse) _____[7] a la capital hace años. Cirilo le (dar) _____[8] a Raquel la dirección de Rosario en Buenos Aires.

En Buenos Aires, Raquel (buscar) _____[9] la calle y el número. Cuando no (encontrar) _____[10] el nombre Castillo, (decidir) _____[11] preguntar por Ángel en una casa. El psiquiatra con quien por fin (hablar) _____[12] fue Arturo Iglesias, hijo de Rosario... y medio hermano de Ángel Castillo. Arturo le (contar) _____[13] que Rosario (morir) _____[14] hace unos años. En cuanto a Ángel, le (decir) _____[15] Arturo, (él: perder) _____[16] contacto con él hace mucho tiempo. Los dos (ir) _____[17] a un cementerio, donde Raquel (sacar) _____[18] fotos de la tumba de Rosario, para mostrárselas a don Fernando.

Now check your answers by listening to the cassette tape.

Actividad B. En la Argentina II

Now complete this part of the summary of events with the phrases given. In some cases, you will both select a phrase and provide the appropriate preterite form of the infinitive.

Frases con verbos: decirles, encontrar a José, ir a La Boca/al puerto, mostrarle a Raquel una foto, poder decirles, reconocerlo

Sustantivos: la búsqueda, una cantina, la casa de Arturo, el hombre de la foto, el nombre de Héctor, la esposa de José

Motivado tal vez por su sentimiento de culpabilidad, Arturo decidió ayudar a Raquel en su _____.[1] Cuando llegó al hotel al día siguiente, _____[2] de Ángel. Con la foto, los dos _____,[3] en busca de Ángel. Allí les preguntaron a varias personas si reconocían[a] a _____.[4] Desgraciadamente, nadie _____.[5]

Por fin un señor _____[6] que tal vez José, un marinero, los podría[b] ayudar. Raquel y Arturo _____[7] en su barco. El marinero no reconoció a Ángel tampoco, pero mencionó _____,[8] otro marinero. José fue a

[a]*they recognized* [b]*could*

buscarlo. No lo encontró, pero sí _____⁹ que lo podrían conocer

mañana por la noche en _____,¹⁰ el Piccolo Navio.

 Now check your answers by listening to the cassette tape.

Actividad C.   En la Argentina III
In this part of the summary, you will form complete sentences by putting the words given in the appropriate order. Scan all of the words in a given item first before trying to put them in order.

Esa noche,

1. en / Arturo / de / cenaron / y / casa / Raquel / Arturo

_____

Durante la cena,

2. vida / poco / le / de / Raquel / su / un / contó / Arturo / a

_____

Al día siguiente,

3. Héctor / cantina / hablar / pudieron / a / y / fueron / con / la

_____

4. sí / marinero / Ángel / este / a / recordó

_____

5. vivir / a / que / dijo / al / fue / Caribe / se / les / Ángel

_____

6. hace / que / carta / mandó / prometió / años / Ángel / una / le / buscarles

_____

_____

7. dirección / la / su / tendría (*would have*) / seguramente / carta

_____

8. Arturo / volvieron / casa / Raquel / y / de / la / Arturo / a

_____

_____

9. Arturo / tenía / que / presentimiento / del / hablaron / mal / allí

_____

_____

¿Estaba muerto Ángel?

Actividad D.   En la Argentina IV
You will hear the speaker on the cassette tape begin the following sentences that continue the summary of the events in Argentina. Complete the sentences with the preterite forms of the infinitives.

Lección 18 Estimada Sra. Suárez

MODELO: (*you see*)   Al día siguiente, mientras esperaban[a] la llamada de Héctor, Raquel y Arturo (*ir*) de compras por la mañana.
                 (*you hear*)   Al día siguiente, mientras esperaban la llamada de Héctor, Raquel y Arturo...
                 (*you say*)   Raquel y Arturo fueron de compras por la mañana.
                 (*you hear*)   Raquel y Arturo fueron de compras por la mañana.

1. Al día siguiente, mientras esperaban[a] la llamada de Héctor, Raquel y Arturo (ir) de compras por la mañana.
2. Héctor (llamar) a Arturo por la tarde.
3. Él (encontrar) la carta.
4. Pero no (poder) hablarles hasta mañana.
5. Por eso, ya que no había nada más que hacer,[b] Raquel y Arturo (pasar) el resto del día juntos.
6. Ellos (divertirse) mucho en el Rosedal.
7. Allí (andar) en mateo y en bote y (tener) un *picnic*.

[a]mientras... *while they were waiting for*   [b]no... *there was nothing else they could do*

Actividad E. En la Argentina V

The following sentences form the conclusion of the events that happened in Argentina, but they are out of order. Can you put them in order in each group?

Parte 1 (1–6)

a. _____ Raquel y Arturo fueron allí para buscarlo.
b. _____ Otra vez tuvo un mal presentimiento sobre la muerte de Ángel.
c. _____ Héctor llamó a Arturo al día siguiente.
d. _____ Arturo la leyó y se quedó muy pensativo.
e. _____ En el puerto, Héctor les dio la carta de Ángel.
f. _____ Le dijo que iba a estar en el puerto.

Parte 2 (1–7)

a. _____ Fueron a muchos sitios de interés histórico y cultural.
b. _____ Estaba (*It was*) claro que Raquel tendría que (*would have to*) salir para Puerto Rico.
c. _____ Allí se despidieron con ternura y Arturo le dio a Raquel una pulsera (*bracelet*) como recuerdo de su visita a la Argentina.
d. _____ Arturo y Raquel lo pasaron muy bien durante su último día en Buenos Aires.
e. _____ Luego Arturo llevó a Raquel al aeropuerto.
f. _____ Eso le gustó mucho a Raquel.
g. _____ A Arturo se le ocurrió la idea de ir a Puerto Rico con Raquel para continuar la búsqueda.

53. *RESUMEN*: PRONOUNS

In the lessons of the Textbook and Workbook you have learned about a number of types of pronouns. What kind of pronoun

1. is the first recipient of the action of the verb?   _____
2. answers the question *to whom* or *for whom* in relation to the verb?   _____
3. must agree in person and number with the subject of the sentence?   _____
4. is used after words like **a**, **de**, **sobre**, and so on?   _____

Now complete the following chart with the missing pronouns. All of the subject pronouns are given for you.

SUBJECT	REFLEXIVE	INDIRECT	DIRECT	OBJECT OF PREP.
yo	_____	me	_____	a _____
tú	te	_____	te	a _____
Ud.	se	_____	_____	a Ud.
él	_____	le	_____	a él
ella	_____	_____	la	a ella
nosotros/as	_____	nos	_____	a _____
vosotros/as	os	os	_____	a vosotros
Uds.	_____	les	_____	a _____
ellos	_____	_____	los	a ellos
ellas	se	_____	_____	a ellas

Now complete the following descriptions. The reflexive, direct, and indirect object pronouns

> follow/precede conjugated verb forms
> come after/in between **no** and a conjugated verb form
> may/must follow and be attached to an infinitive.

Actividad A. Episodios de la búsqueda

The following are brief descriptions of incidents from Raquel and Arturo's meeting and search for Ángel, but there is a lot of repetition in them. Try to eliminate as much repetition as you can by changing nouns to pronouns. **Paso 1** contains brief sentences. **Paso 2** consists of a longer paragraph.

Paso 1

1. En La Boca, Arturo y Raquel les preguntaron a varias personas si reconocían a Ángel. Desgraciadamente, nadie reconoció a Ángel.
2. Los dos fueron a un cementerio, donde Raquel sacó fotos de la tumba de Rosario, para mostrarle las fotos a don Fernando.
3. En el puerto, Héctor le dio a Arturo la carta de Ángel. Arturo leyó la carta y se quedó muy pensativo.

Paso 2

Con una foto de Ángel, Arturo y Raquel fueron a La Boca, en busca de Ángel. Allí les preguntaron a varias personas si reconocían[1] a Ángel. Desgraciadamente, nadie reconoció a Ángel. Por fin un señor les dijo que tal vez José, un marinero, los podría[2] ayudar. Raquel y Arturo encontraron a José en su barco. José no reconoció a Ángel tampoco, pero mencionó el nombre de Héctor, otro marinero. José fue a buscar a Héctor. No encontró a Héctor, pero sí pudo decirles que podrían conocer a Héctor mañana por la noche en una cantina, el Piccolo Navio.

[1]*they recognized* [2]*could*

 Now check your answers by listening to the cassette tape.

Actividad B. Más episodios de la Argentina

Answer the following questions about these photographs from the Argentine video episodes. Use object pronouns as frequently as you can, and feel free to add additional details. (Worksheet)

1. Cuando Raquel llegó al hotel, ¿le dieron su habitación en seguida? ¿Qué le ofreció el recepcionista a Raquel? ¿Tomó la *suite* que le ofreció?

2. ¿Qué le preguntaron Raquel y Arturo a este señor? ¿Reconoció el señor a Ángel? ¿Qué cosa importante les dijo? ¿Adónde los llevó? ¿Dónde encontraron por fin a la persona que buscaban (*they were looking for*)?

3. ¿Quién le preparó la cena a Raquel? ¿Qué le sirvió para la cena? ¿Cómo preparó las brochetas Arturo? ¿Le gustaron a Raquel? ¿Qué le sirvió Arturo con la cena? ¿Qué le contó durante la cena?

4. ¿Quién hizo estas caras? ¿Con qué las hizo? ¿Dónde compró los ingredientes? ¿A quién le gustaron mucho las caras?

UN POCO DE TODO

Actividad A.   Hablando (*Speaking*) de la comida

Paso 1

Here is a breakfast menu from the Hotel Alvear, where Raquel stays while she is in Argentina. You should be able to understand most of it, or at least be able to order breakfast from it! Record your selections directly on the menu, and be sure to decide at what time you would like breakfast to be served, and what newspaper (**diario**) you would like delivered with it.

Pedido de Desayuno

• Por favor colocar en el lado exterior de la puerta antes de las 05:00 A.M.

MARCAR EL HORARIO DESEADO

7:00 ☐	7:30 ☐	8:00 ☐	8:30 ☐	9:00 ☐
9:30 ☐	10:00 ☐	10:30 ☐	11:00 ☐	11:30 ☐

DESAYUNO ALVEAR

JUGOS: NARANJA ☐   POMELO ☐   TOMATE ☐
CAFE ☐   TE ☐
CREMA ☐   LECHE ☐   LIMON ☐
CROISSANTS ☐   TOSTADAS ☐
MANTECA ☐   MERMELADA ☐   DULCE DE LECHE ☐
YOGURT ☐   FRUTAS FRESCAS ☐   CEREALES ☐

DESAYUNO AMERICANO

JUGOS: NARANJA ☐   POMELO ☐   TOMATE ☐
CAFE ☐   TE ☐
CREMA ☐   LECHE ☐   LIMON ☐
CROISSANTS ☐   TOSTADAS ☐
HUEVOS REVUELTOS ☐   HUEVOS FRITOS ☐
HUEVOS CON JAMON ☐   HUEVOS PASADOS POR AGUA ☐
TOCINO FRITO ☐
MANTECA ☐   MERMELADA ☐   DULCE DE LECHE ☐

DESAYUNO CONTINENTAL

JUGO DE NARANJA ☐
CAFE ☐   TE ☐   CHOCOLATE ☐
CREMA ☐   LECHE ☐   LIMON ☐
CROISSANTS ☐   TOSTADAS ☐
MANTECA ☐   MERMELADA ☐   DULCE DE LECHE ☐

DIARIOS

CLARIN ☐   LA NACION ☐   LA PRENSA ☐
AMBITO FINANCIERO ☐   BUENOS AIRES HERALD ☐
OTROS: _____

• Disque 4 ó 5 para hacer su pedido.

Paso 2

Now answer the following questions about the menu.

1. If **leche** means *milk*, what is the Spanish name for a spread made from sweetened condensed milk?
2. What are the Spanish equivalents for *scrambled eggs* and *hard-boiled eggs*?
3. What newspaper would you order if you wanted one written in English? What if you were particularly interested in financial information?

Paso 3

Now that you have ordered breakfast, think about lunch and dinner. What do you most typically eat for those meals? And what is your *ideal* lunch or dinner? Complete the following sentences for either meal. (Worksheet)

Un almuerzo típico/una cena típica consiste en...
Un almuerzo/una cena ideal para mí consiste en...

Paso 4

What you eat or would prefer to eat may not be appropriate for others. What recommendations do you have for the following people? Select at least two types of individuals and suggest what they should eat. (Worksheet)

Personas: Una persona que tiene que engordar (*gain weight*)
Una persona que quiere bajar de peso (*lose weight*)
Un vegetariano/Una vegetariana
Un niño/Una niña de 10 años
Un(a) adolescente de 16 años
Una persona que tiene 80 años
Una persona que quiere comer sólo alimentos naturales

_____ debe comer lo siguiente: ... *No* debe comer...

Actividad B. La familia de Rosario
Paso 1
You have learned a great deal about Rosario's family in Argentina. Can you complete the following family tree? All of the missing characters are men.

En España don Fernando

En la Argentina Rosario

Paso 2
Now pick two characters and write a few sentences about each one. Tell where he or she lives/lived and what his/her relationship is to several of the other characters in the tree. (Worksheet)

Actividad C. En la Argentina
The following photos represent aspects of the major parts of Raquel's search in Argentina. Write at least one sentence about each one, and add additional sentences where you feel they are necessary. When you are finished, you will have a brief summary of Raquel's investigation in Argentina. (Worksheet)

Actividad D. Para investigar
In many of the video episodes you have seen thus far, Raquel has asked many people a lot of questions. Now it is your turn to ask the questions. Create at least five questions about one of the following areas. (Worksheet)

1. What questions didn't Raquel ask in Argentina that you think she should have asked? For example, what might Héctor know that would be of interest to you? What didn't you learn about Arturo that you would like to know?
2. Are you curious about Raquel? What questions would you like to ask her? Remember that Raquel is a lawyer, so she is used to direct questions!

• •

PARA ESCRIBIR

In this activity you will write a short narrative in which you describe Raquel and Arturo's relationship to someone who has not seen the video episodes. You want to tell the reader as much as you can about them and about what happened to them in Buenos Aires, include some interesting information, and make some suggestions about what you think will happen to them in future episodes. Your narrative should be no fewer than 200 and no more than 300 words long.

Thinking About What You Will Write

In order to write this narrative the first thing you must do is think about what information you will include. A good place to begin is with your Textbook and Workbook.

Review the sections called **Preparación** and **¿Tienes buena memoria?** — in particular those in **Lecciones 12–18**—and the review sections in this lesson. You may also want to scan other sections for information about Raquel and Arturo in particular. Be sure to reread the **Más allá del episodio** sections in **Lecciones 4** and **14** in particular, because they are about these two characters.

As you scan all of these sections, note the following useful or interesting information and key phrases. (It is a good idea to do this on a separate sheet of paper. Make one chart for Raquel and another for Arturo.)

Personalidad	Le gusta...
Trabajo	No le gusta...
Familia	

At the same time you should be making a list of only the most important events in **Episodios 12–18**, in order. For now, just jot them down as phrases (**conocer a Arturo, encontrar a Héctor,...**) and don't be concerned about conjugating the verb forms.

You will not necessarily use all of the information or events in your narrative, but that's O.K. For the moment you are just trying to create a bank of ideas upon which to draw.

Organizing Your Narrative

In the first **Para escribir** section you did not have to spend any time at all organizing your narrative, because you were writing about a typical day in your life and the day itself was the organizing principle. For this narrative, however, you will need to spend some time thinking about the organization (order) of what you will write.

Begin by deciding which of the following questions you would like to answer in the narrative.

_____ What things did Raquel and Arturo do together in these video episodes?
_____ Who is Raquel?
_____ Who is Héctor Condotti?
_____ What is Raquel like as a person?
_____ What place is Raquel leaving for and why?
_____ Will Raquel and Arturo ever see each other again? If so, where and when?
_____ What is Arturo like as a person?
_____ Where and when do Raquel and Arturo meet doña Flora?
_____ How did Raquel and Arturo meet?
_____ Who is Arturo?
_____ What is their relationship like?
_____ Why is Raquel in Argentina?
_____ What does their search involve?
_____ Who is Ángel Castillo and why is he important?

There are several items that you probably did not indicate, because they are not important to the topic you are trying to address. Take the items you did select and think about whether any of them form a logical group; then consider the order in which you will present them. What sequence seems to make the most sense to you? Write a brief outline of that sequence.

Drafting

Paso 1

Now draft your narrative. At this stage you should not worry about grammar and spelling. Your goal is to get your ideas down on paper.

Paso 2

After you have completed your draft, look over what you have done. Are you still satisfied with the information you selected? Do you want to add some things and delete others, or go into more detail about certain details or events? Have you included at least one interesting detail about Raquel and one about Arturo? Keep in mind that you are writing for someone who doesn't know anything about them.

Finalizing Your Narrative

If you are satisfied with the information contained in your draft, it is time to look it over for language and style.

Paso 1

First, look at your narration for style. Does the narration flow, or is it disjointed and choppy? Does it contain words and phrases that connect events, or is it mostly an accumulation of sentences?

Here is a list of words and phrases that can help make your narration flow more smoothly.

también	also	**por eso**	that's why, therefore
pero	but	**y**	and

These words and phrases can help you express the sequence of events smoothly.

primero	first	**después**	later (on)
luego	then, next	**por fin**	finally
al día siguiente	the next day	**más tarde**	later
pronto	soon	**de nuevo**	again
cuando	when		

Paso 2

Review your narrative for the following language elements as well.

_____ gender of nouns
_____ adjective agreement
_____ subject-verb agreement
_____ correct tense (present, preterite, **ir** + **a** + *infinitive*)
_____ use of object pronouns

Paso 3

Prepare a clean copy of the final version of your narrative for your instructor.

Have you completed the following sections of the lesson? Check them off here.

_____ **Gramática**   _____ **Para escribir**

_____ **Un poco de todo**

There is no Self-Test for this lesson of the Textbook and Workbook. In preparation for a unit test or just as a general review, it would be a good idea to scan back over the Self-Tests in the previous six lessons. Then you will be ready to continue on with **Lección 19** in the Textbook.

19

POR FIN...

OBJETIVOS

Wheras the materials in the Textbook all had to do with the video episode, the materials in the Workbook will help you expand your knowledge of the Spanish language in general, as well as give you opportunities for self-expression in Spanish. In this lesson you will learn

- how to use the imperfect tense to talk about the activities of others
- more about how to talk about what you and others are doing right now
- more about how to use **por** and **para**, two Spanish prepositions that can express English *for*
- how to pronounce Spanish **x.**

Remember to listen to the tape for **Lección 19** when you see the cassette symbol and to check your answers in Appendix 1.

MÁS ALLÁ DEL EPISODIO

Actividad A.   Ángel Castillo, en Puerto Rico*

PARA PENSAR...

Look over the following questions. You probably cannot answer them now. Keep them in mind as you read the following passage, and answer them after you have finished the reading.

1.   ¿Tuvo Ángel éxito (*success*) cuando llegó a Puerto Rico? ¿Pudo vender sus cuadros?
2.   ¿Cómo y dónde conoció Ángel a María Luisa, su esposa?
3.   Cuando se casaron Ángel y María Luisa, ¿cómo recibió a Ángel la familia de ella? ¿Lo aceptaron con cariño o no le gustó a nadie y lo vieron como a «ese muchacho extranjero que quién sabe quién es»?

---

*From this point on in the Workbook, Más allá del episodio readings will be prefaced only by a brief series of questions. Be sure to read and think about them before you start the reading. Then come back to them and answer them after you have finished the passage.

Para Ángel, los primeros meses en Puerto Rico fueron como un sueño.[1] Vivió plenamente[2] su nueva libertad. Con el poco dinero que tenía, alquiló[3] una pequeña habitación en el último[4] piso de una casa color claro[5] del Viejo San Juan. Era un lugar modesto pero cómodo,[6] y tenía una vista muy hermosa al mar.

Después de instalarse,[7] sacó de sus maletas sus pinturas y pinceles[8] y comenzó a pintar. Al principio fue como una obsesión. Pintaba día y noche, sobre todo escenas del barrio de La Boca que no podía borrar[9] de su memoria. Quiso vender sus pinturas pero, así como en la Argentina, no tuvo éxito.

Dentro de poco se quedó sin dinero... y la isla empezó a perder su encanto. La habitación le pareció muy pequeña. Empezó a extrañar el lujo[10] al que estaba acostumbrado en la estancia. La voz de su padrastro resonaba en su cabeza:[11] «Tienes que trabajar, Ángel. ¡La pintura no te llevará a nada![12]». Solo, lejos de su familia y sin amigos, se sintió por primera vez desamparado.[13] De una cosa estaba seguro:[14] no podía admitir su fracaso y volver a la Argentina.

Ángel estaba muy contento en Puerto Rico.

Una mañana Ángel salió a caminar. En una librería[15] de arte, vio un cartel[16] que decía: «Se necesita joven con conocimientos de arte». Al día siguiente empezó a trabajar en la tienda. Pronto volvió a sentirse feliz en este medio[17] intelectual. Y también volvió a sentir ganas de[18] pintar. Su estilo cambió. Ahora estaba pintando su realidad... el encanto de la isla. El mar le fascinaba y en él encontró su inspiración.

Ángel estaba muy contento, pero todavía le esperaba una sorpresa. Un día en la librería empezó a hablar con una clienta joven. Ángel se sintió inmediatamente atraído[19] por su inteligencia y belleza. La invitó a tomar un café en uno de los restaurantes del barrio. Poco después se enamoraron y decidieron casarse. La familia de María Luisa, que así se llamaba la joven, acogió[20] a Ángel en seguida.

[1]*dream* [2]*fully* [3]*he rented* [4]*top* [5]*color... pastel-colored* [6]*comfortable* [7]*settling in* [8]*brushes* [9]*erase* [10]*luxury* [11]*resonaba... echoed in his mind* [12]*no... will never get you anywhere* [13]*abandoned* [14]*sure* [15]*bookstore* [16]*sign* [17]*environment* [18]*volvió... he felt like . . . again* [19]*attracted* [20]*welcomed, accepted*

Actividad B.

What else would you like to know about Ángel? Listen to the short segment on the cassette tape, then complete the following statements.

1. Ángel... nunca/por fin... tuvo éxito en el mundo artístico.
2. Ángel encontró su inspiración en el mar y en... la cultura puertorriqueña/su esposa.

• •

GRAMÁTICA

 54. *RAQUEL TOMABA UNA FOTOGRAFÍA CUANDO...* : THIRD-PERSON SINGULAR AND PLURAL FORMS (IMPERFECT TENSE)

So far you have learned to talk about the past using the preterite tense. As you know, Spanish has another past tense called the imperfect. In the next lessons you will learn the forms and uses of the imperfect.

Forms

Here are examples of the third-person singular and plural forms of the imperfect for all -ar, -er, and -ir verbs (except ser, ir, and ver).

	caminar	perder	seguir
	-aba(n)	-ía(n)	-ía(n)
él/ella	caminaba	perdía	seguía
ellos/ellas	caminaban	perdían	seguían

Note that the endings for -er and -ir verbs are identical and that they all have a written accent. Note also that there are neither stem changes nor spelling changes in the imperfect.

The imperfect of **hay** is **había** (*there was/were*).

Here are the third-person imperfect forms of **ser, ir,** and **ver,** which have irregularities.

> ser: era(n)   ir: iba(n)   ver: veía(n)

Uses

The imperfect is generally used to talk about events or conditions that were in progress (going on) at a particular point in the past, often while (**mientras**) something else was happening. The English equivalent is often (though not always) expressed with the form *was/were . . . -ing.*

Events (Actions)

Raquel **tomaba** una foto en el cementerio.	*Raquel was taking a photo in the cemetery.*
¿Qué **hacían** Raquel y Ángela mientras **esperaban** la llegada de la familia?	*What did Raquel and Ángela do while waiting for the arrival of the family?*

Conditions

La calle **estaba** bloqueada.	*The street was blocked off.*
Ángela no **sabía** nada de la historia de Rosario y don Fernando.	*Ángela didn't know anything about the story of Rosario and don Fernando.*
¿Y mi abuelo **creía** que Rosario había muerto?	*And my grandfather thought that Rosario had died?*

The past tense of **ir a** + infinitive nearly always uses the imperfect of **ir.**

Los tíos de Ángela **iban** a llegar pronto.	*Ángela's aunts and uncles were going to arrive soon.*

Actividad A.   ¿Qué hacían?

Paso 1

Who was probably doing or feeling the following while Raquel was getting to know Ángela?

a. Arturo
b. don Fernando
c. los tíos de Ángela
d. los hijos de don Fernando

1. ____ Pensaba en Raquel.
2. ____ Comían juntos en La Gavia.
3. ____ Dormía en su habitación.
4. ____ Iban a salir de casa.
5. ____ Hablaban de la investigación de la abogada.
6. ____ Escuchaba los problemas de un paciente.
7. ____ Andaban hacia su carro.
8. ____ No se sentía muy bien.

Paso 2

Now listen as the speaker on the cassette tape repeats the items with an appropriate name.

Actividad B.   Un poco de historia

In this lesson you learned that Ponce de León built a magnificent house in old San Juan in the early 1500s. What else was going on in the world from the early 1500s to the early 1600s? Indicate the appropriate items.

1. _____ Los españoles empezaban a colonizar América.
2. _____ Cleopatra reinaba en Egipto.
3. _____ En España, Fernando e Isabel eran los reyes de Castilla y León y otras partes de la península.
4. _____ En la China y el Japón no existía todavía una civilización avanzada.
5. _____ En Inglaterra (*England*) Henry VIII era el rey.
6. _____ Había colonias inglesas en lo que (*what*) hoy son los Estados Unidos.
7. _____ En lo que hoy es el Perú, los incas tenían una civilización muy avanzada.
8. _____ Muchos ingleses ya vivían en lo que es hoy California.

Now check your answers by listening to the cassette tape.

Actividad C.   Durante el Episodio 19

You know where you were while you were watching **Episodio 19**, but where were your family and friends and what were *they* doing? Select the appropriate answer(s) or provide your own.

1. Mis compañeros de clase
   a. _____ también miraban el episodio
   b. _____ trabajaban
   c. _____ escribían las actividades del Episodio 19
   d. _____ ¿?

2. Mi padre (madre, hermano/a, ...)
   a. _____ no hacía nada en particular
   b. _____ estaba en el trabajo
   c. _____ almorzaba
   d. _____ ¿?

3. Mi mejor amigo/a
   a. _____ veía la televisión
   b. _____ estudiaba en la biblioteca
   c. _____ iba a salir para la universidad
   d. _____ ¿?

4. Mi perro (gato, otro animal doméstico)
   a. _____ dormía
   b. _____ jugaba (*was playing*)
   c. _____ andaba al aire libre
   d. _____ ¿?

Actividad D.   ¿Y tu profesor(a)?

What do you think your Spanish instructor was doing yesterday at different times? Complete each sentence with the appropriate form of one or more of the infinitives given. You can add details if you wish, or use other activities, especially if you know some real information about your instructor. (Worksheet)

1. A las ocho de la mañana...   (dormir, desayunar, ir a la universidad, leer el periódico)
2. A las once de la mañana...   (dar una clase, trabajar en su oficina, hablar con un estudiante, reunirse con unos colegas)
3. A la una de la tarde...   (almorzar en la cafetería, almorzar en su oficina, dar una clase, salir para su casa)
4. A las seis de la tarde...   (mirar las noticias en la televisión, cenar, hacer ejercicio, correr en el parque)
5. A las once de la noche...   (mirar la televisión, dormir, leer en la cama [*bed*], preparar las clases para mañana)

55. ¿QUÉ HACE USTED AQUÍ? —ESTOY TOMANDO UNA FOTO: THE PRESENT PROGRESSIVE

Raquel le **está contando** a Ángela la historia de don Fernando y Rosario. También le **está explicando** los últimos detalles de su investigación. Ángela la **está escuchando** con mucha atención. También **está pensando**: ¡Esta historia parece de novela!

Forms

The present progressive is formed with the present tense of **estar** and the present participle. In English the present participle is the verb form that ends in *-ing*; in Spanish it ends in **-ndo**.

Here are the regular present participle endings.

cruzar	correr	vivir
-ando	-iendo	-iendo
cruzando	corriendo	viviendo

-**Er** verbs that have a stem ending in **-a, -e,** or **-o** replace the **i** in the ending with **y**.

creer → creyendo   traer → trayendo   oír → oyendo

-**Ir** stem-changing verbs show the preterite stem change in the present participle.

dormir → durmiendo   sentir → sintiendo   servir → sirviendo

Some verbs with irregularities in the present have an irregularity in the present participle as well. The most frequently used is **diciendo** (**decir**).

Uses

¿Qué diablos **están haciendo** aquí que todas las calles están bloqueadas?	*What the devil are they doing here that has all the streets closed off?*
Disculpe. **Estoy buscando** la calle Sol.	*Excuse me. I'm looking for Sol Street.*
Raquel se **está despidiendo** (**está despidiéndose**) de Arturo en el aeropuerto.	*Raquel is saying good-bye to Arturo at the airport.*

- The present participle is invariable in form. It never shows agreement in number or gender.
- In Spanish, the progressive is used to stress the ongoing nature of an event or a condition. An event expressed with the progressive is actually in progress.
- When object or reflexive pronouns are used with the progressive, they may either be attached to the participle or precede the conjugated verb. The present participle thus combines with pronouns in the same manner as with the infinitive. When pronouns are attached to the participle, a written accent is required to maintain the stress on the same syllable of the participle.
- Remember that the simple present tense in Spanish often expresses the equivalent of the English progressive, especially in the case of verbs of motion such as **ir** and **venir**. The participles of **ir** (**yendo**) and **venir** (**viniendo**) are used only infrequently. Moreover, the progressive does not express the idea of future intent, as it often does in English. Note the following examples in which the Spanish progressive is *not* used.

I'm going to cross the street.	Voy a cruzar la calle.
I'm leaving for San Germán tomorrow.	Salgo mañana para San Germán.
She's returning to Ángela's house now.	Vuelve ahora a la casa de Ángela.
We are sitting (i.e., we are seated) over there.	Estamos sentados allí.

Actividad A. ¿Quién lo está diciendo?

Which characters could be saying the following things?

a. Ángela   c. Raquel
b. el taxista   d. el amigo de Ángela

1. _____ Estoy tomando una foto de esta tumba.
2. _____ ¿Qué diablos están haciendo aquí? Todas las calles están bloqueadas.
3. _____ Estoy hablando por teléfono con uno de mis tíos.
4. _____ Disculpe. Estoy buscando la calle Sol.
5. _____ Estoy visitando la Casa Blanca.
6. _____ Estoy pensando en Jorge, mi novio.
7. _____ Estoy mostrándole la Casa Blanca a una amiga de Ángela.
8. _____ Estoy hablando por teléfono con Pedro Castillo en México.

Actividad B. ¿Qué están haciendo?

Listen as the speaker on the cassette tape describes the following photographs. Can you match each description with its photo?

a. _____   b. _____   c. _____   d. _____

Actividad C. ¿Quién lo está haciendo?

Can you name someone you think is doing the following things right now? It may be someone you know personally or a famous person.

¿Quién está... ?

1. contando su dinero
2. haciendo una película nueva
3. escribiendo algo sobre los secretos de la gente famosa
4. estudiando español
5. escribiendo una novela nueva
6. dando un discurso (*speech*)
7. celebrando una fiesta
8. visitando otro país

Actividad D. ¿Y tú?

Paso 1

Describe what you are doing right now, using progressive forms. Remember that you are probably doing a number of things at once, not just reading! How many activities can you come up with? (Worksheet)

Paso 2

Now select three or four people whom you know well and describe what they are probably doing at the moment. (Worksheet)

56. *POR SUPUESTO. SIGA POR ESTA CALLE*: *por* AND *para*, TWO MORE IMPORTANT PREPOSITIONS

Raquel buscaba la tumba de Ángel y se encontró con Ángela en el cementerio. Después de hablar un poco, las dos mujeres fueron al apartamento de Ángela. Ella hizo limonada **para** las dos. En el apartamento, había unos cuadros pintados **por** Ángel, y Raquel los admiraba.

Ángela trató de hablar con sus tíos **por** teléfono. Mientras tanto, Raquel salió **para** dar un paseo y visitó una casa construida **para** Ponce de León. Luego Ángela y Raquel caminaron **por** el Parque de las Palomas, donde había pájaros **por** todas partes. Luego volvieron al apartamento, **para** esperar a los tíos de Ángela.

As you know, prepositions express relationships of space, time, means, and purpose between two other elements in a sentence. Two very important prepositions that you have already seen and heard frequently are **por** and **para**. While both are often translated into English as *for*, they are not interchangeable. Here is an example. In these two sentences, "The book is for John" and "I paid two dollars for the book," the word *for* expresses two different relationships. In Spanish the first is expressed with **para** and the second with **por**.

It will take experience and practice for you to be able to use these prepositions accurately. If you can understand the meanings of **por** and **para** in the paragraphs at the beginning of this section, you have a head start. This section will introduce you to the different meanings of **para** and **por**, and it will give you practice with some of the most basic uses.

General Uses of Prepositions

* Remember that, as with all Spanish prepositions, **por** and **para** will always be followed by an object: a noun, pronoun, or an infinitive: **para Julio, por él, para llegar**.
* The pronoun forms used with **por** and **para** are the same as the subject pronouns, except for **mí** and **ti**.

When Not to Use *por* or *para*

* Remember that some Spanish verbs don't require a preposition, whereas their English equivalents do: **esperar** = *to wait for*; **buscar** = *to look for*.
* Remember also that when *for* relates to a verb, it is often expressed with an indirect object rather than with a preposition.

> Arturo **le** compró una campera a Raquel.　　*Arturo bought Raquel a jacket (a jacket for Raquel).*

Using *para*

Para is often the equivalent of English *for*, especially when it involves the notion of a goal or destination. *Para* expresses *for* when *for* means the following:

1. *destined for, to go to* or *be given to* (someone)

   > Antes de ir a su casa, preparé una sorpresa **para** Arturo.　　*Before going to his house I prepared a surprise for Arturo.*

2. *to, in the direction of*

   > Salgo **para** Puerto Rico mañana.　　*I leave for Puerto Rico tomorrow.*

3. *to be used for* or *in*

   > Arturo compró mucha fruta **para** el *picnic*.　　*Arturo bought a lot of fruit for the picnic.*

   > La foto fue útil **para** la búsqueda.　　*The photo was useful for the search.*

4. *in relation to (compared to) others*

   > **Para** (ser un) marinero, Héctor cantaba muy bien.　　*For a sailor, Héctor sang very well.*

Para mí, es una gran sorpresa.	*For me, it's a big surprise.*

In addition, **para** has this very frequent use in Spanish.

5. *in order to* + infinitive (often *in order* is not expressed)

Fuimos al puerto **para** buscarlo.	*We went to the port (in order) to look for him.*
Todo ha sido tan rápido; necesito tiempo para pensar.	*Everything has been so fast. I need time (in order) to think.*

Actividad A.   ¿Qué expresa *para*?

Refer to the preceding numbered explanations to indicate the use of **para** found in the following sentences.

a. _____ Tengo una sed increíble! Voy a traer limonada para las dos.
b. _____ Por fin los tíos de Ángela salieron para el apartamento de Ángela.
c. _____ Esta pulsera (*bracelet*) es para Raquel.
d. _____ Raquel tuvo que andar mucho para llegar a la calle Sol.
e. _____ La despedida fue triste. Especialmente para Arturo.
f. _____ Las verduras que compró Raquel eran para una sorpresa.

Actividad B.   ¿Para qué va la gente a estos lugares?

Why do people usually go to the following places? Create at least seven sentences. (Worksheet)

MODELO: un supermercado → La gente va a un supermercado para comprar comida.

una discoteca		comer
un parque		celebrar algo
una universidad	para	caminar
un museo		prepararse para una carrera
un restaurante		tomar el aire
un cine		comer palomitas (*popcorn*)
una oficina		ver una exposición de arte
		descansar (*to rest*)
		aprender
		ver una película
		bailar
		admirar un cuadro
		conversar con los amigos
		conocer a otra gente
		correr
		trabajar
		estudiar
		¿ ?

Using *por*

Por is also often the equivalent of English *for*. **Por** expresses *for* when *for* means the following:

1. *in exchange for*

Raquel pagó cincuenta mil australes **por** la bolsa de cuero.	*Raquel paid fifty thousand australes for the leather purse.*
«(Muchas) Gracias **por** la campera.»	*"Thank you (very much) for the jacket."*

2. *for the sake of, on behalf of*

Raquel está haciendo el viaje **por** don Fernando.	*Raquel is taking the trip for don Fernando.*

3. *for a period of time*

Los descendientes de Ponce de León ocuparon la casa **por** 250 años.	*The descendants of Ponce de León occupied the house for 250 years.*

In addition, **por** has these very frequent uses in Spanish.

4. *by, by means of*

Ayer, Raquel habló con su madre **por** teléfono.	*Yesterday, Raquel spoke with her mother by telephone.*
Los cuadros fueron pintados **por** Ángel.	*The paintings were painted by Ángel.*

5. *through, along*

Ángel viajó **por** muchos países antes de llegar a Puerto Rico.	*Ángel traveled through a lot of countries before coming to Puerto Rico.*
Siga **por** esta calle.	*Continue along this street.*

6. *during, in* (with morning, afternoon, etc.)

Por la noche Arturo y Raquel fueron al Piccolo Navio.	*In the evening Arturo and Raquel went to the Piccolo Navio.*

7. *because of, on account of, about*

En el episodio previo Raquel se preocupaba **por** Arturo.	*In the previous episode Raquel worried about Arturo.*
Fue difícil llegar a la calle Sol **por** las calles bloqueadas.	*It was difficult to get to Sol Street because of the blocked-off streets.*

8. **Por** is also used in a number of fixed expressions.

por Dios	for heaven's sake	por lo general	generally
por ejemplo	for example	por lo menos	at least
por eso	that's why, for that reason	por primera/última vez	for the first/ last time
por favor	please	por supuesto	of course
por fin	finally	por todas partes	everywhere

Actividad C.   ¿Qué expresa *por*?

Refer to the preceding numbered explanations to indicate the use of **por** found in the following sentences.

a. ____ Raquel y Ángela caminaron por el Parque de las Palomas.
b. ____ Ángela necesita hablar con sus tíos por teléfono.
c. ____ Por favor, señorita, ¿quién es usted?
d. ____ Sigo por esta calle y luego a la derecha, ¿verdad?
e. ____ No podemos seguir por las calles bloqueadas.
f. ____ ¿Por cuánto dinero vendes el apartamento?
g. ____ Por la tarde vienen los tíos de Ángela al apartamento.
h. ____ ¡Ay! ¡Hay palomas por todas partes!
i. ____ Raquel sólo estuvo en la Argentina por unos tres o cuatro días.
j. ____ Don Fernando quiere saber la verdad por sus hijos... y también por sí mismo (*himself*).

Actividad D.   Preocupaciones y sentimientos

Can you explain why certain things are happening in *Destinos*? Create at least five sentences, using a word or phrase from each of the three columns. (Worksheet)

Raquel	se preocupa(n) por	don Fernando
los hijos	empieza a sentir algo por	la salud de su padre
de don Fernando	piensa viajar a Puerto Rico por	Arturo
Rosario	se puso pensativo por	un mal presentimiento
Arturo	nunca se olvidó de su amor por	la opinión de sus tíos
Ángela	hace la investigación por	Raquel
		su amistad con Pedro
		¿ ?

Actividad E. Expresiones

Complete each sentence with one of the following expressions: **por eso, por favor, por lo general, por todas partes, por última vez, por fin, por supuesto, por ejemplo.**

1. Arturo y Raquel buscaron a Ángel _____, pero no lo encontraron.

2. _____, los tíos de Ángela tienen muchas preguntas sobre su vida.

3. A Ángela no le gusta vivir en el apartamento sin sus padres. _____ va a venderlo.

4. Después de cinco llamadas, _____ Ángela pudo hablar con sus tíos.

5. Hay muchas cosas que Raquel quiere saber. _____, ¿por qué Arturo no buscó a Ángel antes de ahora?

6. Rosario vio a don Fernando _____ antes del bombardeo de Guernica.

· ·

PRONUNCIACIÓN: x

The letter **x** is usually pronounced [ks], as in English. However, before a consonant or at the beginning of a word it is often pronounced [s]. In a few special cases (for historical reasons) the **x** is pronounced like the Spanish **j** ([x]).

Actividad.

Repeat the following words and sentences, imitating the speaker.

1. [ks]   existía   examen   exagera   exilio
2. [s]   explicaba   extrañaba   extraordinario   extremo   xerografía   xenofobia   xilófono
3. [x]   México   Texas   Oaxaca
4. Extraño a mis parientes en México.
   No me gustan las temperaturas extremas.
   La medicina no es una ciencia exacta.

Have you completed the following sections of the lesson? Check them off here.

_____ **Más allá del episodio**   _____ **Pronunciación**

_____ **Gramática**

Now scan the words in the **Vocabulario** list to be sure that you understand the meaning of most of them.

Vocabulario

Los verbos

había   there was, there were (*imperfect of* hay)

Las expresiones con *por*

por Dios	for heaven's sake
por ejemplo	for example
por eso	that's why, for that reason
por favor	please
por lo general	generally
por lo menos	at least
por primera/última vez	for the first/last time
por supuesto	of course
por todas partes	everywhere

Repaso: por fin, por teléfono

Now that you have completed the Textbook and Workbook for **Lección 19**, take the Self-Test for that lesson. (It is on page 280.) Remember to listen to the tape when you see the cassette symbol and to check your answers.

_____ **Self-Test**

Now that you have worked through the Textbook and the Workbook and taken the Self-Test, here are some of the things you have accomplished in Spanish.

- You can use and understand vocabulary related to giving directions in Spanish.
- You have learned more about narrating in the past in Spanish.
- You know how to express *for* in a number of ways, as well as additional uses of the important prepositions **por** and **para**.
- You know how Spanish **x** is pronounced.
- You have continued to improve your listening skills.

You are now ready to continue on with **Lección 20** in the Textbook.

20

RELACIONES ESTRECHAS

OBJETIVOS

Whereas the materials in the Textbook all had to do with the video episode, the materials in the Workbook will help you expand your knowledge of the Spanish language in general, as well as give you opportunities for self-expression in Spanish. In this lesson you will learn

- how to use the imperfect to describe what you were doing
- how to talk to your friend about what he or she was doing
- more about the uses of the imperfect
- more about making sentences negative
- more about linking in Spanish.

Remember to listen to the tape for **Lección 20** when you see the cassette symbol and to check your answers in Appendix 1.

MÁS ALLÁ DEL EPISODIO

Actividad A. Ángela y su Titi Olga... y un poco de sicología

PARA PENSAR...

Look over the following questions. You probably cannot answer them now. Keep them in mind as you read the following passage, and answer them after you have finished the reading.

1. ¿Por qué tiene Ángela tanta prisa (*such a rush*) por hablar con sus parientes sobre las noticias de Raquel?
2. ¿Comprende Ángela la reacción de su tía Olga?
3. ¿Son totalmente diferentes Ángela y Olga?
4. En general, ¿se llevan bien o mal las dos mujeres?

La tía Olga y Ángela son muy diferentes, pero se quieren mucho.

Ángela tiene 25 años, pero su familia todavía es muy importante para ella. ¿Por qué tiene tanta prisa por invitar a sus tíos a su casa? ¿Por qué vienen tan rápidamente? ¿Por qué parece que la tía Olga trata de controlarle la vida a Ángela?

Parte de la explicación de todo esto se encuentra en ciertos valores culturales del mundo de habla española. Más que en Norteamérica, la familia es parte importante de la vida diaria y emotiva[1] de una persona hispana. Aunque las generalizaciones siempre son peligrosas, muchos hispanos al llegar[2] a los Estados Unidos notan que las familias norteamericanas no son tan unidas como las familias hispanas.

Las relaciones entre Olga y Ángela también se explican al considerar[3] la personalidad de estas dos mujeres. Ángela siempre vacila entre el «soy independiente» y el «quiero que me necesites». Como muchas personas, ella a veces recurre a[4] la ayuda de su familia (o la de otras personas) sólo para llamar la atención, para asegurarse de que es importante para los otros. La conducta de Ángela no es patológica en este sentido; sus acciones son típicas de muchas personas y son parte de las mil maneras «normales» de adaptarse del ser humano.[5]

Olga también necesita la atención de sus parientes y quiere ser «necesitada[6]». Desde pequeña, Olga ha creído[7] que es la menos querida entre los hijos de doña Carmen. No se creía tan inteligente como Jaime ni tan guapa como Carmen ni tan simpática como Carlos. Por eso Olga siempre ha tratado de dominar a los otros.

Desde que murió la madre de Ángela, Olga se ha visto a sí misma[8] como una madre sustituta para su sobrina. Así, ha tratado de ejercer más y más control sobre la vida de Ángela. Pero al mismo tiempo realmente ha ayudado a Ángela. Cuando Ángel murió, fue Olga quien ayudó con todos los arreglos funerarios. Cuando Roberto se fue a México, Olga le preguntó a Ángela si quería irse a vivir con ella, para que no estuviera[9] tan sola.

Sin embargo, es importante notar que Ángela y Olga se quieren mucho. La familia de doña Carmen Contreras de Soto sí es muy unida. Eso lo ve Raquel perfectamente bien. Cuando Ángela le saca la lengua[10] a Olga, Raquel le asegura que no es para tanto,[11] que la tía sólo está preocupada. Y seguramente la semana que viene—si Ángela no está en México—Olga y Ángela harán planes para ir de compras. Y lo pasarán muy bien juntas.

[1]diaria... *daily and emotional* [2]al... *when they arrive* [3]al... *by considering* [4]resorts to [5]ser... *human being* [6]needed [7]ha... *has believed* [8]se... *has seen herself* [9]para... *so that she wouldn't be* [10]le... *sticks her tongue out* [11]no... *it isn't such a big deal*

Actividad B.

What else would you like to know about Ángela? Listen to the short segment on the cassette tape, then complete the following statements.

1. Durante su infancia y juventud, Ángela y su hermano... no se llevaban bien/casi siempre se llevaban bien.
2. Después de la muerte de sus padres, sus relaciones... cambiaron/no cambiaron nada.
3. Ángela cree que... es posible/es imposible... que su hermano tome mal las noticias.

• •

GRAMÁTICA

57. *MIENTRAS YO TOMABA UNA FOTOGRAFÍA, ¿QUIÉN LLEGÓ AL CEMENTERIO?*: FIRST- AND SECOND-PERSON SINGULAR FORMS (IMPERFECT TENSE)

Forms

In **Lección 19** you learned about the third-person forms of the imperfect tense of Spanish verbs. Here are the first- and second-person singular forms for regular verbs, which are quite similar.

	dar	querer	pedir
	-aba(s)	-ía(s)	-ía(s)
yo	daba	quería	pedía
tú	dabas	querías	pedías
Ud.	daba	quería	pedía

As always, the **Ud.** form is the same as the third-person form.

Remember that the endings for **-er** and **-ir** verbs are identical and that they all have a written accent. Remember also that there are no stem or spelling changes in the imperfect.

Here are the first- and second-person singular imperfect forms of **ser**, **ir**, and **ver**, which have irregularities.

ser	ir	ver
era	iba	veía
eras	ibas	veías
era	iba	veía

Uses

- You probably noticed that the first-person and third-person singular forms are the same. Context will normally tell you which is meant by a form such as **quería**, which can have **yo**, **él**, **ella**, **Ud.**, or a person's name as its subject.
- Remember that the imperfect is used to express events or conditions that were in progress (going on) at a particular point in the past.

Actividad A. Ángela cuenta la historia

After Raquel left with tío Jaime to return to her hotel, Ángela's other aunts and uncle stayed behind. Ángela gave them more details about how she met Raquel. Can you complete her narration with the appropriate forms of the imperfect? You will be expressing what Ángela was doing when other things occurred.

Bueno, esta mañana, cuando salí para el cementerio, no (tener) _____¹ idea de la sorpresa que me esperaba. Cuando llegué, (llevar) _____² flores en la mano, claro, y las (mirar) _____.³ Eran margaritasª y yo (pensar) _____⁴ en cómo eran las flores favoritas de mamá.

Cuando me acerquéᵇ a la tumba, allí estaba Raquel, tomando fotos. Yo no (comprender)_____⁵ por qué una persona querríaᶜ tomar fotos de la tumba. Las dos fuimos a sentarnos en las escaleras de la capilla y Raquel empezó a explicarme qué hacía allí. Cuando yo oí la historia de Rosario, (estar) _____⁶ sorprendida, pero lo que me convencióᵈ fue la carta de una señora en España. ¡Ay, cuántas emociones contradictorias! (Yo: Sentirse) _____⁷ triste, confusa, aprehensiva... todo.

ªdaisies ᵇme... I approached ᶜwould want ᵈlo... what convinced me

 Now check your answers by listening to the cassette tape.

Actividad B.   Preguntas para Raquel

You know what Ángela thought about her meeting with Raquel, but what did Raquel think about the events of the day? Form at least six questions for Raquel using phrases from each column. (Worksheet)

¿Qué pensabas de... ?	la tía Olga
¿Cómo te sentías... ?	la visita a la casa de Ponce de León
¿Qué te parecía... ?	la idea de ir a San Germán
¿Creías que... ?	mientras les contabas la historia
¿Te gustaba... ?	cuando Ángela te habló en el cementerio
	ibas a encontrar a la familia de Ángel tan pronto
	cuando conociste a los tíos de Ángela

Actividad C.   ¿Y tú?

Can you remember where you were and what you were doing at the times indicated? Answer as completely as you can, using the imperfect. (Worksheet)

1. ayer, a las once y media de la mañana
2. ayer, a las diez de la noche
3. hace un año, aproximadamente
4. durante la última serie mundial de béisbol (o el *Superbowl Sunday*)

58. *CUANDO CONOCÍ A ÁNGELA, ELLA NO SABÍA NADA DE LA HISTORIA DE ROSARIO Y FERNANDO*: RELATING TWO OR MORE ACTIONS IN THE PAST

Mientras Raquel **estaba** en el cementerio, **tomaba** una foto de la tumba de Ángel Castillo. En ese momento **llegó** una mujer que **dijo** que **se llamaba** Ángela Castillo. Mientras **hablaban**, Ángela **escuchó** muchas cosas que la **dejaron** sorprendida. Las dos mujeres **seguían conversando** mientras **volvían** al apartamento de Ángela. Cuando **llegaron**, Ángela **trató** de llamar a sus tíos. Siempre **hablaba** con su familia cuando **tenía** un problema o cuando algo importante le **pasaba**.

It is common to relate two or more past actions in the same sentence, using **mientras**. You have already seen that the imperfect is used in a clause that begins with **mientras**. This use of the imperfect indicates that one action was ongoing.

- If the other action in the sentence interrupts the background provided by the **mientras...** clause, it will be in the preterite, as in the first example below.
- If the two actions are simultaneous, the imperfect will be used in the other part of the sentence as well.

Mientras **estaba** en Buenos Aires, **conocí** al medio hermano de Ángel.	*While I was in Buenos Aires, I met Ángel's half brother.*
Raquel **tomaba** limonada mientras **hablaban** de don Fernando.	*Raquel drank lemonade while they spoke about don Fernando.*

In clauses beginning with **cuando...** the preterite is frequently used in combination with the imperfect in the other clause. This combination contrasts one ongoing action (imperfect) with another interrupting action (preterite).

Raquel y Ángela **miraban** unas fotos cuando **llegaron** los tíos.	*Raquel and Ángela were looking at some photos when the aunts and uncles arrived.*

These combinations of the preterite and the imperfect are very common. But you should note that many other combinations of the preterite and imperfect may occur in the same sentence, and you may hear others in the video episodes.

Actividad A. Preguntas y respuestas

Paso 1

Can you match Ángela's questions with Raquel's most likely answers?

Ángela pregunta

1. _____ ¿Dónde estabas cuando la familia Castillo te llamó?
2. _____ ¿Qué hacías cuando recibiste la llamada?
3. _____ Cuando fuiste a Sevilla, ¿qué esperabas hacer?
4. _____ Cuando llegaste a San Juan, ¿qué esperabas encontrar?
5. _____ Cuando te encontré en el cementerio, ¿qué pensabas hacer?

Raquel contesta

a. Pensaba tomar una foto de la tumba para mandársela a don Fernando en México.
b. Estudiaba los documentos para otro caso que tenía.
c. Esa tarde estaba en mi oficina en Los Ángeles.
d. Esperaba usar la dirección en la carta para encontrar a Teresa Suárez muy rápidamente.
e. Pues, pensaba que por fin podría (*I would be able*) hablar con Ángel Castillo.

Paso 2

Now match Raquel's questions with Ángela's likely answers.

Raquel pregunta

1. _____ ¿Qué hacías cuando me viste en el cementerio?
2. _____ ¿Qué te dijo Ángel cuando le preguntaste de dónde era?
3. _____ ¿Dónde estabas cuando murió tu padre?
4. _____ ¿Qué querías oír cuando hablaste con tu abuela?
5. _____ ¿Qué querías decirle a tu hermano cuando lo llamaste?

Ángela contesta

a. Estaba en la universidad, en Río Piedras.
b. Llevaba flores a la tumba de mis padres.
c. Quería contarle la historia de Rosario y Fernando.
d. Quería su permiso para ir a México a conocer a mi abuelo.
e. Dijo que venía del mar. Nunca quería contarnos más detalles.

Actividad B. ¿Y tú?

Paso 1

Think about the last time you received important news about a particular matter. Then answer these questions based on the event you have chosen. (Worksheet)

¿Dónde estabas?	¿Qué hacías?
¿Con quién estabas?	¿Esperabas las noticias o no?
¿Cuántos años tenías?	¿Cómo te sentías en ese momento?

Paso 2

Some notable events are significant for many people. Do you remember where you were and what you were doing when each of the following occurred? Complete as many statements as you can. If you had not been born yet, you can answer with: **Yo no había nacido todavía.**

1. Cuando empezó la guerra contra Irak, yo...
2. Cuando salió el último transbordador espacial (*space shuttle*), yo...
3. Cuando ocurrió el último eclipse de sol, ...
4. Cuando murió el presidente Kennedy, ...
5. Cuando murió John Lennon, ...

Actividad C.   ¿Y tú?

There are other kinds of important moments in life. What were the conditions when the following events occurred? Answer as many as you can. (Worksheet)

1. ¿Qué nota (*grade*) esperabas sacar cuando tomaste tu último examen?
2. ¿Dónde vivías cuando comenzaste los estudios universitarios?
3. ¿Qué esperabas encontrar cuando abriste el último regalo que recibiste?
4. Al principio, ¿qué extrañabas más cuando dejaste la casa de tus padres?
5. ¿Dónde estabas cuando alguien te dio tu primer beso?
6. ¿Cuántos años tenías cuando recibiste tu primer sueldo (*salary*)?
7. ¿Qué llevabas cuando conociste a tu novio/a?
8. ¿Cómo te sentías el día que te graduaste en la escuela secundaria?

59. *EL PADRE DE ÁNGELA NUNCA MENCIONÓ NADA DE SU FAMILIA*: USING INDEFINITE AFFIRMATIVE AND NEGATIVE WORDS

You have already seen and heard a number of indefinite affirmative and negative words. This section summarizes what you already know and adds new information.

Forms

AFFIRMATIVE		NEGATIVE	
algo	something, anything	nada	nothing, not anything
alguien*	someone, anyone	nadie*	no one, nobody, not anybody
algún, alguno/a (algunos/as)	some, any	ningún, ninguno/a†	no, none, not any
sí	yes	no	no
siempre	always	nunca, jamás	never
también	also, too	tampoco	neither, not either

Note that the **alguno/ninguno** pair shows gender and number, whereas the rest of these words are invariable in form. The adjectives **alguno** and **ninguno** shorten to **algún** and **ningún** before masculine singular nouns.

¿Trae **algún** documento?	*Do you have any identification (on you)?*
Si no hay inconveniente...	*If it's no problem . . .*
—**Ninguno**. Será un placer.	*—Not at all. It will be a pleasure.*

---

*Both **alguien** and **nadie** take the personal **a** when they are used as direct objects.

¿Ves a **alguien**?	*Do you see anyone?*
—No, no veo a **nadie**.	*—No, I don't see anybody.*

†The plural forms **ningunos/as** are rarely used.

¿Tienes **algunos** amigos puertorriqueños?	*Do you have any Puerto Rican friends?*
—No, no tengo **ninguno**.	*—No, I don't have any.*

Todavía tengo **algunas** cosas que hacer.	*I still have some things to do.*
¿Desean tomar **algo**?	*Do you want something to drink?*
Llamé a Roberto, pero **nunca** está en su casa.	*I called Roberto, but he's never at home.*

Uses

- In Spanish, only one negative word can precede the verb.

Nadie estaba en la casa de Ángel cuando llegó Raquel.	*Nobody was at Ángel's house when Raquel arrived.*
Raquel **nunca** conoció a Ángel.	*Raquel never got to meet Ángel.*

- Double negatives are common in Spanish. Thus, when **no** precedes the verb, another negative word can appear somewhere after the verb. Such double negatives are grammatically correct in Spanish.

No había **nadie** en la casa de Ángel.	*There wasn't anybody at Ángel's house.*
Raquel **no** conoció **nunca** a Ángel.	*Raquel never got to meet Ángel.*

- When the sentence is negative, any included indefinite word *must* also be negative. Such double negatives are not only grammatically correct, they are obligatory.

Me imagino que tu hermano **no** sabe **nada** de esto.	*I imagine your brother doesn't know anything about this.*
¿Puedes hacer **algo** en este caso? —No, **no** puedo hacer **nada**.	*Can you do anything in this situation? —No, I can't do anything.*

- Note that questions may have a **no** before the verb but not be negative in meaning. In such cases, the affirmative form of the indefinite word is used.

¿**No** quieres llevar **algunos** duraznos o frutillas?	*Don't you want to bring some peaches or strawberries?*
¿**No** quieres vino **también**?	*Don't you want wine too?*

Actividad A.   ¿Quién... ?

Which character is described by the following statements? ¡OJO! You will have to think back over all of the video episodes you have seen so far. And more than one character may be appropriate for some statements.

1. Nunca les dijo nada a sus hijos acerca de Rosario. _____

2. No tenía ninguna idea del paradero de su hermano. _____

3. En La Boca, nadie lo reconocía. _____

4. Siempre se acordaba de su primer esposo. _____

5. No tenía ninguna idea de quién fue Rosario. _____

6. Buscaba a alguien que conociera (*knew*) a Ángel Castillo. _____

7. No sabían nada de la primera esposa de un pariente. _____

8. Encontró algo importante para una persona. _____

Now listen to the statements on the cassette tape and give your answers. Then compare them to the ones given by the speaker.

Actividad B. ¿Qué están diciendo?

Read the following excerpts from Episodio 20 and try to complete them with logical affirmative or negative words. You may wish to scan the list of words at the beginning of this section before you begin.

1. EL NARRADOR: Además de ver lo que sucede en este episodio, _____ vamos a aprender más vocabulario relacionado con la familia.

2. EL NARRADOR: También vamos a aprender _____ sobre la historia de la isla de Puerto Rico.

3. TÍA OLGA: El padre de Ángela, que en paz descanse, _____ mencionó _____ de su familia.

   JAIME: ¿Trae _____ documento?

4. ÁNGELA: ¿Desean tomar _____? Tengo jugo de parcha.

5. TÍA OLGA: Me imagino que tu hermano no sabe _____ de esto.

   ÁNGELA: Llamé a Roberto, pero no estaba en su casa. ¡_____ está en su casa!

   TÍA OLGA: No puedes ir a México sola.

   ÁNGELA: No te preocupes.

   RAQUEL: Si quieren saber _____ más...

   TÍA OLGA: Yo quiero hacerle una pregunta. ¿Por qué Ángel _____ mencionó a su familia?

 Now check your answers by listening to the cassette tape.

Actividad C. ¿Qué va a pasar?

What do you think will happen in the next video episodes of *Destinos*? Indicate the choice that expresses what you think is most likely to happen.

1. Ángela y Raquel van a llegar a San Germán... sin ninguna dificultad / pero con algunas dificultades.
2. Doña Carmen, la abuela de Ángela, ... no va a saber nada / va a saber algo... del pasado de Ángel.
3. En la casa de su abuela, Ángela... va a encontrar algo / no va a encontrar nada... relacionado con el pasado de su padre.
4. Raquel... va a conocer / nunca va a conocer... al novio de Ángela.
5. Ángela... va a viajar / por fin no va a tener ningún interés en viajar... a México con Raquel.

Actividad D. ¿Y tú?

Give the name of a person, place, or thing from your own experience that fits the following categories. (Worksheet)

1. alguien a quien quieres mucho
2. algo que a muchas personas no les gusta hacer y que a ti tampoco te gusta
3. una materia que no te ofrece ninguna dificultad
4. algo que no vas a comer nunca en tu vida
5. algo que siempre haces mal

Pronunciación: More About Linking

As you know, in addition to occurring within words, diphthongs can also occur *between* words, causing the words to be "linked" (pronounced as one long word). A similar type of linking occurs when two identical vowels occur next to each other. (You will practice this usage in items 3–5 below.)

In general, there are no stops between words in Spanish, especially when one of the words begins or ends with a vowel. (You will practice this usage in items 1 and 2.)

 Actividad.

Pronounce the following phrases and sentences as if they were one word, imitating the speaker.

1. el abuelo   el episodio   el hospital
2. los indios   las Antillas   los abuelos
3. no estaba   tú eres   de esto   ¿qué hotel?
4. la isla   la historia   la opinión   la investigación
5. mi hermano   su hermano   mi hotel   me imagino
6. Tengo una foto de mis abuelos.
   ¿Tiene tu abuela un hijo favorito?
   ¿Trae algún documento?
   Creo que eso va a ser imposible.
   Yo voy a hablar con ella primero.

Have you completed the following sections of the lesson? Check them off here.

_____ **Más allá del episodio**   _____ **Pronunciación**

_____ **Gramática**

Now scan the words in the **Vocabulario** list to be sure that you understand the meaning of most of them.

Vocabulario

Las palabras afirmativas y negativas

algo	something, anything	nada	nothing, not anything
alguien	someone, anyone	ningún, ninguno/a	no, none, not any
algún, alguno/a/os/as	some, any	tampoco	neither, not either
jamás	never		

Repaso: nada, nadie, no, nunca, sí, siempre, también

Now that you have completed the Textbook and Workbook for **Lección 20**, take the Self-Test for that lesson. (It is on page 282.) Remember to listen to the tape when you see the cassette symbol and to check your answers.

_____ **Self-Test**

Now that you have worked through the Textbook and the Workbook and taken the Self-Test, here are some of the things you have accomplished in Spanish.

- You have learned about answering the phone in Hispanic countries.
- You can use and understand additional vocabulary related to family members and familial relationships.
- You have learned more about narrating in the past in Spanish, including two ways to use two different past tenses together.
- You know how to express words such as *anybody*, *someone*, *nothing*, and so on, in Spanish.
- You have learned more about how words are linked together in Spanish.
- You have continued to improve your listening skills.

You are now ready to continue on with **Lección 21** in the Textbook.

L E C C I Ó N

21
EL PEAJE

OBJETIVOS

Whereas the materials in the Textbook all had to do with the video episode, the materials in the Workbook will help you expand your knowledge of the Spanish language in general, as well as give you opportunities for self-expression in Spanish. In this lesson you will learn

- how to form the remaining parts of the imperfect
- how to use the verb **tener** to express conditions usually described in English with the verb *to be*
- how to compare one thing or quality with another
- more about intonation and rhythm in spoken Spanish.

Remember to listen to the tape for **Lección 21** when you see the cassette symbol and to check your answers in Appendix 1.

MÁS ALLÁ DEL EPISODIO

Actividad A.   Mientras tanto... en la Argentina: Arturo Iglesias

PARA PENSAR...

Look over the following questions. You probably cannot answer them now. Keep them in mind as you read the following passage, and answer them after you have finished the reading.

1.   Arturo estaba muy triste, muy preocupado, cuando se despidió de Raquel. ¿Sigue así?
2.   ¿Qué está haciendo Arturo para poder estar con Raquel otra vez?
3.   ¿Y Ángel? ¿Sigue Arturo preocupado con el recuerdo de su medio hermano? ¿O ya se ha olvidado de él?

Desde que se despidió de Raquel en el aeropuerto de Buenos Aires, Arturo no ha dejado de[1] pensar en dos personas. Primero, en Raquel. ¡La extraña muchísimo! Piensa en ella constantemente y desea ir a Puerto Rico para volver a verla[2] lo antes posible. Pero hay muchos obstáculos.

Primero, tiene que buscar a alguien que dé sus clases en la universidad. Y luego está el problema de sus pacientes. La ausencia inesperada[3] de su doctor podría ser traumático para muchos, sobre todo para los más delicados, y Arturo es más que nada un médico responsable, todo un profesional. La idea de causarle daño a alguno de sus pacientes le horroriza.

¿Y la segunda persona? Arturo tampoco puede dejar de pensar en Ángel y en su insistente mal presentimiento. Sus sentimientos hacia su hermano son todavía un poco confusos. Ya no lo considera responsable de la muerte de su padre. Pero a pesar de[4] eso no puede olvidar la terrible discusión entre Ángel y Martín... y el ataque cardíaco de su padre.

Y luego está la otra cara[5] de la moneda: su propio sentimiento de culpabilidad por no haber buscado a[6] su medio hermano a lo largo de[7] todos estos años.

Ni Ángel ni él son culpables. Esto es lo que le dice la razón.[8] Pero el corazón, los sentimientos le dicen... otra cosa. Claro, Arturo es psiquiatra. Pero eso no quiere decir que sea capaz de analizarse a sí mismo.

Y luego, volviendo al tema de Raquel... Arturo nunca imaginó que pudiera volver a enamorarse[9]... y mucho menos de una norteamericana. Otra vez, una extranjera. Ojalá que[10] la historia de su primera esposa no se repita...

Arturo espera hablar con Raquel con impaciencia.

[1]no... *hasn't stopped* [2]volver... *to see her again* [3]*unexpected* [4]a... *in spite of* [5]*side* (lit., *face*) [6]por... *about not having looked for* [7]a... *during* [8]*reason* [9]pudiera... *he could fall in love again* [10]Ojalá... *How he hopes that*

 Actividad B.

What else would you like to know about Arturo? Listen to the short segment on the cassette tape, then complete the following statements.

1. A Arturo... le interesa/no le interesa... lo que Raquel sabe ahora acerca de Ángel.
2. Tiene/No tiene... sentimientos ambivalentes acerca de la posibilidad de volver a ver a Ángel, si todavía está vivo.

• •

GRAMÁTICA

 60. *ANDÁBAMOS POR LA AUTOPISTA CUANDO OCURRIÓ UN PROBLEMA CON EL CARRO*: FIRST- AND SECOND-PERSON PLURAL FORMS (IMPERFECT TENSE)

Forms

Here are the forms for the first- and second-person plural of the imperfect tense for regular verbs.

	contar	hacer	decir
nosotros/as	contábamos	hacíamos	decíamos
vosotros/as	contabais	hacíais	decíais
ustedes	contaban	hacían	decían

Note that the first-person plural of all verbs requires a written accent. Note also that the **vosotros/as** endings for -er and -ir verbs have three vowels in a row. The accented **í** combines with a preceding consonant to form one syllable, and the remaining vowels, forming a diphthong, combine with the final -s (-ais) to compose another syllable: **ha-cí-ais.**

As always, the **Uds.** form is the same as the third-person plural (**ellos/as**) form.

Here are the first- and second-person plural imperfect forms of **ser**, **ir**, and **ver**, which have irregularities.

ser	ir	ver
éramos	íbamos	veíamos
erais	ibais	veíais
eran	iban	veían

Uses

¡Miguel y Osito, por fin! ¿Dónde **estabais**, por Dios?	*Miguel and Osito, at last! Where were you two, for heaven's sake?*
Mientras **esperábamos** al hombre del taller, tuvimos un *picnic*.	*While/When we were waiting for the man from the body shop, we had a picnic.*
Mientras **comíamos** la fruta que **llevábamos**, **hablábamos** de muchas cosas.	*While we were eating the fruit we brought, we talked of many things.*

- Remember that the **vosotros** forms are used primarily in Spain, so you will not hear them used by the Puerto Rican characters or by Raquel. In most of Hispanic America the plural of **tú** is **ustedes**.
- Remember that the imperfect is often used in clauses that begin with **mientras**. It may also appear in the other clause if simultaneous actions or conditions are being narrated. However, the verb in the other clause is in the preterite when the action of that verb interrupts the action in the **mientras** clause.

Actividad A. La versión de Arturo

Which of the following sentences would Arturo and Raquel truthfully include if they were telling a friend about the time they spent together in Argentina?

1. _____ Al principio los dos estábamos un poco perdidos. Ella no sabía quién era yo y yo pensaba que ella era una paciente.
2. _____ Los dos estábamos un poco sorprendidos al (*upon*) oír lo que dijo el otro.
3. _____ No nos llevábamos muy bien al principio de la búsqueda.
4. _____ Los dos estábamos muy ansiosos de encontrar a Ángel.
5. _____ Cuando casi estábamos desesperados, un hombre nos habló de un marinero, José.
6. _____ No lo pasábamos muy bien juntos.
7. _____ Desgraciadamente, estábamos ocupados todos los días y Raquel tenía poco tiempo para ver la ciudad.
8. _____ Los dos nos sentimos muy aliviados (*relieved*) cuando por fin teníamos la carta de Ángel.
9. _____ En el aeropuerto, el día que se fue Raquel, estábamos muy tristes.
10. _____ Pero esperábamos volver a vernos (*see each other again*) muy pronto, ya que yo pensaba ir a Puerto Rico.

Now check your answers by listening to the cassette tape.

Actividad B. Preguntas y respuestas

Here are some questions and answers that might have occurred in Rosario's correspondence with a friend after Rosario left for Argentina. How might Rosario have responded to these questions about the period surrounding Martín's death?

La amiga quería saber

1. _____ ¿Dónde vivíais tú, Arturo y Ángel cuando murió Martín?
2. _____ ¿Qué pensabais de las acciones de Ángel?
3. _____ ¿Sabíais que Ángel se embarcó como marinero?
4. _____ ¿Dónde creíais que estaba?
5. _____ ¿No recibíais ninguna carta de él?
6. _____ ¿Qué pensabais cuando recibiste la carta de Ángel?

Rosario le contestó

a. No. Al principio no recibíamos nada de él.
b. Realmente no teníamos ni idea de dónde estaba en esa época.
c. Pensábamos que Ángel era muy egoísta.
d. Vivíamos en la estancia todavía pero Ángel vivía en Buenos Aires. Estudiaba allí.
e. Nos sentíamos... no sé... un poco culpables, pues (*since*) no hicimos nada por buscarlo.
f. No sabíamos nada de esa decisión.

Actividad C.   La tía Olga tenía muchas preguntas

As you know, Ángela's Aunt Olga was not quick to accept Raquel's story. You will hear a series of questions that Olga would have liked to ask Raquel. Can you match her questions with Raquel's probable answers? It is a good idea to scan the answers before beginning.

a. _____ Llevábamos una foto de él que encontró Arturo entre las cosas de su madre.
b. _____ Pues, teníamos una carta que le mandó Ángel a un amigo argentino.
c. _____ Bueno, pensábamos encontrarnos en San Juan, pero ahora... no sé.
d. _____ Al principio le hacíamos preguntas a la gente en las tiendas de La Boca... y ellos nos mandaban siempre a hablar con los marineros.
e. _____ Queríamos llevarlo a México a conocer a su padre.

Actividad D.   ¿Y tú?

Have any of the following situations ever happened to you when you were with others? Select one situation—or think of something similar that happened to you and others— and describe the circumstances of the event. Don't try to narrate the whole event; just answer these questions: ¿Adónde iban Uds.? ¿Por qué iban allí? ¿Qué hora era, más o menos? ¿Qué pasaba o que había en el área? (Worksheet)

1. tener un accidente con el carro en que iban
2. tener una avería (*breakdown*) del carro en que iban
3. perder un autobús, un tren o un avión en un viaje importante
4. perderse (*to lose your way*) en una ciudad
5. quedar separado/a de tus amigos en un concierto
6. tener un encuentro con la policía
7. un incidente ocurrido con unos amigos cuando eras niño/a

61. *YO TENGO MUCHA HAMBRE*: EXPRESSING STATES OF BEING WITH *tener*; ASPECTS OF *hacer* AND *tener* IDIOMS

Idioms* with *tener*

Forms
The verb **tener** is used with nouns in a number of useful expressions. You have already learned some of them.

---

*An idiom (idiomatic expression) is a phrase in one language that does not have the same literal meaning in another. For example: While in English we *pull someone's leg*, in Spanish one *pulls his or her hair* (**tomarle el pelo a alguien**). These two idioms convey a similar idea but are not identical in the two languages.

tener... años	to be . . . years old
tener (mucha) hambre	to be (very) hungry
tener que + *inf.*	to have to (*do something*)
tener (mucha) vergüenza	to be (very) ashamed

Here are some additional idiomatic expressions with **tener.**

tener (mucho) éxito	to be (very) successful
tener (mucho) frío/calor	to be (very) cold/hot
tener (muchas) ganas de + *inf.*	to feel (very much) like (*doing something*)
tener (mucho) miedo de	to be (very) afraid of
tener (mucha) prisa (por + *inf.*)	to be in a (great) hurry (*to do something*)
tener (toda la) razón	to be (completely) right
no tener razón	to be wrong
tener (mucha) sed	to be (very) thirsty
tener (mucho) sueño	to be (very) sleepy
tener (mucha) suerte	to be (very) lucky

Note that the English equivalent of these expressions is usually *to be* plus an adjective: *embarrassed, successful, cold,* and so on.

Uses

Raquel y Ángela **tenían mucha sed** cuando llegaron al apartamento de Ángela.	*Raquel and Ángela were very thirsty when they arrived at Ángela's apartment.*
Ahora **tengo ganas de** comer una ensalada de frutas.	*Now I feel like eating a fruit salad.*
Estuvo delicioso. ¡No sabía que **tenía** tanta **hambre**!	*It was delicious. I didn't know I was so hungry!*
Como psiquiatra, Arturo **tiene** mucho **éxito** en su profesión.	*As a psychiatrist, Arturo is very successful in his practice.*

- These commonly used expressions describe a number of basic emotions, conditions, or states.
- Because the imperfect is usually used to describe emotions and states in the past, these expressions usually occur in the imperfect rather than the preterite when they are in the past.
- The idiom **tener calor** refers only to people. To describe things, use **estar caliente** (*hot*).

Aspects of *hacer* and *tener* Idioms

As you saw with weather expressions in the Un poco de gramática section of **Lección 21** of the Textbook, the adjective mucho/a is used with nouns: **hace mucho frío/calor/sol,** and so on. The same is true for tener + noun idioms: mucho/a is used to express *very* (not muy).

Actividad A.   ¿Qué sienten? ¿Qué sentían?
Match the characters with their probable states of mind at this point in *Destinos.*

a. Arturo   c. Ángela   e. los tíos de Ángela
b. Raquel   d. don Fernando   f. Laura

1. _____ Tiene ganas de conocer a su abuelo en México.
2. _____ Tuvo mucha suerte cuando encontró a Ángela en el cementerio.
3. _____ Tenía mucha hambre en el hotel en Ponce.
4. _____ Tenían miedo de mandar a Ángela a México sola.
5. _____ Tiene ganas de recoger (*pick up*) el coche y seguir con el viaje.
6. _____ Tiene prisa por ver a sus parientes perdidos antes de morir.
7. _____ Tiene ganas de hablar con Raquel, pero ella no está en su hotel cuando él la llama.
8. _____ Tiene que ponerse en contacto con un pariente que está en México.

Now check your answers by listening to the cassette tape.

Actividad B.   ¿Qué hacen?

Choose the phrase that in your opinion best describes what most people do when they experience the following. ¡OJO! There may be more than one correct answer in some cases.

1. Cuando tienen mucho sueño, muchas personas
   a. _____ se acuestan
   b. _____ hacen ejercicio
   c. _____ consultan al médico
   d. _____ ¿ ?

2. Cuando tienen miedo, frecuentemente
   a. _____ buscan una pistola
   b. _____ comienzan a correr con mucha prisa
   c. _____ se duermen
   d. _____ ¿ ?

3. Cuando tienen prisa, muchas personas
   a. _____ toman un taxi
   b. _____ caminan rápidamente
   c. _____ corren por la calle
   d. _____ ¿ ?

4. Cuando tienen frío,
   a. _____ se acuestan temprano
   b. _____ se preparan un chocolate caliente
   c. _____ se ponen un suéter
   d. _____ ¿ ?

5. Cuando tienen mucho éxito en algo,
   a. _____ se lo dicen a todos sus amigos
   b. _____ tienen vergüenza de ello (*about it*)
   c. _____ dicen que fue porque tenían mucha suerte
   d. _____ ¿ ?

6. Si tienen hambre,
   a. _____ almuerzan
   b. _____ tratan de comer menos
   c. _____ toman agua
   d. _____ ¿ ?

Actividad C.   ¿Y tú?

When was the last time you experienced the following or the following happened to you? Describe the circumstances: where you were, what was happening, and so on.
(Worksheet)

1. Tenías mucho calor.
2. No tenías ganas de estudiar.
3. Tenías razón con relación a algo de poca importancia o a algo importante.
4. Tenías miedo.

62. *EN PONCE, HACE MÁS CALOR QUE EN SAN JUAN*: COMPARING AND CONTRASTING

The following conversation might have occurred as Raquel, Ángela, and Laura drove across the island on their way to San Germán.

RAQUEL: Yo no sabía que en Puerto Rico había montañas **tan** altas **como** éstas.
ÁNGELA: Sí, y hace **menos** calor aquí **que** en San Juan.
RAQUEL: Sí, es muy agradable.
ÁNGELA: En Ponce, hace **más** calor **que** en San Juan.

Comparisons of Inequality

Forms

The structure for the comparison of unequal items is as follows:

> **más** + *noun or adjective* + **que**   more + *noun or adjective* + than
>
> **menos** + *noun or adjective* + **que**   less/fewer + *noun or adjective* + than

Note that **más** and **menos** are invariable and show neither gender nor number agreement. Some adjectives have special comparative forms.

mejor (mejores) que	better than
peor (peores) que	worse than
mayor (mayores) que	older than
menor (menores) que	younger than

Note that these have plural forms but do not show gender agreement.

Uses

San Juan es **más** importante **que** Ponce y tiene **más** habitantes **que** la segunda ciudad.	*San Juan is more important than Ponce and has more inhabitants than the second city.*
Hawai tiene **menos** habitantes **que** Puerto Rico.	*Hawaii has fewer inhabitants than Puerto Rico.*
Raquel es **mayor que** Ángela.	*Raquel is older than Ángela.*

- With adjectives, these structures are often (but not always) the equivalent of the English comparative adjectives formed by the suffix *-er* (*taller than, faster than* . . .). No such comparative suffix exists in Spanish.
- *Much more/less* is expressed with **mucho más/menos**. Note that if the comparison is with nouns, **mucho** must agree with the noun.

Olga tiene **mucha menos** paciencia **que** los otros tíos.	*Olga has much less patience than the other aunts and uncles.*

- These structures are also used adverbially, to compare and contrast the actions expressed by verbs or to compare and contrast adverbs.

Raquel trabaja **más que** Arturo, ¿no crees?	*Raquel works more than Arturo, don't you think?*

Jaime estudia **menos que** su hermano Miguel.	*Jaime studies less than his brother Miguel.*
¿Quién corre **más** rápidamente, Jaime o Miguel?	*Who can run faster, Jaime or Miguel?*

- To express *more/less than* + a number, use **más/menos de** + a number.

Puerto Rico tiene **más de tres** millones de habitantes.	*Puerto Rico has more than three million inhabitants.*

Actividad A.   ¿Cierto o falso?

You will hear a series of statements that compare and contrast Raquel and Ángela. Indicate whether the statements are **Cierto (C)** or **Falso (F)**, as far as you know. You should make some educated guesses. You will hear the answers on the cassette tape.

1. C F   2. C F   3. C F   4. C F   5. C F   6. C F   7. C F   8. C F

Comparisons of Equality

Forms

The structure for the comparison of equal items is:

tanto/a/os/as + *noun* + **como**	as much/many + *noun* + as
tan + *adjective or adverb* + **como**	as + *adjective or adverb* + as

The word **tanto**, an adjective, modifies nouns; it agrees in number and gender with the noun it modifies. The word **tan**, an adverb, is invariable in form.

Uses

Ángel no tenía **tantos** hermanos **como** su esposa.	*Ángel didn't have as many brothers and sisters as his wife.*
Olga no tenía **tanta** información **como** Ángela.	*Olga didn't have as much information as Ángela.*
¿Es **tan** alta Ángela **como** Raquel?	*Is Ángela as tall as Raquel?*
¿Pintaba Ángel **tan** bien **como** Picasso?	*Did Ángel paint as well as Picasso?*

- This structure is the equivalent of the English *as . . . as*, but the distinction is made in Spanish as to whether what is being compared is a quantity (a noun) or a quality (an adjective or adverb).
- When the second element of the comparison is not expressed after **tan** or **tanto**, the word **como** is omitted.

Llueve mucho en El Yunque, pero en San Juan no llueve **tanto**.	*It rains a lot in El Yunque, but in San Juan it doesn't rain as much.*
San Juan es una capital como Buenos Aires, pero no es **tan** grande.	*San Juan is a capital like Buenos Aires, but it isn't as large.*

Actividad B.   ¿Sabías esto?

Combine phrases from the lefthand column with those from the right to create true statements about the places Raquel has visited during her investigation.

1. _____ En Puerto Rico en verano no hace tanto calor
2. _____ Los argentinos creen que Buenos Aires es tan elegante
3. _____ La gente de España es tan simpática
4. _____ Hay tantos turistas en Puerto Rico en el invierno

5. _____ La isla de Puerto Rico no está tan lejos de Nueva York
6. _____ La peseta puertorriqueña tiene tanto valor (*value*)
7. _____ Las Pampas de la Argentina son tan productivas
8. _____ La población de Buenos Aires es casi tan grande

a. como los llanos (*plains*) del medioeste de los Estados Unidos
b. como en el «Valle de la Muerte» de California
c. como en el sur de la Florida
d. como las islas del estado de Hawai
e. como la (*that*) de Nueva York
f. como el *quarter* porque ¡son la misma moneda (*same coin*), con dos nombres diferentes!
g. como la gente del Caribe
h. como París

Actividad C.   Opiniones personales
Do you agree with the following statements? If not, change the sentences to indicate your personal opinion. Use **más/menos... que** and **tanto/tan... como,** as needed.

1. Los deportes (*sports*) son tan importantes como los estudios.
2. La física es más interesante que la literatura.
3. Los profesores tienen más trabajo que los estudiantes.
4. Hay tantas mujeres como hombres que estudian ingeniería.
5. El español es menos difícil que el inglés.
6. El dinero es tan importante en la vida como la amistad (*friendship*).
7. Los hombres son tan románticos como las mujeres.
8. Las mujeres practican tantos deportes como los hombres.
9. Hay más personas que hablan español que inglés.
10. Los profesores no deben ganar (*earn*) tanto dinero como los médicos.

Actividad D.   ¿Quién tiene más? ¿Quién tiene menos?
Create at least six comparative statements about don Fernando and Arturo. Use **más/ menos... que** and **tanto/tan... como,** as needed. Think about the following aspects of their lives and compare any other aspects of their lives that you can think of. (Worksheet)

hijos, nietos, secretos, dinero, cartas viejas, tierra (*land*), problemas, preguntas, memorias tristes, criados (*servants*) en casa, médicos, fotos de Ángel

 ### Actividad E.   ¿Y tú?
You will hear some questions about aspects of your life. Answer the questions in complete sentences and with real information. (Worksheet)

1. ...   2. ...   3. ...   4. ...   5. ...

Actividad F.   ¿Y tú?
Describe yourself by comparing yourself with whomever you wish: friends, famous personalities, your professors, and so on. Create at least four sentences in each group. (Worksheet)

Soy...   generoso/a, guapo/a, inteligente, estudioso/a, trabajador(a), joven, buena persona, cariñoso/a, gruñón (gruñona), pensativo/a, ¿ ?

Tengo...   paciencia, buenas ideas, talento, éxito, amigos, dinero, suerte, problemas, cursos, ¿ ?

PRONUNCIACIÓN: Intonation and Rhythm

The intonation and rhythm of spoken Spanish are different from those of spoken English. One of the best ways to learn about these differences is to listen carefully to, then imitate, native speakers of Spanish.

Actividad A.

Repeat the following questions and exclamations after the speaker. Pay particular attention to punctuation, intonation, and rhythm.

1. ¿Con quién vas a cenar esta noche?
2. ¿Dónde vas a estar mañana a las tres?
3. ¿Ya hablaste con tus tíos?
4. ¿Pudiste hablar por fin con Arturo?
5. Van a llegar por la tarde, ¿no?
6. Es el tío de Ángela, ¿verdad?
7. ¡Es imposible verlos esta tarde!
8. ¡Por Dios! ¡Eso es horroroso!

Actividad B.

When you hear the corresponding number, say the following sentences. Then repeat them, imitating the speaker.

1. Enero es el primer mes del año.
2. No comprendí lo que me dijiste.
3. Se casó el catorce de abril.
4. Ocurrió en el año mil novecientos.
5. Estábamos en Puerto Rico en mayo.
6. Ponía flores en la tumba cuando la vi.

Have you completed the following sections of the lesson? Check them off here.

_____ **Más allá del episodio**   _____ **Pronunciación**

_____ **Gramática**

Now scan the words in the **Vocabulario** list to be sure that you understand the meaning of most of them.

VOCABULARIO

Los adjetivos

caliente — hot (*not used with weather or people*)

Las comparaciones (Comparisons)

más... que	more . . . than
menos... que	less/fewer . . . than
tan... como	as . . . as
tanto/a/os/as... como	much/many . . . as
mayor(es)	older
mejor(es)	better
menor(es)	younger
peor(es)	worse

Las expresiones con *tener*

tener (mucho) éxito	to be (very) successful
tener (mucho) frío/calor	to be (very) cold/hot
tener (muchas) ganas de + *inf.*	to feel (very much) like (*doing something*)
tener (mucho) miedo de	to be (very) afraid of
tener (mucha) prisa por + *inf.*	to be in a (great) hurry (*to do something*)
tener (toda la) razón	to be (completely) right
no tener razón	to be wrong
tener (mucha) sed	to be (very) thirsty
tener (mucho) sueño	to be (very) sleepy
tener (mucha) suerte	to be (very) lucky

Repaso: tener... años, tener hambre, tener que + *inf.*, tener vergüenza

Las palabras adicionales

al principio — at first, at the beginning

Now that you have completed the Textbook and Workbook for **Lección 21**, take the Self-Test for that lesson. (It is on page 284.) Remember to listen to the tape when you see the cassette symbol and to check your answers.

_____ **Self-Test**

Now that you have worked through the Textbook and the Workbook and taken the Self-Test, here are some of the things you have accomplished in Spanish.

- You can use and understand additional vocabulary related to weather conditions.
- You have learned more about narrating in the past in Spanish.
- You know how to express conditions such as being hungry, sleepy, successful, and so on, in Spanish.
- You know how to compare equal items and contrast unequal items in Spanish.
- You have learned more about intonation and rhythm in Spanish.
- You have continued to improve your listening skills.

You are now ready to continue on with **Lección 22** in the Textbook.

22

RECUERDOS

OBJETIVOS

Whereas the materials in the Textbook all had to do with the video episode, the materials in the Workbook will help you expand your knowledge of the Spanish language in general, as well as give you opportunities for self-expression in Spanish. In this lesson you will learn

- more about an additional use of the imperfect, as well as review the uses you already know
- about using **estar** to describe conditions
- more about verbs that describe changes of state or condition
- more about word stress and written accents in Spanish.

Remember to listen to the tape for **Lección 22** when you see the cassette symbol and to check your answers in Appendix 1.

MÁS ALLÁ DEL EPISODIO

Actividad A. Doña Carmen, suegra de Ángel

PARA PENSAR...

Look over the following questions. You probably cannot answer them now. Keep them in mind as you read the following passage, and answer them after you have finished the reading.

1. Es obvio que doña Carmen sabía algo del pasado de Ángel, pero ¿qué es lo que sabía exactamente?
2. ¿Cómo lo supo? ¿Se lo dijo Ángel? ¿O es que doña Carmen se enteró por su propia cuenta (*found out on her own*)?

Doña Carmen es una mujer serena y comprensiva, el alma[1] de su familia. Al mismo tiempo, es una persona dinámica, jovial; da gusto[2] estar con ella... y todos los parientes lo reconocen. Al mismo tiempo que buscan sus consejos, también buscan su compañía. La respetan, pero también la quieren. Visitar a la abuela es un deber,[3] claro, pero en este caso es un deber ameno.

Doña Carmen adoraba a su hija María Luisa. Cuando ésta[4] se enamoró de repente de Ángel, pensaba que ella había encontrado[5] en ese ex marinero argentino al compañero ideal. Su hija y su yerno venían con frecuencia a San Germán a visitarla.

A Ángel le gustaba mucho pintar, pero sobre todo en el pueblo colonial donde vivía su suegra. Se sentaba en el jardín y pintaba todo el día; le gustaba sobre todo la luz de ese lugar, por la mañana o al anochecer.[6] A veces se quedaba en su cuarto y pintaba toda la noche. Doña Carmen perdonaba esa manía de su yerno porque le gustaban mucho sus pinturas; creía que realmente tenía talento. Y cuando María Luisa criticaba a su esposo en broma[7] por pasar tanto tiempo pintando, su madre la silenciaba. La suegra sí comprendía lo que era ser pintor. Así nació entre doña Carmen y Ángel una gran amistad.[8]

Doña Carmen se llevaba muy bien con su hija y su yerno.

Doña Carmen observaba a Ángel y María Luisa y veía que eran muy felices. Pero su instinto de madre le decía que algo triste había ocurrido[9] en el pasado de Ángel. Un día lo encontró contemplando unos retratos que él había pintado. Vio emoción en su rostro[10] y lágrimas en sus ojos.[11] Le preguntó: «¿Quiénes son estas personas, Ángel?» Ángel no contestó inmediatamente. Doña Carmen no insistió, pero se quedó a su lado. Después de un largo silencio, Ángel la miró y murmuró: «Son mi madre y mi hermano.»

Doña Carmen no sabía qué decir. Se quedó sorprendida, esperando una explicación. Ángel, por su parte, sintió la necesidad de confiarle su secreto. Entonces le contó la historia de la muerte de su padrastro y cómo se sintió culpable... de cómo se fue de Buenos Aires y nunca quiso regresar. También le pidió que guardara[12] su secreto. No quería ni que María Luisa supiera[13] la verdad.

Doña Carmen le prometió no decirle nada a nadie. Ángel se sintió aliviado[14] y mucho más tranquilo. A los pocos días Ángel le confió a doña Carmen una pequeña caja. Le explicó el significado de su contenido y le pidió que se la entregara[15] a sus hijos cuando ella lo creyera[16] necesario.

[1]*soul* [2]*da... it is a pleasure* [3]*duty* [4]*the latter* [5]*había... had found* [6]*al... at nightfall* [7]*en... jokingly* [8]*friendship* [9]*había... had happened* [10]*face* [11]*lágrimas... tears in his eyes* [12]*she keep* [13]*to know* [14]*relieved* [15]*she hand over* [16]*believed*

Actividad B.

What else would you like to know about doña Carmen and her relationship with her daughter and son-in-law? Listen to the short segment on the cassette tape, then complete the following statements.

1. Al principio de la enfermedad de María Luisa, la vida de la familia... sufrió grandes trastornos (*disruptions*)/era casi normal.
2. Después de la muerte de su esposa, Ángel... seguía visitando a su suegra/no venía con la misma frecuencia.

• •

GRAMÁTICA

63. *EL PADRE DE ÁNGELA VENÍA TODOS LOS FINES DE SEMANA*: USING THE IMPERFECT TO EXPRESS HABITUAL ACTIONS IN THE PAST

Read the following dialogue that might have occurred between Ángela and her grandmother.

ÁNGELA: A mi padre le **gustaba** pintar cuando **venía** aquí.

DOÑA CARMEN: Sí. Se **sentaba** en el jardín y **pintaba** todo el día.

ÁNGELA: Le **gustaba** la luz del jardín.

DOÑA CARMEN: A veces **pintaba** de noche.

ÁNGELA: No recuerdo eso.

DOÑA CARMEN: Ah, sí. Se **quedaba** en su cuarto y **pintaba** toda la noche.

In addition to describing an ongoing action, another frequent use of the imperfect is to describe actions that occurred repeatedly or habitually in the past. This is often expressed in English with *would* or *used to*.

¿A qué se dedicaba su esposo?	*What did your husband use to do?*
Ángel venía aquí todos los fines de semana.	*Ángel would (used to) come here every weekend.*

A number of time expressions are frequently used with the imperfect to talk about habitual actions in the past. Here are some of the most common.

todos los días/meses/años	every day/month/year
todos los fines de semana	every weekend
todas las noches/semanas/tardes	every night/week/afternoon
cada* hora/día/noche/semana/mes/ año	each (every) hour/day/night/week/month/ year
con frecuencia, frecuentemente	frequently
a ratos, a veces	at times
muchas veces	many times, often
pocas veces	seldom
de vez en cuando	from time to time
en aquel entonces	back then, at that time, in those days
de niño/a / joven	as a child/young person

Actividad A.   Cuando venía a visitar Ángel...

The following sentences form a description of Ángel's visits to San Germán to see María Luisa and the rest of the family, but they are out of order. Can you put them in order, from 1 to 12?

a. _____ Bajaba de su apartamento a la calle, donde estaba el carro.
b. _____ Después de comer, pasaba unas horas con su mujer antes de acostarse.
c. _____ Luego iba con sus hijos a la plaza para pasear y ver a la gente.
d. _____ Con frecuencia pintaba toda la noche del sábado.
e. _____ Ángel hacía el viaje casi todos los viernes por la tarde.
f. _____ Los domingos por la tarde volvía a San Juan.
g. _____ Siempre salía de San Juan por la autopista de Ponce.
h. _____ Generalmente pasaba los sábados con su esposa también.
i. _____ Por la enfermedad de su esposa, muchas veces era un día triste.
j. _____ A veces se paraba en un lugar cerca de Ponce para tomar un café.
k. _____ Cada domingo iba a la iglesia con Ángela y Roberto.
l. _____ Cuando por fin llegaba a la casa, siempre lo recibía Dolores con algo de comer.

Actividad B.   ¿Y tú?

Which of the following activities did you do when you were a child? And how often?

De niño/a...   mucho   a veces   nunca

1. Veía a mis abuelos.
2. Iba a nadar (*to swim*) cuando hacía calor.   _____   _____   _____
3. Iba al parque con mis amigos.   _____   _____   _____
4. Veía los dibujos animados (*cartoons*) los sábados por la mañana.   _____   _____   _____
5. Veía fútbol en la televisión.   _____   _____   _____

---

*The adjective cada (*each, every*) is invariable in form. It modifies both masculine and feminine singular nouns.

6. Cuando nevaba, iba a esquiar con mis padres.
7. Visitaba los centros comerciales (*malls*).
8. Pensaba en el futuro.
9. Molestaba a mis padres.
10. Estudiaba todo el día.

_____ _____ _____
_____ _____ _____
_____ _____ _____
_____ _____ _____
_____ _____ _____

Actividad C. Un poco de historia

Paso 1
Listen as the speaker on the cassette tape describes one aspect of the history of Puerto Rico.

Paso 2
Now, based on what you have heard, unscramble the following words to reconstruct the narration. (Worksheet)

Durante muchos años

1. colonia / era / Puerto Rico / una / española

Después de la guerra entre España y los Estados Unidos

2. norteamericano / la Isla / territorio / pasó a ser

En aquel entonces

3. la Isla / producto / importante / el / era / más / azúcarª / el / de
4. cañaᵇ / había / de / azúcar / grandes / de / fincas
5. esas / de / dueños / una / eran / esposo / doña Carmen / fincas / su / y / de

En esa época

6. una / su / grandes / era / más / de / finca / las
7. doscientos / a / trabajaban / veces / finca / de / la / hombres / en / más
8. ganadoᶜ / también / la / en / había / finca

Poco a poco, sin embargo,

9. vendiendo / iban / parcelas / en / esposo / doña Carmen / finca / y / su / la

En los años 40,

10. la Isla / diversificar / de / economía / la / el / trataba / gobiernoᵈ / de

Pero la industria del azúcar

11. economía / seguía / parte / puertorriqueña / la / de / siendo / una / importante

ª*sugar* ᵇ*cane* ᶜ*cattle* ᵈ*government*

Actividad D. ¿Y tú?
Read through the following groups of questions. Then select one group and answer the questions thoroughly. (Worksheet)

1. ¿Cómo eras cuando tenías diez años? ¿Eras más alto/a que tus compañeros/as? ¿Eras tímido/a? ¿travieso/a (*naughty*)? ¿muy obediente? ¿Molestabas a tus padres con frecuencia? ¿Qué hacías que les molestaba?
2. ¿Veías mucho la televisión cuando eras pequeño/a? ¿Qué programa(s) veías que ahora no ves? ¿Qué programa(s) siempre querías ver pero no te lo permitían tus padres? ¿Cuál era tu programa favorito? ¿tu actor favorito (actriz favorita)?
3. ¿Te gustaba ir a la escuela? ¿Cuál era tu materia favorita? ¿Qué materia detestabas? ¿Eras buen(a) estudiante? ¿Cómo se llamaba tu maestro favorito (maestra favorita)? ¿Hablabas mucho a veces en clase?

4. ¿Tenías muchos amigos (muchas amigas)? ¿Salías con ellos con frecuencia? ¿Adónde iban todas las tardes después de la escuela? ¿Cómo se llamaba tu mejor amigo/a? ¿Qué hacían juntos/as?

64. *A MIS PADRES LES ENCANTABA ESTA CASA*: SUMMARY OF THE USES OF THE IMPERFECT

You have learned to use the imperfect to perform a number of functions. Here is a summary of them, along with some additional examples.

* To describe conditions that were ongoing in the past

   This includes physical characteristics, states of mind, and emotions, as well as age.

Ángela **era** una joven lista y simpática. **Tenía** 25 años, más o menos.	*Ángela was a bright and pleasant young woman. She was about 25 years old.*
Se sentía muy frustrada por lo del coche.	*She felt very frustrated by the situation with her car.*
Hacía muy buen tiempo durante el viaje a San Germán, pero **hacía** mucho calor.	*The weather was very nice during the trip to San Germán, but it was very hot.*

* To talk about events that were ongoing (in progress) in the past

   This includes simultaneous ongoing events, usually expressed with **mientras**.

Raquel **escuchaba** con atención **mientras** doña Carmen **hablaba** de Ángel.	*Raquel listened (was listening) attentively while (as) doña Carmen talked (was talking) about Ángel.*

   Note, however, that **cuando** can have the meaning of **mientras** and thus can be followed by the imperfect.

Cuando hablaba con Olga, Raquel se **sentía** un poco incómoda.	*When (While) she was speaking with Olga, Raquel felt a little uncomfortable.*

   The imperfect also expresses actions in progress that were interrupted by another action (expressed with the preterite).

Mientras **íbamos** a San Germán, el carro **empezó** a funcionar mal.	*While we were going to San Germán, the car began to run badly.*
Salíamos del peaje cuando **se paró** el carro.	*We were leaving the tollbooth when the car stopped.*

   The **ir a** + infinitive structure is almost always in the imperfect.

Ángela **iba a llamar** a su hermano otra vez.	*Ángela was going to call her brother again.*

* To talk about habitual events in the past

   Often (but not always) this use of the imperfect is signaled by the use of words and phrases that emphasize the habitual nature of the action: **todos los días, siempre**, and so on.

De niña, Ángela **visitaba** a su abuela **con frecuencia**.	*As a child, Ángela visited (used to visit) her grandmother often.*

An Additional Use of the Imperfect

The imperfect is always used to tell time in the past in Spanish.

¿Qué hora **era** cuando Ángela,
Raquel y Laura llegaron a la casa
de la abuela?

*What time was it when Ángela, ,
Raquel and Laura arrived at the
grandmother's house?*

Eran las once de la mañana.

It was eleven A.M.

Actividad.   ¿Quién lo diría?

Which of these characters might have made the following statements? ¡OJO! There may
be more than one person for some statements.

a.   doña Carmen   b.   Raquel   c.   Ángela

1. _____ Íbamos a viajar a México si doña Carmen pensaba que era una buena idea.
2. _____ Era muy temprano cuando llegamos al taller para recoger (*to pick up*) el carro.
   Yo estaba de mal humor.
3. _____ Todavía no comprendo por qué mi papá nunca nos decía nada de su familia en
   Buenos Aires.
4. _____ Mientras esperaba a mis nietas y la abogada, fui a la iglesia. Estaba un poco
   pensativa.
5. _____ Eran las dos de la tarde cuando por fin terminamos de almorzar.
6. _____ De niña, me gustaba mucho venir a esta casa. También asistía a la universidad
   en este pueblo.
7. _____ Éste era el baúl de mi padre. No sabía que estaba aquí todavía.
8. _____ Íbamos a salir cuando doña Carmen nos dijo que nos quería dar algo.

65. *Y AQUÍ ESTAMOS, CANSADAS Y LISTAS PARA DORMIR:* EXPRESSING EMOTIONS AND STATES OF BEING WITH *estar* AND *sentirse*

You have already learned how to express a number of conditions and emotions in Spanish
by using **tener** with nouns: **tener miedo** (*to be afraid*), **tener hambre** (*to be hungry*), and
so on. Other feelings and conditions can be expressed in Spanish by using adjectives with
the verbs **estar** and **sentirse** (**ie, i**).

Doña Carmen **está** preocupada.   *Doña Carmen is worried.*

Arturo **se sentía** culpable.   *Arturo felt guilty.*

Here are some adjectives frequently used with **estar** to express conditions and states of
mind. You already know the meaning of many of them.

aburrido/a	bored	**nervioso/a**	nervous
cansado/a	tired	**ocupado/a**	busy, occupied
contento/a	happy, content	**pensativo/a**	pensive
enfermo/a	sick, ill	**preocupado/a**	worried
enojado/a	angry	**sorprendido/a**	surprised
furioso/a	furious	**sospechoso/a**	suspicious
muerto/a	dead	**triste**	sad

Adjectives often used with **sentirse** include **aburrido/a, (in)cómodo/a**
(*[un]comfortable*), **culpable, frustrado/a, nervioso/a,** and **preocupado/a.**

Note: As you learned in the Textbook, adjectives are used with verbs such as **ponerse**, **quedarse**, and **volverse** to express a *change* in state of mind or condition. Compare these sentences.

> Don Fernando **se puso** enfermo hace unos meses.
> Todavía **está** enfermo.

Ponerse expresses the onset of the illness, whereas **estar** describes the resulting condition.

Actividad A. ¿Cómo están?

You will hear a series of sentences on the cassette tape. Each one will be said twice. Write them down, then indicate the character you think each sentence describes. Pay attention to the adjective endings because they convey information about gender and number. (Worksheet)

a. don Fernando
b. doña Carmen
c. Ángela

d. Raquel
e. Arturo
f. los tíos de Ángela

Actividad B. ¿Cómo se sentía Raquel?

Paso 1

Do you remember how Raquel felt when she encountered these situations? Complete the following sentences with **sentirse** or **estar** and an appropriate adjective to describe her feelings. ¡OJO! Use the imperfect of both verbs.

1. En Sevilla Jaime se perdió dos veces. Raquel...
2. Raquel dejó su cartera en el taxi en Madrid. (Ella)...
3. Supo que Rosario vivía en la Argentina. (Ella)...
4. En la estancia Santa Susana Cirilo le dijo que Rosario se mudó a Buenos Aires. Raquel...
5. Cuando conoció a Arturo, él le dijo que Ángel era su hermano. Raquel...
6. Arturo la llevó al aeropuerto y se despidió de ella. Raquel...
7. En San Juan le informó una vecina que Ángel estaba muerto. Raquel...
8. Raquel tenía que contarles a los tíos la historia de Ángel y don Fernando. (Ella)...
9. En Puerto Rico algo le pasó al coche y tenían que pasar la noche en Ponce. Raquel...
10. Doña Carmen le dio a Ángela permiso de ir a México con Raquel. (Ella)...

Paso 2

Now check your answers by listening to the cassette tape. First you will hear each sentence. Give your answer, then listen to the possible answer given on the tape.

Actividad C. ¿Y tú?

Describe how you feel in these situations by combining items from each column.

Cuando	tengo que ir al dentista	estoy	preocupado/a
	vi el último examen de español	estaba	triste
	hablo con mis profesores	me siento	alegre
	se fue un buen amigo mío (*of mine*)	me sentía	nervioso/a
	tuve un accidente		culpable
	pago la matrícula (*tuition*)		contento/a
	estudio hasta las dos de la mañana		terrible
	llega el verano		sorprendido/a
	se murió mi (perro, gato, ...)		solo/a
			cansado/a
			enojado/a

Actividad D. ¿Y tú?

Describe how you feel or felt and why, for several days this week. Contrast your current feelings with your previous ones. You may follow these models if you wish. (Worksheet)

MODELO: Hoy me siento/estoy _____ porque _____.

Ayer me sentía/estaba _____ porque _____.

El viernes pasado me sentía/estaba _____ porque

_____.

Esta semana me siento/estoy _____ porque _____.

La semana pasada me sentía/estaba _____ porque

_____.

- -

PRONUNCIACIÓN: More on Stress and the Written Accent

Before beginning the following activities, complete the three simple rules for accentuation in Spanish as a review.

Rule #1: If a word ends in a vowel, -n, or -s, stress normally falls on the . . . last/next-to-the-last . . . syllable.

Rule #2: If a word ends in any other consonant, stress normally falls on the . . . last/next-to-the-last . . . syllable.

Rule #3: Any exception to rules 1 and 2 will have a written accent mark on the stressed . . . consonant/vowel.

Actividad A.

Repeat the following words after the speaker, paying close attention to stress and the written accent.

1. moneda paradero escaleras puertos empiezan

2. señal ciudad bailar responder \ taller

3. película semáforo periódico búsqueda máquina

4. Ángel inglés avión después San Germán

As you know, the written accent mark is important for maintaining the original sound of a word to which syllables have been added. It can also change the pronunciation and the meaning of words that are spelled alike except for the accent: **como** versus **¿cómo?**.

Actividad B.

When you hear the corresponding number, read the following pairs of words. Then repeat the correct pronunciation, imitating the speaker.

1. hablo / habló
2. llamo / llamó
3. búsqueda / buscábamos
4. nación / naciones
5. lápiz / lápices
6. avión / aviones
7. preguntar / preguntárselo
8. buscando / buscándolo

When some words (primarily one-syllable words) have accents, they are to distinguish them from other words that sound like them. This accent is called a *diacritical* accent.

Repeat the following pairs of words, then provide the meanings that are missing.

1. mi _____ / mí (*me*)
2. tu (*your*) / tú _____
3. el (*the*) / él _____
4. si _____ / sí (*yes*)

5. se (*oneself*) / sé _____
6. te _____ / té (*tea*)
7. que (*that, which*) / ¿qué? _____
8. este _____ / éste (*this one*)

Have you completed the following sections of the lesson? Check them off here.

_____ **Más allá del episodio**   _____ **Pronunciación**

_____ **Gramática**

Now scan the words in the **Vocabulario** list to be sure that you understand the meaning of most of them.

• •

Vocabulario

¿Con qué frecuencia... ? (How Often . . . ?)

a ratos/veces	at times
cada (*inv.*)	each
de niño/a / joven	as a child/young person
en aquel entonces	back then, at that time, in those days
el fin de semana	weekend
frecuentemente	frequently
la vez*	time, occasion
de vez en cuando	from time to time
muchas/pocas veces	often/seldom
todos/as...	every

Repaso: el año, con frecuencia, el día, la hora, el mes, la noche, la semana, la tarde

Los adjetivos

cansado/a	tired
contento/a	happy, content
enfermo/a	sick
enojado/a	angry
frustrado/a	frustrated
furioso/a	furious
(in)cómodo/a	(un)comfortable
nervioso/a	nervous
ocupado/a	busy

Repaso: aburrido/a, culpable, muerto/a, pensativo/a, preocupado/a, sorprendido/a, sospechoso/a, triste

---

Now that you have completed the Textbook and Workbook for **Lección 22**, take the Self-Test for that lesson. (It is on page 286.) Remember to listen to the tape when you see the cassette symbol and to check your answers.

_____ **Self-Test**

---

*Note that la vez means *time* in the sense of occurrence or event. El tiempo means *time* in the general sense (el tiempo vuela = *time flies*). La hora refers to clock time.

Now that you have worked through the Textbook and the Workbook and taken the Self-Test, here are some of the things you have accomplished in Spanish.

- You can use and understand vocabulary useful for describing changes in physical and mental conditions.
- You have learned more about the language functions you can perform with the imperfect, including describing in the past and talking about habitual actions.
- You know how to express additional conditions such as *worried, angry, sad,* and so on, in Spanish.
- You have learned more about spoken stress and the written accent mark in Spanish.
- You have continued to improve your listening skills.

You are now ready to continue on with **Lección 23** in the Textbook.

23

VISTA AL MAR

OBJETIVOS

Whereas the materials in the Textbook all had to do with the video episode, the materials in the Workbook will help you expand your knowledge of the Spanish language in general, as well as give you opportunities for self-expression in Spanish. In this lesson you will learn

- how to use forms of **estar + -ndo** to talk about what was happening at a given moment in the past
- more about using the preterite and the imperfect together to talk about past events
- how to use the verb phrase **acabar de** to talk about what just happened.

Remember to listen to the tape for **Lección 23** when you see the cassette symbol and to check your answers in Appendix 1.

MÁS ALLÁ DEL EPISODIO

Actividad A. Ángela y el apartamento

This section of the Workbook will be different from previous **Más allá del episodio** sections. Instead of reading about a character or characters from the series, you will listen to a brief narration on the cassette tape. Read through the **Para pensar...** section before listening to the tape.

PARA PENSAR...

Look over the following questions. You probably cannot answer them now. Keep them in mind as you listen to the narration, and answer them after you have finished listening.

1. ¿Por qué quiere Ángela vender el apartamento de sus padres? ¿Qué motivos tiene?
2. ¿Es posible que su deseo de vender el apartamento tenga algo que ver con (*has to do with*) la muerte de su padre? ¿con el hecho de que (*the fact that*) su hermano ya no pasa tanto tiempo con ella? ¿Es posible que necesite dinero por otra razón?

Now listen to the narration on the cassette tape.

Actividad B.
Answer the following questions about the narration you have just heard.

1. De los siguientes títulos, ¿cuál es el más apropiado para la narración?
   a. ____ La tristeza de Ángela
   b. ____ Motivos para vender
   c. ____ Calle Sol, 4

2. Las razones de Ángela para vender el apartamento tienen que ver con (*have to do with*)...
   a. ____ la familia y el trabajo
   b. ____ el trabajo y su vida personal
   c. ____ la familia y su vida personal

¿Es buena idea que Ángela venda el apartamento?

GRAMÁTICA

66. *JORGE ESTABA TRABAJANDO EN UNA PELÍCULA*: THE PAST PROGRESSIVE

You have already learned that you can describe an action that is in progress at the moment by using **estar** plus the **-ndo** form (present participle) of a verb. The progressive may also be used when referring to the past.

Forms
The past progressive is formed with the past tense of **estar**—usually the imperfect—and the present participle. As with the present progressive, an object or reflexive pronoun may precede **estar** or follow and be attached to the present participle.

Laura **estaba mirando** el mapa.	*Laura was looking at the map.*
¿Me **estaba proponiendo** matrimonio?	*Was he proposing marriage to me?*
Ángela **estaba enseñándole** (le estaba enseñando) la copa.	*Ángela was showing him the goblet.*

Uses
When speaking about the past, it is not always necessary to use the past progressive to express English *was/were -ing*. The simple imperfect can do that. Here are the preceding examples with the imperfect tense.

> Laura miraba el mapa.
> ¿Me proponía matrimonio?
> Ángela le enseñaba la copa.

In addition, remember that there are some cases in which the use of the progressive—present or past—is not appropriate.

- The progressive is almost never used with verbs of motion such as **ir** or **venir**. However, the corresponding English verbs are frequently used in the progressive.

Íbamos para San Germán cuando se descompuso el carro.	*We were going to San Germán when the car broke down.*

- The progressive does not express futurity.

Salíamos para San Germán   *We were going to leave (leaving) for*
al día siguiente.   *San Germán the next day.*

Actividad A. ¿Qué estaban haciendo?

Select the most appropriate completion for each sentence. ¡OJO! Some items refer to things you have seen in the video episode; others ask you to predict what the characters might have been doing.

Cuando Ángela, Raquel y Laura llegaron a San Germán...

1. doña Carmen estaba

   a. _____ escribiéndole una carta a una amiga
   b. _____ pintando unas hojas en el cuarto de Ángel
   c. _____ rezando (*praying*) en la iglesia

2. Dolores no estaba con ella. Estaba

   a. _____ trabajando en la casa
   b. _____ haciendo las compras
   c. _____ jugando con Laura

3. En ese momento Jorge y sus estudiantes estaban

   a. _____ aprendiendo un nuevo drama
   b. _____ actuando en una película
   c. _____ cantando en el coro de la universidad

4. Al mismo tiempo Arturo estaba

   a. _____ caminando en el Rosedal
   b. _____ hablando con su madre
   c. _____ preparando su viaje a Puerto Rico

5. Los tíos de Ángela estaban

   a. _____ comprando sus billetes (*tickets*) para México
   b. _____ hablando de la nueva situación
   c. _____ llamando a don Fernando

Now listen to the items on the cassette tape and give your answers. You will hear the correct answer on the tape.

Actividad B. ¿Y tú?

Paso 1

Indicate what some of your friends and family were doing during the following time frames. Select one person for each item. (Worksheet)

1. La última vez que yo lo/la llamé, mi _____ estaba...

2. Mientras yo estaba mirando el **Episodio 23** de *Destinos*, mi _____ estaba...

3. Esta mañana, mientras yo todavía estaba dormida, mi _____ estaba...

Paso 2

Now indicate what you were doing at the following times. (Worksheet)

4. Anoche, a las diez de la noche...
5. Este mismo día (¡más o menos!) el año pasado, ...
6. Ayer, a las once de la mañana...

67. ¡ARTURO ME DIJO QUE ME QUERÍA MUCHO!: USING THE PRETERITE AND IMPERFECT TOGETHER

RAQUEL: En el hotel, **hice** una llamada de larga distancia. **Llamé** a Buenos Aires para hablar con Arturo. Y **tuve** suerte. Arturo **estaba** en casa cuando lo **llamé**. **Hablamos** un rato, unos minutos. ¡Y qué sorpresa! Arturo me **dijo** algo que realmente me **sorprendió**. Me **dijo** que me **quería** mucho. ¿Qué voy a hacer?

You have learned to use and recognize the preterite and imperfect forms to talk about the past. In addition, in **Lección 22**, you read a summary of the uses of the imperfect. Stated briefly, they are to express events in progress, habitual or repeated events, descriptions, and conditions.

Uses of the Preterite

In general, functions in the past other than those just summarized are expressed with the preterite.* The preterite is used

- to talk about distinct, individual actions or events in the past

These may have occurred only once or be seen as having happened individually a number of times.

Fuimos a San Germán y **hablamos** con mi abuela.	*We went to San Germán and talked with my grandmother.*
Le **dije** el número como mil veces.	*I told him the number about a thousand times.*
Olga **empezó** inmediatamente a hacerle preguntas a Raquel.	*Olga immediately began to ask Raquel questions.*
La conversación **terminó** tarde.	*The conversation ended late.*

- to talk about changes in conditions

Ángela **se enojó** cuando su abuela criticó a Jorge, y luego **se puso** triste.	*Ángela got mad when her grandmother criticized Jorge, and then she became sad.*

- to describe actions that occured within a defined period of time

A time phrase, such as **por una hora** or **por un año**, is often used in these cases.

¿**Estuvo** en Nueva York? —Sí, **estuve** por unos días.	*Were you in New York? —Yes, I was there for a few days.*
Durante unos años **vivieron** en la estancia Santa Susana.	*For a few years they lived on the Santa Susana Ranch.*

Preterite and Imperfect Together

When a sentence contains more than one verb, any sequence or combination of tenses is possible, depending on what you wish to express: all preterite, all imperfect, or a combination of the two. Remember that a frequent pattern is as follows: the imperfect describes what was happening when another action (expressed in the preterite) occurred.

---

*There are, of course, other past tenses, which you will learn to use as you progress through the *Destinos* Textbook and Workbook.

Raquel **viajó** a Puerto Rico, **buscó** la casa de Ángel y **habló** con una vecina de Ángela.	*Raquel traveled to Puerto Rico, looked for Ángel's house, and spoke with Ángela's neighbor.*
Eran las diez y Ángela **tenía** una cita para ver unos apartamentos a las diez y media.	*It was ten o'clock and Ángela had an appointment to see some apartments at ten-thirty.*
Arturo **estaba** en casa cuando lo **llamé**.	*Arturo was at home when I called him.*
Cuando nosotras **llegamos**, Jorge **daba** una clase.	*When we arrived, Jorge was teaching a class.*

Actividad A. ¿En qué orden?

The following events all happened in **Episodio 23**, but they are out of order. Can you put them in chronological order, from 1 to 8?

a. _____ Ángela le prometió a su jefa que iba a volver al trabajo en dos semanas.
b. _____ Raquel llamó a Arturo y le dijo que Ángel estaba muerto.
c. _____ Mientras hablaban en el patio de la universidad, Ángela le mostró a Jorge la copa de bodas de su abuela, Rosario.
d. _____ Raquel conoció a Jorge Alonso, que era el novio de Ángela.
e. _____ Ángela y Raquel vieron un apartamento y un *town house* que le interesaban mucho a Ángela.
f. _____ Raquel se despidió de Ángela y Laura en el hotel.
g. _____ Ángela decidió tomar el apartamento porque la vista al mar era fenomenal.
h. _____ Arturo le prometió a Raquel reunirse con ella en México y le dijo que la quería.

Actividad B. ¿Qué dijeron?

Here are three segments of dialogue from **Episodio 23**. Can you complete each segment in the manner indicated in the directions in each part?

Parte A. Raquel y Arturo hablan por teléfono. Completa el diálogo con las frases apropiadas.

Frases útiles: ella murió, era un artista, estaba casado, estaban con él, murió solo, tenía dos hijos

RAQUEL: Ángel... ya...

ARTURO: ¿Cuándo?

RAQUEL: Hace unos meses. _____[1] muy conocido en Puerto Rico. Y

_____.[2]

ARTURO: ¿Has hablado[a] con su esposa?

RAQUEL: No. _____[3] hace unos años.

ARTURO: Ángel _____,[4] entonces.

RAQUEL: No. Sus hijos _____.[5]

ARTURO: ¿Sus hijos? Raquel...

RAQUEL: Sí. Ángel _____.[6] Su hija Ángela es una mujer atractiva y simpática.

[a]¿Has... *Have you spoken*

 Now check your answers by listening to the cassette tape.

Parte B: Ángela habla con Raquel y luego con su tío Jaime, que llama por teléfono. Pon las palabras en orden.

ÁNGELA: Raquel, ¿puedes ir conmigo a la universidad? Quiero que conozcas[a] a Jorge, mi novio. Acaba de[b] llegar de Nueva York.
RAQUEL: ¿Jorge trabaja en la universidad?
ÁNGELA: Sí, él es profesor de teatro.
RAQUEL: 1. ¿ Nueva York / qué / y / en / hacía?

_____

ÁNGELA: 2. película[c] / en / trabajando / estaba / una

_____

RAQUEL: ¿De verdad?
ÁNGELA: Sí. Jorge trabaja a menudo[d] en Nueva York. Pasa mucho tiempo allá. [*Suena el teléfono.*] Hola, tío Jaime. ¿Cómo estás?
JAIME: Ángela, tengo a alguien que está muy interesado en comprar la casa.
3. mucho / gustó / le

_____

ÁNGELA: ¿El hombre del otro día?
JAIME: El mismo. 4. casa / le / la / mucho / impresionó

_____

[a]Quiero... *I want you to meet*   [b]Acaba... *He's just*   [c]*movie*   [d]a... con frecuencia

Now check your answers by listening to the cassette tape.

Parte C. Raquel habla de lo que hizo con Ángela este día. Pon las oraciones en orden (1–7).

a. _____ Fuimos al banco porque Ángela tenía que hablar con la supervisora.
b. _____ Cuando llegamos aquí a la universidad, ¿qué hacía Jorge?
c. _____ Finalmente, vinimos aquí a la universidad.
d. _____ Hoy fui con Ángela al banco donde trabaja.
e. _____ Ángela quería ver a su novio, Jorge.
f. _____ Cuando nosotras llegamos, Jorge daba una clase.
g. _____ Ángela quería ver a una persona aquí.

Now check your answers by listening to the cassette tape.

Actividad C. ¿Por qué?

23.4
OPTIONAL
PHOTO

Indicate why the following things happened by selecting the logical completion for each sentence.

1. _____ Raquel, Ángela y Laura se sentaron bajo un árbol (*tree*)...
2. _____ Ángela quería vender el apartamento...
3. _____ Raquel llamó a Arturo en Buenos Aires...
4. _____ Ángela paró el carro y compró refrescos (*soft drinks*)...
5. _____ Jorge iba frecuentemente a Nueva York...
6. _____ Ángela y Raquel pasaron por unos apartamentos...
7. _____ Ángela decidió tomar el apartamento...
8. _____ Ángela y Jorge salieron del teatro...

a. porque le recordaba mucho a sus padres
b. porque allí había más oportunidades de trabajar
c. porque Ángela quería contarle a Jorge la historia de su padre
d. porque hacía mucho calor en la autopista de Ponce
e. porque quería informarle sobre la muerte de Ángel
f. porque todas tenían mucha sed
g. porque tenía una magnífica vista al mar
h. porque Ángela pensaba mudarse

Actividad D. Un viaje a Nueva York

Jorge has just returned from New York. What might he say about his trip? Based on the phrases provided, form complete sentences with the appropriate imperfect or preterite form of the infinitives. (Worksheet)

1. la semana pasada / yo hacer un viaje / Nueva York

   _____

2. estar en la ciudad / por cuatro días

   _____

3. mientras estar allí / trabajar en una película

   _____

4. también / ir a muchas fiestas

   _____

5. cenar / tres restaurantes fabulosos / y / ver / tres obras de teatro en Broadway

   _____

   _____

6. todos las noches / salir / con personas interesantes

   _____

7. todos / ser / actores y actrices atractivos

   _____

8. gustar mucho / el viaje / y / aceptar otro trabajo / para el mes que viene (*coming*)

   _____

   _____

Actividad E. ¿Y tú?

Indicate some habits you have recently changed. Follow the model if you wish. Create at least three sentences. (Worksheet)

> MODELO: El año pasado siempre estudiaba en la biblioteca.
> Este semestre empecé a estudiar más en casa.

Frases útiles: almorzar en... , tomar clases de... , estudiar por la tarde... , no estudiar mucho... , salir todas las noches, trabajar en... , ir al cine con frecuencia... , mirar mucho la televisión

El tiempo: el año pasado, durante el invierno, el semestre (trimestre) pasado

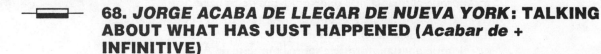

68. *JORGE ACABA DE LLEGAR DE NUEVA YORK*: TALKING ABOUT WHAT HAS JUST HAPPENED (*Acabar de* + INFINITIVE)

The expression **acabar de** + infinitive is used in either the present or imperfect tense to describe what just happened.

Blanca, **acabo de decidirme.**	*Blanca, I have just decided.*
Acabábamos de llegar de San Germán cuando llamé a Arturo.	*We had just returned from San Germán when I called Arturo.*

Note that this expression is not used to express English *I have decided* or *We had returned.* Its use is limited to the meaning of the special expression *have/had just (done something).*

 ### Actividad A.   ¿Quién?

Listen as the narrator makes a series of statements. Which of the characters listed would be most likely to make them? ¡OJO! Some characters are appropriate for more than one statement.

a.   Raquel
b.   Arturo
c.   Ángela
d.   doña Carmen

e.   la jefa de Ángela
f.   los tíos de Ángela
g.   Laura
h.   el mecánico de Ponce

1. __   2. __   3. __   4. __   5. __   6. __   7. __   8. __   9. __   10. __

Actividad B.   ¿Y tú?

What always happens just after you've washed the car? stepped into the shower? Combine the elements from the three columns to describe the experiences that you think are most annoying. Create at least five sentences. (Worksheet)

Cuando

acabo de lavar el carro	frecuentemente	suena (*rings*) el teléfono
acabo de estudiar mucho	a veces	alguien me llama para
acabo de acostarme	siempre	invitarme a cenar
acabo de salir de la casa	nunca	llaman a la puerta
acabo de recibir el sueldo (*salary*)	muchas veces	cancelan el examen
acabo de preparar la cena		empieza a llover
acabo de entrar en la ducha (*shower*)		llegan las cuentas (*bills*)
acaba de empezar mi programa favorito		se me descompone el carro
acabo de gastar (*spend*) mi dinero		pierdo mi cartera
		se pone enfermo mi perro/ gato
		¿ ?

Have you completed the following sections of the lesson? Check them off here.

_____   **Más allá del episodio**   _____   **Gramática**

Now scan the words in the **Vocabulario** list to be sure that you understand the meaning of them.

• •

VOCABULARIO

Los verbos
acabar de + *inf.*   to have just (*done something*)

Los sustantivos
la película   movie

Now that you have completed the Textbook and Workbook for **Lección 23**, take the Self-Test for that lesson. (It is on page 288.) Remember to listen to the tape when you see the cassette symbol and to check your answers.

_____ **Self-Test**

Now that you have worked through the Textbook and the Workbook and taken the Self-Test, here are some of the things you have accomplished in Spanish.

- You can use and understand vocabulary useful for describing the rooms and other parts of a house, and a number of domestic appliances.
- You have learned more about the language functions you can perform with the preterite.
- You have learned more about using the preterite and the imperfect to narrate in the past in Spanish.
- You know how to express actions that were ongoing, as well as those that have or had just happened.
- You have continued to improve your listening skills.

You are now ready to continue on with **Lección 24** in the Textbook.

24

EL DON JUAN

OBJETIVOS

Whereas the materials in the Textbook all had to do with the video episode, the materials in the Workbook will help you expand your knowledge of the Spanish language in general, as well as give you opportunities for self-expression in Spanish. In this lesson you will learn

- more about using the preterite and imperfect together to talk about past events
- about the special uses of some verbs (such as **saber** and **conocer**) in the preterite
- about the use of **hace... que...** to tell how long something has been going on.

Remember to listen to the tape for **Lección 24** when you see the cassette symbol and to check your answers in Appendix 1.

MÁS ALLÁ DEL EPISODIO

Actividad A.   Jorge Alonso

PARA PENSAR...

Look over the following questions. You probably cannot answer them now. Keep them in mind as you listen to the narration, and answer them after you have finished listening.

1. En este episodio, Jorge trata de insinuarse con (*get close to*) Raquel. ¿Es siempre así Jorge? ¿Es un mujeriego, como dice Raquel?
2. ¿Qué sabe la abuela, doña Carmen, de Jorge? (Recuerda que en el **Episodio 22** doña Carmen le dijo a Ángela: «Verás (*You'll see*) si no es verdad lo que te digo de Jorge.»
3. Como dice Ángela, «todo el mundo se opone» a sus relaciones con Jorge. ¿Por qué será? (*Why do you suppose that is?*)

Now listen to the narration on the cassette tape.

Actividad B.

Answer the following questions about the narration you have just heard.

Jorge, ¿un hombre oportunista o un novio cariñoso?

Sí   No   1. Raquel tiene razón en pensar así de Jorge.
Sí   No   2. Si Raquel y doña Carman hablaran (*were to talk*) de Jorge, no estarían de acuerdo (*they wouldn't agree*).
Sí   No   3. Jorge sí quiere casarse con Ángela.

• •

GRAMÁTICA

 69. *EN LA UNIVERSIDAD CONOCÍ AL NOVIO DE ÁNGELA*: DIFFERENCES BETWEEN THE PRETERITE AND IMPERFECT OF *conocer*, *saber*, *querer*, *poder*, AND *hay*

These verbs have different English equivalents depending on whether they are used in the preterite or the imperfect. Note the following translations. You may want to familiarize yourself with them by listening for them in native speech and watching for them in reading materials.

The Verb *conocer*

- preterite = *met* (*Note:* **conocer** can also mean *meet* in the present.)

Raquel **conoció** a los tíos de Ángela.	*Raquel met Ángela's uncles and aunts.*
Voy a la universidad para **conocer** a Jorge.	*I'm going to the university to meet Jorge.*

- imperfect = *knew, was acquainted with*

Arturo no **conocía** bien a su medio hermano.	*Arturo didn't know his half-brother well.*

The Verb *saber*

- preterite = *found out, learned*

Raquel llegó a la casa de Ángel y **supo** que estaba muerto.	*Raquel arrived at Ángel's house and found out he was dead.*

- imperfect = *knew about, had knowledge of*

Ángela no **sabía** que tenía un tío en la Argentina.	*Ángela didn't know she had an uncle in Argentina.*

The Verb *querer*

- affirmative preterite = *tried, made an attempt*

Raquel **quiso** avisar a Ángela sobre la personalidad de Jorge.	*Raquel tried to warn Ángela about Jorge's personality.*

- negative preterite = *refused*

> Pero Ángela **no quiso** oír la crítica de su novio. | *But Ángela refused to hear any criticism of her boyfriend.*

- imperfect (affirmative and negative) = *wanted (didn't want)*

> Raquel **no quería** meterse en sus relaciones con Jorge. | *Raquel didn't want to get involved in her relationship with Jorge.*

The Verb *poder*

- affirmative preterite = *succeeded in*

> Raquel **pudo** convencer a doña Carmen de que el viaje era muy urgente. | *Raquel succeeded in convincing doña Carmen that the trip was very urgent.*

- negative preterite = *failed to*

> Jorge **no pudo** impresionar a Raquel. | *Jorge failed to impress Raquel.*

- imperfect (affirmative and negative) = *was (not) able to*

> Ángela **no podía** comprender por qué todos se oponían a sus relaciones con Jorge. | *Ángela couldn't understand why everyone was opposed to her relationship with Jorge.*

The verb *hay (haber)*

- preterite = *there was/were* in the sense of *occurred, happened*

> **Hubo** un accidente en el sitio de la excavación. | *An accident occurred at the excavation site.*

- imperfect = *there was/were, there existed*

> **Había** muchas cosas que hacer. | *There were many things to do.*

Actividad A.   ¿Cuánto recuerdas?

How much do you remember about Jorge and the events that surround him? Indicate whether the statements you hear are Cierto (C) or Falso (F).

1. C F   2. C F   3. C F   4. C F   5. C F   6. C F   7. C F   8. C F

Actividad B.   ¿A quién se refiere?

Answer the following questions about recent events in *Destinos* with the name of the appropriate person or place. If you need help, some choices are given in parentheses, but you should try to answer without looking at them.

1.   ¿Quién no quiso creer la historia que Raquel les contó a los tíos de Ángela? (¿tía Olga o tío Jaime?)

2. ¿Quiénes no pudieron arreglar (*fix*) el carro en la autopista? (¿los mecánicos o Raquel y Ángela?)
3. ¿A quién conoció Raquel en San Germán? (¿a tía Olga o a doña Carmen?)
4. ¿Quién pudo conseguir el permiso de doña Carmen para el viaje de Ángela a México? (¿Raquel o Ángela?)
5. ¿Quién quiso coquetear (*flirt*) con Raquel? (¿tío Jaime o Jorge?)
6. ¿Quién no quiso escuchar nada malo sobre Jorge? (¿doña Carmen o Ángela?)
7. ¿Dónde hubo un accidente? (¿en México o en San Germán?)
8. ¿Quién dio la noticia que hubo un accidente en la excavación? (¿Jorge o tío Jaime?)

Actividad C.   ¿Y tú?

Create at least five accurate statements about yourself by combining one element from each group. Complete the sentences with information based on your own experience, as needed. (Worksheet)

1. Supe un secreto
2. No quise hacer algo que me pidieron mis padres (hijos)
3. Pude convencer a mis padres (hijos) de algo importante
4. Hubo una sorpresa muy grande en mi vida
5. Conocí a mi primer novio (primera novia)
6. No pude expresarme muy bien
7. Una vez quise

pero lo hice de todas formas (*anyway*)
pero no pude
cuando les dije que (no) _____
cuando tuve (que) _____
cuando un amigo me dijo que _____
cuando tenía _____ años
cuando alguien me dio/dijo _____
cuando estaba en la escuela primaria/secundaria

70. *HACE CUATRO DÍAS QUE ESTOY EN PUERTO RICO*: TALKING ABOUT HOW LONG SOMETHING HAS BEEN HAPPENING

You have already learned that **hace** (plus time) expresses *ago* when used with a preterite tense verb.

La esposa de Ángel murió hace unos años. (Hace unos años que la esposa de Ángel murió.)	*Ángel's wife died a few years ago.*
Hace cuatro días que Raquel llegó a Puerto Rico. (Raquel llegó a Puerto Rico hace cuatro días.)	*Raquel arrived in Puerto Rico four days ago.*

When **hace** (plus time) is used with a verb in the present tense, it expresses how long something has been going on.

Hace varias semanas que Raquel conoce a Arturo.	*Raquel has known Arturo for a few weeks.*
Hace sólo unos días que Raquel conoce a Ángela.	*Raquel has known Ángela for only a few days.*
¿Cuánto tiempo hace que tiene la copa doña Carmen?	*How long has doña Carmen had the goblet?*

Note that **¿Cuánto tiempo hace que...?** expresses *How long has it been that . . . ?*

Actividad A. ¿Cuánto tiempo hace?

Match the beginning of each sentence with its logical conclusion.

1. _____ Hace apenas (*barely*) unas horas que...
2. _____ Hace más de cincuenta años que...
3. _____ Hace casi (*almost*) dos semanas que...
4. _____ Hace poco menos de un año que...
5. _____ Hace casi quinientos años que...

a. Raquel conoce a Jorge
b. Ángela y Jorge son novios
c. Raquel conoce a Arturo
d. hablan español en Puerto Rico
e. don Fernando vive en México

 On the cassette tape you will hear the beginning of each sentence. Say the sentence's conclusion of your choice, then listen for the correct answer on the tape.

 ## Actividad B. ¿Qué ocurrió primero?

Listen to the narrations on the cassette tape, then indicate whether the statements are **Cierto (C)** or **Falso (F)**.

C F 1. Entre los dos estados, Arizona es el estado más viejo.
C F 2. Los dos eran territorio español en una época, pero España perdió a Puerto Rico primero.
C F 3. Nueva York lleva más tiempo como estado que California.
C F 4. El tren es una forma más reciente de transporte que el avión.
C F 5. Sabemos más sobre los viajes por mar que sobre los viajes por el espacio.

Actividad C. Un poco de historia

 How long ago did the following events take place? First, match the sentences that describe the events with the drawings. Then complete the sentences based on information in the drawings.

a.

b.   c.   d.   e.   f.

1. _____ Colón llegó a América hace _____ siglos.

2. _____ John Hancock firmó la Declaración de la Independencia hace más de _____ años.

3. _____ Alexander Graham Bell inventó el teléfono hace unos _____ años.

4. _____ Magallanes navegó el estrecho (*strait*) que lleva su nombre hace un poco menos de _____ siglos.

5. _____ Los mexicanos ganaron (*won*) la batalla de Puebla hace más de _____ años.

6. _____ Fidel Castro capturó la Habana hace más de _____ años.

Actividad D. ¿Y tú?

Choose five of the following experiences, or any other ones, and indicate how long they have been going on. Follow the model if you wish. (Worksheet)

MODELO: Ya hace... años que...

Frases útiles: vivir en la misma casa, estar en esta universidad, trabajar en la misma compañía, tener el mismo novio/esposo (la misma novia/esposa), manejar el mismo carro, ponerse este/a suéter (camisa, vestido), almorzar con frecuencia en el mismo sitio

71. *AL LLEGAR A PUERTO RICO, DESCUBRÍ QUE ÁNGEL ESTABA MUERTO*: ANOTHER USE OF THE INFINITIVE

You have already learned that, in Spanish, the infinitive is used after certain verbs (**Necesito dormir...**) and after prepositions (**Después de dormir...**). Here are some additional uses of the infinitive. Note that the English equivalent for both employs the *-ing* form. You will frequently see and hear these uses of the infinitive.

- **al** + infinitive = *on/upon . . . -ing*

Al conocer a Jorge, Raquel notó que era mujeriego.	*On meeting Jorge, Raquel noted that he was a womanizer.*
Al terminar la clase, Jorge les dio una tarea a los alumnos.	*On finishing the class, Jorge gave the students an assignment.*

- infinitive = noun subject of a sentence (. . . *-ing*)

(El) Pintar era la pasión de Ángel.	*Painting was Ángel's passion.*
(El) Manejar puede ser difícil en las ciudades grandes.	*Driving can be difficult in large cities.*

Note that the use of the article (**el**) is optional.

You are already familiar with this use of the infinitive in conjunction with the verb **gustar** (and verbs like it). In these sentences the infinitives are the subject of the verb **gustar**. The article (**el**) is not used in this construction.

A Ángel le gustaba mucho **pintar**.	*Ángel used to like to paint a lot.*
A Ángela le gusta mucho **manejar**.	*Ángela likes to drive a lot.*

Actividad A.   ¿Qué ocurrió?

Can you match the following events from **Episodio 24** with what happened immediately after them?

1. _____ Al llegar a la universidad,
2. _____ Al salir del teatro,
3. _____ Al encontrar una tienda en Río Piedras,
4. _____ Al terminar de hacer las compras,
5. _____ Al llegar a su habitación, Raquel
6. _____ Al escuchar el plan de Ángela, Raquel
7. _____ Al escuchar las ideas de Raquel, Ángela
8. _____ Al salir todos para el aeropuerto,

a. todos fueron al hotel para nadar
b. llegó el tío Jaime con malas noticias
c. llamó a su mamá en Los Ángeles
d. las mujeres fueron al museo de arte
e. dijo que Ángela debía pensar bien en lo que quería hacer
f. se enojó con ella
g. Raquel y Ángela fueron a la clase de Jorge
h. Raquel compró unos cassettes de música puertorriqueña.

Actividad B. ¿Qué hacen?

Identify the activity that best fits each description. ¡OJO! Sometimes you will answer based on things you have seen in the video episodes; at other times, you will have to decide based on what you know about the characters or the plot.

1. _____ es algo que a Raquel le gusta mucho.
   a. Cantar (*singing*)   b. Nadar   c. Viajar

2. _____ es la actividad principal del coro de la universidad.
   a. Viajar   b. Cantar   c. Servir

3. _____ es algo que le gusta mucho a Jorge.
   a. Visitar museos   b. Estar en Nueva York   c. Leer

4. _____ es una cosa que Raquel hace todo el tiempo.
   a. Hacer llamadas telefónicas   b. Visitar los bares   c. Dormir

5. _____ es una actividad frecuente de doña Carmen.
   a. Viajar   b. Pensar en el pasado con nostalgia   c. Estudiar ciencias naturales

6. _____ las opiniones sobre Jorge es difícil para Ángela.
   a. Buscar   b. Revelar   c. Aceptar

7. _____ es lo que van a hacer las mujeres ahora.
   a Nadar   b. Volver a San Germán   c. Ir a México

8. _____ es su primera obligación al llegar a México.
   a. Ir a ver a Roberto   b. Probar la comida   c. Ir de compras

Actividad C. ¿Y tú?

Painting was Ángel's passion. Getting involved in the affairs of others is Raquel's problem. What are your passions and problems? What do you really love to do? What do you do too much of (**demasiado**)? What shouldn't you do at all? Create statements by using at least six of the following items, or by referring to your own particular habits and actions. (Worksheet)

MODELOS: ...es una de mis pasiones
...les apasiona a muchas personas, pero a mí no
...(demasiado) es uno de mis problemas
...es un problema para muchos, pero no para mí

1. mirar la televisión
2. fumar cigarrillos
3. comer (chocolate, patatas fritas...)
4. beber cerveza (*beer*)
5. meterse en la vida de otras personas
6. enfadarse con otros
7. hablar de (la política, la historia, el cine, el béisbol...)
8. leer (poesías, novelas, revistas...)
9. chismear (*to gossip*) con los amigos
10. salir por la noche

Have you completed the following sections of the lesson? Check them off here.

_____ **Más allá del episodio**   _____ **Gramática**

Now scan the words in the **Vocabulario** list to be sure that you understand the meaning of them.

VOCABULARIO

Expresiones con *hace*

¿Cuánto tiempo hace que... ?	How long has it been that . . . ?
hace (*time*) que + *present tense*	I (you, he . . .) have/ has been . . .-ing for (*time*)

Repaso: hace... + *preterite* (*ago*)

Las palabras adicionales

casi	almost
demasiado	too much

Now that you have completed the Textbook and Workbook for **Lección 24**, take the Self-Test for that lesson. (It is on page 290.) Remember to listen to the tape when you see the cassette symbol and to check your answers.

_____ **Self-Test**

Now that you have worked through the Textbook and the Workbook and taken the Self-Test, here are some of the things you have accomplished in Spanish.

- You have learned several ways to express strong positive and negative reactions.
- You can use and understand vocabulary to describe people's personalities.
- You have learned more about the language functions you can perform with the preterite.
- You have learned more about using the preterite and the imperfect to narrate in the past in Spanish.
- You know how to express actions that have been going on for a period of time.
- You have learned about some additional uses of the infinitive in Spanish.
- You have continued to improve your listening skills.

You are now ready to continue on with **Lección 25** in the Textbook.

25

REFLEXIONES I

OBJETIVOS

Whereas the materials in the Textbook all had to do with the video episode, the materials in the Workbook will help you expand your knowledge of the Spanish language in general, as well as give you opportunities for self-expression in Spanish. In this lesson you will review

- what you have learned about narrating in the past, using imperfect verb forms
- what you have learned about past-tense narration, using both the preterite and the imperfect.

Remember to listen to the tape for **Lección 25** when you see the cassette symbol and to check your answers in Appendix 1.

GRAMÁTICA

 72. RESUMEN: IMPERFECT TENSE FORMS

You have learned the imperfect forms for all types of Spanish verbs.

Regular Verbs

Can you complete the following table with the forms of these three verbs that are regular in the imperfect tense?

cenar		correr		decidir	
cen____	cenábamos	corría	corr____	decid____	decidíamos
cenabas	cen____	corr____	corríais	decidías	decid____
cen____	cenaban	corr____	corr____	decid____	decid____

Verbs with Irregularities

You have learned that only three Spanish verbs have irregularities in the imperfect tense. Review what you know by supplying the yo forms of these verbs.

ser: _____   ir: _____   ver: _____

73. *RESUMEN*: USES OF THE PRETERITE AND THE IMPERFECT

You have learned to perform the following language functions with the imperfect (I) or the preterite (P) in Spanish. Can you tell which tense should be used in each instance?

I   P   1. to talk about distinct, individual actions in the past
I   P   2. to tell time in the past
I   P   3. to describe conditions that were in progress at a given point in the past, including physical appearance and emotions
I   P   4. to tell someone's age
I   P   5. to talk about distinct events, no matter how many times they happened
I   P   6. to talk about events that were ongoing (in progress) in the past
I   P   7. to talk about changes in conditions
I   P   8. to talk about simultaneous events
I   P   9. to express the action that interrupts another (ongoing) action
I   P   10. to express what someone *was going* to do
I   P   11. to describe actions that occurred within a defined period of time (**por una hora, por un año, ...**)
I   P   12. to talk about habitual events in the past

74. *RESUMEN*: ADDITIONAL VERB FORMS AND STRUCTURES

In the last six lessons of the Textbook and Workbook, you have learned to use several verbs and structures to express the Spanish equivalents of the following English verb forms. Can you match these English sentences with the Spanish equivalents that would be used to express them?

1. _____ I am watching television.
2. _____ I have just eaten.
3. _____ I was reading a book.
4. _____ I had just finished the exercise.
5. _____ I went there some years ago.
6. _____ I have been living here for some time.

a. Acabo de comer.
b. Fui allí hace unos años.
c. Estaba leyendo un libro.
d. Hace mucho tiempo que vivo aquí.
e. Acababa de terminar el ejercicio.
f. Estoy mirando la televisión.

Actividad A.   Al llegar a Buenos Aires
Now that you have reviewed the forms of the imperfect, combine them with the preterite to tell what happened to Raquel in Buenos Aires. Can you fill in the blanks with the appropriate preterite and imperfect forms of the verbs in parentheses, using them in the order given?

1. Cuando Raquel _____ a Buenos Aires, _____ muy cansada. Al principio no hizo nada sino (*but*) descansar. (llegar, estar)

2. Al día siguiente, _____ a la estancia Santa Susana, donde creía que Rosario _____ . (ir, vivir)

3. El señor que _____ la puerta le dijo que Rosario ya no _____ allí. (contestar, vivir)

4. Afortunadamente, _____ otro señor, Cirilo, que _____ a Rosario. (hay, recordar)

5. Según Cirilo, Rosario _____ a la capital hace muchos años y _____ ahora en Buenos Aires, en la calle Gorostiaga. (mudarse, vivir)

6. Raquel le _____ a Cirilo las gracias por la información y _____ para la ciudad. (dar, salir)

7. Con el chofer, Raquel _____ el número y la calle que le había dado (*had given*) Cirilo, pero no _____ nada de lo que buscaba. (buscar, encontrar)

8. Por fin, (ella) _____ preguntar en la casa de un tal Dr. Iglesias, que _____ en esa calle. (decidir, estar)

9. Un ama de casa la _____ entrar. Raquel _____ hablar con el doctor. (dejar, esperar)

Actividad B. En España y en la Argentina

The following are segments from previous video episodes of *Destinos*, but they are incomplete. Can you complete them with the appropriate form of the infinitives in the preterite or imperfect?

Segment 1. En Sevilla, Raquel encuentra a Jaime en la Plaza de las Tres Cruces.

RAQUEL: ¡Jaime! ¡Te hemos buscado[a] por todo el barrio de Santa Cruz! ¿Dónde (encontrar: tú) _____[1] a Osito?

JAIME: Este señor lo (encontrar) _____.[2]

RAQUEL: Muchas gracias, señor. (Estar: Nosotros) _____[3] todos muy preocupados.

CIEGO: No hay de qué. Realmente (ser) _____[4] el perro quien me (encontrar) _____[5] a mí. ¿Es Ud. la madre de este niño?

RAQUEL: No, no. Soy una amiga de la familia.

[a]hemos... *we've looked*

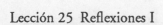

Now check your answers by listening to the cassette tape.

Segment 2:   En Madrid, Raquel y el reportero hablan frente al hotel.

ALFREDO: ¿Qué ocurre?

RAQUEL: Me siento como una tonta. (Dejar: Yo) _____[1] mi cartera en el taxi.

ALFREDO: ¿En el taxi que (tomar) _____[2] en la estación?

RAQUEL: Sí.

ALFREDO: Nosotros lo (ver) _____.[3] Creo que (ser) _____[4] el número 7096.

RAQUEL: ¿Sí? ¿Sabe en qué dirección (ir: el taxi) _____[5]?

Now check your answers by listening to the cassette tape.

Segment 3:   En Madrid, Raquel habla con la Sra. Suárez.

RAQUEL: ¿(Casarse: Ella) _____[1] de nuevo?

SRA. SUÁREZ: Pues, sí. Rosario (ser) _____[2] muy atractiva... y muy simpática. Y como (creer) _____[3] que Fernando había muerto... Ya tiene Ud. la información que (buscar) _____.[4]

Now check your answers by listening to the cassette tape.

Segment 4:   En Buenos Aires, Arturo habla de su medio hermano, Ángel Castillo.

ARTURO: Mi padre (ser) _____[1] un hombre muy estricto. (Querer) _____[2] que Ángel estudiara Ciencias Económicas, pero Ángel (tener) _____[3] otras inclinaciones.... (Hay) _____[4] una escena terrible. Pues mi padre (estar) _____[5] furioso.

Now check your answers by listening to the cassette tape.

Segment 5:   En Buenos Aires, Arturo le indica a Raquel el lugar en que van a empezar la búsqueda de Ángel.

ARTURO: Ésa es la calle Caminito. La última vez que (ver: yo) _____[1] a mi hermano, (ser) _____[2] aquí. Sus amigos (vivir) _____[3] por aquí. El problema es encontrar a alguien que lo recuerde.

Now check your answers by listening to the cassette tape.

Segment 6:   Arturo habla con José, que posiblemente conoce a su hermano.

JOSÉ: ¿Ángel Castillo?

ARTURO: Sí, es mi hermano. (Perder: Nosotros) _____[1] contacto hace muchos años. (Tener: Él) _____[2] amigos acá. (Pintar) _____.[3] Le (gustar) _____[4] los barcos.

JOSÉ: Lo siento, no lo conozco. ¿Ya (hablar: Uds.) _____[5] con Héctor?

Now check your answers by listening to the cassette tape.

Segment 7: En casa de Arturo, Raquel y él hablan de su primer matrimonio.

RAQUEL: ¿Y tú? ¿Cuánto tiempo (estar) _____¹ casado?

ARTURO: Cinco años. Mi esposa (ser) _____² del Perú.

RAQUEL: ¿Y qué (hacer) _____³? ¿(Tener) _____⁴ alguna profesión?

ARTURO: No, creo que eso (ser) _____⁵ la razón de nuestra incompatibilidad. En esa época (vivir: yo) _____⁶ obsesionado con mi trabajo.

RAQUEL: (Extrañar: Ella) _____⁷ mucho el Perú, me imagino.

ARTURO: Sí. Al final (decidir) _____⁸ regresar a su país.

RAQUEL: Habrá sido doloroso.ª

ARTURO: Lo (ser) _____⁹ ... pero ya (pasar) _____.¹⁰ ¡Ya deben estar listas las *brochettes*!

ªHabrá... *It must have been painful.*

 Now check your answers by listening to the cassette tape.

• •

Un poco de todo

Actividad A. Un poco de geografía

Paso 1
Raquel's brief trip to Sevilla has taken her farther than she anticipated. Can you indicate the most important points of her trip on the following map? Indicate the names both of countries and cities. You should also indicate Raquel's destination at the end of this review video episode and any other city you can think of that is important to the story.

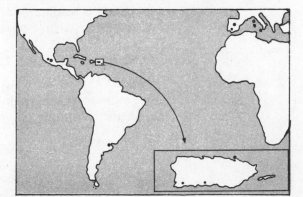

Paso 2
The following families and people have played an important role in *Destinos* in the different locations seen in the shows so far. Place them in their correct locations on the map.

la familia Castillo
la familia Ruiz
la familia Iglesias
la Sra. Suárez

Actividad B. Los personajes de *Destinos*

Paso 1

As you watched the first video episodes of *Destinos* (and reviewed parts of some of the shows), you became acquainted with the members of two families whose histories are interconnected. Using the symbols indicated below, construct a family tree that shows the relationship between these families: la familia Castillo, la familia Iglesias. Label all of the characters that you include in your diagram. (Worksheet)

Paso 2

Now choose one branch of the families you have diagrammed and write a brief paragraph that describes that branch as fully as you can. Be sure to indicate where the characters live, who is married to whom (who is the child of whom, and so on), and which characters are no longer living. (Worksheet)

Actividad C. ¿Y tú?

Answer at least two of the following groups of questions as fully as you can. You may add additional details if you wish. (Worksheet)

1. Piensa en una carta importante que recibiste recientemente. ¿De quién era? ¿Por qué te la escribió? ¿De qué se trataba (*What was it about*)? ¿de un asunto de familia? ¿de amor? ¿asuntos académicos? ¿de dinero? ¿de algo relacionado con tus estudios? (O, al contrario, ¿le escribiste tú una carta importante a alguien recientemente?)
2. Piensa en el viaje más largo que has hecho (*you've taken*) en tu vida. ¿Adónde fuiste? ¿Por qué? ¿Con quién? ¿Te divertiste? ¿Qué te gustó más del viaje? ¿Qué te gustó menos? ¿Te gustaría regresar a ese sitio que visitaste?
3. Piensa en tu primer beso de amor. ¿Cuánto tiempo hace que ocurrió? ¿Dónde estabas? ¿A quién besaste o quién te besó? ¿Te gustó la experiencia? ¿Qué sentiste en ese momento? ¿Todavía te relacionas con la persona a quien besaste o que te besó?
4. Piensa en la cosa más importante que perdiste últimamente. ¿Qué era? ¿Cómo y dónde la perdiste? ¿Por qué era importante para ti? ¿La encontraste por fin? ¿Cómo y dónde? ¿Quién la encontró?

Actividad D. Las Lecciones 1–18

Paso 1

The following photographs represent some highlights of the first eighteen video episodes of *Destinos*. Put them in order, from 1 to 8.

a. _____

b. _____

c. _____

d. _____

e. _____

f. _____

g. _____

h. _____

Paso 2

Now, based on the sequence of events you have established in **Paso 2**, write a brief summary of **Lecciones 1–18**. To make your version of the story flow smoothly, remember to use words and phrases such as the following: **primero, luego, después, por fin; también, pero, por eso, y.** (Worksheet)

• •

PARA ESCRIBIR

In this activity you will write a short letter that Raquel might send to a friend named Susan Winters, who lives in Los Angeles. Susan is a colleague at Raquel's law firm, and she is also interested in learning Spanish. Susan is currently taking a second-year Spanish course at a local college. Raquel will write to her in Spanish.

This is the first letter that Raquel has sent to Susan since leaving the United States, and, although Raquel and Susan are good friends as well as colleagues, she was not able to talk to Susan before she left. So Susan knows nothing about the case nor about Raquel's trip so far, and she has never traveled either to Spain or Argentina.

As you write from Raquel's point of view, tell Susan as much as you can about the important events that have happened, and include interesting information whenever you can. Your letter should be no fewer than 200 and no more than 300 words long.

Thinking About What You Will Write

In order to write this letter, you must first of all think about what information you will include. A good place to begin is with your Textbook and Workbook.

Look over the section called **Repaso de los Episodios 12–17** in the Textbook for **Lección 18**. The activities in that section are based on Raquel's letter to Sra. Suárez, written from the airport in Buenos Aires. That letter was written to someone who has a very different relationship to Raquel than Susan—and very different interests in Raquel's trip—but still the information in it may be useful. You may also want to look back at what you wrote in the **Para escribir** section in **Lección 18**, because it was about Raquel and Arturo. And you should reread what you just wrote in **Actividad D** in the **Un poco de todo** section in this lesson, because it provides a general summary, in your own words, of the major events of Raquel's trip so far.

As you scan all of these sections, note the following useful or interesting information and key phrases. (It is a good idea to do this on a separate sheet of paper.)

Background information	Important people
Major events	Things enjoyed
Major problems	Arturo

For now, just jot down information in the six categories as phrases (**perder mi cartera, conocer a la mujer que escribió la carta,** and so on), and don't be concerned about conjugating the verb forms.

You will not necessarily use all of the information or events in your letter, but that is O.K. For the moment, you are just trying to create a "bank" of ideas upon which to draw.

Organizing Your Letter

In order to begin to write this letter, you must decide how you will address Susan. Because this is a letter, you will address Susan directly, but will you use **tú** or **Ud.**? And how do letters start in Spanish? Look back at the letter that Raquel wrote to Sra. Suárez in **Episodio 18** (Textbook). Will Raquel address Susan in the way in which she addressed Teresa Suárez? Or will she use a more relaxed greeting such as **Querida...** (*Dear...*)? Note also for the heading of your letter that the date in Spanish should be written in the following manner: (15) de (octubre) de (199–).

The next thing you need to do is to spend some time thinking about the organization (order) of what you will write. Begin by deciding in which of the six categories of information Susan is most likely to be interested. Because this will not be a long letter, you cannot give her lots of details or develop all of the categories. Here they are again.

____ Background information	____ Important people
____ Major events	____ Things enjoyed
____ Major problems	____ Arturo

Look at the categories you selected and think about whether any of them group together logically, then consider the order in which you will present them. What sequence seems to make the most sense to you? Write a brief outline of that sequence.

Now look at the categories you didn't select and see whether there is an important piece of information or two that can fit into the categories you have outlined.

Finally, note that one common way to end a letter between friends is to use the Spanish phrase **Abrazos** (*Hugs*) **de tu amiga** _____.

Drafting

Paso 1

Now draft your letter. At this stage you should not worry about grammar and spelling. Your goal is to get your ideas down on paper.

Write the date and the greeting you have chosen. Then begin to write the letter. If you wish, you may select one of the following as your opening sentence. Doing so may help you get started.

¡Te va a parecer imposible el viaje que estoy haciendo!

Saludos desde la Argentina. Aquí te mando unos detalles interesantes de este viaje de sorpresa.

Te extraño mucho, pero lo estoy pasando muy bien. Te estoy escribiendo hoy desde...

Paso 2

After you have completed your draft, look over what you have done. Are you still satisfied with the information you selected? Do you want to add some things and delete others or go into more detail about certain events? Have you included at least one interesting detail in each of the major topics about which you have written? Keep in mind that you are writing for someone who knows nothing about your trip and who has not visited the places that Raquel has visited.

Finalizing Your Letter

If you are satisfied with the information contained in your draft, it is time to look it over for style and language.

Paso 1

First, look at your letter for style. Have you been consistent throughout in the way in which you have addressed Susan? Does the letter flow, or is it disjointed and choppy? Does it contain words and phrases that connect events, or is it mostly an accumulation of sentences? Remember to use words and phrases that can smooth out the flow of a composition and help express the sequence of events clearly.

Paso 2

Review your letter for the following language elements.

_____ gender of nouns
_____ adjective agreement
_____ subject-verb agreements
_____ correct tense (present, **ir** + **a** + infinitive, preterite, imperfect, progressive forms)
_____ use of object pronouns
_____ use of **por** and **para**
_____ comparisons

Paso 3

Prepare a clean copy of the final version of your letter for your instructor.

Have you completed the following sections of the lesson? Check them off here.

_____ **Gramática**   _____ **Para escribir**

_____ **Un poco de todo**

There is no Self-Test for this lesson of the Textbook and Workbook. In preparation for a unit test or just as a general review, take a moment to scan back over the Self-Tests in the previous six lessons. Then you will be ready to continue on with **Lección 26** in the Textbook.

26
REFLEXIONES II

OBJETIVOS

Whereas the materials in the Textbook all had to do with the video episode, the materials in the Workbook will help you expand your knowledge of the Spanish language in general, as well as give you opportunities for self-expression in Spanish. In this lesson you will review

• what you have learned about past-tense narration using both the preterite and the imperfect.

Remember to listen to the tape for **Lección 26** when you see the cassette symbol and to check your answers in Appendix 1.

GRAMÁTICA

Note: In the Gramática section of Lección 25 you reviewed the most important functions of the imperfect and the preterite tenses, as well as their forms. Return to that section, if necessary, to review the information briefly. Then do the following activities.

Actividad A.   Un cuento para una niña

In Episodio 20 you heard Ángela read from a storybook that her father had made for her when she was a child. Here is the part of the story that you have heard. Can you complete it with the appropriate preterite or imperfect form of the infinitives?

EL COQUÍ Y LA PRINCESA

A nuestra hija, Ángela, nuestra princesa

Érase una vez[a] un coquí. Le (gustar) _____gustaba_____[1] pintar. Su padre y su madre (querer) _____querían_____[2] mandarlo a la escuela. Pero el pequeño coquí no (querer) _____quería_____[3] estudiar. Sólo (querer) _____quería_____[4] pintar. Los padres (regañar[b]) _____regañaban_____[5] al pequeño coquí. Le (gritar[c]) _____gritaban_____[6] y (gritar) _____gritaban_____[7]

Una noche, el pequeño coquí (embarcarse) _____se embarcó_____[8]... y nunca (volver) _____volvió_____[9] a ver a sus padres ni a su hermanito. El coquí (pasar) _____pasó_____[10] muchos días y noches en un barco hasta llegar a una bella isla llamada Puerto Rico.

Al coquí le (gustar) _____gustó_____[11] mucho la vieja ciudad y allí (quedarse) _____se quedó_____[12] y (dedicarse) _____se dedicó_____[13] a pintar.

[a]Érase... *Once upon a time*   [b]*to scold*   [c]*to shout*

Now check your answers by listening to the cassette tape.

Actividad B. El resto del cuento

Here is the rest of the coquí story, which you did not hear in **Episodio 20**. Complete it by selecting the correct words from those in parentheses. Because you have not heard this part of the story yet, it is a good idea to scan through the whole narration before starting the activity.

Un día una hermosa princesa (pasaba/pasó)[1] por el estudio del coquí y vio sus cuadros. (Les/Le)[2] gustaron tanto que los elogió[a] con mucho entusiasmo. El pequeño coquí (era/fue)[3] tímido... y se (ponía/puso)[4] rojo con los elogios de la princesa.

«(Soy/Estoy)[5] un pequeño coquí a quien le gusta pintar. ¿Por qué me dice Ud. esas cosas (tan/tantas)[6] bonitas?»

«Porque», dice la princesa, «es evidente que Ud. es (tanto como/más que)[7] un coquí. Es un maestro, un artista de sueños, (alguno/alguien)[8] que ilumina nuestra Isla con su arte maravilloso.»

Y entonces la princesa (hacía/hizo)[9] algo inesperado.[b] Se inclinó[c] y (lo/le)[10] dio un beso al pequeño coquí. Y de repente el pequeño coquí se (convertía/convirtió)[11] en un príncipe. La princesa y el nuevo príncipe (estaban/estuvieron)[12] tan contentos que se (casaban/casaron)[13] ese día.

Entonces el príncipe, que antes (era/fue)[14] un pequeño coquí, vivió feliz con su princesa para siempre en su hermosa Isla, Puerto Rico.

El verdadero[d] príncipe y la verdadera princesa con su hija, Ángela.

Una leyenda:[e] El coquí de Puerto Rico vive en los bosques tropicales. El coquí no puede salir (siempre/nunca)[15] de la Isla. Si sale, se (muere/murió).[16]

[a]*she praised*   [b]*unexpected*   [c]Se... *She bent down*   [d]*real*   [e]*legend*

Now check your answers by listening to the cassette tape.

¡Un desafío! *El coquí y la princesa* is an allegory, a story whose characters represent other people. Can you identify the individuals upon whom the story is based?

el padre del coquí: _____Mentira Iglesias pero verdad Don Fernando_____

la madre del coquí: _____Rosario_____

el hermanito del coquí: _Arturo_

el coquí mismo: _Ángel_

la princesa: _~~Angela~~ María Luisa_

la hija del príncipe y la princesa: _~~Roberto~~ Ángela_

Why do you think Ángela read this story to herself on the evening of the day she met Raquel?

• •

UN POCO DE TODO

Actividad A. Un poco de geografía

In Lección 25 you indicated the stopping points of Raquel's trip on a map (on page 233). Go back to that map now and indicate any additional cities or countries that you can think of after having seen this review episode.

You should also place an additional family on that map in its proper location: **la familia de Ángela Castillo.**

Actividad B. Los personajes de *Destinos*

Paso 1

There is now an additional branch of the Castillo family that you can add to the family tree you diagrammed in Lección 25 (it is on the Worksheet for Lección 25). Using the same symbols you used in that lesson, add the most important members of Ángel's family to that diagram.

Paso 2

Now write a brief paragraph that describes Ángel's family as fully as you can. Be sure to indicate where the characters live, who is married to whom (who is the child of whom, and so on), and which characters are no longer living. You should also indicate the relationship of this family to the rest of the Castillo family. (Worksheet)

Actividad C. ¿Cómo es?

Select at least two of the following characters that were introduced in Puerto Rico and write a brief description of their personalities. Before you begin to write, review the adjectives introduced in Lección 24 of the Textbook. Don't forget to use the feminine forms of the adjectives when describing a female character. You may also wish to describe how the characters react—or reacted—in a particular situation that you have seen or heard about in *Destinos*. (Worksheet)

Personajes de Puerto Rico: Ángel Castillo, Ángela Castillo, tía Olga, doña Carmen, Laura, Jorge Alonso

Actividad D. En Ponce

Paso 1

Here is a map of the downtown area of Ponce, where Raquel, Ángela, and Laura spent the night on their way to San Germán. Look at the map briefly to familiarize yourself with the names of the streets, and scan the legend for the points of interest indicated on the map.

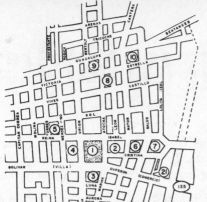

SITIOS DE INTERES

1. **Plaza de las Delicias, Catedral, Antiguo Parque de Bombas, Calle Isabel y Reina, Tiendas, Bancos y Restaurantes, Hotel Meliá**
2. **Museo de La Danza**
3. **Casa Alcaldía**
4. **Casa Armstrong**
5. **Museo de Arquitectura**
6. **Teatro La Perla y el Museo de la Historia de Ponce**
7. **Casa Serrallés (Museo de Artes Plásticas)**
8. **El Centro de los Artesanos**
9. **Correo**
10. **Plaza de Mercado Nueva**

Paso 2

Now imagine that you are in **la Plaza de las Delicias.** Find it on the map.

Paso 3

On the cassette tape, you will hear the speaker give you directions for getting from **la Plaza** to one of the locations on the map. Listen carefully, then indicate what your destination would be if you followed the directions. Listen to the directions as many times as you need to.

Destination: _____

Actividad E.   ¿Y tú?

Answer at least two of the following groups of questions as fully as you can. You may add additional details if you wish. (Worksheet)

1. Piensa en un pariente con quien siempre tienes conflictos. ¿Quién es esta persona? ¿Cómo es, en tu opinión? ¿Cuál es la razón de los conflictos que tienes con él/ella? ¿Cuándo ocurrió el último choque que Uds. tuvieron? ¿De qué se trataba? (*What was it about?*) ¿Quién tuvo la culpa?
2. Piensa en alguna ocasión en que tú le diste o querías darle consejos a un amigo (una amiga). ¿Cuáles eran las circunstancias? ¿Por qué creías que necesitaba tus consejos esa persona? ¿Cuál fue la reacción de esa persona? ¿Aceptó tus consejos y te lo agradeció (*thanked*) o se enfadó contigo?
3. Piensa en el novio (la novia) o el esposo (la esposa) de un amigo (una amiga) que no te gusta para nada. ¿Quién es esta persona? ¿Cómo es, en tu opinión? ¿Por qué no te gusta? ¿Tuviste una vez algún conflicto con él/ella? ¿Cuáles fueron las circunstancias de ese conflicto?
4. Piensa en alguna persona de tu familia que conocías muy bien y que ya murió. ¿Quién era? ¿Lo/La querías mucho? ¿Dónde estabas tú cuando esa persona murió? ¿Cómo te afectó su muerte? ¿Todavía piensas en esa persona?

Have you completed the following sections of the lesson? Check them off here.

_____ **Gramática**

_____ **Un poco de todo**

There is no Self-Test for this lesson of the Textbook and Workbook. In preparation for a unit test or just as a general review, take a moment to scan back over the Self-Tests in **Lecciones 19–24** and the activities in the previous lesson. Then you will be ready to continue on with **Lección 27** in the Textbook.

WORKSHEETS AND SELF-TESTS

This section of the Workbook contains Worksheets coordinated with each lesson of the Workbook together with Self-Tests for most lessons. If your instructor asks you to do so, you should tear these pages out and hand them in to him or her. Note the following points about these materials:

- Possible answers to some of the Worksheet activities are included in Appendix 1.
- Answers to most of the items in the Self-Tests are given in Appendix 2.
- The total number of points in each Self-Test is included at the top. Consult with your instructor to determine what is an acceptable percentage. Seventy percent is often viewed as the lowest acceptable percentage.

WORKSHEET: LECCIÓN 1

Gramática 1: Actividad C

_____

_____

_____

WORKSHEET: LECCIÓN 2

Gramática 2: Actividad B

Personas	Lugares	Cosas	Conceptos
_____	_____	_____	_____
_____	_____	_____	_____
_____	_____	_____	_____
_____	_____	_____	_____

Gramática 3: Actividad B

_____

_____

_____

_____

_____

_____

_____

_____

Gramática 3: Actividad C

_____

_____

_____

_____

_____

_____

_____

SELF-TEST: LECCIONES 1 y 2 (52 puntos) NOMBRE _____

I.   El episodio y los personajes

A.   Who is described in the following sentences about characters from *Destinos*? (6 puntos)

_____ 1. Esta persona es hijo de don Fernando. No vive en México. Vive en Miami. Tiene una esposa y dos hijos.

_____ 2. Esta persona es hermano de don Fernando y es profesor en la universidad. Vive en México.

_____ 3. Esta persona vive en La Gavia, en México. Sus hijos son Ramón, Mercedes, Juan y Carlos. Tiene una carta importante.

B.   ¿Cierto (C) o falso (F)? (4 puntos)

____ 1. Rosario es la esposa de don Fernando y vive en La Gavia.
____ 2. Juan es hijo de don Fernando y vive en Nueva York.
____ 3. Pedro es hijo de don Fernando y vive en México.
____ 4. Raquel es abogada y vive en Miami.

II.   El vocabulario

A.   Complete the sentences with the appropriate family member term. (6 puntos)

1. Pati es la _____ de Juan.   2. Mercedes es la _____ de don Fernando.

3. Don Fernando es el _____ de Ramón.   4. Juan es el _____ de Carlos.

5. Pedro es el _____ de Ramón.   6. Carlos y Mercedes son los _____ de don Fernando.

B.   Listen as a woman named Graciela tells you something about herself. Then fill in the blanks according to what you have heard. (6 puntos)

1. El _____ de Graciela se llama Antonio.

2. Profesiones: Graciela es _____ , Antonio es _____ y Roberto es _____ .

3. Elena vive también en la _____ y es la _____ de Graciela.

C.   Using the verbs **soy** and **tengo**, write three sentences similar to Graciela's about yourself and your family. (9 puntos)

_____

_____

III.   La gramática

A.   Write the correct words in the blanks for each of these nouns. (16 puntos)

the	a/an/ some	my	his	
1. ____	____	____	____	profesoras
2. ____	____	____	____	ciudad
3. ____	____	____	____	padres
4. ____	____	____	____	esposo

B.   Complete the sentences with the correct form of **ser**. (5 puntos)

1. Juan y Pati _____ esposos.   2. Yo _____ estudiante de español.   3. Ramón: «Carlos y yo _____ hermanos.»   4. Pedro: «Don Fernando _____ mi hermano.»   5. Carlos: «Pedro _____ mi tío.»

WORKSHEET: LECCIÓN 3

Gramática 5: Actividad C

_____
_____
_____
_____
_____
_____
_____

Gramática 5: Actividad D

_____
_____
_____
_____

Gramática 6: Actividad C

_____
_____
_____
_____
_____

Gramática 6: Actividad D

1. _____
_____

2. _____
_____

3. _____

Gramática 7: Actividad

1. _____
_____

2. _____
_____

I.   El episodio y los personajes

A.   Which character in **Episodio 3** said or might have said the following? (6 puntos)

_____ 1. Mamá. Hay una señorita aquí que busca a la abuela Teresa.

_____ 2. Mi cliente, don Fernando, vive en México.

_____ 3. Mi esposo trabaja ahora. Esta noche habla con Ud.

B.   Tell which of these things happened in **Episodio 3** by indicating **Sí** or **No**. (4 puntos)

Sí   No 1. Raquel habla con Teresa Suárez.
Sí   No 2. Miguel y Jaime le explican a Raquel que Teresa es su abuela.
Sí   No 3. Elena Ramírez revela que Teresa vive en México.
Sí   No 4. Raquel le pregunta unas cosas al esposo de Elena.

II.   El vocabulario

A.   The sentences you will hear contain numbers. Write the numbers in words. (8 puntos)

1. _____   2. _____   3. _____   4. _____

B.   Match words from the two groups. The words in the second group are not translations but rather items related to the words in the first group. (8 puntos)

_____ 1. abuela   _____ 2. nombre   _____ 3. apellido   _____ 4. iglesia   _____ 5. chicos

_____ 6. revelar   _____ 7. mercado   _____ 8. barrio

a. secret   b. Raquel   c. Triana   d. worship   e. food   f. la Sra. Suárez   g. Ramírez   h. Jaime y Miguel

III.   La gramática

A.   Complete the paragraph with the correct form of a verb from the list. Be sure that the verb form fits the paragraph: **buscar, creer, desear, escribir, estar, hablar, necesitar, preguntar, revelar, tomar, trabajar, viajar, visitar, vivir.** (14 puntos)

En Sevilla, Raquel _____[1] un taxi para ir (*go*) al Barrio de Triana. Raquel _____[2] que la Sra. Suárez _____[3] todavía (*still*) en la calle Pureza. Ella _____[4] hablar con Teresa Suárez porque su cliente, don Fernando, desea saber si Rosario y su hijo _____[5] vivos o muertos. En el barrio de Triana, Raquel habla con Elena Ramírez y sus hijos, Miguel y Jaime. Raquel le _____[6] a Elena si sabe algo (*if she knows something*) de Rosario. Raquel _____[7] el secreto de don Fernando.

B.   Use these verbs to write three original sentences about your family: **estar, trabajar, vivir.** (9 puntos)

_____

_____

_____

WORKSHEET: LECCIÓN 4

Gramática 8: Actividad C

_____

_____

_____

_____

_____

SELF-TEST: LECCIÓN 4 (43 puntos)   NOMBRE _____

I.   El episodio y los personajes

A. Choose the correct answers to these questions according to **Episodio 4**. (4 puntos)

1. ¿Quién habla por teléfono con su madre?
    a. Raquel   (b.) Miguel padre   c. Miguel hijo
2. ¿Adónde decide viajar Raquel ahora para hablar con Teresa?
    a. a Barcelona   b. a Sevilla   (c.) a Madrid
3. ¿Adónde lleva la familia Ruiz a Raquel?
    a. a casa   b. a un restaurante muy elegante   (c.) al mercado de los animales
4. ¿Qué compra Miguel en el mercado de animales?
    (a.) un perro   b. unos peces   c. un pájaro

B. Who said or might have said the following in **Episodio 4**? (4 puntos)

Raquel   1. Debo viajar a Madrid y buscar a la Sra. Suárez.

Miguel hijo   2. Bueno, realmente me gustan todas. Pero la verdad es que mi favorita es ciencias naturales.

II.   El vocabulario

A. Write the Spanish name of the courses where you would study the following. (6 puntos)

1. $\sqrt{230}$=? *la matematicas*   4. Wall Street _____
2. L. da Vinci *el arte*   5. Shakespeare _____
3. S. Freud *la /*   6. Plato _____

B. Use the following words and expressions to write three sentences about yourself: **estudiar, mi curso favorito, sacar ... notas en.** (9 puntos)

_____

_____

_____

III.   La gramática

A. Miguel is talking about school. Complete the paragraph with the correct form of a verb from the list: **ser, estar, estudiar, sacar.** (12 puntos)

Yo _____¹ estudiante de colegio. Tú, Jaime, _____² en el primer año (*first year*). Yo _____³ ciencias naturales y _____⁴ buenas notas. Tú _____⁵ ciencias naturales también pero no _____⁶ muy buenas notas.

B. Complete the following sentences with what you hear on the tape. (8 puntos)

1. A Jaime *le gusta* el perro.   2. Los perros son *animales carñinosos* 3. Miguel tiene *muchas* asignaturas.   4. Al final del episodio, Osito *esta perdido* .

WORKSHEET: LECCIÓN 5

Gramática 11: Actividad C

_____

_____

_____

_____

_____

Gramática 14: Actividad B

1. _____
2. _____
3. _____
4. _____
5. _____
6. _____
7. _____

Gramática 14: Actividad C

_____

_____

_____

_____

_____

_____

_____

_____

_____

_____

_____

Gramática 14: Actividad D

_____

_____

_____

_____

_____

SELF-TEST: LECCIÓN 5 (41 puntos)   NOMBRE _____

I. El episodio y los personajes

Match the following characters with the statement that describes something they do in **Episodio 5**.
(8 puntos)

a. Raquel   b. el ciego   c. Miguel padre   d. Elena   e. Jaime   f. Miguel hijo

_(c) b_ 1. El primero que encuentra a Osito en la calle.
_e_ 2. Se pierde cuando busca a Osito.
_a_ 3. Busca a Jaime en la catedral.
_d_ 4. Es mujer y busca a su hijo en el Barrio de Santa Cruz.
_b_ 5. Vende cupones de lotería.
_f_ 6. Busca a Jaime con su padre.
_a_ 7. Encuentra a Jaime con Osito y el ciego.
_a_ 8. Va a Madrid a ver a la Sra.Teresa Suárez.

II. El vocabulario

A. Listen to a description of some of Elena's activities. Then match the activity and time. (8 puntos)

____ 1. Estudio literatura
____ 2. Hablamos mamá y yo
____ 3. Voy al mercado
____ 4. Vamos a un restaurante

a. los martes a las nueve de la mañana.
b. los lunes a las siete de la tarde.
c. los jueves a las cuatro de la tarde.
d. el domingo a las dos de la tarde.

B. Use the following verbs to write three sentences about yourself and your friends: **cenar, ir a, ver.**
(9 puntos)

_____

_____

_____

III. La gramática

A. Rewrite the verbs in the following sentences to make them express the future with **ir a.** (8 puntos)

1. Cenamos en el Café Giralda. _Vamos ir a cenar en el café Giralda_
2. Ven a Gloria Estefan en Miami. _Van a venir a Gloria Estefan en Miami_
3. Corro a las siete de la mañana. _Voy a ~~ir~~ correr a las siete de la mañana._
4. Comprendéis las oraciones, ¿no? _Vosotros vais ~~es~~ a comprender las oraciones ¿no?_

B. Complete the paragraph with the correct form of a verb from the list: **cenar, deber, desear, ir.**
(8 puntos)

Miguel padre: ¿Por qué no _deseamos_ ¹ (nosotros) a cenar? Jaime y Miguel, _deben_ ² llevar
el perro a casa. Elena y yo _vamos a_ ³ llevar a Raquel al hotel. A las nueve todos _cenen_ ⁴
en el Restaurante Río Grande.

WORKSHEET: LECCIÓN 6

Un poco de todo: Actividad A

_____

_____

_____

_____

_____

_____

_____

_____

_____

Un poco de todo: Actividad B

_____

_____

_____

_____

_____

_____

Un poco de todo: Actividad D

Paso 1

1. _____

2. _____

3. _____

4. _____

5. _____

Paso 2 _____

_____

_____

_____

_____

_____

_____

_____

WORKSHEET: LECCIÓN 7

Gramática 17: Actividad D

_____

_____

_____

_____

Gramática 19: Actividad C

1. _____
2. _____
3. _____
4. _____
5. _____
6. _____

Gramática 19: Actividad D

_____

_____

_____

_____

_____

_____

SELF-TEST: LECCIÓN 7 (44 puntos)   NOMBRE _____

I. El episodio y los personajes

Complete the description of Episodio 7 with appropriate words from the list: **cartera, encuentra, Federico, llevar, mensaje, puede, salen, Sánchez, taxi, trae.** (10 puntos)

Raquel pierde su _____¹ pero sabe que está en el taxi. El reportero Alfredo _____² dice que va a buscar el _____.³ Raquel necesita ver la ropa que trae para el viaje. _____,⁴ el hijo de Teresa Suárez, llega al hotel. Desea _____⁵ a Raquel a casa a cenar con su madre. Hay mucha confusión en el hotel. Alfredo _____⁶ la cartera pero no _____⁷ a Raquel. Federico no _____⁸ hablar con Raquel por teléfono. Finalmente Raquel y Federico _____⁹ y Raquel tiene que dejar un _____¹⁰ para Alfredo.

II. El vocabulario

A. You will hear the names of clothing. Indicate with **H** (Hombre) or **M** (Mujer) which is *most likely* to wear each one. ¡OJO! Both may be appropriate in some cases. (7 puntos)

1. H M   2. H M   3. H M   4. H M   5. H M   6. H M   7. H M

B. Write three sentences about what you are wearing now. (9 puntos)

_____

_____

_____

III. La gramática

Complete the sentences with the correct form of a verb from the list: **conocer, decir, hacer, oír, saber, salir, tener, traer, venir.** (18 puntos)

1. El tren para Madrid _____ a las once y media.
2. Yo no _____ dónde está la cartera.
3. Yo _____ una reservación.
4. Raquel _____ a Madrid de Sevilla.
5. ¿_____ tú a la ganadora de la lotería?
6. Perdón, yo no _____ bien. ¿Puede repetir, por favor?
7. ¿Cuándo _____ tú un viaje a México?
8. Yo _____ un suéter aquí en la maleta (*suitcase*).
9. Teresa _____ que Raquel tiene que venir a Madrid.

WORKSHEET: LECCIÓN 8

Gramática 20: Actividad D

1. _____
   _____

2. _____
   _____

3. _____
   _____

4. _____
   _____

5. _____
   _____

6. _____
   _____

7. _____
   _____

8. _____
   _____

Gramática 22: Actividad C

_____
_____
_____
_____
_____

SELF-TEST: LECCIÓN 8 (38 puntos)   NOMBRE _____

I. El episodio y los personajes

Put these events from **Episodio 8** in order (1–9). (9 puntos)

_____ a. La Sra. Suárez empieza a contar la historia de Rosario.
_____ b. La Sra. Suárez dice que Rosario vive en la Argentina.
_____ c. Raquel y la Sra. Suárez se sientan a hablar.
_____ d. Raquel piensa llamar a Elena del hotel.
_____ e. Raquel cuenta la historia de Jaime y el perro.
_____ f. Raquel dice que va a traer la foto mañana.
_____ g. La Sra. Suárez dice que el hijo de Rosario se llama Ángel.
_____ h. El botones trae un mensaje para Raquel.
_____ i. Federico hace las presentaciones.

II. El vocabulario

A. Complete the questions with the interrogative words that would produce the answers. (8 puntos)

1. ¿_____ sales para la Argentina? —Salgo mañana.
2. ¿_____ está hoy? —Muy bien, gracias. ¿Y Ud.?
3. ¿_____ vive Rosario ahora? —Vive en la Argentina.
4. ¿_____ es Federico? —Es el hijo de Teresa Suárez.
5. ¿_____ quieres ver a Alfredo ahora? —Él tiene mi cartera.
6. ¿_____ hijos tiene don Fernando? —Tiene cuatro.
7. ¿_____ piensa hacer Raquel ahora? —Piensa ir a la Argentina.
8. ¿_____ es el apellido de Raquel? —Es Rodríguez.

B. Use the following words to write three sentences about what your friend(s) do or don't do: **olvidarse, pedir, perder, recordar.** (9 puntos)

_____
_____
_____

III. La gramática

You will hear the following questions on the tape. Complete the answers. If the question uses the **ir a** form, answer without it, and vice versa. (12 puntos)

1. ¿Cuándo empieza el viaje?   _____ esta noche.
2. ¿Qué van a pedir ellos?   _____ la dirección.
3. ¿Dónde se va a sentar ella?   _____ aquí.
4. ¿Cuándo van a volver?   _____ a las nueve.
5. ¿Quiénes se casan hoy?   _____ María y Juan.
6. ¿Qué encuentra en el hotel?   _____ un mensaje.

WORKSHEET: LECCIÓN 9

Gramática 23: Actividad B

Paso 2

_____

_____

_____

_____

_____

_____

Gramática 24: Actividad E

1. _____

_____

2. _____

_____

3. _____

_____

4. _____

_____

Gramática 25: Actividad B

Paso 1 _____

_____

_____

Paso 2 _____

_____

Gramática 25: Actividad D

Paso 2

1. _____

2. _____

3. _____

4. _____

5. _____

6. _____

SELF-TEST: LECCIÓN 9 (44 puntos)   NOMBRE _____

I. El episodio y los personajes

Match the actions with the person who does them in **Episodio 9**. Not all names may be used, and some may be used more than once. (10 puntos)

a. Federico   b. Raquel   c. Teresa Suárez   d. Pedro Castillo   e. Elena   f. Alfredo   g. el Sr. Díaz   h. Miguel Ruiz

_____ 1. Va al mercado y a la farmacia.
_____ 2. Se prepara para hacer un viaje a la Argentina.
_____ 3. Desayuna con Raquel.
_____ 4. Dice que es el ganador de la lotería.
_____ 5. Va al taller de Federico.
_____ 6. Tiene unos amigos que forman una tuna.
_____ 7. Recuerda que es primavera en la Argentina.
_____ 8. Compra un cupón de la lotería.
_____ 9. Dice que don Fernando está en el hospital.
_____ 10. Recibe un telegrama de Pedro Castillo.

II. El vocabulario

A. The sentences you will hear contain demonstratives. Write the form of the demonstrative you hear. (5 puntos)

1. _____   2. _____   3. _____   4. _____

5. _____

Now write the form of the possessive adjective you hear. (5 puntos)

6. _____   7. _____   8. _____   9. _____

10. _____

B. Match the months with the seasons. (6 puntos)

_____ 1. enero   a. verano
_____ 2. mayo   b. primavera
_____ 3. noviembre   c. otoño
_____ 4. junio   d. invierno
_____ 5. diciembre
_____ 6. marzo

III. La gramática

Answer these questions about yourself. (18 puntos)

1. ¿A qué hora te levantas, generalmente?

_____

2. ¿A qué hora te despiertas, generalmente?

_____

3. Cuando te acuestas, ¿te duermes inmediatamente?

_____

4. ¿A qué hora vuelves a casa los martes?

_____

5. ¿Qué cosas pierdes frecuentemente?

_____

6. Cuando te levantas, ¿te vistes inmediatamente?

WORKSHEET: LECCIÓN 10

Gramática 27: Actividad E

_____

_____

_____

_____

_____

_____

_____

_____

_____

_____

Gramática 28: Actividad B

1. _____

2. _____

3. _____

4. _____

5. _____

6. _____

Gramática 28: Actividad C

1. _____

2. _____

3. _____

4. _____

5. _____

6. _____

7. _____

8. _____

SELF-TEST: LECCIÓN 10 (49 puntos)   NOMBRE _____

I. El episodio y los personajes

Indicate which characters do these things in Episodio 10. Note that more than one character does them. (8 puntos)

a. Raquel   b. Alfredo   c. Federico   d. el Sr. Díaz   e. Teresa Suárez   f. María

_____ 1. Van al Museo del Prado.

_____ 2. Van a una escuela de baile.

_____ 3. Van a cenar en un restaurante.

_____ 4. Dicen que están impresionados por los cuadros de Goya.

II. El vocabulario

A. Complete the sentences with the correct form of adjectives from the list. (16 puntos)

alto, bajo, bonito, canoso, delgado, grande, gordito, rubio

1. Julia Roberts es una mujer _____.

2. En un equipo (*team*) de básquetbol, hay hombres _____.

3. Los Siete Enanos (*Dwarfs*) son _____.

4. Arnold Schwarzenegger es un hombre _____.

5. Roseanne Barr no es una mujer _____.

6. Michelle Pfeiffer tiene el pelo _____.

7. Las personas viejas tienen el pelo _____.

8. Los luchadores (*wrestlers*) sumo son hombres _____.

B. Write three sentences that describe yourself. Use at least six of the adjectives from **Lección 10**. (9 puntos)

_____

_____

_____

III. La gramática

A. Answer the following questions for yourself and a classmate with the "we" form of the verb. Use information that is true for you. (8 puntos)

1. ¿A qué hora se acuestan Uds.?

_____

2. ¿Se despiertan Uds. temprano?

_____

3. ¿Se duermen Uds. en la clase?

_____

4. ¿Quiénes se visten primero?

_____

B. You will hear a series of phrases on the tape. Write what you hear, including the correct form of the adjective listed here. (8 puntos)

1. (bonito) _____

2. (grande) _____

3. (joven) _____

4. (guapo) _____

WORKSHEET: LECCIÓN 11

Un poco de todo: Actividad A

1. _____
2. _____
3. _____
4. _____
5. _____
6. _____
7. _____
8. _____

Un poco de todo: Actividad C

Paso 2 _____

_____

_____

_____

_____

_____

Un poco de todo: Actividad D

_____

_____

_____

_____

_____

_____

_____

_____

_____

_____

Un poco de todo: Actividad E

_____

_____

_____

_____

_____

_____

WORKSHEET: LECCIÓN 12

Gramática 34: Actividad E

1. _____
2. _____
3. _____
4. _____
5. _____
6. _____
7. _____
8. _____
9. _____
10. _____

Gramática 35: Actividad E

1. _____
   _____
2. _____
   _____
3. _____
   _____
4. _____
   _____
5. _____
   _____
6. _____
   _____

SELF-TEST: LECCIÓN 12 (39 puntos)   NOMBRE _____

I.   El episodio y los personajes

A. Put the events from Episodio 12 in order (1–8). (8 puntos)

_____   a. Raquel toma un taxi a la estancia.
_____   b. Raquel encuentra al doctor Arturo Iglesias.
_____   c. Arturo dice que va a ayudar a Raquel.
_____   d. Arturo y Raquel van al cementerio.
_____   e. Raquel busca el número 900 de la calle Gorostiaga.
_____   f. Cirilo le da a Raquel la dirección de Rosario.
_____   g. Raquel llega al hotel, pero hay error en su reserva.
_____   h. Raquel sube a su habitación y cuenta su dinero.

B. Match the characters with the corresponding description. (5 puntos)

a. Cirilo   b. Ángel   c. Arturo   d. Martín Iglesias   e. Rosario

_____   1. Padre de Arturo y segundo esposo de Rosario.
_____   2. Medio hermano de Arturo.
_____   3. Madre de Arturo y de Ángel.
_____   4. Un gaucho de la estancia Santa Susana.
_____   5. Segundo hijo de Rosario; médico de Buenos Aires.

II.   El vocabulario

A. Answer these questions by writing out the numbers in words. (9 puntos)

1. ¿En qué año llegó Colón (*Columbus*) a América?

_____

2. ¿Cuántos son 350 más (*plus*) 260?

_____

3. ¿Cuándo declararon su independencia los Estados Unidos?

_____

B. Translate the words in parentheses into Spanish. (3 puntos)

1. Don Fernando, el (*first*) _____ esposo de Rosario.
2. La Argentina, el (*third*) _____ país que visitó Raquel.
3. Cirilo, un (*good*) _____ gaucho de la Estancia Santa Susana.

III.   La gramática

A. Answer the questions you hear with the correct preterite forms. (8 puntos)

1. Ya _____.   3. Ya _____.
2. Ya _____.   4. Ya la _____.

B. Answer these questions truthfully using the appropriate object pronouns in your answers. (6 puntos)

1. ¿Dónde tienes el dinero (*money*)? _____
2. ¿Dónde llevas la cartera? _____
3. ¿Dónde compras los libros? _____

WORKSHEET: LECCIÓN 13

Gramática 37: Actividad D

1. _____
2. _____
3. _____
4. _____
5. _____
6. _____

Gramática 38: Actividad D

1. _____
2. _____
3. _____
4. _____
5. _____
6. _____

SELF-TEST: LECCIÓN 13 (37 puntos)   NOMBRE _____

I. El episodio y los personajes

Match the question with the character who asked or might have asked it. Some of the characters may be used more than once. (8 puntos)

_____ 1. ¿Y si preguntamos en las tiendas?
_____ 2. ¿Seguro que no quieren un pescado?
_____ 3. ¿Y no lo buscaron en el bar?
_____ 4. ¿Ya hablaron con Héctor?
_____ 5. ¿Quién es Héctor?
_____ 6. ¿Necesitan algo más?
_____ 7. ¿Ya probaste la parrillada?
_____ 8. ¿No me invitas a pasar?

a. el vendedor de pescado
b. Arturo
c. Raquel
d. el hombre del restaurante
e. José
f. doña Flora

II. El vocabulario

A. The sentences you will hear contain the names of fish, shellfish, or other foods. Write the names you hear. (8 puntos)

1. _____ 2. _____ 3. _____ 4. _____
5. _____ 6. _____ 7. _____ 8. _____

B. Use the following words and phrases to write three sentences about your likes and dislikes in food: **almorzar, (no) me gusta(n), preferir.** (9 puntos)

_____

_____

_____

III. La gramática

Answer these questions in the preterite, using the cues. (12 puntos)

1. ¿Decidiste dónde comenzar? (sí/ calle Caminito)

    _____

2. ¿Te conocí ayer? (sí/ en la estancia)

    _____

3. ¿Te vi en el Piccolo Navio anoche? (sí/ allí)

    _____

4. Te invité a mi casa, ¿no? (sí/ ayer)

    _____

WORKSHEET: LECCIÓN 14

Gramática 40: Actividad D

1. _____
2. _____
3. _____
4. _____

Gramática 41: Actividad C

important _____

annoying _____

Gramática 41: Actividad D

1. _____
2. _____
3. _____
4. _____
5. _____
6. _____
7. _____

Gramática 42: Actividad C

_____
_____
_____
_____
_____
_____

SELF-TEST: LECCIÓN 14 (39 puntos)　　　NOMBRE _____

I.　El episodio y los personajes

A.　Tell who said or might have said the following to whom in **Episodio 14**. (6 puntos)

1.　_____ → _____ Sí, estoy divorciado. Me organizo bastante bien solo.

2.　_____ → _____ No, no. Es para Ud. Es de su hermano.

3.　_____ → _____ Sí, quisiéramos hablar con Ud., pero con este ruido
(*noise*)... ¿Podemos hablar afuera?

B.　Write the correct character's name. (4 puntos)

Ya hay ahora dos cartas importantes en la historia. Una es la carta de _____[1] a

_____[2] que dice que Rosario no está muerta y que tiene un hijo. La segunda carta es de

_____[3] a _____[4] que puede llevar la dirección de Ángel.

II.　El vocabulario

A.　You will hear a list of meats. Put the letter of the source next to the number of each item in the list.
(8 puntos)

a.　　　　　b.　　　　　c.　　　　　d.　　　　　e.

1. ____　2. ____　3. ____　4. ____　5. ____　6. ____　7. ____　8. ____

B.　Write two sentences about meat you and/or your friends ate this week. (6 puntos)

_____

_____

III.　La gramática

A.　Answer these questions with either the **nosotros** or the **vosotros** form of the preterite. (9 puntos)

1.　¿Vosotros nos comprendisteis? Claro que_____.

2.　¿Nos invitasteis al Piccolo Navio? Sí, _____.

3.　¿Os conocimos ayer? Sí, _____ ayer.

B.　Complete the paragraph with the appropriate preposition: **antes de, cerca de, durante, entre, hasta, sin, sobre.** (6 puntos)

Arturo y Raquel llegaron al Piccolo Navio para hablar con Héctor. _____[1] hablar con ellos

Héctor cantó. _____[2] la primera conversación con Héctor, Arturo y Raquel aprendieron unas

cosas nuevas _____[3] Ángel. La casa de Héctor está _____[4] la cantina. Pero ahora

tienen que esperar _____[5] mañana para hablar con Héctor de nuevo. Se van _____[6]

saber dónde está Ángel.

WORKSHEET: LECCIÓN 15

Gramática 43: Actividad D

_____

_____

_____

_____

_____

Gramática 43: Actividad E

1. _____
2. _____
3. _____
4. _____
5. _____
6. _____
7. _____

Gramática 44: Actividad C

_____

_____

_____

_____

_____

_____

_____

_____

Gramática 45: Actividad B

Paso 2 _____

_____

_____

Gramática 45: Actividad C

_____

_____

_____

_____

_____

_____

SELF-TEST: LECCIÓN 15 (34 puntos)   NOMBRE _____

I. El episodio y los personajes

Choose the best answer to these questions about Episodio 15. (5 puntos)

1. ¿Por qué se siente culpable Arturo?
   a. Conoció a su madre.   b. No buscó a Ángel.   c. No conoce a don Fernando.
2. ¿Qué mal presentimiento tiene Arturo?
   a. Que Ángel puede estar muerto.   b. Que se va Raquel.   c. Que él va a morir.
3. ¿Qué esperan Raquel y Arturo en la casa de Arturo? Esperan _____.
   a. a Ángel   b. las fotos   c. la llamada de Héctor
4. ¿Adónde va Raquel ahora? Va _____.
   a. a la Gavia   b. a Puerto Rico   c. a La Boca
5. ¿Por qué tiene que ir de compras Raquel?
   a. Le gusta Arturo.   b. Porque va a hacer otro viaje.   c. Para buscar a Ángel.

II. El vocabulario

A. You will hear a list of names of fruits. Write the number you hear with the appropriate drawing. (6 puntos)

a. _____   b. _____   c. _____   d. _____   e. _____   f. _____

B. Indicate your preferences between three of the following pairs of fruits by writing three sentences: piña/naranja, sandía/melón, cereza/uva, manzana/pera. (9 puntos)

_____

_____

_____

III. La gramática

A. Answer these questions in the preterite, using the cues. (8 puntos)

1. ¿Cuándo le vas a dar el cuadro? (ya/ ayer) _____

   _____

2. ¿Uds. le van a decir todo? (ya/ anoche) _____

   _____

3. ¿Les vas a traer la carta de Ángel? (ya/ el martes) _____

   _____

4. ¿Les vas a dar la dirección? (ya/ ayer) _____

   _____

B. Express how these characters react to certain things, using the verbs gustar, encantar, and molestar. (6 puntos)

1. a Raquel, los obstáculos _____

2. a Arturo, Raquel _____

3. a Héctor, las fiestas _____

WORKSHEET: LECCIÓN 16

Gramática 46: Actividad D

_____

_____

_____

_____

_____

_____

_____

Gramática 46: Actividad E

1. _____

2. _____

3. _____

4. _____

5. _____

Gramática 47: Actividad C

_____

_____

_____

_____

Gramática 47: Actividad D

Paso 1 _____

_____

_____

Paso 2 _____

_____

_____

_____

Gramática 48: Actividad C

_____

_____

_____

_____

I.   El episodio y los personajes

A.   Put the following events from Episodio 16 in chronological order (1–6). (6 puntos)

_____ a. Arturo y Raquel van a bailar el tango.
_____ b. Arturo y Raquel van a la casa de Arturo para revelar fotos.
_____ c. Arturo decide ir a Puerto Rico con Raquel.
_____ d. Raquel va al supermercado a comprar legumbres.
_____ e. Raquel y Arturo van al puerto a ver a Héctor.
_____ f. Raquel va a la casa de Arturo a esperar a Héctor.

B.   Indicate with **Sí** or **No** whether the following information was in Ángel's letter. (5 puntos)

Sí   No   1. Ángel no piensa volver más a la Argentina.
Sí   No   2. Rosario también está en Puerto Rico.
Sí   No   3. Ángel visitó muchos países como marinero.
Sí   No   4. Vivió en España por mucho tiempo.
Sí   No   5. Dijo que no es realmente marinero. Es pintor.

II. El vocabulario

A.   You will hear a list of vegetables. Match the number of each with its English equivalent. (10 puntos)

_____ a. peas   _____ b. corn   _____ c. carrot   _____ d. celery   _____ e. mushroom
_____ f. squash   _____ g. olives   _____ h. potato   _____ i. beans   _____ j. lettuce

B.   Answer these questions about your preferences in vegetables. Mention at least two in each answer. (9 puntos)

1.   ¿Qué legumbres te gusta poner en la ensalada?

_____

2.   ¿Qué legumbres te gusta comer con bistec?

_____

3.   ¿Cuáles son tus legumbres favoritas?

_____

III. La gramática

A.   Answer these questions, using the cues and including two object pronouns. (6 puntos)

1.   ¿Cuándo le diste la dirección? (ayer)

_____

2.   ¿Cuándo te mandó la carta? (el año pasado)

_____

3.   ¿Cuándo te dio el cuadro? (hace mucho tiempo)

_____

B.   Complete the sentences with the correct preterite form of the verb. (4 puntos)

1.   ¿Qué _____ Raquel y Arturo anoche? (hacer)
2.   Por la tarde (ellos) _____ al puerto. (ir)
3.   ¿Cuándo _____ Raquel a Buenos Aires? (venir)
4.   ¿Cómo _____ tú dónde vive Ángel ahora? (saber)

WORKSHEET: LECCIÓN 17

Gramática 49: Actividad C

_____
_____
_____
_____
_____
_____
_____
_____

Gramática 50: Actividad C

_____
_____
_____
_____

Gramática 50: Actividad D

1. _____
2. _____
3. _____
4. _____

Gramática 51: Actividad C

_____
_____
_____
_____

SELF-TEST: LECCIÓN 17 (33 puntos)   NOMBRE _____

I.   El episodio y los personajes

A. Match the descriptions with the places from Episodio 17. (4 puntos)

_____ 1. Lugar donde vivió un escritor argentino famoso en todo el mundo.
_____ 2. Lugar donde unas mujeres protestan por la desaparición de sus hijos.
_____ 3. Un lugar donde dan conciertos, ópera, ballet y otros espectáculos.
_____ 4. Un lugar donde vive un psiquiatra de Buenos Aires.

a. una casa de la calle Gorostiaga   b. el Teatro Colón   c. la Plaza de Mayo   d. la casa de Jorge Luis
  Borges

B. Which of the following statements describe Raquel's experiences and feelings? (4 puntos)

Sí No 1. Tuvo un novio que la abandonó para aceptar un trabajo en Nueva York.
Sí No 2. Quiere a Arturo y ya piensa en el matrimonio.
Sí No 3. Le gusta Arturo, pero dice que necesita más tiempo.
Sí No 4. Está muy contenta con su trabajo.

II.   El vocabulario

A. Match the descriptions you hear with the appropriate form of writing. (5 puntos)

1. _____   2. _____   3. _____   4. _____   5. _____

a. un poema   b. una novela   c. una comedia   d. un artículo   e. un cuento

B. Write three sentences about your reading preferences. Try to use these words: escritor, novela, poesía, artículo. (9 puntos)

_____

_____

_____

III.   La gramática

A. Complete the sentences with the correct preterite form of the verb. (5 puntos)

1. Mis padres _____ hace unos años. (morir)

2. ¿Qué le _____ Arturo a Raquel la primera noche? (servir)

3. Raquel le _____ a Arturo más tiempo para pensar. (pedir)

4. ¿_____ Ángel ya o todavía no? (morir)

5. ¿A qué hora (tú) te _____ anoche? (dormir)

B. Answer these questions using the cues and including two object pronouns. (6 puntos)

1. ¿Os dio el artículo? (sí / ayer)

_____

2. ¿Nos pidieron la dirección? (sí / ya)

_____

3. ¿Os regaló los cuadros? (sí / anoche)

_____

WORKSHEET: LECCIÓN 18

Gramática 53: Actividad B

1. _____
   _____

2. _____
   _____

3. _____
   _____

4. _____
   _____

Un poco de todo: Actividad A

Paso 3 _____

_____

_____

Paso 4 _____

_____

_____

_____

Un poco de todo: Actividad B

Paso 2 _____

_____

_____

Un poco de todo: Actividad C

_____

_____

_____

_____

Un poco de todo: Actividad D

1. _____
2. _____
3. _____
4. _____
5. _____

WORKSHEET: LECCIÓN 19

Gramática 54: Actividad D

1. _____

2. _____

3. _____

4. _____

5. _____

Gramática 55: Actividad D

Paso 1 _____

_____

_____

_____

Paso 2 _____

_____

_____

_____

_____

Gramática 56: Actividad B

_____

_____

_____

_____

_____

_____

_____

_____

Gramática 56: Actividad D

1. _____

2. _____

3. _____

4. _____

5. _____

I. El episodio y los personajes

Raquel has been looking for several people in several places. First indicate the order of her searches (1–8), then match the places with each search until it ends. (16 puntos)

Action	Order	Place
A. Buscaba a Ángel.	_____ _____	a. en el cementerio del Morro en San Juan
B. Buscaba la casa de Ángel.	_____ _____	b. en la Estancia Santa Susana
C. Buscaba a Héctor.	_____ _____	c. en la calle Sol en el Viejo San Juan
D. Buscaba a Teresa Suárez.	_____ _____	d. en el puerto de Buenos Aires
E. Buscaba la tumba de Rosario.	_____ _____	e. en Madrid
F. Buscaba a Rosario y a su hijo.	_____ _____	f. en el barrio de Triana de Sevilla
G. Buscaba la tumba de Ángel.	_____ _____	g. en un barrio de Buenos Aires
H. Buscaba de nuevo a Teresa Suárez.	_____ _____	h. en el cementerio de Buenos Aires

II.   El vocabulario

A. Answer these questions about places to which you go. (6 puntos)

1. ¿En qué calles tienes que doblar a la derecha y en cuáles a la izquierda para llegar a la universidad (al trabajo)?

_____

2. ¿A cuántas cuadras vives de la universidad (del trabajo)? _____

_____

B. You will hear a series of sentences. Write the **por** expression you hear. (6 puntos)

1. _____   3. _____   5. _____

2. _____   4. _____   6. _____

III. La gramática

A. Answer these questions in the imperfect, using the cues. (12 puntos)

1. ¿Por qué preguntó Raquel por el número 4 de la calle Sol? (ser/direccion /de/Ángel)

_____

2. ¿Por qué fue Raquel al cementerio del Morro? (buscar/tumba/de/Ángel)

_____

3. ¿Qué hacía Raquel cuando llegó Ángela a la tumba de sus padres? (tomar/foto/de/tumba)

_____

4. ¿Por qué llamó Ángela a sus tíos? (querer/contarles/historia)

_____

B. Complete the present progressive forms in these sentences with the correct form of one of these verbs: **decir, escribir, esperar, servir.** (3 puntos)

1. Ahora Raquel y Ángela están _____ a los tíos de Ángela.

2. Creo que Raquel está _____ en su computadora ahora.

3. No oigo lo que les está _____ Ángela a sus tíos.

WORKSHEET: LECCIÓN 20

Gramática 57: Actividad B

1. _____
2. _____
3. _____
4. _____
5. _____
6. _____

Gramática 57: Actividad C

1. _____
2. _____
3. _____
4. _____

Gramática 58: Actividad B

Paso 1 _____

_____

_____

_____

_____

Gramática 58: Actividad C

1. _____
2. _____
3. _____
4. _____
5. _____
6. _____
7. _____
8. _____

Gramática 59: Actividad D

1. _____
2. _____
3. _____
4. _____
5. _____

I.   El episodio y los personajes

A.   How are the following pairs of characters related? In some cases, both answers may be the same terms. (10 puntos)

1.   Ángel - doña Carmen   _____ - _____
2.   Olga - Ángela   _____ - _____
3.   Ángela - doña Carmen   _____ - _____
4.   Arturo - Ángela   _____ - _____
5.   Ángel - Arturo   _____ - _____

B.   Which of the new characters in **Episodio 20** is described by these sentences? (6 puntos)

_____ 1.   La persona que parecía tener más influencia sobre Ángela.

_____ 2.   La persona que acompaña a Raquel y Ángela a San Germán.

_____ 3.   La persona que le hace muchas preguntas a Raquel.

II.   El vocabulario

A.   Listen to the descriptions of some kinship terms and write the term described. (6 puntos)

1.   Es mi _____.   4.   Es mi _____.
2.   Es mi _____.   5.   Son mis _____.
3.   Es mi _____.   6.   Es mi _____.

B.   Complete the sentences with the correct form of one of the words from the list: **algo, nada, alguno, ninguno.** (4 puntos)

1.   ¿Tenías _____ para mí? —No, no tenía _____ para ti.
2.   ¿Tienes _____ libros de Borges? —No, no tengo _____.

III.   La gramática

A.   Complete these three sentences about your activities and those of your friends. (6 puntos)

1.   Anoche, mientras yo estudiaba español, mis amigos _____.
2.   Ayer, mientras mi amigo/a miraba la tele, yo _____.
3.   Cuando llamó mi amigo/a la última vez, yo _____.

B.   Complete these sentences with the correct imperfect form of the verbs in parentheses. (4 puntos)

1.   Yo _____ a caminar pero tú _____ tomar un taxi. (ir, querer)
2.   Yo no _____ que tú _____ la hija de Ángel. (saber, ser)

WORKSHEET: LECCIÓN 21

Gramática 60: Actividad D

_____

_____

_____

_____

_____

Gramática 61: Actividad C

1. _____

2. _____

3. _____

4. _____

Gramática 62: Actividad D

1. _____

2. _____

3. _____

4. _____

5. _____

6. _____

Gramática 62: Actividad E

1. _____

2. _____

3. _____

4. _____

5. _____

Gramática 62: Actividad F

_____

_____

_____

_____

_____

_____

_____

_____

SELF-TEST: LECCIÓN 21 (44 puntos)   NOMBRE _____

I. El episodio y los personajes

A. Put the following events from Episodio 21 in the order in which they occurred (1–6). (6 puntos)

_____ a. Laura pagó el peaje.   _____ d. Le pusieron gasolina al carro.
_____ b. Ángela compró refrescos.   _____ e. Llamaron al mecánico en Ponce.
_____ c. Las tres se acostaron en Ponce.   _____ f. Salieron las tres de San Juan.

B. Match the following places from Episodio 21 with their descriptions. (4 puntos)

_____ 1. la segunda ciudad de Puerto Rico   a. va de una ciudad a otra
_____ 2. lugar de reparaciones   b. Ponce
_____ 3. una gasolinera   c. donde se compra gasolina
_____ 4. la autopista   d. un taller

II. El vocabulario

A. Write three sentences about the weather where you live. Use these expressions: **más (menos) calor,** **más (menos) frío.** (9 puntos)

_____

_____

_____

B. You will hear a series of sentences. Listen, then complete these sentences with a **tener** expression that explains what you heard. (12 puntos)

1. La persona _____.   4. Las personas _____.
2. Las personas _____.   5. La persona _____.
3. La persona _____.   6. La persona _____.

III. La gramática

A. Answer these questions with complete sentences. (9 puntos)

1. ¿Quién tiene menos hermanos, Ángela o la tía Olga?

_____

2. ¿Quién tenía menos hijos, Rosario o don Fernando?

_____

3. ¿Dónde hace más calor, en San Juan o en Ponce?

_____

B. Complete these sentences with the correct imperfect form of the verbs in parentheses. (4 puntos)

1. (Nosotras) _____ mucha hambre cuando _____ por la autopista hacia Ponce. (tener, ir)

2. Y Uds., ¿qué _____ cuando _____ niños? (hacer, ser)

WORKSHEET: LECCIÓN 22

Gramática 63: Actividad C

Paso 2

1. _____
2. _____
3. _____
4. _____
5. _____
6. _____
7. _____
8. _____
9. _____
10. _____
11. _____

Gramática 63: Actividad D

_____
_____
_____
_____
_____
_____

Gramática 65: Actividad A

1. _____ *Personaje* _____
2. _____ *Personaje* _____
3. _____ *Personaje* _____
4. _____ *Personaje* _____
5. _____ *Personaje* _____
6. _____ *Personaje* _____

Gramática 65: Actividad D

_____
_____
_____
_____
_____

SELF-TEST: LECCIÓN 22 (27 puntos)   NOMBRE _____

I. El episodio y los personajes

Match the items from the two groups to describe some of the events in **Episodio 22**. (8 puntos)

_____ 1. Las tres se alegran cuando llegan al taller porque...
_____ 2. Ángela no comprende por qué...
_____ 3. La primera persona que Raquel conoce en San Germán es...
_____ 4. Doña Carmen y su esposo tenían antes...
_____ 5. Cuando se enfermó su madre, ...
_____ 6. Durante esa época Ángel vivía en San Juan y...
_____ 7. Raquel y Ángela buscaban entre las cosas de Ángel y...
_____ 8. Antes de volver a San Juan, Ángela...

a. Dolores Acevedo.
b. una gran finca de caña de azúcar.
c. todos los fines de semana venía a San Germán.
d. encontraron unos dibujos con el nombre de "Recuerdos".
e. recibió una copa de bodas como recuerdo de Rosario.
f. pueden seguir hacia San Germán.
g. Ángela se quedó en San Germán para ayudar a la abuela.
h. su padre no le habló de su vida.

II. El vocabulario

A. Answer these questions about your experiences. (6 puntos)

1. ¿Con quién te enfadas frecuentemente?

   _____

2. ¿Qué te gusta hacer cuando estás enfermo/a?

   _____

B. You will hear a series of statements. Listen, then complete these sentences with the correct form of one of the adjectives from the list: **cansado, contento, nervioso, triste.** (8 puntos)

1. Ángela: Yo estoy _____.   3. Estoy _____.
2. Están _____.   4. Están _____.

III. La gramática

Complete the sentences with the correct imperfect form of the verbs in parentheses. (5 puntos)

1. Cuando yo _____ cinco años, _____ en México. (tener, vivir)
2. De niña, Ángela _____ a veces en el carro. (enfermarse)
3. Mi madre _____ cuando yo _____ las cosas. (enojarse, perder)

WORKSHEET: LECCIÓN 23

Gramática 66: Actividad B

Paso 1

1. _____
   _____

2. _____
   _____

3. _____
   _____

Paso 2

4. _____
   _____

5. _____
   _____

6. _____
   _____

Gramática 67: Actividad E

_____
_____
_____
_____
_____
_____

Gramática 68: Actividad B

_____
_____
_____
_____
_____
_____
_____

SELF-TEST: LECCIÓN 23 (41 puntos)   NOMBRE _____

I. El episodio y los personajes

A. Match the items from the two columns to describe some of the events of **Episodio 23**. (6 puntos)

_____ 1. Cuando volvió de San Germán, Raquel...
_____ 2. Raquel le dijo a Arturo que Ángel estaba muerto y...
_____ 3. Al día siguiente Ángela y Raquel fueron primero...
_____ 4. Ángela quería vender su apartamento y tenía que...
_____ 5. Ángela se decidió por el apartamento porque...
_____ 6. Las dos mujeres fueron a la universidad porque...

a. Ángela quería contarle a Jorge la historia de Ángel.
b. buscar una nueva residencia.
c. llamó a Arturo para decirle lo que pasaba.
d. tenía una vista maravillosa al mar.
e. que él tenía dos sobrinos.
f. al banco para hablar con la jefa de Ángela.

B. Listen to the short descriptions of the new characters and match the character with the description. (3 puntos)

_____ a. la Sra. Isabel Santiago   _____ b. Jorge Alonso   _____ c. Blanca Núñez

II. El vocabulario

A. Describe your own living situation. Write three sentences about 1) rooms you have; 2) appliances you have; 3) what you can see from your window(s). (9 puntos)

_____

_____

_____

B. Match the item in column A with its use in column B. (5 puntos)

A	B
_____ 1. la nevera	a. para mirar y hacer vídeos
_____ 2. la videocasetera	b. para preparar la comida normalmente
_____ 3. la estufa	c. para escuchar música
_____ 4. el horno de microondas	d. para tener fríos los alimentos
_____ 5. el estéreo	e. para preparar la comida rápidamente

III. La gramática

Complete the sentences with the correct imperfect or preterite form of the verbs in parentheses. (18 puntos)

Las mujeres _____^{1} (volver) de San Germán cuando Ángela le _____^{2} (preguntar) a Raquel sobre sus impresiones de Arturo. Raquel le _____^{3} (decir) que Arturo _____^{4} (ser) un hombre simpático y guapo. Ángela le _____^{5} (recordar) que la _____^{6} (ir) a recoger a las nueve de la mañana. Raquel le _____^{7} (hablar) a Arturo cuando él le _____^{8} (decir) que la _____^{9} (querer).

WORKSHEET: LECCIÓN 24

Gramática 69: Actividad C

_____

_____

_____

_____

_____

_____

_____

_____

_____

_____

_____

Gramática 70: Actividad D

_____

_____

_____

_____

_____

_____

_____

_____

Gramática 71: Actividad C

1. _____

2. _____

3. _____

4. _____

5. _____

6. _____

SELF-TEST: LECCIÓN 24 (37 puntos)   NOMBRE _____

I. El episodio y los personajes

Indicate who said the following to whom in **Episodio 24**. (14 puntos)

1. _____ → _____   Me puedes tutear. El tuteo es más íntimo, ¿no?

2. _____ → _____   Llévala tú, mi amor. Acabo de recordar que un estudiante quería verme en la oficina.

3. _____ → _____   ¿Por qué no regresamos al hotel? Después de recoger los boletos, podemos descansar... tomar el sol... nadar, si quieres.

4. _____ → _____   Pero... la pobre me parece tan inocente, no sabe lo que ocurre.

5. _____ → _____   Ah, sí, se me olvidaba. Nosotras las madres no debemos preocuparnos por los hijos cuando ya están grandes.

6. _____ → _____   Cuando venda mi casa, quiero darle a Jorge una parte del dinero.

7. _____ → _____   Su hermano... Hubo un accidente en la excavación.

II. El vocabulario

A. Write three sentences describing yourself, your best friend, and someone you don't like. Use at least two adjectives in each sentence. (9 puntos)

_____

_____

_____

B. You will hear a series of descriptions. Listen, then complete these sentences with a word from the list: **desconfiado, ingenuo, mujeriego, pesimista, terco**. (8 puntos)

1. ¡Qué _____ es!

2. ¡Qué _____ es!

3. ¡Qué _____ es!

4. ¡Qué _____ es!

III. La gramática

Complete the sentences with the correct preterite form of the verb in parentheses. Then give the English equivalent of the verb form. (6 puntos)

1. Yo _____ a Jorge ayer. (conocer) I _____

2. Jorge no _____ ir al museo. (querer) Jorge _____

3. Raquel _____ lo que pensaba hacer Ángela. (saber) Raquel _____

WORKSHEET: LECCIÓN 25

Un poco de todo: Actividad B

Paso 1

Paso 2 _____
_____
_____
_____
_____
_____
_____

Un poco de todo: Actividad C

1. _____
_____
_____
_____

2. _____
_____
_____
_____

Un poco de todo: Actividad D

Paso 2 _____
_____
_____
_____
_____
_____
_____
_____
_____
_____

WORKSHEET: LECCIÓN 26

Un poco de todo: Actividad B

Paso 2 _____

_____

_____

_____

_____

_____

Un poco de todo: Actividad C

_____

_____

_____

_____

_____

_____

_____

Un poco de todo: Actividad E

1. _____

_____

_____

_____

_____

2. _____

_____

_____

_____

_____

APPENDIX 1: ANSWER SECTION

LECCIÓN 1

MÁS ALLÁ DEL EPISODIO

Actividad A. 1. Cierto. 2. Falso. La Gavia es una hacienda histórica. 3. Falso. La Gavia es grande. 4. Cierto. 5. Falso. Hay una capilla en La Gavia. **Actividad B.** Here are the English equivalents of the list of places. You may want to check your comprehension of them before checking your answers to the activity. 1. a patio 2. a hospital 3. a chapel 4. a library 5. an airport 6. an entrance 7. a restaurant 8. a stable 9. a pharmacy 10. a hotel 11. a garage 12. a supermarket

   Places from **Actividad A** that are found at La Gavia, according to the reading passage and the photo captions, are (1) un patio, (3) una capilla, (4) una biblioteca, and (6) una entrada. It is also a reasonably safe bet that there are (8) un establo and (11) un garaje, but they are not mentioned in the passage. A sumptuous hacienda might even have (5) un aeropuerto (albeit a small one).

GRAMÁTICA

Actividad A. 1. Raquel 2. don Fernando 3. Ramón 4. Mercedes 5. Ramón **Actividad B.** 1. Soy 2. es 3. somos Soy Ramón. 4. Soy 5. Soy 6. soy 7. es Soy Raquel.

PRONUNCIACIÓN

Actividad B. 1. Cierto. 2. Cierto. 3. Falso. 4. Falso.

¡AUMENTA TU VOCABULARIO!

Actividad A. 1. una condición mental 2. una persona 3. información

LECCIÓN 2

GRAMÁTICA

SECTION 2 Actividad A. 1. el hombre 2. la mujer 3. el estudiante 4. la estudiante 5. los tíos 6. las tías 7. el director 8. la directora 9. los clientes 10. las abogadas 11. la compañía 12. la universidad 13. las oficinas 14. las ciudades 15. la hacienda 16. las cartas 17. la columna 18. la memoria 19. los modelos 20. el futuro 21. la tensión 22. las relaciones 23. la rivalidad

   1. un hombre 2. una mujer 3. un estudiante 4. una estudiante 5. unos tíos 6. unas tías 7. un director 8. una directora 9. unos clientes 10. unas abogadas 11. una compañía 12. una universidad 13. unas oficinas 14. unas ciudades 15. una hacienda 16. unas cartas 17. una columna 18. una memoria 19. unos modelos 20. un futuro 21. una tensión 22. unas relaciones 23. una rivalidad

   1. hombres 2. mujeres 3. estudiantes 4. estudiantes 5. tío 6. tía 7. directores 8. directoras 9. cliente 10. abogada 11. compañías 12. universidades 13. oficina 14. ciudad 15. haciendas 16. carta 17. columnas 18. memorias 19. modelo 20. futuros 21. tensiones 22. relación 23. rivalidades **Actividad B.** Personas: los tíos, los esposos Lugares: una compañía, la universidad Cosas: una columna Conceptos: el español *Note:* You may have put una columna and el español into the opposite categories, depending on how you view them. That's OK, as long as you know what they mean.

SECTION 3 Actividad A. 1. don Fernando 2. Ramón 3. Raquel 4. Gloria 5. Juan 6. Carlos 7. los hijos de don Fernando 8. Mercedes **Actividad B.** Don Fernando tiene una familia muy grande. Sus cuatro hijos viven en distintas partes del mundo. Su hija, Mercedes, vive en La Gavia. No tiene hijos. Su hijo Ramón también vive en La Gavia, con su esposa, Consuelo, y su hija, Maricarmen. Su hijo Carlos vive en Miami, con su esposa, Gloria, y sus dos (2) hijos, Juanita y Carlitos. Su hijo Juan vive en Nueva York con su esposa, Pati. No tienen hijos. Su esposa, Carmen, ya murió; está muerta.

PRONUNCIACIÓN

Letters of the Spanish alphabet that are different: ch, ll, ñ, rr.

¡AUMENTA TU VOCABULARIO!

Actividad A. You probably answered the questions this way. 1. Cierto. 2. Cierto. 3. Falso. Hay muchos mexicoamericanos en Los Ángeles. 4. Cierto. 5. Cierto. 6. Falso. La opresión sí tiene solución. **Actividad B.** 1. universidad 2. profesión 3. especialización 4. presiones 5. tensión 6. personalidades 7. rivalidad

LECCIÓN 3

GRAMÁTICA

SECTION 4 Actividad A. 1. Falso. Hay pocas industrias en el sur de España. 2. Cierto. 3. Falso. Hay muchas iglesias y hay una catedral muy grande en Sevilla. 4. Cierto. 5. Falso. En Sevilla hay muchas iglesias y varias tradiciones religiosas, como la Semana Santa. **Actividad B.** *Possible answers:* 1. No hay muchas personas en la familia. 2. Hay dos hijos. 3. No, no hay un abuelo, pero hay una abuela. 4. No, no hay hermanas, pero hay hermanos. 5. Es la familia Ruiz, de Sevilla.

SECTION 5 Actividad A. 1. ¿Cómo estás? 2. ¿Cómo está usted? Answers 1 and 2 are based on actual usage in video episodes you have seen. Carlos uses the informal question with Ofelia and she addresses him with the more formal forms. Another boss and secretary might address each other in different ways. 3. ¿Cómo estás? 4. ¿Cómo está usted? Again, these answers are based on actual usage in the video episodes. Pedro, older than Raquel and a senior colleague, addresses her informally. Raquel uses formal forms to show deference to Pedro. This is a choice made by these individuals at this time. 5. ¿Cómo está usted? When you don't know someone very well, it is better to err on the side of formality. If your instructor wants you to address him or her with the informal forms, that will be made clear to you. **Actividad C.** *Possible answers:* 1. Raquel está en el mercado de Triana, en la calle Pureza, con Elena, con los chicos, con el taxista. 2. Don Fernando está en La Gavia, en su habitación. 3. Elena y Raquel están en el mercado de Triana. 4. Los hijos de don Fernando están en el patio de La Gavia, con sus hermanos. 5. Raquel y los chicos están en la calle Pureza. 6. Los chicos están en la calle Pureza, con Raquel.

SECTION 6 Actividad A. 1. Teresa Suárez escribe una carta. 2. Raquel viaja a Sevilla. 3. Raquel busca a Rosario. Don Fernando también busca a Rosario. 4. Miguel y Jaime hablan con Raquel en la calle. 5. Ramón y Mercedes viven en La Gavia, con su padre. 6. Raquel y el taxista entran en el barrio de Triana en taxi. 7. Don Fernando cree que Rosario está en España. Raquel también cree que Rosario está en España. 8. Raquel llega al mercado de Triana con dos chicos. 9. Raquel investiga el secreto de don Fernando. 10. Don Fernando revela un secreto a su familia. **Actividad B.** 1. Ramón y Mercedes no trabajan en Miami. Trabajan en La Gavia. 2. Mercedes y don Fernando no viajan con frecuencia. 3. Carlos también visita a don Fernando en La Gavia. 4. Sus hijos no toman muchas medicinas. 5. Miguel y Jaime no explican la historia. 6. Raquel pregunta dónde vive Teresa Suárez.

SECTION 7   Actividad.   *Possible answers:* Raquel necesita hablar con Teresa Suárez. Debe buscar a Rosario. Desea visitar los monumentos históricos de Sevilla.   Miguel y Jaime necesitan buscar a su madre en el mercado. Deben estudiar mucho. Desean visitar a su abuela.

¡AUMENTA TU VOCABULARIO!

Actividad A.   a. 5   b. 1   c. 3   d. 4   e. 2   Actividad B.   1. estudioso   2. escuela   3. estudiante   4. teorías   5. especialmente   6. biología
7. totalmente   8. estudiar   9. realmente   10. fantasías

LECCIÓN 4

GRAMÁTICA

SECTION 8   Actividad A.   1. Pati   2. Raquel   3. Raquel   4. Elena   5. Pati   6. Raquel   7. Elena   8. Raquel   Actividad B.   1. camino
2. Estudio   3. saco   4. trabajo (estudio)   5. escribo   6. Visito   7. deseo   8. debo   9. soy   10. creo   11. necesito
SECTION 9   Actividad A.   1. d   2. g   3. a   4. e   5. c   6. b   7. f   Actividad B.   1. Debes   2. crees   3. Hablas   4. escribes   5. visitas
6. llamas   7. llevas   8. eres   9. sacas   10. deseas   11. hablas
SECTION 10   Actividad.   1. serio   2. bueno   3. buenas   4. favorita   5. naturales   6. famoso   7. importantes   8. desobediente   9. mediocres
10. favorita   11. física   12. domésticos   13. fieles   14. cariñosos

PRONUNCIACIÓN

Actividad B.   1. Miguel y Elena   2. Raquel y el taxista   3. Pati es la esposa de Juan.   4. No está ahora en Madrid.   5. Vive ahora en Los Ángeles.

¡AUMENTA TU VOCABULARIO!

Actividad A.   1. egoísmo   2. dentista   3. programador   4. realista   5. pintor

LECCIÓN 5

GRAMÁTICA

SECTION 11   Actividad A.   1. c   2. a   3. b   Actividad B.   1. estudiamos   2. Usamos   3. buscamos   4. investigamos   5. Deseamos
6. escribimos   7. sacamos   8. comprendemos   9. Somos
SECTION 12   Actividad A.   1. Raquel   2. Elena   3. Raquel   4. Elena   5. Elena   6. Raquel   Actividad B.   1. vivís   2. Creéis   3. debéis
4. Comprendéis   ¡Un desafío! Sí, vivimos en esta calle (en la calle Pureza). No. No vive aquí. Vive en Madrid. Sí, señor, comprendemos.
Actividad C.   1. f. Habla Miguel.   2. d. Hablan los dos.   3. e. Hablan los dos.   4. c. Habla Elena.   5. g. Hablan los dos.   6. b. Hablan los dos.
7. h. No sabes quién habla aquí. Posiblemente los dos.   8. a. Hablan los dos.
SECTION 13   Actividad.   1. a   2. a   3. a   4. a   5. al   6. nothing   7. a   8. nothing   9. nothing   10. a   11. a   12. a   13. a
SECTION 14   tú vas, vosotros vais, Ud. va, Uds. van   Actividad A.   1. voy   2. ir   3. va   4. vamos   5. vamos   6. voy   Actividad B.   *Possible answers:* 1. Voy a Madrid.   3. Voy al mercadillo de los animales.   4. Voy a la oficina.   5. Vamos a un restaurante elegante.   6. Vamos a la Plaza de las Tres Cruces.   7. Voy a la estación.   Actividad C.   *Possible answers:* 1. Raquel va a viajar a Madrid en tren y va a ver a la Sra. Suárez.   2. Jaime y Miguel van a ir a la escuela el lunes. Van a correr con Osito. Y van a visitar a su tía el domingo.   3. Miguel y Elena van a cenar en un restaurante, con sus hijos.   4. Mercedes va a hablar con don Fernando y va a llamar al médico.   5. El ciego va a vender cupones de la lotería.   6. Miguel hijo va a sacar buenas notas (¡pero Jaime no!).   7. Voy a estudiar mucho.   8. Voy a comprar un cupón.   9. Voy a buscar un teléfono.   10. Voy a ir a un restaurante.   11. Voy a comprar un pez tropical.

PRONUNCIACIÓN

Actividad B.   está   música   miércoles   Rodríguez   también   conversación   química   informática

¡AUMENTA TU VOCABULARIO!

1. dominante   2. arquitectura   3. figura   4. pintura   5. escultura   6. fascinante   7. cultura   8. tolerante

LECCIÓN 6

GRAMÁTICA

SECTION 15   buscar: -as, -amos; creer: -e, -en; vivir: -o, -imos   Actividad A.   1. d   2. a   3. b   4. f, h   5. b   6. f, h   7. d   8. e   9. c, g   10. e

UN POCO DE TODO

Actividad A.   *Possible answers:* 1. Raquel viaja a Madrid en tren, corre por las calles.   2. Jaime estudia ciencias naturales, corre por las calles.   3. Teresa Suárez escribe una carta a don Fernando.   4. A Miguel le gusta estudiar ciencias naturales.   5. Raquel necesita (desea) hablar con Teresa, saber dónde vive Rosario.   6. Miguel va a la escuela de San Francisco de Paula, desea ser científico.   7. Miguel y Jaime van a la escuela de San Francisco de Paula.   8. Don Fernando desea (necesita) saber donde vive Rosario.   Actividad C.   1. 21 (Raquel, al taxista)   2. 13, 14, 15 (el recepcionista, a Raquel)   3. 2-21-30-12 (Raquel, al recepcionista)   4. 12, 15 (el reportero, a su asistente y a Raquel)   Actividad D.   *Possible answers: Note:* Some details have been added.   El jueves, hablo con Pedro y acepto el caso de don Fernando. El viernes, voy a Sevilla en avión y llego al hotel Doña María. El sábado, voy al Barrio de Triana. Hablo con los miembros de la familia Ruiz y descubro que Teresa Suárez ya no vive en Sevilla. El domingo, acompaño a la familia al mercadillo de los animales. Compramos un perro y el perro se escapa. Corro por las calles del Barrio Santa Cruz y busco a Jaime. Visito el Alcázar y ceno con la familia en un restaurante elegante. El lunes, voy a la estación con la familia y tomo el tren para Madrid.   Actividad E.   7:30 : a la universidad   8:00: _química_   9:30 : inglés   10:45 : informática   1:00 : en la cafetería   3:30: _a casa_   6:00: _cena con Jorge_

LECCIÓN 7

GRAMÁTICA

SECTION 17   Actividad A.   1. Raquel Rodríguez   2. Teresa Suárez, Raquel Rodríguez (Pero ellas saben su nombre. Los otros no saben quién es.)
3. Teresa Suárez, Federico Ruiz   4. Miguel y Jaime   5. Raquel Rodríguez   Actividad B.   1. sé   2. saber   3 conocen   4. sé   5. conocer   6. sabe
7. conozco   8. sé   9. conocer   Actividad C.   1. Conozco...   2. Ya sé... (Be positive! Don't make this sentence negative!)   3. Sé...   4. Sé...
5. Sé...   6. No conozco...
SECTION 18   hacer hacemos   dar dais   traer traen   salir sale   poner pones   ver vemos   Actividad.   1. Raquel Rodríguez   2. el recepcionista, el botones   3. Raquel Rodríguez   4. Alfredo Sánchez   5. el botones (No damos propina al recepcionista.)   6. Raquel Rodríguez   7. Teresa Suárez
8. el Sr. Díaz
SECTION 19   Actividad A.   1. Raquel Rodríguez, el Sr. Díaz   2. el recepcionista   3. Raquel Rodríguez   4. Teresa Suárez   5. Raquel Rodríguez
6. Federico Ruiz   7. Raquel Rodríguez   8. Teresa Suárez   Actividad B.   1. tengo   2. salen   3. hago   4. dice   5. tiene   6. viene   7. tengo
8. veo   9. vengo

LECCIÓN 8

GRAMÁTICA

SECTION 20 **Actividad A.** 1. S 2. Q 3. Q 4. S 5. Q 6. Q 7. S 8. Q **Actividad B.** 1. e 2. h 3. g 4. c 5. b 6. a 7. l 8. f 9. k 10. d 11. i 12. j **Actividad C.** 1. a. ¿De dónde b. ¿Dónde c. ¿Por qué d. ¿Cuánto e. ¿Qué f. ¿Cuándo 2. a. ¿Por qué (¿Qué) b. ¿Cuántas c. ¿Por qué d. ¿Cuál e. ¿Cuál 3. a. ¿Qué b. ¿A quién c. ¿Con quién d. ¿Adónde e. ¿Qué f. ¿Cuál

SECTION 21 **Actividad A.** *Paso 2* 1. Cierto. 2. Falso. Sí recuerda que se fue a vivir a la Argentina. 3. Falso. Piensan que es muy simpática. 4. Cierto. 5. Cierto. 6. Falso. Raquel pierde su cartera. 7. Falso. La investigación es fascinante para Raquel. 8. Falso. Raquel sabe que tiene que ir a la Argentina. 9. Falso. Encuentran la cartera en un taxi. 10. Falso. Don Fernando no muere... todavía.

SECTION 22 **Actividad A.** 1. Raquel se sienta al lado de la Sra. Suárez. No se olvida de llamar a Elena. 2. La Sra. Suárez se acuerda de Rosario con nostalgia. 3. Rosario y Martín Iglesias se casan en Buenos Aires. 4. Don Fernando se casa dos veces, no se siente bien, se acuerda de Rosario con nostalgia. 5. Raquel y la Sra. Suárez se sientan a hablar. 6. El hijo de Rosario y don Fernando se llama Ángel. 7. Rosario se casa dos veces, se va a la Argentina.

LECCIÓN 9

GRAMÁTICA

SECTION 23 **Actividad A.** *Paso 1* 1. Encuentro 2. quiero 3. tengo 4. Quiero 5. quiero 6. Empiezo 7. pido 8. sigo 9. encuentro 10. pienso 11. pienso 12. puedo **Actividad B.** *Paso 1* 1. Sigo 2. cuento 3. Pienso 4. Pierdo 5. Sigo 6. Empiezo 7. Recuerdo 8. Quiero *Paso 2* 1. ¿Sigues... 2. ¿A veces cuentas... 3. ¿Piensas... 4. ¿Pierdes... 5. ¿Sigues... 6. ¿Empiezas... 7. ¿Recuerdas... 8. ¿Quieres...

SECTION 24 **Actividad A.** You should have checked off these activities: 2, 3, 5, 7. 1. C 2. C 3. F 4. F 5. F 6. C **Actividad B.** 1. Teresa 2. Federico 3. Federico 4. Federico 5. Teresa 6. Federico

SECTION 25 **Actividad A.** 1. P 2. IMP Los hijos de Teresa Suárez viven en Sevilla, Madrid y Barcelona. 3. P 4. P 5. P 6. IMP Teresa cree que los perros dan problemas. **Actividad B.** *Paso 1* Nuestra abuela vive en Madrid, con nuestro tío, Federico. Nuestro perro se llama Osito. Nuestros padres todavía piensan mucho en Raquel. Nuestra escuela se llama el Colegio de San Francisco de Paula. Nuestra calle está en el Barrio de Triana. Nuestros amigos van a la misma escuela. *Paso 2 Possible answers:* ¿Con quién vive vuestra (su) abuela? ¿Cómo se llama vuestro (su) perro? ¿En quién piensan vuestros (sus) padres? ¿Cómo se llama vuestra (su) escuela? ¿Dónde está vuestra (su) calle? ¿A qué escuela van vuestros (sus) amigos? **Actividad C.** 1. Mi 2. Su (*His*) 3. su (*his*) 4. Sus (*His*) 5. su (*their*) 6. su (*their*) 7. su (*his*)

SECTION 26 **Actividad.** *Paso 2* 1. b (NC) 2. f (F) 3. e (C) 4. a (NC) 5. g (C) 6. d (C) 7. c (F)

LECCIÓN 10

GRAMÁTICA

SECTION 27 **Actividad A.** 1. don Fernando 2. Manuel Díaz 3. Elena Ramírez **Actividad C.** 1. mexicoamericana 2. mexicanos 3. mexicana 4. española 5. españoles 6. argentino 7. español 8. mexicanas **Actividad D.** alemán = *German* 1. francesa 2. ingleses 3. rusos 4. inglesa y norteamericana 5. portugués 6. alemanes 7. italiano (Miguel Ángel = Michelangelo) 8. chino 9. japonés

SECTION 28 *Uses* ser: a. 1, 5, 6, 7, 10 b. 15, 16 c. 3 d. 2 e. 13 f. 14 g. 12 h. 11 estar: a. 4, 9 b. 8 **Actividad A.** 1. d 2. f 3. e 4. i 5. g 6. b 7. h 8. j 9. c 10. a **Actividad B.** 1. España y Portugal están en la Península Ibérica. 2. Andalucía está en el sur de España. Es una comunidad autónoma. 3. El Alcázar está en Sevilla. Es un monumento de gran interés histórico. 4. El Prado y el Parque del Retiro están en Madrid. 5. El catalán y el gallego son dos lenguas. 6. Madrid es la capital de España.

SECTION 29 **Actividad A.** 1. c 2. e 3. f 4. b 5. a 6. d **Actividad B.** 1. Nos despertamos 2. nos levantamos 3. Nos vestimos 4. vestirse 5. desayunamos 6. levantarme (¡OJO! Habla Pati.) 7. nos despedimos 8. Queremos 9. volvemos 10. contamos 11. nos sentamos 12. empezamos 13. nos acostamos 14. Nos dormimos

LECCIÓN 11

GRAMÁTICA

SECTION 30 yo form _x_ tú form _x_ Ud. form _x_ él/ella form _x_ nosotros form ___ vosotros form ___ Uds. form _x_ ellos/ellas form _x_ The stem change occurs in present-tense stem-changing verbs in a pattern that reminds some people of a shoe. For this reason, stem-changing verbs are sometimes called "shoe verbs."
empezar: empiezas, empieza, empezáis pedir: pido, pide, pedimos contar: cuenta, contamos, cuentan

SECTION 31 casarse: se casa, os casáis acostarse: me acuesto, te acuestas, nos acostamos, se acuestan

SECTION 32 conocer *to know* conozco, conoce dar *to give* doy, dan decir *to say, to tell* digo, decimos estar *to be* estoy, están hacer *to do; to make* hago, hacéis ir *to go* voy, vamos oír *to hear* oigo, oye poner *to put; to place* pongo, pone saber *to know* sé, sabes salir *to leave* salgo, salimos ser *to be* soy, son tener *to have* tengo, tiene traer *to bring* traigo, traes venir *to come* vengo, vienen ver *to see* veo, vemos **Actividad A.** 1. d 2. c, g 3. a 4. f, h 5. a 6. b 7. c, g 8. a 9. f, h 10. c, g **¡Un desafío!** 1. Raquel, la Sra. Suárez, Federico, María 2. Raquel 3. Raquel, el Sr. Díaz, Alfredo Sánchez 4. Federico y María 5. don Fernando 6. Federico, hablando con Raquel 7. el Sr. Díaz, hablando del (o con el) reportero 8. la Sra. Suárez, hablando de Raquel 9. Federico, hablando con su madre y Raquel 10. Federico **Actividad B.** 1. encuentro 2. tengo 3. puedo 4. pasar 5. estoy 6. Debo 7. Salgo

SECTION 33 rojo: rojos azul: azul, azules realista: realista, realistas mexicano: mexicanos, mexicanas español: española, españoles mi: mi, mis nuestro: nuestra, nuestros este: esta, estos **Actividad.** 1. atractiva, educada, imposible 2. musicales, universitarios, medievales, típica, medieval 3. bonitos, bonitos, expresivos, feo, feo 4. gris, neoclásico, grecorromanas, grandes

UN POCO DE TODO

Actividad B. 1. ropa de señora, ropa de caballero (= *gentleman*) 2. lavado o plancha, limpiar y planchar; planchar 3. jersey, suéter 4. pañuelo, camisa de noche, pijama **Actividad C.** *Paso 1* 1. enero 2. junio, en verano 3. julio 4. abril 5. no se menciona 6. enero 7. diciembre 8. la primavera

LECCIÓN 12

GRAMÁTICA

SECTION 34 **Actividad A.** 1. d, h 2. j 3. c 4. d 5. a, d 6. b 7. d, f 8. e 9. g 10. i **Actividad B.** 1. Present 2. Past 3. Past 4. Present 5. Past 6. Present 7. Past 8. Past 9. Present 10. Present **Actividad C.** a. 6 b. 10 c. 8 d. 5 e. 1 f. 7 g. 2 h. 3 i. 9 j. 4 **Actividad D.** 1. salieron 2. Llegaron 3. se casó 4. vivieron 5. Empezó 6. abandonó 7. se dedicó 8. visitaron 9. se enteró 10. sufrió 11. se mudó 12. perdonó 13. perdieron

SECTION 35 **Actividad A.** *Paso 1* 1. la 2. los 3. la 4. la 5. los 6. Los 7. La 8. la 9. lo **Actividad B.** 1. la *suite* 2. la dirección de Rosario 3. a Raquel (= *It's a pleasure to meet you.*) 4. Rosario 5. a Raquel (= *How can I help you?*) 6. Ángel **Actividad C.** a. 6 b. — c. 3

d. 1 e. 5 f. 2 g. 4 **Actividad D.** 1. la 2. encontrarla 3. los (¡OJO! Rosario y su hijo) 4. la 5. lo 6. conocerlo

SECTION 36 **Actividad A.** 1. b, b 2. c, b

LECCIÓN 13

GRAMÁTICA

SECTION 37 **Actividad A.** 1. A 2. A 3. A 4. A 5. R 6. R **Actividad B.** a. 9 b. 5 c. 3 d. 6 e. 1 f. 8 g. 4 h. 7 i. 10 j. 2 **Actividad C.** *Paso 1* 1. e 2. g 3. a 4. b 5. f 6. d 7. c

SECTION 38 **Actividad A.** 1. R 2. O (Cirilo) 3. A 4. A 5. A 6. O (un marinero) 7. R 8. R **Actividad B.** *Paso 1* 1. c 2. e 3. a 4. a 5. b 6. a 7. a

SECTION 39 **Actividad B.** 1. se sentó 2. se acostó 3. se durmió 4. se despidió 5. la invitó a sentarse 6. se contaron 7. se escucharon 8. fueron

LECCIÓN 14

GRAMÁTICA

SECTION 40 **Actividad A.** 1. No. Raquel y Arturo comenzaron la búsqueda en La Boca. 2. Sí. 3. No. Probaron unos pescados deliciosos. 4. Sí. 5. Sí. 6. Sí. 7. Sí. 8. No. Ángel le escribió una carta a Héctor. Héctor cree que desde Puerto Rico, pero no está seguro. 9. No. Héctor subió a su casa, pero Arturo y Raquel no subieron con él. 10. Sí. **Actividad B.** 1. d 2. i 3. j 4. a 5. h 6. b 7. f 8. c 9. g 10. e

SECTION 41 **Actividad A.** 1. b 2. b 3. a 4. b 5. a **Actividad B.** 1. b 2. d 3. c 4. a

SECTION 42 **Actividad A.** 1. No. Arturo trabaja en su casa. 2. Sí. 3. No. Vive en La Boca. 4. Sí. 5. No. Yo regresé a mi hotel y llamé a Pedro. 6. Sí. 7. Sí. 8. Sí. **Actividad B.** 1. en 2. cerca del 3. con 4. al lado de 5. cerca del 6. antes de 7. entre 8. durante 9. lejos de 10. sin

PRONUNCIACIÓN

Actividad B. 1. b 2. a 3. b 4. b

LECCIÓN 15

GRAMÁTICA

SECTION 43 **Actividad A.** 1. a, b 2. d 3. b 4. c 5. d 6. a, b 7. e 8. b 9. f 10. d **Actividad B.** *Paso 2* a. 3 b. 6 c. 2 d. 7 e. 9 f. 5 g. 8 h. 1 i. 10 j. 4 **Actividad C.** a. 1 b. 5 c. 7 d. 2 e. 4 f. 6 g. 3

SECTION 44 **Actividad A.** 1. b 2. d, g 3. g 4. c 5. f 6. e 7. b 8. a 9. a 10. h **Actividad B.** 1. Le mandó una carta, desde el Caribe. 2. Le regaló una campera negra muy bonita. 3. Le contó una historia... la historia de don Fernando. 4. Le dio la dirección de Rosario en Buenos Aires. 5. Les dio el nombre de Héctor. 6. Le regaló un cuadro de Ángel. 7. Le trajo fruta, pan y queso... en una canasta. 8. Le contó una historia... la historia de su medio hermano Ángel.

SECTION 45 **Actividad A.** 1. d, g, k 2. c, k 3. a, b, j 4. a 5. e, f, g (pero lo hace de todas formas) 6. f, h, i 7. k 8. f 9. a **Actividad B.** *Paso 1* 1. A, R 2. A 3. R 4. R 5. A 6. R 7. R 8. A 9. A 10. A, R 11. R

PRONUNCIACIÓN

Actividad B. 1. pena 2. uña 3. leña 4. suena 5. tino

LECCIÓN 16

GRAMÁTICA

SECTION 46 **Actividad A.** 1. R 2. A 3. OP 4. R 5. A 6. OP 7. A, R 8. A, R 9. OP 10. A (o R) ¡Un desafío! 3. Héctor 6. Héctor 9. unas personas de La Boca **Actividad B.** 1. pudimos hablar con él 2. Vine a la casa 3. quiso sacar una foto 4. se puso muy enfadado 5. tuvimos noticias 6. Fuimos allí 7. se puso muy pensativo 8. supo algo definitivo 9. tuvo un mal presentimiento 10. fui al hotel 11. tuvo un mal presentimiento 12. fui a una tienda 13. le hice una sorpresa

SECTION 47 **Actividad A.** 1. a. Le = a él (a Héctor) 2. a. me = a mí 3. a. Te = a ti b. Te = a ti 4. a. Le = a él (a Ramón) b. Le = a él (a Ramón) c. me = a mí 5. a. Te = a ti b. lo = que ella sale mal en las fotos c. la = la foto **Actividad B.** 1. d 2. e 3. a 4. f 5. a 6. c 7. g 8. b

SECTION 48 **Actividad A.** 1. te las 2. te la 3. te la 4. te lo 5. te lo **Actividad B.** 1. don Fernando, el secreto de su pasado 2. Arturo, la campera (a Raquel) 3. Teresa Suárez, la carta (a don Fernando) 4. Ángel, la carta (a Héctor) 5. Arturo, las brochetas (a Raquel) 6. Arturo, todo el mal presentimiento (a Raquel) 7. Raquel, las caras (a Arturo) 8. Héctor, el cuadro (a Arturo)

LECCIÓN 17

GRAMÁTICA

SECTION 49 **Actividad A.** *Paso 1* 1. murió, murió 2. seguí 3. sirvió 4. consiguió, conseguí 5. pedimos, pedí, pidió

SECTION 50 **Actividad A.** 1. f 2. d 3. b 4. a 5. g 6. e 7. c **Actividad B.** ¿Qué os parecen... , Os compré... , Voy a mandároslo...

SECTION 51 **Actividad A.** 1. h 2. b 3. g 4. f 5. e 6. a 7. c 8. i 9. d

PRONUNCIACIÓN

Actividad B. 1. ll 2. l 3. ll 4. ll 5. l 6. l

LECCIÓN 18

GRAMÁTICA

SECTION 52 *Regular Verbs:* cenar: cené, cenó, cenasteis correr: corriste, corrió, corrimos, corrieron decidir: decidí, decidió, decidisteis, decidieron *Spelling Change Verbs:* busqué, llegué, empecé; leyó, oyeron *-ir Stem-Changing Verbs:* X = Ud. and él/ella form, Uds. and ellos/ellas form pedir: pedí, pidió, pedimos, pidieron dormir: dormí, durmió, dormimos, durmieron *Verbs with Irregularities:* anduve dijeron estuvo hizo fuimos pudiste puse quisieron supe fueron tuvisteis trajo viniste **Actividad A.** 1. llegó 2. fue 3. salió 4. dio 5. habló 6. se acordó 7. se mudó 8. dio 9. buscó 10. encontró 11. decidió 12. habló 13. contó 14. murió 15. dijo 16. perdió 17. fueron 18. sacó **Actividad B.** 1. búsqueda 2. le mostró a Raquel una foto 3. fueron a La Boca 4. al hombre de la foto 5. lo reconoció 6. les dijo

7. encontraron a José   8. el nombre de Héctor   9. pudo decirles   10. una cantina   **Actividad C.**   1. Esa noche, Arturo y Raquel cenaron en casa de Arturo.   2. Durante la cena, Arturo le contó a Raquel un poco de su vida.   3. Al día siguiente fueron a la cantina y pudieron hablar con Héctor.   4. Este marinero sí recordó a Ángel.   5. Les dijo que Ángel se fue a vivir al Caribe.   6. Prometió buscarles una carta que Ángel le mandó hace años.   7. Seguramente la carta tendría su dirección.   8. Arturo y Raquel volvieron a la casa de Arturo.   9. Allí hablaron del mal presentimiento que tenía Arturo: ¿Estaba muerto Ángel?   **Actividad E.**   *Parte 1*   a. 3   b. 6   c. 1   d. 5   e. 4   f. 2   *Parte 2*   a. 5   b. 1   c. 7   d. 4   e. 6   f. 3   g. 2

SECTION 53   1. direct object pronouns   2. indirect object pronouns   3. reflexive pronouns   4. pronouns that serve as the object of a preposition   yo me, me, a mí   tú te, a ti   Ud. le, lo/la   él se, lo   ella se, le   nosotros nos, nos, a nosotros   vosotros os   Uds. se, los/las, a Uds.   ellos se, les   ellas les, las   *Position:* precede, come in between, may

Actividad A.   *Paso 1*   1. reconoció a Ángel → lo reconoció   2. para mostrarle las fotos → para mostrárselas   3. leyó la carta → la leyó   *Paso 2*   *Note:* Suggested changes are indicated in italics.   Con una foto de Ángel, Arturo y Raquel fueron a La Boca, en busca de *él.* Allí les preguntaron a varias personas si *lo* reconocían. Desgraciadamente, nadie *lo* reconoció. Por fin un señor les dijo que tal vez José, un marinero, los podría ayudar. Raquel y Arturo encontraron a José en su barco. *Él (Éste)* no reconoció a Ángel tampoco, pero mencionó el nombre de Héctor, otro marinero. José fue a buscar*lo.* No *lo* encontró, pero sí pudo decirles que podrían conocer*lo* mañana por la noche en una cantina, el Piccolo Navio.

UN POCO DE TODO

Actividad A.   *Paso 2*   1. dulce de leche   2. huevos revueltos, huevos pasados por agua   3. Buenos Aires Herald, **Ámbito financiero**   **Actividad B.**   *Paso 1*   don Fernando + Rosario → Ángel Castillo   Rosario + Martín Iglesias → Arturo Iglesias

LECCIÓN 19

MÁS ALLÁ DEL EPISODIO

Actividad B.   1. por fin   2. su esposa

GRAMÁTICA

SECTION 54   **Actividad A.**   *Paso 1*   1. a (o posiblemente b)   2. d   3. b   4. c   5. d   6. a   7. c (o posiblemente d)   8. b   **Actividad B.**   You should have indicated 1, 3, 5, 6, and 7.

SECTION 55   **Actividad A.**   1. c   2. b   3. a   4. c   5. c   6. a   7. d   8. c   **Actividad B.**   a. —   b. 3   c. 1   d. 4   e. 2

SECTION 56   **Actividad A.**   a. 1   b. 2   c. 1   d. 5   e. 4   f. 3   **Actividad C.**   a. 5   b. 4   c. 8   d. 5   e. 7   f. 1   g. 6   h. 8   i. 3   j. 2

Actividad E.   1. por todas partes   2. Por lo general   3. Por eso   4. por fin   5. Por ejemplo   6. por última vez

LECCIÓN 20

MÁS ALLÁ DEL EPISODIO

Actividad B.   1. casi siempre se llevaban bien   2. cambiaron   3. es posible

GRAMÁTICA

SECTION 57   **Actividad A.**   1. tenía   2. llevaba   3. miraba   4. pensaba   5. comprendía   6. estaba   7. Me sentía

SECTION 58   **Actividad A.**   *Paso 1*   1. c   2. b   3. d   4. e   5. a   *Paso 2*   1. b   2. e   3. a   4. d   5. c

SECTION 59   **Actividad A.**   1. don Fernando (y también Teresa Suárez)   2. Arturo   3. Ángel Castillo   4. Rosario   5. Elena Ramírez o Miguel Ruiz   6. Arturo o Raquel   7. los hijos de don Fernando   8. el reportero, Alfredo Sánchez   **Actividad B**   1. también   2. algo   3. nunca (jamás), nada, algún   4. algo   5. nada, Nunca (Jamás), algo, nunca (jamás)

LECCIÓN 21

MÁS ALLÁ DEL EPISODIO

Actividad B.   1. le interesa   2. Tiene

GRAMÁTICA

SECTION 60   **Actividad A.**   You should have indicated 1, 2, 4, 5, 9, and 10.   **Actividad B.**   1. d   2. c   3. f   4. b   5. a   6. e   **Actividad C.**   1. b   2. d   3. a   4. e   5. c

SECTION 61   **Actividad A.**   1. c   2. b   3. f   4. e   5. c   6. d   7. a   8. c   **Actividad B.**   *Possible answers:*   1. a   2. b   3. a, b, c   4. b, c   5. a, c   6. a

SECTION 62   **Actividad A.**   1. Cierto.   2. Falso.   3. Cierto.   4. Cierto.   5. Falso.   6. Falso.   7. Falso.   8. Cierto.   **Actividad B.**   1. b   2. h   3. g   4. c   5. d   6. f   7. a   8. e

LECCIÓN 22

MÁS ALLÁ DEL EPISODIO

Actividad B.   1. era casi normal   2. no venía con la misma frecuencia

GRAMÁTICA

SECTION 63   **Actividad A.**   a. 2   b. 6   c. 11   d. 9   e. 1   f. 12   g. 3   h. 7   i. 8   j. 4   k. 10   l. 5   **Actividad C.**   *Paso 2*   1. Puerto Rico era una colonia española.   2. La Isla pasó a ser territorio norteamericano.   3. El azúcar era el producto más importante de la Isla.   4. Había grandes fincas de caña de azúcar.   5. Doña Carmen y su esposo eran dueños de una de esas fincas.   6. Su finca era una de las más grandes.   7. A veces trabajaban en la finca más de doscientos hombres.   8. También había ganado en la finca.   9. Doña Carmen y su esposo iban vendiendo la finca en parcelas.   10. El gobierno trataba de diversificar la economía de la Isla.   11. Seguía siendo una parte importante de la economía puertorriqueña.

SECTION 64   **Actividad A.**   1. c   2. c   3. c   4. a   5. a, b, c   6. c   7. c   8. b, c

SECTION 65   **Actividad A.**   1. Debe estar preocupado porque no tiene noticias de Raquel. e   2. Se sentían sospechosos de Raquel. f   3. Está muy enfermo y quiere saber algo de la investigación de Raquel. a   4. Se siente triste cuando piensa en la muerte de su hija. b   5. Estaba sorprendida cuando oyó la historia de su abuelo que vivía en México. c   6. Está preocupada. Quiere que don Fernando conozca a sus nietos antes de morir. d   **Actividad B.**   *Paso 1*   *Possible answers:*   1. Raquel estaba/se sentía preocupada... ¡y enojada!   2. Estaba/se sentía preocupada.   3. Estaba/se sentía sorprendida.   4. Raquel estaba/se sentía contenta, porque sabía dónde buscarla.   5. Raquel estaba/se sentía *muy* sorprendida.   6. Raquel estaba/se sentía muy triste... y un poco pensativa.   7. Raquel estaba/se sentía muy triste.   8. Estaba/se sentía un poco incómoda.   9. Raquel estaba/se sentía muy cansada.   10. Estaba/se sentía muy contenta.

PRONUNCIACIÓN

Rule #1: next-to-the-last   *Rule #2:* last   *Rule #3:* vowel   **Actividad C.**   1. my   2. you (subject pronoun)   3. he; him (object of a preposition)   4. if   5. I know   6. you; to/for you   7. what?, which?   8. this (demonstrative adjective); east

LECCIÓN 23

MÁS ALLÁ DEL EPISODIO

Actividad B 1. b 2. c

GRAMÁTICA

SECTION 66 Actividad A. 1. c 2. a 3. a 4. c 5. b

SECTION 67 Actividad A. a. 4 b. 2 c. 8 d. 7 e. 5 f. 1 g. 6 h. 3 Actividad B. *Parte A* 1. Era un artista 2. estaba casado 3. Ella murió 4. murió solo 5. estaban con él 6. tenía dos hijos *Parte B* 1. ¿Y qué hacía en Nueva York? 2. Estaba trabajando en una película. 3. Le gustó mucho. 4. Le impresionó mucho la casa. *Parte C* a. 2 b. 6 c. 3 d. 1 e. 5 f. 7 g. 4 Actividad C. 1. d 2. a 3. e 4. f 5. b 6. h 7. g 8. c Actividad D. 1. La semana pasada hice un viaje a Nueva York. 2. Estuve en la ciudad por cuatro días. 3. Mientras estaba allí, trabajaba en una película. 4. También fui a muchas fiestas. 5. Cené en tres restaurantes fabulosos y vi tres obras de teatro en Broadway. 6. Todas las noches salía con personas interesantes. 7. Todos eran actores y actrices atractivos. 8. Me gustó mucho el viaje y acepté otro trabajo para el mes que viene.

SECTION 68 Actividad A. 1. c 2. a 3. d 4. g 5. e 6. a 7. h 8. d 9. f 10. b

LECCIÓN 24

MÁS ALLÁ DEL EPISODIO

Actividad B. 1. Sí. 2. No. Estarían de acuerdo porque tienen la misma opinión de Jorge. 3. No. Jorge anda con otras mujeres, no solamente con Ángela. Sólo le interesa el dinero que Ángela le puede ofrecer.

GRAMÁTICA

SECTION 69 Actividad A. 1. Falso. Raquel conoció a Jorge en un salón de clase (*classroom*) de la universidad. 2. Falso. Raquel no tenía mucho interés en Jorge. 3. Cierto. 4. Falso. Las mujeres querían que él las acompañara (*him to go with them*), pero él no quiso. 5. Cierto. 6. Cierto. 7. Cierto. 8. Falso. Ángela le habló de este plan. Actividad B. 1. tía Olga 2. Los mecánicos y Raquel y Ángela 3. a doña Carmen 4. Raquel 5. Jorge 6. Ángela 7. en México 8. tío Jaime

SECTION 70 Actividad A. 1. a 2. e 3. c 4. b 5. d Actividad B. 1. Cierto. 2. Falso. España perdió a México primero. 3. Cierto. 4. Falso. El tren fue inventado en el siglo XIX. 5. Cierto. Actividad C. *Note:* Exact answers will vary depending on the year in which you are studying this text. 1. e. hace casi cinco siglos 2. f. hace más de doscientos años 3. b. hace unos ciento veinte años 4. a. hace un poco menos de cinco siglos 5. c. hace más de ciento treinta años 6. d. hace más de treinta años

SECTION 71 Actividad A. 1. g 2. d 3. h 4. a 5. c 6. e 7. f 8. b Actividad B. 1. c 2. b 3. b 4. a 5. b 6. c 7. c 8. a

LECCIÓN 25

GRAMÁTICA

SECTION 72 *Regular Verbs:* cenar: cenaba, cenaba, cenabais correr: corrías, corría, corríamos, corrían decidir: decidía, decidía, decidíais, decidían *Verbs with Irregularities:* ser: era ir: iba ver: veía

SECTION 73 1. P 2. I 3. I 4. I 5. P 6. I 7. P 8. I 9. P 10. I 11. I 12. I

SECTION 74 1. f 2. a 3. c 4. e 5. b 6. d

SECTION 72-74 Actividad A. 1. llegó, estaba 2. fue, vivía 3. contestó, vivía 4. había, recordó 5. se mudó, vivía 6. dio, salió 7. buscó, encontró 8. decidió, estaba 9. dejó, esperaba Actividad B. *Segment 1* 1. encontraste 2. encontró 3. Estábamos 4. fue 5. encontró *Segment 2* 1. Dejé 2. tomó 3. vimos 4. era 5. iba *Segment 3* 1. Se casó 2. era 3. creía 4. buscaba *Segment 4* 1. era 2. Quería 3. tenía 4. Hubo 5. estaba *Segment 5* 1. vi 2. fue 3. vivían *Segment 6* 1. Perdimos 2. Tenía 3. Pintaba 4. gustaban 5. hablaron *Segment 7* 1. estuviste 2. era 3. hacía 4. Tenía 5. era 6. vivía 7. Extrañaba 8. decidió 9. fue 10. pasó

UN POCO DE TODO

Actividad A. *Paso 1* You might have indicated the following places: los Estados Unidos: Los Ángeles México: la Ciudad de México España: Madrid (en el centro), Sevilla (en el sur) la Argentina: Buenos Aires Puerto Rico: San Juan *Paso 2* la familia Castillo: México, España (don Fernando) la familia Ruiz: Madrid y Sevilla la familia Iglesias: la Argentina, España (Rosario) *Note:* Of course, Rosario was not part of the Iglesias family when she was living in Spain, but, because of her, you may have thought to include that family with Spain on the map. **Actividad B.** *Paso 1* la primera familia Castillo: don Fernando y Rosario → Ángel la segunda familia Castillo: don Fernando y doña Carmen → Ramón (y Consuelo → Maricarmen), Mercedes, Carlos (y Gloria → Carlitos y Juanita), Juan (y Pati) la familia Iglesias: Rosario y Martín Iglesias → Arturo, con Ángel, su medio hermano **Actividad D.** *Paso 1* 1. c 2. e 3. h 4. a 5. d 6. g 7. b 8. f

LECCIÓN 26

GRAMÁTICA

Actividad A. 1. gustaba 2. querían 3. quería 4. quería 5. regañaban 6. gritaban 7. gritaban 8. se embarcó 9. volvió 10. pasó 11. gustó 12. se quedó 13. se dedicó **Actividad B.** 1. pasó 2. Le 3. era 4. puso 5. Soy 6. tan 7. más que 8. alguien 9. hizo 10. le 11. convirtió 12. estaban 13. casaron 14. era 15. nunca 16. muere ¡Un desafío! el padre = Martín Iglesias la madre = Rosario el hermanito = Arturo el coquí = Ángel la princesa = María Luisa, la esposa de Ángel la hija = Ángela Because Ángel never talked about his life in Argentina nor about his family, it is likely that Ángela is understanding the full meaning of the story for the first time.

UN POCO DE TODO

Actividad A. *Paso 1* You might have indicated the following places: San Juan, Ponce, San Germán. la familia de Ángel Castillo = Puerto Rico **Actividad B.** *Paso 1* la familia Castillo Soto: Ángel y María Luisa → Roberto y Ángela **Actividad D.** *Paso 3* You have arrived at number 10 on the map, la Plaza de Mercado Nueva.

APPENDIX 2: ANSWERS TO SELF-TESTS

LECCIONES 1 y 2

I. El episodio y los personajes
A. 1. Carlos (Castillo)   2. Pedro (Castillo)   3. Fernando (Castillo)   B.   1. F   2. C   3. F   4. F

II. El vocabulario
A. 1. esposa   2. hija   3. padre   4. hermano   5. tío   6. hijos   B.   1. esposo   2. abogada, profesor, estudiante   3. ciudad, hermana

III. La gramática
A. 1. las, unas, mis, sus   2. la, una, mi, su   3. los, unos, mis, sus   4. el, un, mi, su   B.   1. son   2. soy   3. somos   4. es   5. es

LECCIÓN 3

I. El episodio y los personajes
A. 1. Miguel   2. Raquel   3. Elena Ramírez   B.   1. No.   2. Sí.   3. No.   4. Sí.

II. El vocabulario
A. 1. veintiuno (veinte y uno)   2. cuatro   3. diecinueve (diez y nueve)   4. quince   B.   1. f   2. b   3. g   4. d   5. h   6. a   7. e   8. c

III. La gramática
A. 1. toma   2. cree   3. vive   4. desea   5. están   6. pregunta   7. revela

LECCIÓN 4

I. El episodio y los personajes
1. b   2. c   3. c   4. a   B.   1. Raquel   2. Miguel hijo

II. El vocabulario
A. 1. las matemáticas   2. el arte   3. la sicología   4. el comercio   5. la literatura   6. la filosofía

III. La gramática
A. 1. soy   2. estás   3. estudio   4. saco   5. estudias   6. sacas   B.   1. le gusta   2. animales cariñosos   3. muchas   4. está perdido

LECCIÓN 5

I. El episodio y los personajes
A. 1. b   2. e   3. a   4. d   5. b   6. f   7. a   8. a

II. El vocabulario
A. 1. b   2. c   3. a   4. d

III. La gramática
A. 1. Vamos a cenar...   2. Van a ver...   3. Voy a correr...   4. Vais a comprender...   B.   1. vamos   2. debéis   3. deseamos/debemos   4. cenamos

LECCIÓN 7

I. El episodio y los personajes
1. cartera   2. Sánchez   3. taxi   4. Federico   5. llevar   6. trae (encuentra)   7. encuentra   8. puede   9. salen   10. mensaje

II. El vocabulario
A. 1. M   2. H   3. H   4. M   5. M   6. H, M   7. M

III. La gramática
1. sale   2. sé   3. tengo   4. viene   5. Conoces   6. oigo   7. haces   8. traigo (tengo)   9. dice

LECCIÓN 8

I. El episodio y los personajes
a. 3   b. 4   c. 2   d. 8   e. 6   f. 7   g. 5   h. 9   i. 1

II. El vocabulario
A. 1. Cuándo   2. Cómo   3. Dónde   4. Quién   5. Por qué   6. Cuántos   7. Qué   8. Cuál

III. La gramática
1. Va a empezar   2. Piden   3. Se sienta   4. Vuelven   5. Se van a casar   (Van a casarse)   6. Va a encontrar

LECCIÓN 9

I. El episodio y los personajes
1. c   2. b   3. f   4. g   5. b   6. a   7. b   8. c   9. d   10. b

II. El vocabulario
A. 1. ese   2. esta   3. este   4. aquella   5. esa   6. tu   7. vuestra   8. su   9. nuestra   10. sus   B.   1. d   2. b   3. c   4. a   5. d   6. b

III. La gramática
Answers will vary. The verbs should be: 1. Me levanto   2. Me despierto   3. Me acuesto, Me duermo   4. Vuelvo   5. Pierdo   6. Me levanto, Me visto

LECCIÓN 10

I. El episodio y los personajes
1. a, b, d   2. a, c, e, f   3. a, c, e, f   4. a, d

II. El vocabulario
A. 1. bonita   2. altos   3. bajos   4. grande   5. delgada   6. rubio   7. canoso   8. gorditos

III. La gramática
A. Answers will vary. The verb forms should be: 1. Nos acostamos   2. Nos despertamos   3. Nos dormimos   4. Nos vestimos   **B.** 1. unos bailes bonitos   2. el museo grande   3. unas mujeres jóvenes   4. la profesora guapa

LECCIÓN 12

I. El episodio y los personajes
A. a. 3   b. 6   c. 8   d. 7   e. 5   f. 4   g. 1   h. 2   **B.** 1. d   2. b   3. e   4. a   5. c

II. El vocabulario
A. 1. mil cuatrocientos noventa y dos   2. seiscientos diez   3. mil setecientos setenta y seis   **B.** 1. primer   2. tercer   3. buen

III. La gramática
A. 1. Ya llegó.   2. Ya se mudó.   3. Ya decidieron.   4. Ya la oyó.   **B.** Answers will vary. They should begin as follows: 1. Lo tengo   2. La llevo   3. Los compro

LECCIÓN 13

I. El episodio y los personajes
A. 1. b, c   2. a   3. f   4. e   5. b   6. d   7. b   8. c

II. El vocabulario
A. 1. calamares   2. mejillones   3. atún   4. lenguado   5. ensalada   6. salmón   7. pan   8. arroz

III. La gramática
1. Sí, decidí comenzar en la calle Caminito.   2. Sí, me conociste ayer en la estancia.   3. Sí, me viste allí.   4. Sí, me invitaste a tu casa ayer.

LECCIÓN 14

I. El episodio y los personajes
A. 1. Arturo a Raquel   2. Héctor a Arturo   3. Arturo a Héctor.   **B.** 1. Teresa Suárez   2. don Fernando   3. Ángel   4. Héctor

II. El vocabulario
A. 1. b   2. a   3. b   4. d   5. c   6. a   7. b   8. e

III. La gramática
A. 1. los (os) comprendimos   2. los (os) invitamos   3. nos conocisteis ayer   **B.** 1. antes de   2. Durante   3. sobre   4. cerca de   5. hasta   6. sin

LECCIÓN 15

I. El episodio y los personajes
A. 1. b   2. a   3. c   4. b   5. b

II. El vocabulario
A. a. 2   b. 5   c. 3   d. 6   e. 1   f. 4

III. La gramática
A. 1. Ya le di el cuadro ayer.   2. Ya le dijimos todo anoche.   3. Ya les traje la carta de Ángel el martes.   4. Ya les di la dirección ayer.   **B.** Answers may vary. Here are the most likely ones: 1. A Raquel le molestan los obstáculos.   2. A Arturo le encanta Raquel.   3. A Héctor le gustan las fiestas.

LECCIÓN 16

I. El episodio y los personajes
A. a. 6   b. 5   c. 3   d. 4   e. 2   f. 1   **B.** 1. Sí.   2. No.   3. Sí.   4. No.   5. Sí.

II. El vocabulario
A. a. 5   b. 8   c. 9   d. 2   e. 7   f. 6   g. 3   h. 1   i. 10   j. 4

III. La gramática
A. 1. Se la di ayer.   2. Me la mandó el año pasado.   3. Me lo dio hace mucho tiempo.   **B.** 1. hicieron   2. fueron   3. vino   4. supiste

LECCIÓN 17

I. El episodio y los personajes
A. 1. d   2. c   3. b   4. a   **B.** 1. Sí.   2. No.   3. Sí.   4. Sí.

II. El vocabulario
A. 1. d   2. b   3. a   4. e   5. c

III. La gramática
A. 1. murieron   2. sirvió   3. pidió   4. Murió   5. dormiste   **B.** 1. Sí, nos lo dio ayer.   2. Sí, ya nos la pidieron.   3. Sí, anoche nos los regaló.

LECCIÓN 19

I. El episodio y los personajes
A. 5/g   **B.** 7/c   **C.** 6/d   **D.** 1/f   **E.** 4/h   **F.** 3/b   **G.** 8/a   **H.** 2/e

II. El vocabulario
B. 1. por ejemplo   2. por primera vez   3. por todas partes   4. por eso   5. por supuesto   6. por favor

III. La gramática
A. Answers may vary slightly. Here are the most likely ones: 1. Era la dirección de Ángel.   2. Buscaba la tumba de Ángel.   3. Tomaba una foto de la tumba.   4. Quería contarles la historia.   **B.** 1. esperando   2. escribiendo   3. diciendo

LECCIÓN 20

I. El episodio y los personajes
A. 1. el yerno - la suegra   2. la tía - la sobrina   3. la nieta - la abuela   4. el tío - la sobrina   5. el medio hermano - el medio hermano   **B.** 1. doña Carmen   2. Laura   3. Olga

II. El vocabulario
A. 1. nuera   2. hermanastra   3. suegro   4. cuñada   5. sobrinos   6. prima   **B.** 1. algo, nada   2. algunos, ninguno

III. La gramática
B. 1. iba, querías   2. sabía, eras

LECCIÓN 21

I. El episodio y los personajes
A. a. 4   b. 3   c. 6   d. 2   e. 5   f. 1   **B.** 1. b   2. d   3. c   4. a

II. El vocabulario
B. 1. tiene frío   2. tienen prisa   3. tiene sueño   4. tienen sed   5. tiene hambre   6. tiene (mucha) suerte

III. La gramática
A. 1. Ángela tiene menos hermanos que la tía Olga.   2. Rosario tenía menos hijos que don Fernando.   3. En Ponce, hace más calor que en San Juan.
B. 1. teníamos, íbamos   2. hacían, eran

LECCIÓN 22

I. El episodio y los personajes
1. f   2. h   3. a   4. b   5. g   6. c   7. d   8. e

II. El vocabulario
B. 1. nerviosa   2. cansados   3. triste   4. contentas

III. La gramática
1. tenía, vivía   2. se enfermaba   3. se enojaba, perdía

LECCIÓN 23

I. El episodio y los personajes
A. 1. c   2. e   3. f   4. b   5. d   6. a   **B.** a. 2   b. 1   c. 3

II. El vocabulario
B. 1. d   2. a   3. b   4. e   5. c

III. La gramática
1. volvían   2. preguntó   3. dijo   4. era   5. recordó   6. iba   7. hablaba   8. dijo   9. quería

LECCIÓN 24

I. El episodio y los personajes
1. Jorge → Raquel   2. Jorge → Ángela   3. Raquel → Ángela   4. Raquel → su madre   5. su madre → Raquel   6. Ángela → Raquel
7. Jaime → Raquel

II. El vocabulario
B. 1. desconfiado   2. terca   3. mujeriego   4. ingenua

III. La gramática
A. 1. conocí; *met*   2. quiso; *refused*   3. supo; *found out*

APPENDIX 3
VERB CHARTS

A. Regular Verbs: Simple Tenses

INFINITIVE PRESENT PARTICIPLE PAST PARTICIPLE	INDICATIVE					SUBJUNCTIVE		IMPERATIVE
	PRESENT	IMPERFECT	PRETERITE	FUTURE	CONDITIONAL	PRESENT	IMPERFECT	
hablar hablando hablado	hablo hablas habla hablamos habláis hablan	hablaba hablabas hablaba hablábamos hablabais hablaban	hablé hablaste habló hablamos hablasteis hablaron	hablaré hablarás hablará hablaremos hablaréis hablarán	hablaría hablarías hablaría hablaríamos hablaríais hablarían	hable hables hable hablemos habléis hablen	hablara hablaras hablara habláramos hablarais hablaran	habla tú, no hables hable Ud. hablemos hablen
comer comiendo comido	como comes come comemos coméis comen	comía comías comía comíamos comíais comían	comí comiste comió comimos comisteis comieron	comeré comerás comerá comeremos comeréis comerán	comería comerías comería comeríamos comeríais comerían	coma comas coma comamos comáis coman	comiera comieras comiera comiéramos comierais comieran	come tú, no comas coma Ud. comamos coman
vivir viviendo vivido	vivo vives vive vivimos vivís viven	vivía vivías vivía vivíamos vivíais vivían	viví viviste vivió vivimos vivisteis vivieron	viviré vivirás vivirá viviremos viviréis vivirán	viviría vivirías viviría viviríamos viviríais vivirían	viva vivas viva vivamos viváis vivan	viviera vivieras viviera viviéramos vivierais vivieran	vive tú, no vivas viva Ud. vivamos vivan

B. Regular Verbs: Perfect Tenses

INDICATIVE					SUBJUNCTIVE	
PRESENT PERFECT	PAST PERFECT	PRETERITE PERFECT	FUTURE PERFECT	CONDITIONAL PERFECT	PRESENT PERFECT	PAST PERFECT
he has ha hemos habéis han + hablado comido vivido	había habías había habíamos habíais habían + hablado comido vivido	hube hubiste hubo hubimos hubisteis hubieron + hablado comido vivido	habré habrás habrá habremos habréis habrán + hablado comido vivido	habría habrías habría habríamos habríais habrían + hablado comido vivido	haya hayas haya hayamos hayáis hayan + hablado comido vivido	hubiera hubieras hubiera hubiéramos hubierais hubieran + hablado comido vivido

C. Irregular Verbs

INFINITIVE PRESENT PARTICIPLE PAST PARTICIPLE	INDICATIVE					SUBJUNCTIVE		IMPERATIVE
	PRESENT	IMPERFECT	PRETERITE	FUTURE	CONDITIONAL	PRESENT	IMPERFECT	
andar andando andado	ando andas anda andamos andáis andan	andaba andabas andaba andábamos andabais andaban	anduve anduviste anduvo anduvimos anduvisteis anduvieron	andaré andarás andará andaremos andaréis andarán	andaría andarías andaría andaríamos andaríais andarían	ande andes ande andemos andéis anden	anduviera anduvieras anduviera anduviéramos anduvierais anduvieran	anda tú, no andes ande Ud. andemos anden
caer cayendo caído	caigo caes cae caemos caéis caen	caía caías caía caíamos caíais caían	caí caíste cayó caímos caísteis cayeron	caeré caerás caerá caeremos caeréis caerán	caería caerías caería caeríamos caeríais caerían	caiga caigas caiga caigamos caigáis caigan	cayera cayeras cayera cayéramos cayerais cayeran	cae tú, no caigas caiga Ud. caigamos caigan
dar dando dado	doy das da damos dais dan	daba dabas daba dábamos dabais daban	di diste dio dimos disteis dieron	daré darás dará daremos daréis darán	daría darías daría daríamos daríais darían	dé des dé demos deis den	diera dieras diera diéramos dierais dieran	da tú, no des dé Ud. demos den
decir diciendo dicho	digo dices dice decimos decís dicen	decía decías decía decíamos decíais decían	dije dijiste dijo dijimos dijisteis dijeron	diré dirás dirá diremos diréis dirán	diría dirías diría diríamos diríais dirían	diga digas diga digamos digáis digan	dijera dijeras dijera dijéramos dijerais dijeran	di tú, no digas diga Ud. digamos digan
estar estando estado	estoy estás está estamos estáis están	estaba estabas estaba estábamos estabais estaban	estuve estuviste estuvo estuvimos estuvisteis estuvieron	estaré estarás estará estaremos estaréis estarán	estaría estarías estaría estaríamos estaríais estarían	esté estés esté estemos estéis estén	estuviera estuvieras estuviera estuviéramos estuvierais estuviera	está tú, no estés esté Ud. estemos estén
haber habiendo habido	he has ha hemos habéis han	había habías había habíamos habíais habían	hube hubiste hubo hubimos hubisteis hubieron	habré habrás habrá habremos habréis habrán	habría habrías habría habríamos habríais habrían	haya hayas haya hayamos hayáis hayan	hubiera hubieras hubiera hubiéramos hubierais hubieran	
hacer haciendo hecho	hago haces hace hacemos hacéis hacen	hacía hacías hacía hacíamos hacíais hacían	hice hiciste hizo hicimos hicisteis hicieron	haré harás hará haremos haréis harán	haría harías haría haríamos haríais harían	haga hagas haga hagamos hagáis hagan	hiciera hicieras hiciera hiciéramos hicierais hicieran	haz tú, no hagas haga Ud. hagamos hagan

C. Irregular Verbs (continued)

INFINITIVE PRESENT PARTICIPLE PAST PARTICIPLE	INDICATIVE					SUBJUNCTIVE		IMPERATIVE
	PRESENT	IMPERFECT	PRETERITE	FUTURE	CONDITIONAL	PRESENT	IMPERFECT	
ir yendo ido	voy vas va vamos vais van	iba ibas iba íbamos ibais iban	fui fuiste fue fuimos fuisteis fueron	iré irás irá iremos iréis irán	iría irías iría iríamos iríais irían	vaya vayas vaya vayamos vayáis vayan	fuera fueras fuera fuéramos fuerais fueran	ve tú, no vayas vaya Ud. vayamos vayan
oír oyendo oído	oigo oyes oye oímos oís oyen	oía oías oía oíamos oíais oían	oí oíste oyó oímos oísteis oyeron	oiré oirás oirá oiremos oiréis oirán	oiría oirías oiría oiríamos oiríais oirían	oiga oigas oiga oigamos oigáis oigan	oyera oyeras oyera oyéramos oyerais oyeran	oye tú, no oigas oiga Ud. oigamos oigan
poder pudiendo podido	puedo puedes puede podemos podéis pueden	podía podías podía podíamos podíais podían	pude pudiste pudo pudimos pudisteis pudieron	podré podrás podrá podremos podréis podrán	podría podrías podría podríamos podríais podrían	pueda puedas pueda podamos podáis puedan	pudiera pudieras pudiera pudiéramos pudierais pudieran	
poner poniendo puesto	pongo pones pone ponemos ponéis ponen	ponía ponías ponía poníamos poníais ponían	puse pusiste puso pusimos pusisteis pusieron	pondré pondrás pondrá pondremos pondréis pondrán	pondría pondrías pondría pondríamos pondríais pondrían	ponga pongas ponga pongamos pongáis pongan	pusiera pusieras pusiera pusiéramos pusierais pusieran	pon tú, no pongas ponga Ud. pongamos pongan
querer queriendo querido	quiero quieres quiere queremos queréis quieren	quería querías quería queríamos queríais querían	quise quisiste quiso quisimos quisisteis quisieron	querré querrás querrá querremos querréis querrán	querría querrías querría querríamos querríais querrían	quiera quieras quiera queramos queráis quieran	quisiera quisieras quisiera quisiéramos quisierais quisieran	quiere tú, no quieras quiera Ud. queramos quieran
saber sabiendo sabido	sé sabes sabe sabemos sabéis saben	sabía sabías sabía sabíamos sabíais sabían	supe supiste supo supimos supisteis supieron	sabré sabrás sabrá sabremos sabréis sabrán	sabría sabrías sabría sabríamos sabríais sabrían	sepa sepas sepa sepamos sepáis sepan	supiera supieras supiera supiéramos supierais supieran	sabe tú, no sepas sepa Ud. sepamos sepan
salir saliendo salido	salgo sales sale salimos salís salen	salía salías salía salíamos salíais salían	salí saliste salió salimos salisteis salieron	saldré saldrás saldrá saldremos saldréis saldrán	saldría saldrías saldría saldríamos saldríais saldrían	salga salgas salga salgamos salgáis salgan	saliera salieras saliera saliéramos salierais salieran	sal tú, no salgas salga Ud. salgamos salgan

C. Irregular Verbs (continued)

INFINITIVE / PRESENT PARTICIPLE / PAST PARTICIPLE	PRESENT	IMPERFECT	PRETERITE	FUTURE	CONDITIONAL	PRESENT (SUBJ.)	IMPERFECT (SUBJ.)	IMPERATIVE
ser / siendo / sido	soy / eres / es / somos / sois / son	era / eras / era / éramos / erais / eran	fui / fuiste / fue / fuimos / fuisteis / fueron	seré / serás / será / seremos / seréis / serán	sería / serías / sería / seríamos / seríais / serían	sea / seas / sea / seamos / seáis / sean	fuera / fueras / fuera / fuéramos / fuerais / fueran	sé tú, no seas / sea Ud. / seamos / sean
tener / teniendo / tenido	tengo / tienes / tiene / tenemos / tenéis / tienen	tenía / tenías / tenía / teníamos / teníais / tenían	tuve / tuviste / tuvo / tuvimos / tuvisteis / tuvieron	tendré / tendrás / tendrá / tendremos / tendréis / tendrán	tendría / tendrías / tendría / tendríamos / tendríais / tendrían	tenga / tengas / tenga / tengamos / tengáis / tengan	tuviera / tuvieras / tuviera / tuviéramos / tuvierais / tuvieran	ten tú, no tengas / tenga Ud. / tengamos / tengan
traer / trayendo / traído	traigo / traes / trae / traemos / traéis / traen	traía / traías / traía / traíamos / traíais / traían	traje / trajiste / trajo / trajimos / trajisteis / trajeron	traeré / traerás / traerá / traeremos / traeréis / traerán	traería / traerías / traería / traeríamos / traeríais / traerían	traiga / traigas / traiga / traigamos / traigáis / traigan	trajera / trajeras / trajera / trajéramos / trajerais / trajeran	trae tú, no traigas / traiga Ud. / traigamos / traigan
venir / viniendo / venido	vengo / vienes / viene / venimos / venís / vienen	venía / venías / venía / veníamos / veníais / venían	vine / viniste / vino / vinimos / vinisteis / vinieron	vendré / vendrás / vendrá / vendremos / vendréis / vendrán	vendría / vendrías / vendría / vendríamos / vendríais / vendrían	venga / vengas / venga / vengamos / vengáis / vengan	viniera / vinieras / viniera / viniéramos / vinierais / vinieran	ven tú, no vengas / venga Ud. / vengamos / vengan
ver / viendo / visto	veo / ves / ve / vemos / veis / ven	veía / veías / veía / veíamos / veíais / veían	vi / viste / vio / vimos / visteis / vieron	veré / verás / verá / veremos / veréis / verán	vería / verías / vería / veríamos / veríais / verían	vea / veas / vea / veamos / veáis / vean	viera / vieras / viera / viéramos / vierais / vieran	ve tú, no veas / vea Ud. / veamos / vean

D. Stem-changing and Spelling Change Verbs

INFINITIVE / PRESENT PARTICIPLE / PAST PARTICIPLE	INDICATIVE PRESENT	IMPERFECT	PRETERITE	FUTURE	CONDITIONAL	SUBJUNCTIVE PRESENT	IMPERFECT	IMPERATIVE
construir (y) / construyendo / construido	construyo / construyes / construye / construimos / construís / construyen	construía / construías / construía / construíamos / construíais / construían	construí / construiste / construyó / construimos / construisteis / construyeron	construiré / construirás / construirá / construiremos / construiréis / construirán	construiría / construirías / construiría / construiríamos / construiríais / construirían	construya / construyas / construya / construyamos / construyáis / construyan	construyera / construyeras / construyera / construyéramos / construyerais / construyeran	construye tú, no construyas / construya Ud. / construyamos / construyan
dormir (ue, u) / durmiendo / dormido	duermo / duermes / duerme / dormimos / dormís / duermen	dormía / dormías / dormía / dormíamos / dormíais / dormían	dormí / dormiste / durmió / dormimos / dormisteis / durmieron	dormiré / dormirás / dormirá / dormiremos / dormiréis / dormirán	dormiría / dormirías / dormiría / dormiríamos / dormiríais / dormirían	duerma / duermas / duerma / durmamos / durmáis / duerman	durmiera / durmieras / durmiera / durmiéramos / durmierais / durmieran	duerme tú, no duermas / duerma Ud. / durmamos / duerman

D. Stem-changing and Spelling Change Verbs (continued)

INFINITIVE / PRESENT PARTICIPLE / PAST PARTICIPLE	INDICATIVE					SUBJUNCTIVE		IMPERATIVE
	PRESENT	IMPERFECT	PRETERITE	FUTURE	CONDITIONAL	PRESENT	IMPERFECT	
pedir (i, i) / pidiendo / pedido	pido pides pide pedimos pedís piden	pedía pedías pedía pedíamos pedíais pedían	pedí pediste pidió pedimos pedisteis pidieron	pediré pedirás pedirá pediremos pediréis pedirán	pediría pedirías pediría pediríamos pediríais pedirían	pida pidas pida pidamos pidáis pidan	pidiera pidieras pidiera pidiéramos pidierais pidieran	pide tú, no pidas pida Ud. pidamos pidan
pensar (ie) / pensando / pensado	pienso piensas piensa pensamos pensáis piensan	pensaba pensabas pensaba pensábamos pensabais pensaban	pensé pensaste pensó pensamos pensasteis pensaron	pensaré pensarás pensará pensaremos pensaréis pensarán	pensaría pensarías pensaría pensaríamos pensaríais pensarían	piense pienses piense pensemos penséis piensen	pensara pensaras pensara pensáramos pensarais pensaran	piensa tú, no pienses piense Ud. pensemos piensen
producir (zc) / produciendo / producido	produzco produces produce producimos producís producen	producía producías producía producíamos producíais producían	produje produjiste produjo produjimos produjisteis produjeron	produciré producirás producirá produciremos produciréis producirán	produciría producirías produciría produciríamos produciríais producirían	produzca produzcas produzca produzcamos produzcáis produzcan	produjera produjeras produjera produjéramos produjerais produjeran	produce tú, no produzcas produzca Ud. produzcamos produzcan
reír (i, i) / riendo / reído	río ríes ríe reímos reís ríen	reía reías reía reíamos reíais reían	reí reíste rió reímos reísteis rieron	reiré reirás reirá reiremos reiréis reirán	reiría reirías reiría reiríamos reiríais reirían	ría rías ría riamos riáis rían	riera rieras riera riéramos rierais rieran	ríe tú, no rías ría Ud. riamos rían
seguir (i, i) (ga) / siguiendo / seguido	sigo sigues sigue seguimos seguís siguen	seguía seguías seguía seguíamos seguíais seguían	seguí seguiste siguió seguimos seguisteis siguieron	seguiré seguirás seguirá seguiremos seguiréis seguirán	seguiría seguirías seguiría seguiríamos seguiríais seguirían	siga sigas siga sigamos sigáis sigan	siguiera siguieras siguiera siguiéramos siguierais siguieran	sigue tú, no sigas siga Ud. sigamos sigan
sentir (ie, i) / sintiendo / sentido	siento sientes siente sentimos sentís sienten	sentía sentías sentía sentíamos sentíais sentían	sentí sentiste sintió sentimos sentisteis sintieron	sentiré sentirás sentirá sentiremos sentiréis sentirán	sentiría sentirías sentiría sentiríamos sentiríais sentirían	sienta sientas sienta sintamos sintáis sientan	sintiera sintieras sintiera sintiéramos sintierais sintieran	siente tú, no sientas sienta Ud. sintamos sientan
volver (ue) / volviendo / vuelto	vuelvo vuelves vuelve volvemos volvéis vuelven	volvía volvías volvía volvíamos volvíais volvían	volví volviste volvió volvimos volvisteis volvieron	volveré volverás volverá volveremos volveréis volverán	volvería volverías volvería volveríamos volveríais volverían	vuelva vuelvas vuelva volvamos volváis vuelvan	volviera volvieras volviera volviéramos volvierais volvieran	vuelve tú, no vuelvas vuelva Ud. volvamos vuelvan

INDEX

In this index, **Conversaciones** (functional expressions), **Notas culturales** (both country-specific and general), and vocabulary topics appear as groups; items in those lists are not cross-referenced. Abbreviations in the index are identical to those used in the Textbook end vocabulary. The indication "WB1" precedes page references to this *Destinos* Workbook I. Page references without "WB1" before them refer to the *Destinos* Textbook.

Index

About the Authors

Bill VanPatten is Associate Professor of Spanish at the University of Illinois at Urbana–Champaign, where he also directs the graduate program in Spanish. He received his Ph.D. in Spanish from the University of Texas in Austin in 1983. His areas of specialty are input and input processing in second language acquisition, the impact of instruction on second language acquisition, and the acquisition of Spanish syntax and morphology. He has published numerous articles and chapters in books, and he is also the co-author of several McGraw-Hill Spanish textbooks for the college level, including *Puntos de partida*, *¿Qué tal?*, and *¿Sabías que... ?* Professor VanPatten is the designer of *Destinos*, a telecourse for PBS television stations.

Martha Alford Marks received her Ph.D. in Spanish Literature from Northwestern University in 1978. She subsequently served on the faculties of Kalamazoo College and Northwestern University, where she coordinated the first- and second-year Spanish programs, supervised teaching assistants, appeared consistently on the Faculty Honor Roll, and won the 1982 Outstanding Teaching Award. Nationally known for her work as an ACTFL Oral Proficiency tester and trainer, Dr Marks is also the co-author of several other McGraw-Hill Spanish textbooks for the college level, including *¿Qué tal?* and *Al corriente*.

Richard V. Teschner is Professor of Language and Linguistics at the University of Texas-El Paso, where he has taught since 1976. He received his Ph.D. in Spanish Linguistics from the University of Wisconsin-Madison in 1972. His publications range from bibliographies and textbooks (in particular, Spanish for native speakers) to numerous reviews, articles, and monographs. In 1988 he served as President of the American Association of Teachers of Spanish and Portuguese. He was Secretary-Treasurer, then President, of the Linguistic Association of the Southwest.